Recommendation on Social Protection Floors

Studies in Employment and Social Policy

VOLUME 50

Editors

Professor Alan Neal (founding editor of the *International Journal of Labour Law and Industrial Relations*, and Convenor of the European Association of Labour Law Judges); Professor Manfred Weiss (past president of the International Industrial Relations Association); and Professor Birgitta Nyström (professor of private law at the Law Faculty, University of Lund, Sweden, and member of the European Committee of Social Rights).

Objective

Studies in Employment and Social Policy series seeks to provide a forum for highlighting international and comparative research on contemporary areas of significance for evaluation and regulation of the world of work.

Introduction

Launched in 1997, the Studies in Employment and Social Policy Series now boasts over forty titles, addressing key policy and development issues in the fields of industrial relations, labour law, social security, and international labour regulation.

Content

With contributions from leading figures in the field, the series brings together key policymakers, academics, and regulators, providing a unique context in which to analyse and evaluate the rapid and dramatic work and social policy developments taking place around the globe.

The titles published in this series are listed at the end of this volume.

Recommendation on Social Protection Floors

Basic Principles for Innovative Solutions

Edited by

Tineke Dijkhoff
Letlhokwa George Mpedi

Published by:
Kluwer Law International B.V.
PO Box 316
2400 AH Alphen aan den Rijn
The Netherlands
Website: www.wolterskluwerlr.com

Sold and distributed in North, Central and South America by:
Wolters Kluwer Legal & Regulatory U.S.
7201 McKinney Circle
Frederick, MD 21704
United States of America
Email: customer.service@wolterskluwer.com

Sold and distributed in all other countries by:
Quadrant
Rockwood House
Haywards Heath
West Sussex
RH16 3DH
United Kingdom
Email: international-customerservice@wolterskluwer.com

MIX
FSC® C103993
Printed on acid-free paper.

ISBN 978-90-411-8623-2

e-Book: ISBN 978-90-411-8633-1
web-PDF: ISBN 978-90-411-8634-8

© 2018 Kluwer Law International BV, The Netherlands

All rights reserved. No part of this publication may be reproduced, stored in a retrieval system, or transmitted in any form or by any means, electronic, mechanical, photocopying, recording, or otherwise, without written permission from the publisher.

Permission to use this content must be obtained from the copyright owner. Please apply to: Permissions Department, Wolters Kluwer Legal & Regulatory U.S., 76 Ninth Avenue, 7th Floor, New York, NY 10011-5201, USA. Website: www.wolterskluwerlr.com

Printed in the United Kingdom.

Editors

Tineke Dijkhoff, Senior Researcher at the Max Planck Institute for Social Law and Social Policy, Munich (Germany).

Letlhokwa George Mpedi, Professor and Executive Dean of the Faculty of Law and Director of the Centre for International and Comparative Labour and Social Security Law, University of Johannesburg, Johannesburg (South Africa).

Contributors

Tania Abbiate, Senior Researcher at the Max Planck Institute for Social Law and Social Policy, Munich (Germany).

Pablo Arellano Ortiz, Professor of Labour Law and Social Security at the Pontificia Universidad Católica de Valparaíso, Valparaíso (Chile).

Christina Behrendt, Senior Social Policy Specialist at the Social Protection Department of the International Labour Organisation, Geneva (Switzerland).

Stephen Devereux, Research Fellow at the Institute of Development Studies, Brighton (United Kingdom) and holder of the South African Research Chair in Social Protection for Food Security, hosted by the Centre of Excellence in Food Security at the University of the Western Cape, Cape Town (South Africa).

Gabriela Mendizábal Bermúdez, Professor and Researcher at the Faculty of Law and Social Sciences of the Autonomous University of the State of Morelos in Cuernavaca, Morelos (Mexico).

Mathias Nyenti, Senior Lecturer and Research Associate at the Centre for International and Comparative Labour and Social Security Law, University of Johannesburg, Johannesburg (South Africa).

Laura Pautassi, Professor of Economic, Social and Cultural Rights at the University of Buenos Aires/UBA Law School, Researcher at the National Council of Scientific and Technical Research, and at the A. Gioja Institute of Legal and Civil Research in the Law Faculty of the Universidad de Buenos Aires, Buenos Aires (Argentina).

Babu P. Remesh, Professor at the School of Development Studies, Ambedkar University Delhi (AUD), Delhi (India).

Contributors

Emmanuelle Saint-Pierre Guilbault, Legal Specialist at the Social Protection Department of the International Labour Organisation, Geneva (Switzerland).

Maya Stern-Plaza, Legal Officer at the Social Protection Department of the International Labour Organisation, Geneva (Switzerland).

Worawet Suwanrada, Professor at the Faculty of Economics, Chulalongkorn University, Bangkok (Thailand).

Victoire Umuhire, Social Protection Policy Officer at the Social Protection Department of the International Labour Organisation, Geneva (Switzerland).

Veronika Wodsak, Social Security Expert at the Social Protection Department of the International Labour Organisation, Geneva (Switzerland).

Summary of Contents

Editors	v
Contributors	vii
Preface	xxi
List of Abbreviations and Acronyms	xxiii

PART I
Introduction to the Social Protection Floors: Basic Principles and Broader Context   1

CHAPTER 1
Recommendation on Social Protection Floors and Basic Principles for Innovative Solutions: General Introduction
Tineke Dijkhoff & Letlhokwa George Mpedi   3

CHAPTER 2
Principles for National Social Protection Floors
Tineke Dijkhoff   13

CHAPTER 3
Implementing the Principles of Social Protection Floors Recommendation, 2012 (No. 202)
Christina Behrendt, Emmanuelle Saint-Pierre Guilbault, Maya Stern-Plaza, Victoire Umuhire & Veronika Wodsak   41

CHAPTER 4
Social Protection Floors and the Right to Food
Stephen Devereux   71

Summary of Contents

PART II
Implementation of the Basic Principles: Case Studies 87

CHAPTER 5
The Child Support Grant in the Republic of South Africa
Letlhokwa George Mpedi 89

CHAPTER 6
Conditional Cash Transfers for Families and Children under Mexico's PROSPERA Programme
Gabriela Mendizábal Bermúdez 115

CHAPTER 7
Argentina: From an Emblematic Case to Its Institutionalization – An Analysis of the Universal Child Allowance for Social Protection
Laura Pautassi 145

CHAPTER 8
Tunisian National Programme for Assistance to Families in Need
Tania Abbiate 169

CHAPTER 9
Chile Solidario CCT Programme: New Logic Behind Chilean Social Protection Programmes
Pablo Arellano Ortiz 197

CHAPTER 10
Does Employment Guarantee Support a Social Protection Floor?: A Case Study of Mahatma Gandhi National Rural Employment Guarantee Scheme (MGNREGS) in India
Babu P. Remesh 219

CHAPTER 11
Namibia National Pension Scheme
Mathias Nyenti 237

CHAPTER 12
Old-Age Allowance Scheme in Thailand
Worawet Suwanrada 261

PART III
Conclusions 291

CHAPTER 13
A Framework of Principles as a Policy and Assessment Tool:
Conclusions
Tineke Dijkhoff & Letlhokwa George Mpedi   293

Appendix   301

Table of Contents

Editors   v

Contributors   vii

Preface   xxi

List of Abbreviations and Acronyms   xxiii

PART I
Introduction to the Social Protection Floors: Basic Principles and Broader Context   1

CHAPTER 1
Recommendation on Social Protection Floors and Basic Principles for Innovative Solutions: General Introduction
Tineke Dijkhoff & Letlhokwa George Mpedi   3

1.1	The Road Towards National Social Protection Floors: A General Overview		3
	1.1.1	The Global Protection Gap and the Birth of Recommendation	3
	1.1.2	The Broader Perspective of the Joint United Nations Social Protection Floor Initiative	5
1.2	A Set of Principles As Policy Tool and Assessment Framework		6
1.3	Objectives, Methods and Design of the Book		7
	1.3.1	Objectives	7
	1.3.2	Methods and Choices	9
	1.3.3	Structure of the Book	10
Bibliography			10

Table of Contents

CHAPTER 2
Principles for National Social Protection Floors
Tineke Dijkhoff   13

2.1	Introduction		13
2.2	Recommendation 202: An Overview		13
	2.2.1	Preamble	13
	2.2.2	Part I: Objectives, Scope, and Principles	14
	2.2.3	Part II: National Social Protection Floors	16
	2.2.4	Part III: National Strategies for the Extension of Social Security	16
	2.2.5	Part IV: Monitoring	17
2.3	Preliminary Observations		17
	2.3.1	The National Floor: Social Protection or Social Security?	17
	2.3.2	Binding Force Versus Political Support	20
2.4	Classifying and Clarifying the Principles		21
	2.4.1	Selection of 'Umbrella Principles'	21
	2.4.2	State Responsibility	24
	2.4.3	Universality of Protection	26
	2.4.4	Entitlements Based on Law	28
	2.4.5	Adequacy and Predictability of Benefits	30
	2.4.6	Non-discrimination	31
	2.4.7	Financial Solidarity	32
	2.4.8	Good Governance	34
	2.4.9	Coherence of Policies	36
	2.4.10	Social Participation	37
Bibliography			38

CHAPTER 3
Implementing the Principles of Social Protection Floors Recommendation, 2012 (No. 202)
Christina Behrendt, Emmanuelle Saint-Pierre Guilbault, Maya Stern-Plaza, Victoire Umuhire & Veronika Wodsak   41

3.1	Introduction		41
3.2	SPFs and the Human Right to Social Security		44
3.3	How Do the Principles of Recommendation No. 202 Inform the Implementation of Nationally Defined SPFs?		46
	3.3.1	State Responsibility	47
	3.3.2	Universality of Protection, Comprising At Least a Basic Set of Social Security Guarantees for All	48
	3.3.3	Anchoring Social Protection Systems in Law	51
	3.3.4	Adequacy and Predictability of Benefits (Accessibility, Responsiveness to Special Needs)	53

		3.3.5	Non-discrimination (Gender, Nationality and Status in Employment)	55
		3.3.6	Financial and Economic Management, and Financial Solidarity	56
		3.3.7	Good Governance	59
		3.3.8	Coherence of Policies	60
		3.3.9	Social Participation	63
3.4	The Way Ahead: Progress Towards Realizing the Right to Social Security for All			65
Bibliography				66

CHAPTER 4
Social Protection Floors and the Right to Food
Stephen Devereux 71

4.1	Introduction	71
4.2	Coverage: How to Ensure That Everyone Is Income Secure?	73
4.3	Adequacy: How Much Income Do People Need for Food Security?	75
4.4	Stability: How to Allow for Variability In Needs over Time?	77
4.5	Intra-household Issues: Is Household Food Security Sufficient for Individual Nutrition Security?	79
	4.5.1 Gender	79
	4.5.2 Care	81
4.6	Conclusion	82
Bibliography		84

PART II
Implementation of the Basic Principles: Case Studies 87

CHAPTER 5
The Child Support Grant in the Republic of South Africa
Letlhokwa George Mpedi 89

5.1	Introduction	89
5.2	Assessment of the Scheme on the Basis of the Principles	91
	5.2.1 State Responsibility	91
	5.2.2 Universality of Protection	93
	5.2.3 Entitlements Based on Law	95
	5.2.4 Adequacy and Predictability of Benefits	96
	5.2.5 Non-discrimination	97
	5.2.6 Financial Solidarity	99
	5.2.7 Good Governance	99
	5.2.8 Coherence in Policies	101
	5.2.9 Social Participation	102
5.3	Legislative Deficits	105

Table of Contents

5.4	Implementation Failures		106
	5.4.1	Supporting Documents	107
	5.4.2	The Urban-Rural Divide	108
	5.4.3	Minor PCGs	109
	5.4.4	Children Living on the Streets	110
	5.4.5	Other Impediments to Access	111
5.5	Conclusion		111
Bibliography			111

CHAPTER 6
Conditional Cash Transfers for Families and Children under Mexico's PROSPERA Programme
Gabriela Mendizábal Bermúdez   115

6.1	Introduction		115
	6.1.1	Social Security in Mexico	115
	6.1.2	PROSPERA as a Means to Combat Poverty	116
	6.1.3	Mexico and the ILO	118
	6.1.4	The Structure of This Chapter	118
6.2	PROSPERA'S Background		119
	6.2.1	Social Security Through Social Security and Assistance Programmes	119
	6.2.2	PROSPERA and Its Scope of Application	121
	6.2.3	PROSPERA's Impact on Poverty	125
6.3	Assessment of PROSPERA on the Basis of the Principles		127
	6.3.1	State Responsibility	127
	6.3.2	Universality of Protection	128
	6.3.3	Entitlements Based on Law	130
	6.3.4	Adequacy and Predictability of Benefits	132
	6.3.5	Non-discrimination	133
	6.3.6	Financial Solidarity	134
	6.3.7	Good Governance	135
	6.3.8	Coherence of Policies	136
	6.3.9	Social Participation	137
6.4	Legislative Deficits and Implementation Failures		139
6.5	Conclusions		140
Bibliography			142

CHAPTER 7
Argentina: From an Emblematic Case to Its Institutionalization – An Analysis of the Universal Child Allowance for Social Protection
Laura Pautassi   145

7.1	Introduction	145

7.2	The Process of Incorporating a Social Protection Floor		148
	7.2.1	Background	148
	7.2.2	Universal Child Allowance for Social Protection (AUH)	149
7.3	Assessment of the AUH on the Basis of the Principles		151
	7.3.1	State Responsibility	151
	7.3.2	Universality of Protection	152
	7.3.3	Entitlements Based on Law and Non-discrimination	154
	7.3.4	Adequacy and Predictability of Benefits	155
	7.3.5	Non-discrimination	156
	7.3.6	Financial Solidarity	159
	7.3.7	Good Governance	160
	7.3.8	Coherence of Policies	160
	7.3.9	Social Participation	162
7.4	Legislative Deficits and Implementation Failures		162
7.5	Conclusions		164
Bibliography			166

CHAPTER 8
Tunisian National Programme for Assistance to Families in Need
Tania Abbiate 169

8.1	Introduction		169
	8.1.1	Overview of Tunisian Social Protection Schemes	170
	8.1.2	Socio-Economic Rights Guarantees in the 2014 Constitution	172
	8.1.3	Tunisian Compliance with ILO and Steps Towards the Implementation of SPFs	174
	8.1.4	Background of the PNAFN	175
8.2	Assessment of the Scheme on the Basis of Principles		177
	8.2.1	State Responsibility	177
	8.2.2	Universality of Protection	178
	8.2.3	Entitlements Based on Law	180
	8.2.4	Adequacy and Predictability of Benefits	182
	8.2.5	Non-discrimination	183
	8.2.6	Financial Solidarity	186
	8.2.7	Good Governance	187
	8.2.8	Coherence of Policies	188
	8.2.9	Social Participation	189
8.3	Legislative Deficits		190
8.4	Conclusions		191
Bibliography			192

Table of Contents

CHAPTER 9
Chile Solidario CCT Programme: New Logic Behind Chilean Social Protection Programmes
Pablo Arellano Ortiz 197

9.1	Background from Chile Solidario Programme to Oportunidades Y Seguridades Programme		197
	9.1.1	Key Factors in the Latin American Context	198
	9.1.2	Origin and Evolution: From Chile Solidario to Securities and Opportunities	202
	9.1.3	The Mechanism for Measuring Poverty: A Determinant of Protection	207
9.2	Assessment of Chile Solidario on the Basis of the Principles		209
	9.2.1	State Responsibility	210
	9.2.2	Universality of Protection	210
	9.2.3	Entitlements Based on Law	211
	9.2.4	Adequacy and Predictability of Benefits	212
	9.2.5	Non-discrimination	212
	9.2.6	Financial Solidarity	213
	9.2.7	Good Governance	214
	9.2.8	Coherence of Policies	214
	9.2.9	Social Participation and Freedom of Association	214
9.3	Discussion of Legislative Deficits and/or Implementation Failures Flowing from the Assessment		215
9.4	Reformulation of the Programme and Policy		216
Bibliography			216
Legislation			218

CHAPTER 10
Does Employment Guarantee Support a Social Protection Floor?:
A Case Study of Mahatma Gandhi National Rural Employment Guarantee Scheme (MGNREGS) in India
Babu P. Remesh 219

10.1	Introduction		219
10.2	MGNREGS: A Profile		221
10.3	Viewing MGNREGS Through the Lens of National Social Protection Floor		222
	10.3.1	State Responsibility	223
	10.3.2	Universality of Protection	224
	10.3.3	Legal Entitlements	226
	10.3.4	Adequacy and Predictability of Benefits	227
	10.3.5	Non-discrimination	229
	10.3.6	Financial Solidarity	229
	10.3.7	Good Governance	230

	10.3.8	Coherence of Policies	231
	10.3.9	Social Participation	232
10.4		Performance Analysis and Conclusion	233
Bibliography			234

CHAPTER 11
Namibia National Pension Scheme
Mathias Nyenti 237

11.1	Introduction		237
11.2	Assessment of the Old-Age Pension on the Basis of the Principles		240
	11.2.1	State Responsibility	240
	11.2.2	Universality of Protection	242
	11.2.3	Entitlements Based on Law (Incl. Inspection, Enforcement, Effective and Accessible Complaint, and Appeal Procedures)	243
	11.2.4	Adequacy and Predictability of Benefits (Accessibility, Sufficiency, and Responsiveness to Specific Needs)	246
	11.2.5	Non-discrimination (Including Gender, Nationality, and Status of Employment)	249
	11.2.6	Financial Solidarity	250
	11.2.7	Good Governance	250
	11.2.8	Coherence of Policies	253
	11.2.9	Social Participation (Both in the Design and Administration of a Scheme) and Freedom of Association	255
11.3	Legislative Deficits and/or Implementation Failures of the Old-Age Pension		256
11.4	Conclusions		257
Bibliography			258

CHAPTER 12
Old-Age Allowance Scheme in Thailand
Worawet Suwanrada 261

12.1	Introduction		261
12.2	Historical Background, Development and Context of the Old-Age Allowance Scheme		263
	12.2.1	Historical Background and Development of the Scheme	263
	12.2.2	Context of Old-Age Allowance Scheme in the Public Pension Systems	268
12.3	Economic and Social Impact of Old-Age Allowance		271
12.4	Assessment of the Old-Age Allowance Scheme on the Basis of Nine Principles		276
	12.4.1	State Responsibility	276
		12.4.1.1 Establishment and Maintenance	276

Table of Contents

	12.4.1.2 Implementation	278
	12.4.1.3 Monitoring Mechanisms	278
12.4.2	Universality of Protection	280
12.4.3	Entitlement Based on Law	281
12.4.4	Complaint and Appeal Procedures	282
12.4.5	Adequacy and Predictability of Benefits	284
12.4.6	Non-discrimination	285
12.4.7	Financial Solidarity	286
12.4.8	Coherence of Policies	287
12.4.9	Social Participation	287
12.4.10	Good Governance	288
12.5	Challenges of Old-Age Allowance in the Future	288
Bibliography		289

PART III
Conclusions   291

CHAPTER 13
A Framework of Principles as a Policy and Assessment Tool: Conclusions
Tineke Dijkhoff & Letlhokwa George Mpedi   293

13.1	Introduction	293
13.2	Principles	294
	13.2.1 State Responsibility	294
	13.2.2 Universality of Protection	295
	13.2.3 Entitlement Based on Law	296
	13.2.4 Adequacy and Predictability of Benefits	297
	13.2.5 Non-discrimination	297
	13.2.6 Financial Solidarity	298
	13.2.7 Good Governance	298
	13.2.8 Coherence of Policies	299
	13.2.9 Social Participation	299
13.3	Legislative Deficits and Implementation Failures	300
13.4	Conclusion	300

Appendix   301

Preface

This book focuses on the International Labour Organisation Social Protection Floors Recommendation 202 of 2012 (hereinafter 'the Recommendation'). It pays particular attention on key basic principles contained in the Recommendation, namely: State responsibility, universality of protection, entitlement based on law, adequacy and predictability of benefits, non-discrimination, financial solidarity, good governance, coherence of policies and social participation. The publication is divided into three parts, Part I provides a general framework on the recommendation and delineates the pertinent principles. In addition, it examines the principle of coherence of policies with a particular focus on social protection floors and the right to food.

Part II of the publication contains case studies which focus on children and families (i.e., Child Support Grant in South Africa, *PROSPERA* in Mexico, Universal Child Allowance in Argentina, and Cash Transfer Programme in Tunisia), persons of a working age (*Chile Solidario* in Chile and Mahatma Gandhi National Rural Employment Guarantee Scheme in India), and elderly persons (National Pension in Namibia and 500 Bath Pension Scheme in Thailand). Part III consists of concluding observations and lessons (to be) learnt.

We wish to express our heartfelt appreciation to the following organizations that sponsored the workshop which was held in Johannesburg on 12 and 13 September 2016 to discuss the preliminary papers which later evolved into the chapters contained in this publication: Max Planck Institute for Social Law and Policy (Munich, Germany), Centre for International and Comparative Labour and Social Security Law (Johannesburg, South Africa), South African Research Chair in Social Protection and Food Security, hosted by the Centre of Excellence in Food Security at the University of the Western Cape (Cape Town, South Africa) and Fritz Thyssen Foundation (Cologne, German). It goes without saying that the opinions expressed in this publication are in actual fact those of the authors. They do not in any sense represent the views of the aforementioned organizations.

This publication would have not materialized had it not been for the hard work and dedication of all the contributors who were thoughtful, prompt and professional in their interaction with the editors. We thank them all from the bottom of our hearts. Dr Stephen Devereux served as a project advisor and liberally shared his wisdom by giving

Preface

valuable comments and feedback on several chapters contained in this volume. Last but by no means least, we would like to express words of profound gratitude to our publisher, Wolters Kluwer, and all the persons, especially Fiona McGrath, who diligently toiled behind the scenes to ensure that this book is linguistically accurate, of sound editorial quality and, most importantly, sees the light of day.

Munich/Johannesburg, July 2017
Tineke Dijkhoff
Letlhokwa George Mpedi

List of Abbreviations and Acronyms

AMG	*Assistance médicale gratuite*
AMGII	*Assistance médicale à* tarifs réduits
ANSES	National Social Security Administration
ARS	Argentine Pesos
ASEAN	Association of Southeast Asian Nations
AUE	Universal Allowance for Pregnant Women
AUH	Universal Child Allowance for Social Protection
BIG	Basic Income Grant
BRICS	Brazil, Russia, India, China and South Africa
CCT	Conditional Cash Transfer
CGD	Care Dependency Grant
CELS	*Centro de Estudios Legales y Sociales*
CESCR	Committee on Economic, Social and Cultural Rights
CICLASS	Centre for International and Comparative Labour and Social Security Law
CLP	Chilean Peso
CNAM	National Health Insurance Fund
CNRPS	National Pension and Social Insurance Fund
CNSS	National Social Security Fund
CONEVAL	*Consejo Nacional de Evaluación de la Política de Desarrollo Social*
CPI	Consumer Price Index
CSG	Child Support Grant
DOLA	Department of Local Administration
DPA	Department of Public Assistance

List of Abbreviations and Acronyms

ECOWAS	Economic Community of West African States
e-FMS	e-Financial Management System
ESS	Extension of Social Security
ECLAC	Economic Commission for Latin America and the Caribbean
FAO	Food and Agriculture Organization
FES	*Friedrich-Ebert-Stiftung*
FGS	Sustainability Guarantee Fund
FPS	*Ficha de Proteccion Social*
FS	*Ficha Social*
GDP	Gross Domestic Product
HIV/AIDS	Human Immunodeficiency Virus / Acquired Immunodeficiency Syndrome
ICESCR	International Covenant on Economic, Social and Cultural Rights
ICROP	Integrated Community Registration Outreach Programme
ILC	International Labour Conference
ILO	International Labour Organization
INDEC	*Instituto de Estadísticas y Censos*
IMSS	*Instituto Mexicano del Seguro Social*
INR	Indian Rupees
IOE	International Organisation of Employers
ISSA	International Social Security Association
ISSFAM	*Instituto de Seguridad Social para las Fuerzas Armadas Mexicanas*
ISSSTE	*Instituto de Seguridad y Servicios Sociales de los Trabajadores del Estado*
JBY	*Janashree BimaYojana*
MAS	Department of Social Promotion of the Ministry of Social Affairs
MDGs	Millennium Development Goals
MGNREGS	Mahatma Gandhi National Rural Employment Guarantee Act
MPI	Max Planck Institute
MSD	Maternity, Sick Leave and Death Benefit
MXN	Mexican Peso
NAD	Namibian Dollars

List of Abbreviations and Acronyms

NADLEC	National Economic, Development and Labour Council
NCE	National Committee on the Elderly
NESDB	National Economic and Social Development Board
NFFWP	National Food for Work Campaign
NGOs	Non-Governmental Organisations
NRA	National Reform Assembly
NREGA	National Rural Employment Guarantee Act
NREGS	National Rural Employment Guarantee Scheme
OBCs	Other Backward Castes
OECD	Organisation of Economic Co-operation and Development
OHCHR	United Nations High Commissioner for Human Rights
OIT	*Organisation internationale du travail*
PAJA	Promotion of Access to Justice Act
PAMI	National Institute of Social Services for Retirees and Pensioners
PCG	Primary Care Giver
PER/PELJ	Potchefstroom Electronic Law Journal/*Potchefstroomse Elektroniese Regsblad*
PJJHD	*Plan Jefes y Jefas de Hogar Desocupados*
PLW	Pregnant and Lactating Women
PNAFN	*Programme National d'Aide aux Familles Nécessiteuses*
PNRT	National Employment Regularization Plan
PROGRESA	*Programa de Educación, Salud y Alimentación*
PSNP	Productive Safety Net Programme
RSBY	*Rashtriya Swasthya BimaYojana*
RSH	Social Registry of Homes
SADC	Southern African Development Community
SALC	South African Law Commission
SAPs	Structural Adjustment Programmes
SASSA	South African Social Security Agency
SCs	Scheduled Castes
SDGs	Sustainable Development Goals
SEWA	Self-Employed Women's Association
SMIG	*Salaire Minimum Interprofessionnel Garanti*
SPER	Social Protection Expenditure Review
SPiA	Social Protection in Action

List of Abbreviations and Acronyms

SPFs	Social Protection Floors
STs	Scheduled Tribes
THB	Thai Baht
TFR	Total Fertility Rate
TND	Tunisian Dinar
UDHR	Universal Declaration of Human Rights
UGTT	*Union Génerale des Travailleurs Tunisiens*
UK	United Kingdom
UN	United Nations
UNDP	United Nations Development Programme
UNICEF	United Nations Children's Fund
UNRISD	United Nations Research Institute for Social Development
UPA	United Progressive Alliance
USD	United States Dollars
UTICA	*Union Tunisienne de l'Industrie, du Commerce et de l'Artisanat*
WHO	World Health Organization
ZAR	South African Rand
ZIAS	*Zeitschrift für ausländisches und internationales Abreits-und Sozialrecht*

PART I Introduction to the Social Protection Floors: Basic Principles and Broader Context

CHAPTER 1
Recommendation on Social Protection Floors and Basic Principles for Innovative Solutions: General Introduction

Tineke Dijkhoff & Letlhokwa George Mpedi

1.1 THE ROAD TOWARDS NATIONAL SOCIAL PROTECTION FLOORS: A GENERAL OVERVIEW

1.1.1 The Global Protection Gap and the Birth of Recommendation

It was acknowledged that despite the recognition of social security as a human right and the development of social security Conventions and Recommendations by the International Labour Organization (hereinafter the ILO), the vast majority of the world's population still had no access to social security protection, or very little.[1] To address this global protection gap, the International Labour Conference in 2001 decided to give the highest priority to bringing social security to those who are not covered by existing schemes.[2] In 2003, the ILO launched the Global Campaign on Social Security and Coverage for All, and initiated several studies on this issue.[3] It was concluded that 'the basic deficiency of the existing ILO instruments lies in the lack of the requirement of universal access to at least

---

1. *See* Behrendt s. 3.1.
2. ILO, *Social Security: A New Consensus* (International Labour Office 2001). For a more elaborate description of the development towards the Social Protection Floor Initiative, *see*: ILO, *Social Protection Floors for Social Justice and a Fair Globalization*, International Labour Conference, 101st Session, 2012, Report IV(1), 5-8 (International Labour Office 2011).
3. For an overview, *see*: ILO, *Social Security for All. Investing in Global Social and Economic Development. A Consultation* Discussion Paper 16 (Social Security Department 2006).

a basic set of benefits'.[4] It was broadly acknowledged that the various social security Conventions do not sufficiently promote the extension of social security to the informal economy in the developing world.

As a result, the International Labour Conference adopted in 2008 the Declaration on Social Justice for a Fair Globalization, which reaffirmed the commitment to extend social security to all in need of such protection in the framework of the Decent Work Agenda.[5] In the light of this Declaration, the ILO undertook a General Survey on the application of its social security instruments and indeed concluded in its report that the current social security Conventions did not sufficiently address poverty and informal employment:[6]

> [T]he current ILO mandate in social security, as reaffirmed and updated by the Declaration on Social Justice for a Fair Globalization of 2008, has largely outgrown the standards with which it has to be implemented. The available means are no more sufficient to meet the new ends. This is particularly evident as regards the objective of extending social security coverage to all, beyond the formal economy to the masses of population living in abject poverty and insecurity, which is placed at the heart of the ILO's mandate and mission.

The International Labour Conference, in 2011, recognized that 'the task of globalizing social security requires the ILO to complement the current set of up-to-date standards with a new high-impact instrument' and embraced the idea of establishing national social protection floors. It was decided that a new Recommendation was needed to complement the existing standards and to provide 'flexible but meaningful guidance to Member States in building social protection floors within comprehensive social security systems tailored to national circumstances and levels of development'.[7]

The main objective of this Recommendation would be 'to protect in the first place the presently unprotected, the poor and the most vulnerable, including workers in the informal economy and their families, to ensure that they can enjoy effective essential social security throughout the life cycle'.[8] Consequently, in June 2012, the International Labour Conference adopted the autonomous Social Protection Floors Recommendation 202 of 2013 (hereinafter the Recommendation) with an impressive tripartite consensus: 452 votes in favour, 0 against, and 1 abstention.

---

4. ILO, *Setting Social Security Standards in a Global Society* 34 (International Labour Office 2008). See also ILO, *Social Security and the Rule of Law* 48-151 (International Labour Office 2011).
5. ILO, *Declaration on Social Justice for a Fair Globalization Adopted by the International Labour Conference at its 97th Session* (10 Jun. 2008).
6. ILO, *Social Security and the Rule of Law*, para. 30 (2011). See also ILO, *Social Protection Floors for Social Justice and a Fair Globalization*, International Labour Conference, 101st Session, 2012, Report IV(1), para. 15 (International Labour Office 2011).
7. *Ibid.*, paras 15-17.
8. *Ibid.*, para. 39.

1.1.2 The Broader Perspective of the Joint United Nations Social Protection Floor Initiative

Simultaneous to the standard-setting developments, but in a broader context, the Joint UN Social Protection Floor Initiative had been launched in 2009.[9] The ILO and the World Health Organization (hereinafter the WHO) were leading the initiative and managed to build a global coalition for this subject, including many other UN agencies (including the International Monetary Fund and the World Bank), developing partners and Non-governmental Organizations.

Calculations showed that a basic set of social transfers would be affordable, over time, even for low-income developing countries.[10] The initiative specifically addressed the issue of informal employment, emphasizing the vulnerable position, and the lack of social protection of informal workers:[11]

> [C]ash benefit coverage is still largely concentrated on urban-based workers and their families in the formal economy, and even then migrant workers have little access. Most people in the informal economy, where women and smallholder farmers are disproportionally represented, have only rudimentary access – if they have access at all – to basic cash benefits or transfers. Their access to affordable essential social and health services (including safe water supply) is equally deficient.

The concept of a national social protection floor was envisaged to consist of two main elements that help to realize the respective human rights:[12]

- *Essential Services*: ensuring the availability, continuity, and access to public services (such as water and sanitation, health, education, and family-focused social work support).
- *Social Transfers*: a basic set of essential social transfers, in cash and in kind, paid to the poor and vulnerable to enhance food security and nutrition, provide a minimum income security and access to essential services, including education and health care.

It was stated that the 'ILO is already promoting the social transfer component of the social floor, i.e. a basic set of essential social guarantees realized through transfers in cash and in kind …'[13] 'These transfers should be complemented by a number of essential social services, such as health, education, supply of safe water and housing.'[14] At a later stage, the services component has been explained as the 'supply' side of the social protection floor, i.e., 'activities

---

9. ILO and WHO, *The Social Protection Floor. A Joint Crisis Initiative of the UN Chief Executives Board for Co-ordination on the Social Protection Floor* (ILO & WHO 2009).
10. *Ibid.*, 10-11.
11. *Ibid.*, 8.
12. *Ibid.*, 2. The respective human rights are laid down in the Universal Declaration of Human Rights, paras 22, 25 and 26.
13. *Ibid.*, 6.
14. *Ibid.*, 7.

to develop the means to ensure the availability of goods and services in areas of health, water and sanitation, housing, education, food and related information, etc.'.[15] This could involve, for example, the development of infrastructures.

Unfortunately, the idea that income security and the availability, continuity, and access to essential services are two different elements of social protection, is not reflected in the title or the content of Recommendation 202. In fact, Recommendation 202 'only' covers the social transfer part of a social protection floor although this has not been made explicit.[16]

1.2 A SET OF PRINCIPLES AS POLICY TOOL AND ASSESSMENT FRAMEWORK

The main objective of the Recommendation is to provide guidance to Member States in establishing and maintaining social protection floors as a fundamental element of their national social protection systems.[17] It describes a number of basic guarantees – involving health care and income protection – a social protection floor should offer.[18] The way to realize these guarantees and the means to be used are left open, while innovative measures that fit with national characteristics and circumstances are promoted. National authorities are free to choose which forms of social protection they consider expedient, as long as the citizens effectively have access to a basic benefit package during their life cycle that enables them to live their lives in dignity.

Unlike the social security Conventions, the Recommendation does not set out concrete standards to be met, nor does it prescribe specific techniques to be used; it rather promotes innovative measures that fit in with national characteristics and circumstances. Because of the wide variety of possible schemes, the different techniques that can be employed to administer the scheme, and the emphasis on innovation, there is a genuine risk that important values relating to social security will be overlooked or made subordinate to realizing the objectives of the schemes concerned. For example, conditional cash transfers are often designated to mothers. The designation of a mother as a recipient, however, can limit a woman's opportunities and functions other than being a caregiver.[19] Although it has been shown that these forms of cash transfers can be effective in combatting poverty and improving education and health of the children and provide for basic needs of informal workers, it is equally important to ensure that women are able to develop other skills and have access to the labour market – all the more since they are role models for their daughters.

---

15. International Organisation of Employers, *The Concept of the Social Protection Floor. Explanatory Note for Employers* 3 (IOE 2011).
16. *See* further Dijkhoff, s. 2.3.1.
17. ILO Recommendation No. 202, Art. 1.
18. Dijkhoff, s. 2.2.3.
19. *See*, for example: R. Antonopoulos, *Expanding Social Protection in Developing Countries; A Gender Perspective*, Working Paper No. 757, 19 (Levy Economics Institute 2013).

Chapter 1: Social Protection Floors and Basic Principles for Innovative Solutions

In order to advance the creation of fair, equitable and universal social protection schemes, the Recommendation contains an extensive list of principles that should be applied in respect of all elements of a national social protection floor.[20] This list reflects what the international community considers important for social protection measures to comply with. Especially because the Recommendation does not prescribe pre-designed schemes that implicitly embody important values and legal principles – as is the case in the Conventions – but rather advocates new approaches, a set of explicit principles seems very useful; it could serve as a starting point and policy guideline for the creation of social protection floors. Considering the Recommendation's objective of providing basic social security for all, it is imperative that the set of principles must be particularly adequate in the context of developing countries with large informal economies, poor infrastructures, and weak administrations.

The question may be raised whether the principles summed up in the Recommendation constitutes an adequate and practicable list indeed; at first sight, it does not come across as a systematic and coherent one. In fact, it is a projection of principles and values put forward during the drafting process of the Recommendation by the different stakeholders – the ILO Office, governments, employers, and employees – with their different backgrounds, expertise, and interests. This is illustrated by the fact that the initial questionnaire prepared by the ILO Office addressed twelve principles while the final text includes nineteen principles. The need for consensus has made the list lengthy, a bit rambling, and sometimes overlapping. Moreover, the various principles and their relevance for a social protection floor are not systematically explained.

The lack of consistency and transparency regarding the fundamental values underlying social security may affect the applicability and the impact of the Recommendation in practice, and hamper the development of social protection for informal workers. In this book, a practicable set of principles is formulated that can be used both as a policy tool and an assessment framework for the creation, maintenance, and supervision of the different schemes that together make out a national social protection floor.

1.3 OBJECTIVES, METHODS AND DESIGN OF THE BOOK

1.3.1 Objectives

This book aims at providing insight in and understanding of the fundamental principles which implementation and application are prerequisite to a social protection floor. A practicable set of principles is composed and commented (Chapter 2) in order to create a clear framework of principles for the creation, implementation, maintenance, and supervision of national social protection floors. This framework may promote and strengthen the guiding function of

---

20. ILO Recommendation No. 202, Art. 3.

Recommendation 202 and serve as a tool for policymakers in their search for closing social protection gaps in their countries.

Within the context of this objective, the book assesses the principles included in the Recommendation and shows how, and to what extent, they are implemented in selected national schemes. The study focusses on the suitability and implementability of the principles with the view to extending social security, particularly to informal workers. This book, in light of the preceding overview, strives to address, among others, the following questions: What is the meaning of the principles with respect to the extension of social protection to informal workers? How and to what extent are these principles implemented in national schemes? What are the legislative deficits and/or implementation failures facing social protection schemes pertinent to the establishment of social protection floors? What are the lessons to be learnt from the experiences of schemes discussed as case studies?

This study is inspired by different studies recently conducted within the framework of the research agenda of the Max Planck Institute for Social Law and Social Policy (Munich) and the Centre for International and Comparative Labour and Social Security Law (Johannesburg).[21] In the research project on 'International Standard Setting and Innovation in Social Security' which was finalized in 2013, it has been established that, among other things, the existing international standards do not cover several social risks in a holistic manner.[22] Such risks include poverty, HIV/AIDS, and migration. In addition, it was found that new methods of social protection fall outside the scope of the existing social protection Conventions, which are predominantly based on traditional concepts of social insurance and social assistance.[23] In that project, it has also been concluded that the ILO Recommendation on national social protection floors may constitute a positive response to various observed problems. The research project at hand, with this book as its final product, expands on these conclusions.

---

21. U. Becker, D. Pieters, F. Ross, P. Schoukens (eds), *Security: A General Principle of Social Security Law in Europe* (Europe Law Publishing 2010); C. Mesa Lago, et al., *Re-reforms of Privatized Pension Systems*, 2012/3 ZIAS, 189-316 (2012); M. Nyenti & L.G. Mpedi, *The Impact of SADC Social Protection Instruments on the Setting Up of a Minimum Social Protection Floor in Southern African Countries*, 15 PER/PELJ (2012).
22. U. Becker, F. Pennings, T. Dijkhoff (eds), *International Standard Setting and Innovation in Social Security* (Wolters Kluwer 2013).
23. For studies on the social security standards, *see*: T. Dijkhoff, *International Social Security Standards in the European Union. The Cases of the Czech Republic and Estonia* (diss.) Social Europe Series vol. 28 (Intersentia 2011); F. Pennings (ed.) *International Social Security Standards. Current Views and Interpretation Matters* (Intersentia 2007); F. Pennings, *General Introduction* 15-37 (U. Becker, F. Pennings, T. Dijkhoff eds, Wolters Kluwer 2013).

1.3.2 Methods and Choices

The study is conducted from a legal perspective. It focusses primarily on the regulatory framework of social protection floors. The point is that without a sound legal framework, social protection schemes cannot be effective, operationalized, exist and, most importantly, a basic floor cannot be constructed. Furthermore, the Recommendation is, although soft law, a legal instrument that requires insertion into national laws and regulations. At the same time, the subjects 'social protection' and 'social security' are closely intertwined with economics, public finances, social policy, and development studies. By involving in the project not only lawyers, but also economists from different backgrounds, the book takes an interdisciplinary approach towards the social protection floor. For example, next to the legal examination of the social protection system, each case study also addresses the financial costs of the system, its impact in terms of poverty reduction, and implementation issues.

A literature review is the main research method used for the different chapters, which includes the use of primary sources such as national and international databases, international treaties, and national laws and regulations. The study uses case studies as a method to test the application of the defined principles in practice. This is the set of principles which have been formulated in Chapter 2 and used as an assessment framework. The selected cases (social protection schemes) reflect the context within which these principles are meant to support and safeguard basic social protection for all. The study does not involve comparative law. For that reason, the different case studies are solely meant to give an insight into the application of the principles in different schemes and under different circumstances.

The selection of the cases is based on a mix of criteria and arguments. The main criterion was the connection of a social protection scheme with the idea of social protection floors. Therefore, most selected cases are examples of successful social protection floor experiences put forward by the ILO and United Nations Development Programme.[24] All these schemes are specifically designed to extend social protection to vulnerable groups of persons that are not protected by employment-related social insurance, notably informal workers.

Second, the selected schemes cover different risks, corresponding with the risks addressed in the Recommendation. Nevertheless, it was resolved to concentrate on cash transfer benefits (unconditional as well as conditional) and thus leave out health care schemes, because of the different nature of benefits in kind and the limited scale of the current project.

Furthermore, the book covers schemes from both developing countries and emerging economies in different parts of the world.[25] The primary aim of this approach is to ensure that a global perspective and not regional picture is

---

24. UNDP, *Sharing Innovative Experiences* vol. 18 (UNDP 2011).
25. Covered in Chapters 5-12.

established. Within the borders of these choices, we have selected the cases, as elaborated in the Chapters 5-12.

1.3.3 Structure of the Book

The book is compartmentalized into three parts: (I) an introduction on the concept of social protection floors from different perspectives; (II) case studies assessing the implementation of the principles in selected schemes; and (III) conclusions.

Part 1 comprises four chapters providing a general introduction, the principles for social protection floors, implementing the principles of Social Protection Floors Recommendation, and social protection floors and the right to food. It starts with a brief overview and discussion of the Recommendation and the presentation of nine principles derived from the Recommendation and previous international instruments (Chapter 2). These principles are generally accepted as being prerequisite to basic social security for all; therefore, any social protection floor should reflect and apply these principles. The following chapters place the principles in a broader context. Chapter 3 focuses on the implementation of the principles, while Chapter 4 touches on the limitations of the Recommendation by only focussing on income security and health care. As a result of the focus on the social security component of social protection, other basic needs may not sufficiently be secured by a social protection floor that is nevertheless in line with the Recommendation. The example of food security makes perfectly clear the need for a broad approach of a social protection floor as a coherent package of measures of which income security is an important, but not the only, part.

Part II of the publication consists of eight case studies focusing on children and families (Chapters 5-8), working age (Chapters 9-10), and old age (Chapters 11-12). All case studies are structured around the principles as discussed in Chapter 2. The authors examine to what extent the principles are applied within social protection schemes that are considered as parts of national social protection floors. Related legislative deficits and/or implementation failures are identified and discussed.

Part III of the book is made of one chapter which is the conclusion. This chapter (Chapter 13) brings the conclusions of the case studies together and highlights the lessons learnt.

BIBLIOGRAPHY

Antonopoulos R., *Expanding Social Protection in Developing Countries; A Gender Perspective*, Working Paper No. 757 (Levy Economics Institute 2013).

Becker U., F. Pennings, T. Dijkhoff (eds), *International Standard Setting and Innovation in Social Security* (Wolters Kluwer 2013).

Becker U., et al. (eds), *Security: A General Principle of Social Security Law in Europe* (Europe Law Publishing 2010).

Dijkhoff T., *International Social Security Standards in the European Union. The Cases of the Czech Republic and Estonia* (diss.) Social Europe Series vol. 28 (Intersentia 2011).

ILO and WHO, *The Social Protection Floor. A Joint Crisis Initiative of the UN Chief Executives Board for Co-ordination on the Social Protection Floor* (2009).

ILO, *Setting Social Security Standards in a Global Society* (International Labour Office 2008).

ILO, *Social Security and the Rule of Law* (International Labour Office 2011).

ILO, *Social Security for All. Investing in Global Social and Economic Development. A Consultation* Discussion Paper 16 (Social Security Department 2006).

ILO, *Declaration on Social Justice for a Fair Globalization Adopted by the International Labour Conference at its 97th Session* (10 June 2008).

ILO, *Social Protection Floors for Social Justice and a Fair Globalization*, International Labour Conference, 101st Session, 2012, Report IV(1) (International Labour Office 2011).

ILO, *Social Security: A New Consensus* (International Labour Office 2001).

International Organisation of Employers, *The Concept of the Social Protection Floor. Explanatory Note for Employers* (IOE 2011).

Mesa Lago C., et al., *Re-reforms of Privatized Pension Systems*, 2012/3 ZIAS, 189-316 (2012).

Nyenti M. & L.G. Mpedi, *The Impact of SADC Social Protection Instruments on the Setting Up of a Minimum Social Protection Floor in Southern African Countries*, 15 PER/PELJ (2012).

Pennings F. (ed.), *International Social Security Standards. Current Views and Interpretation Matters* (Intersentia 2007).

Pennings F., *General Introduction* (U. Becker, F. Pennings, T. Dijkhoff eds, Wolters Kluwer 2013).

UNDP, *Sharing Innovative Experiences* vol. 18 (UNDP 2011).

CHAPTER 2
Principles for National Social Protection Floors

Tineke Dijkhoff

2.1 INTRODUCTION

In this chapter, the principles that are included in Recommendation 202[1] as being imperative for the creation and implementation of social protection floors are central. From the nineteen principles listed in Article 3, we have composed a shortlist of, what we call, 'umbrella principles' (section 2.4.1). Each of the umbrella principles is discussed in view of the context of a social protection floor (section 2.4.2-2.4.10). These principles make out the assessment framework for the case studies (Chapters 5-12). In the case studies, the extent to which and in what way the principles are applied in the creation, implementation, and administration of the schemes under review will be examined. Before elaborating on the principles, a brief overview of the content of the Recommendation is given (section 2.2.1-2.2.4). This is followed by some general observations that are important to consider before elaborating on the principles.

2.2 RECOMMENDATION 202: AN OVERVIEW

2.2.1 Preamble

In the Preamble, important principles and conclusions on the right to social security are restated and it reflects, in part, the evolution from the Declaration of Philadelphia to the present Recommendation. It starts by reaffirming the right to

---

1. Recommendation concerning National Floors of Social Protection, adoption: Geneva, 101st ILC session (14 Jun. 2012), *see* the Appendix of this volume.

social security as a human right and an economic and social necessity for development and progress.[2] Furthermore, it reaffirms the importance of social security in preventing and reducing poverty, in supporting the transition from informal to formal employment, in empowering people to adjust to changes in the economy and the labour market, and in creating sustainable long-term growth and social inclusion.

Specific reference is made to Articles 22 and 25 of the Universal Declaration of Human Rights and Articles 9, 11, and 12 of the International Covenant on Economic, Social and Cultural Rights, which do not only contain the right to social security,[3] but also elaborate the right of everyone to an adequate standard of living for themselves and their families, including adequate food, clothing, and housing,[4] and the right of everyone to the enjoyment of the highest attainable standard of physical and mental health.[5]

The Preamble also refers to several ILO Declarations and resolutions on the extension of social security and to the continuing relevance of the Income Security Recommendation (1944) and the Medical Care Recommendation (1944) that, in fact, already provide a sketch of a basic social protection floor. Furthermore, the pertinence of Convention No. 102 on Minimum Standards of Social Security for the development of comprehensive national social security systems is emphasized.

2.2.2 Part I: Objectives, Scope, and Principles

The main objective of the Recommendation is to provide guidance to Member States in:[6]

- establishing and maintaining social protection floors as a fundamental element of their national social security systems; and
- implementing social protection floors within strategies for the extension of social security that progressively ensure higher levels of social security to as many people as possible, guided by ILO social security standards.

This dualistic aim reflects the horizontal extension of social security (increase of the *number of persons* covered) on the one hand and a vertical extension (increase of the *level* of protection) on the other hand.[7] Whereas the

---

2. The notion of 'social progress and development' refers to the UN Declaration on Social Progress and Development, Res. G.A. 2542 (XXIV) of 11 Dec. 1969.
3. Universal Declaration of Human Rights (UDHR), UN GA res. 217A (III), 1948, Art. 22; International Covenant on Economic, Social and Cultural Rights (ICESCR), Art. 9.
4. UDHR, Art. 25; ICESCR, Art. 11.
5. UDHR, Art. 25; ICESCR, Art. 11.
6. Recommendation 202, Art. 1.
7. For an explanation of the horizontal and vertical dimension of social security extension, *see*: ILO, *Social Security for Social Justice and a Fair Globalization*. Report VI 135-136 (ILO 2011).

Chapter 2: Principles for National Social Protection Floors

existing social security Conventions with their concrete norms and their system of minimum and higher standards rather focus on the vertical dimension, the new Recommendation concentrates first and foremost on the horizontal dimension. The inclusion of the second objective is obviously meant to prevent countries from settling with the establishment of a social floor and to instead keep them working on a comprehensive social security system.[8]

Article 2 explains that social protection floors should be understood as 'nationally defined sets of basic social security guarantees which secure protection aimed at preventing or alleviating poverty, vulnerability and social exclusion'. The term 'guarantee' is used to reflect a focus on outcomes and not on methods or techniques. It includes 'either universal or means-tested benefits as long as the objective, i.e., a minimum level of income security for all residents, is achieved'.[9]

In Article 3, nineteen principles are formulated to be applied while creating a protection floor. The first principle is put in the opening sentence of this Article: 'Recognizing the overall and primary responsibility of the State in giving effect to this Recommendation, Members should apply the following principles:'

(a) universality of protection, based on social solidarity;
(b) entitlement to benefits prescribed by national law;
(c) adequacy and predictability of benefits;
(d) non-discrimination, gender equality, and responsiveness to special needs;
(e) social inclusion, including of persons in the informal economy;
(f) respect for the rights and dignity of people covered by the social security guarantees;
(g) progressive realization, including by setting targets and time frames;
(h) solidarity in financing while seeking to achieve an optimal balance between the responsibilities and interests among those who finance and benefit from social security schemes;
(i) consideration of diversity of methods and approaches, including financing mechanisms and delivery systems;
(j) transparent, accountable, and sound financial management and administration;
(k) financial, fiscal, and economic sustainability with due regard to social justice and equity;
(l) coherence with social, economic, and employment policies;
(m) coherence across institutions responsible for delivery of social protection;
(n) high-quality public services that enhance the delivery of social security systems;

---

8. ILO, *Social Protection Floors for Social Justice and a Fair Globalization*, Report IV(1) para. 11 (ILO 2012).
9. ILO, *Social Security for Social Justice and a Fair Globalization*. Report VI 151 (ILO 2011).

(o) efficiency and accessibility of complaint and appeal procedures;
(p) regular monitoring of implementation and periodic evaluation;
(q) full respect for collective bargaining and freedom of association for all workers; and
(r) tripartite participation with representative organizations of employers and workers, as well as consultation with other relevant and representative organizations of persons concerned.

2.2.3 Part II: National Social Protection Floors

In the second part, the concept of national social protection floors is specified in more detail. A national social protection floor should comprise four basic social security guarantees, to be defined at a nationally defined minimum level:[10]

- access to a nationally defined set of goods and services, constituting essential health care, including maternity care, that meets the criteria of availability, accessibility, acceptability, and quality;
- basic income security for children, at least at a nationally defined minimum level, providing access to nutrition, education, care, and any other necessary goods and services;
- basic income security, at least at a nationally defined minimum level, for persons in active age who are unable to earn sufficient income, in particular in cases of sickness, unemployment, maternity, and disability; and
- basic income security, at least at a nationally defined minimum level, for older persons.

It is emphasized that countries should consider different approaches in providing the basic guarantees, so as to implement the most effective and efficient combination of benefits and schemes in the national context.[11] It is specifically expressed that implementation of the different measures should 'promote productive economic activity and formal employment'.[12] Several further specifications directly follow from the principles listed in Part I (e.g., concerning universality, diversity of methods, economic sustainability, and good governance, including fraud prevention).

2.2.4 Part III: National Strategies for the Extension of Social Security

Part III goes more deeply into the implementation process of the different strategies used for the building of a national social protection floor. It starts by

---

10. Recommendation 202, Art. 5.
11. Recommendation 202, Art. 9.
12. Recommendation 202, Art. 10(b).

prescribing Member States to formulate and implement national social security extension strategies based on social dialogue and social participation.[13] For this purpose, national priorities regarding measures to be taken should be formulated on the basis of identified protection gaps; appropriate schemes should be developed or extended, either contributory or non-contributory, or both; a solid financial plan should be made, including a time frame; and information programmes to raise awareness about the extension strategies should be undertaken. These strategies are to be applied to persons 'both in the formal and informal economy', and should support the growth of formal employment and the reduction of informality.[14] The strategies should include the objective of achieving the range and levels of benefits set out in Convention No. 102, or in the instruments setting out more advanced standards.

2.2.5 Part IV: Monitoring

The last part stipulates that countries should monitor the progress in implementing social protection floors through appropriate, nationally defined mechanisms.[15] These mechanisms should include the collecting, compiling, analysing and publishing of social security data and indicators on a regular basis, following the guidance provided by the ILO. Furthermore, the Member States are encouraged to exchange information, experiences, and expertise on social security strategies, policies, and practices among themselves and with the ILO.

2.3 PRELIMINARY OBSERVATIONS

2.3.1 The National Floor: Social Protection or Social Security?

The term 'social protection' in the title of Recommendation 202 promises a broad interpretation of what a national floor should contain: more than merely social security. Social protection includes social security, but 'given the dimension of the informal economy and the massive and persistent poverty, the concept of social protection has to include the idea of productive employment and poverty reduction'.[16] In the ILO Report on decent work and the informal economy, the distinction between social protection and social security has been explained as follows:[17]

> However, there has been growing recognition of the need to broaden the concept of social security to take account of the problems faced by developing

---

13. Recommendation 202, Art. 13.
14. Recommendation 202, Art. 15.
15. Recommendation 202, Art. 19.
16. J. Unni & U. Rani, *Social Protection for Informal Workers: Insecurities, Instruments and Institutional Mechanisms* 3 (ILO 2002).
17. ILO, *Decent Work and the Informal Economy* 56-57 (ILO 2002).

countries and the realities of the informal economy. With flexible and unstable employment and many more workers in the informal economy, what is needed is a broader concept of 'social protection' which covers not only social security but also non-statutory schemes, including various types of new contributory schemes, mutual benefit societies and grass-roots and community schemes for workers in the informal economy.

Reference in the Preamble of the Recommendation to other human rights than social security, such as the right to an adequate standard of living, including adequate food, clothing, and housing, is in line with the expectations raised by the title. It is clear that a national social protection floor should not only consist of 'traditional' social security schemes that are usually limited to formal employees but also that it refers to a broader sense of social protection – broader in terms of personal scope and in terms of risks covered.

Looking at the specification of national protection floors given in Part II of the Recommendation, we can see that the approach is broader indeed than the approach of Convention 102. The latter includes strict definitions for each social risk, and provides for three cash transfer methods: social insurance, social assistance (means-tested), and universal benefits, with certain preference for social insurance. The formulation 'basic income security' used in the Recommendation, on the other hand, may involve all possible kinds of measures as long as they serve the objective. Also, the target groups 'children', 'persons in active age who are unable to earn sufficient income' and 'older persons' are, in principle, not further specified or subject to limitations. The term 'guarantee' reflects a focus on outcomes and not on methods or techniques, as is the case in Convention No. 102.

Income security for persons in active age, for example, may also include insurance for the loss of crop due to a natural disaster, or the loss of tools; or training programmes to enhance productivity. Article 10 requires Member States 'to combine preventive, promotional and active measures, benefits and social services', and a wide variety of possible measures is mentioned throughout the Recommendation which should be tailored to national economic and social realities.

However, the focus on 'social security guarantees' and income security and basic health care being the core of the Recommendation is confusing in this respect, as it refers to the traditional and narrow idea of social security and does not reflect the broader concept of social protection. In fact, in previous ILO publications on the social floor idea, the term 'social security floor' was used instead of 'social protection floor'.[18] The ambivalence towards the concept of the social protection floor may flow from the fact that the protection of workers – in

---

18. *See*, for example: M. Cichon & K. Hagemejer, *Changing the Development Policy Paradigm: Investing in a Social Security Floor for All* 60 International Social Security Review 169-196 (2007); ILO, *Setting Social Security Standards in a Global Society* 22 (ILO 2008); For an extensive overview of the development of the social security towards social protection concept, *see* B. Deacon, *Global Social Policy in the Making. The Foundation of the Social Protection Floor Making* (Policy Press 2013).

the sense of employees – has always been the ILO's centre of interest and activity. It may be true that the conservative stance from the side of trade unions and employers' organizations are a part of the barrier to the development of an instrument that goes further beyond worker protection.[19]

Taking a closer look at the structure of the Recommendation, the different status of social security guarantees and other measures are clearly visible. The four core provisions specified in Article 5 (access to essential health care and basic income security for the three target groups) are the guarantees; any social protection floor should comprise at least these core guarantees. Article 9 adds that benefits following from the basic social security guarantees may include the whole range of benefits provided for in Convention No. 102, 'as well as any other social benefits in cash or in kind'. Then, Article 10 does not deal with social security guarantees, but with permissive policies, Members may take into account while designing and implementing national social protection floors, including, for example, labour inspection, labour market policies, promotion of education, and coordination with other policies that enhance formal employment.

It may be concluded that:

- A social protection floor envisaged by the Recommendation is a set of national *social security measures* (guarantees) established by law, which relate to the traditional concept of social security, however, focused on the outcomes and not on the methods.
- Simultaneous to the implementation of social security measures, State Members may take into account *other measures*, which cover the broader spectrum of *social protection*, that is, beyond social security. These measures are different from the 'guarantees'; they are permissive and depending on the national situation and level of development.

In fact, the Recommendation deals with the social security part of social protection. Other elements envisaged to be covered by a social protection floor according to the Social Protection Floors Initiative, such as food security, access to potable water and sanitation, are not explicitly addressed, nor are issues relating to labour rights, such as the right to work and safety in the work place.

Of course, income security helps to obtain sufficient food, potable water and sanitation, which the Recommendation emphasizes by stating that '[t]he guarantees should ensure at a minimum that, over the life cycle, all in need have access to essential health care and to basic income security which together secure effective access to goods and services defined as necessary at the national level'. However, social protection in the broader sense depends on many more factors than a minimum income, such as the availability of necessary resources

---

19. On the conservative role of the social partners, see also s. 2.4.10.

as such, a working infrastructure and distribution system, and political stability.[20]

In spite of its title and the broad ambitions laid down in the Preamble, the core of the Recommendation is limited to basic health care and income security. The ILO Conference has not made a clear choice for either social security or social protection. The title and the Preamble promise more than the Recommendation makes true. A clear delineation of the scope and task of the Recommendation, namely promoting social security as a key element of the social protection floor, might have made the instrument clearer, easier to apply, and more powerful.

2.3.2 Binding Force Versus Political Support

The ILO Conference has opted for a Recommendation as an instrument and not for a Convention. This is not an obvious choice. In most cases, a Recommendation is adopted to support and elaborate a Convention on the same subject that lays down the basic principles to be implemented by ratifying countries. The Recommendation on national social protection floors, however, is an autonomous instrument not linked to any specific Convention.

Because a Recommendation is an instrument without binding force and Recommendation 202 does not have a binding Convention as its counterpart, it has very little legal significance.[21] There is no regular supervision on the implementation of Recommendations, and there are no sanctions for non-compliance. Member States are free to use the included suggestions and guidelines fully, partly or not at all. This was the reason in the first instance that it was noted that for the development of social protection floors, a Recommendation would provide insufficient legal basis. The problem was formulated as follows: 'It is rather Recommendations Nos. 67 and 69 that lay down the relevant standards for implementing this minimum social security floor. Due to their legal nature, however, they do not provide binding obligations for ILO member States in this regard.'[22] This point of view was dropped at a later stage of the decision-making process.[23]

The choice in the end for, again, a Recommendation has not been clearly and sufficiently motivated. Tapiola argues that the new social protection floors instrument were to promote Convention 102, and that the aim of a Convention

---

20. *See* also Chapter 4.
21. T. Dijkhoff, *Supervision of Social Security Standards: Between Law and Politics* (F. Pennings & G. Vonk eds., Edward Elgar Publishing 2015).
22. ILO, *Setting Social Security Standards in a Global Society* 22 (ILO 2008). Also, for the development of the Recommendation: B. Deacon, *Global Social Policy in the Making* 37-59 (Policy Press 2013).
23. K. Tapiola, *Global Standards: The Policy of the ILO* (U. Becker, F. Pennings, T. Dijkhoff eds., Kluwer International 2013).

could not be to implement the provisions of another Convention.[24] Deacon extensively describes the history of the development of the Recommendation, but at this point, he only states that '[a] convention was not acceptable so another recommendation was all that could be achieved'.[25]

Probably various reasons have led to the choice of a Recommendation, such as the lack of political will to accept a binding instrument and the low ratification rate of the existing social security Conventions in developing countries. It must be realized that the financial impact and administrative burden flowing from the obligation to establish regular reports on the application of a Convention is difficult to overcome for many developing countries, where administration systems are often very weak and financial resources short.

It is true, of course, that a Convention is more powerful from a legal perspective; however, a Recommendation may be preferable from a policy perspective. Precisely the lack of an international supervisory system and the broad margin of appreciation of national and local authorities may be an incentive for governments to make commitments regarding a gradual creation of a national social protection floor.

The almost unanimous adoption of the instrument is illustrative of the broad political support of the idea of social protection floors. Furthermore, it appears from the standard-setting history of the ILO that Recommendations can be very influential on national policies. Exemplary are the previously mentioned Philadelphia Recommendations from 1944 that worldwide have served as a starting point for a broader concept of social security, and eventually have played a leading role in the creation of the idea of social protection floors.

2.4 CLASSIFYING AND CLARIFYING THE PRINCIPLES

2.4.1 Selection of 'Umbrella Principles'

As noted in the previous Chapter (section 1.2), the list of principles laid down in Part I of the Recommendation is a result of discussions during the drafting process by different stakeholders with diverging interests. Several of these principles reflect the well-established principles set out in the social security Conventions – notably Convention 102 – such as State responsibility, financial solidarity, tripartite participation, financial sustainability, predictability of benefits, non-discrimination, and regular monitoring of implementation. They are generally recognized as conditional for social security.

Other principles have been added in view of the specific aim of social protection floors: coverage, through a wide range of measures, of those who are

---

24. *Ibid.*, 48.
25. B. Deacon, *Global Social Policy in the Making* 40 (Policy Press 2013).

not protected by traditional (mostly employment related) social security. Examples are the principles that deal with good governance (involving transparency, accountability, and efficiency), coherence of policies, and social inclusion. The formulation of these 'new' principles of social security within the framework of a social protection floor is a very good idea considering the broad and innovative character of such floor that should be geared with the specific national situation and needs. It is necessary to depart from the path of long-standing insurance methods in order to protect those who cannot be reached through these established methods.

However, the formulation of the list of principles laid down in Article 3 is not obvious. The nineteen principles do not constitute a clear and practicable set of basic values to serve as a guideline for policymakers and administrations. In the following, a more concise and manageable list is presented that serves as a gauge for the assessment of the selected social security schemes in different countries (Chapters 5–12).

The formulation of these 'umbrella principles' is based on different human rights treaties and explanatory documents related to social protection – for example, General Comment No. 19 on the Right to Social Security of the International Committee on Economic, Social and Cultural Rights. Furthermore, categorizations or clarifications of principles have been made by scholars previously, which have also been taken into account.[26]

Studying the documents and literature, it appeared that Article 3 of the Recommendation contains all the principles that have been drawn up elsewhere, although sometimes worded slightly differently. The next step was to make a consistent, less possible overlapping, and workable list out of the nineteen principles enumerated in the Recommendation by classifying them under a limited number of umbrella principles.

It should be noted that different categorizations are possible and that a categorization of the principles is not an objective as such; it is rather a tool to be able to approach them in a more effective manner. Important is that the list is complete in the sense that it contains all generally acknowledged basic values for social security that are relevant for a social protection floor. The 'shortlist' is as follows (the letters between brackets refer to the letters of the principles used in Article 3):

---

26. For example: U. Becker et al., *Security. A General Principle of Social Security Law in Europe* (Europe Law Publishing 2010); C. Mesa Lago, et al., *Re-reforms of Privatized Pension Systems*, 3 ZIAS 189-316 (2012); M. Mikkola, *Social Human Rights of Europe* (Bookwell Ltd 2010); A.M. Fischer, *Inequality and the Universalistic Principle in the Post-2015 Development Agenda* (Erasmus University Rotterdam, November 2012); G. Vonk, *The 2012 Recommendation Concerning National Floors of Social Protection (No 202), The Human Rights Approach to Social Security in ILO Wrapping Paper*, 4 International Journal of Social Security and Workers Compensation 49-59 (2012-2013).

Chapter 2: Principles for National Social Protection Floors

1. *state responsibility*	Article 3
2. *universality of protection*	(a) universality of protection, based on social solidarity; (e) social inclusion, including of persons in the informal economy; (g) progressive realization, including by setting targets and time frames; (i) consideration of diversity of methods and approaches, including of financing mechanisms and delivery systems;
3. *entitlements based on law*	(b) entitlement to benefits prescribed by national law; (o) efficiency and accessibility of complaint and appeal procedures;
4. *adequacy and predictability of benefits*	(c) adequacy and predictability of benefits; (f) respect for the rights and dignity of people covered by the social security guarantees;
5. *non-discrimination*	(d) non-discrimination, gender equality and responsiveness to special needs;
6. *financial solidarity*	(h) solidarity in financing while seeking to achieve an optimal balance between the responsibilities and interests among those who finance and benefit from social security schemes;
7. *good governance*	(f) respect for the rights and dignity of people covered by the social security guarantees; (i) consideration of diversity of methods and approaches, including of financing mechanisms and delivery systems; (j) transparent, accountable and sound financial management and administration; (k) financial, fiscal and economic sustainability with due regard to social justice and equity; (m) coherence across institutions responsible for delivery of social protection; (n) high-quality public services that enhance the delivery of social security systems; (p) regular monitoring of implementation, and periodic evaluation;
8. *coherence of policies*	(i) consideration of diversity of methods and approaches, including of financing mechanisms and delivery systems; (l) coherence with social, economic and employment policies; (m) coherence across institutions responsible for delivery of social protection;
9. *social participation*	(q) full respect for collective bargaining and freedom of association for all workers; and (r) tripartite participation with representative organizations of employers and workers, as well as consultation with other relevant and representative organizations of persons concerned.

In the following sections, each principle is discussed in the light of a social protection floor, and possible questions that may be relevant for the case studies are formulated.

2.4.2 State Responsibility

The Recommendation explicitly assigns the 'overall and primary responsibility' for effectuation of the social protection to the Member States. It could be argued that this principle is superfluous. The Recommendation addresses the Member States as duty bearers, which makes them responsible by definition. And there is broad consensus on the idea that the human right to social security imposes three obligations to the State, namely, the obligation to respect, to protect, and to fulfil.[27] This may be the reason that State responsibility was not included in the text of the initial draft of the Recommendation. Still, it is appropriate to explicitly mention this principle and distinguish it from all other principles by not putting it in the list but above the list. After all, it is the State that must ensure that the entire list of principles will be implemented and applied regarding all aspects of the social protection floor.

State responsibility can have different forms and differ in extent, depending on the context.[28] The term 'overall and primary responsibility' does not paint a clear picture of how far the responsibility reaches. The formulation does not necessarily seem to imply that the State itself must be the provider of the benefits or the administrator of the schemes. For example, the question to what extent private actors may be involved has not been addressed.

Some indications as to the extent of State responsibility can be found in relation to ILO Convention No. 102 on minimum standards of social security, in which this principle is also incorporated.[29] According to this Convention, State responsibility does not, for example, rule out the use of voluntary and/or private schemes for the fulfilment of its obligations, providing that the government is involved by setting a legislative framework that requires participation of insured persons in the administration of the scheme concerned.[30]

This could imply that a social protection floor should not necessarily merely consist of public schemes, but that there is also room for private schemes. However, the 'good experiences' highlighted by the ILO so far are all State-run schemes, which may reflect a disfavour for private schemes in respect

---

27. For example, CESCR, General Comment No. 19: *The right to social security* 50 (2008); ILO, *Social Security and the Rule of Law* 66 (ILO 2011); G. Vonk, *The 2012 Recommendation Concerning National Floors of Social Protection (No 202)*, 4 International Journal of Social Security and Workers Compensation 53-54 (2012-2013).
28. G. Vonk, *The 2012 Recommendation Concerning National Floors of Social Protection (No. 202)*, 4 International Journal of Social Security and Workers Compensation 52-54 (2012-2013); T. Dijkhoff, *International Social Security Standards in the European Union. The Cases of the Czech Republic and Estonia* Social Europe Series vol. 28, 35 (Intersentia 2011).
29. ILO Convention 102, Art. 71(3).
30. ILO Convention 102, Art. 72(1).

of social security. Nevertheless, the wording of the Recommendation does not rule out private schemes to play a part within a social protection floor.

It was furthermore made clear by the ILO in an explanatory memorandum to ILO Convention No. 102 that the general responsibility of the State 'would not necessarily bind the Member to meet any deficit occurring in the agency administering a scheme [...], but it would oblige it to take measures to ensure that the benefits are duly provided'.[31] Examples of such measures would be for the government to grant a subsidy to meet the deficit, or to secure the provision of the benefits by arranging a loan.

From the State's responsibility to establish and maintain a social protection floor, it follows that the State must durably provide sufficient financial means to fulfil its duties.[32] The State must also ensure a balance between the resources raised for social security and benefits delivered, allowing for redistribution between different groups in accordance with the solidarity principle. It has been emphasized in this respect that resources envisaged for social security cannot be used to finance non-social security expenditure such as a deficit in the State budget.[33] In relation to privatized schemes, this would imply a prohibition on profit-seeking for insurance funds.

In spite of many open questions, the Recommendation provides some clarity concerning the specific fields, or objects, of a State's responsibility. First, the State is responsible for the establishment and maintenance of a social protection floor (Article 4) and obliges the State to establish the basic social security guarantees by law (Article 7). This stresses the role of the State as initiator and main actor, and as the provider of the legislative framework. Second, the State should formulate and implement social protection floor strategies (Article 13). This means that the elaboration and interpretation of the legal framework cannot be left to other actors and stakeholders, but that the government itself must design a 'master plan' – setting objectives and defining priorities – along which the floor must be built and implemented. Third, the State should monitor the developments of the social protection floor and define proper monitoring mechanisms (Article 19).

The case studies in the second part of this book will reveal how the various States interpret their 'overall and primary responsibility' to the schemes that may constitute a part of national social protection floors in the making. Questions will be addressed as to the specific role of the State in the different phases

---

31. ILO, *Report V (a) (2): Minimum Standards of Social Security* International Labour Conference, 35th Session, 231. (ILO 1952).
32. *See also* P. Schoukens, *Social Security Law Instruments of the Next Generation* 550-551 (F. Pennings & G. Vonk eds., Edward Elgar 2015).
33. T. Dijkhoff, *The Introduction of Private Elements in National Social Security and the Role of International Standards* (K. Koldinska & M. Štefko eds., Auditorium 2010); M. Humblet & R. Silva, *Standards for the XXIst Century, Social Security* 12 (ILO 2002); M. Humblet & M. Zarka-Martres, *ILO Standards Policy* 447 (International Labour Office ed., ILO 2001). ILO, *Social Security: Issues, Challenges and Prospects* 57-58 (ILO 2001).

of development, whether or not private actors are involved and to what extent the State actually guarantees the provision of the benefits.

2.4.3 Universality of Protection

The first principle listed in Article 3 reads: 'universality of protection, based on social solidarity'. This principle is a derivative of the very idea of a social protection floor – a floor implies a basis for all. It is closely connected with another principle in the list: 'social inclusion, including of persons in the informal economy'. The principle of universality reflects the universal right to social security as proclaimed by the Declaration of Philadelphia and incorporated in the International Covenant on Economic, Social and Cultural rights.

In the past, the ILO has elaborated the human right to social security through the different social security Conventions that translate human rights aspirations into concrete legal standards. For these standards to have any practical significance, they must be set at a level that would be attainable in the short term by a substantial number of countries, and at the same time, they should embody achievable objectives for less-developed countries. Setting unattainable standards would have been senseless.

This normative approach of the ILO social security Conventions makes it possible to monitor compliance of these norms and to call Member States to account in cases of infringements of the norms. However, at the same time, the setting of legally binding and achievable norms does not go together with the ultimate goal of 100% coverage. Because the minimum norms of ILO Convention No. 102 can generally be met by covering 50% of salaried workers or 20% of the economically active population, this Convention is not instrumental in further extending social protection – in spite of its reference to the universal right to social security.[34]

The Recommendation returns to the human rights approach in the sense that its objective is full coverage – through a floor of basic social protection. It should be noted, however, that Article 6 adds that the social security guarantees should be provided to 'at least all residents and children, as defined in national laws and regulations'. This obviously does not imply universality, since this definition exclusively refers to persons legally residing in the country. The wording of this Article was the subject of intense debate and several amendments during the 2012 ILO Conference. In spite of the efforts of the workers' representatives to have an amendment adopted that the guarantees should apply 'as a priority step towards the realization of the right of everyone to social

---

34. *See*, for example F. Pennings, *Historical and Theoretical Background of Standard Setting in Social Security* (U. Becker et al. eds, Wolters Kluwer 2013); T. Dijkhoff, *International Social Security Standards in the European Union* 351-354 (Intersentia 2011).

security' instead of the current formulation, this aspiration to cover all was not accepted.[35]

Unfortunately, the actual formulation is not only contradictory to the universal concept of a social protection floor, it is also not very clear. It was explained at a later stage that it 'should be interpreted to read that the floor would indeed be available to all children subject only to national laws *about the age at which persons are regarded as children.*'[36] This means that to any child, legally or not legally residing in the country, basic income security must be secured. It also means that adult irregular migrants and other persons illegally residing and/or working in a country fall outside the scope of a social protection floor. The addition of 'at least' indicates that a broader scope may be strived for, but it is not a requirement. This is difficult to understand because in many developing and emerging countries, illegal migrants make up an important part of the informal economy.

Principle (g) requires 'progressive realization, including by setting targets and time frames'. Typical of human rights instruments, no standards are given as to the time frame a State should set, or the minimum amount of effort, to be delivered. Still, the principle of progressive realization is inextricably bound with a human right in general since, in practice, they are never fully attained.

It can be argued that contributory schemes, targeted schemes, and conditional schemes are in breach of the principle of universality since they exclude large groups of persons in need of social security. However, from the idea of universality as a future prospect follows naturally that a social protection floor does not necessarily consist of merely universal schemes. In the context of the Recommendation as one of the guiding instruments for the realization of the human right to social security, it seems acceptable to interpret universality in the light of progressive realization. Universal coverage can also be strived for through targeted schemes and benefits regarding specific contingencies if those schemes cover existing gaps in protection.

In fact, to attain universality, the Recommendation promotes a combination of different benefits and schemes that is most effective in the national context. This is emphasized through principle (i): 'consideration of diversity of methods and approaches, including of financing mechanisms and delivery systems'. However, it should be stressed that for universal coverage, non-contributory schemes are indispensable.[37]

Questions to be addressed in the case studies include to what extent the scheme at hand fills gaps in protection, especially regarding informal workers and non-legal residents and their children; whether further extension of the personal scope is envisaged in the future; and whether the scheme under review is embedded in a coherent range of measures that together constitute an extensive floor developing towards universality.

---

35. B. Deacon, *Global Social Policy in the Making* 90 (Policy Press 2013).
36. *Ibid.*, 92.
37. CESCR, General Comment No. 19: *The right to social security* para. 23 (2008).

2.4.4 Entitlements Based on Law

First, it has to be realized that the 'rights-based' concept can be interpreted in different ways. A rights-based approach is often linked to human rights. For example, Vonk counter poses a rights-based approach and a State duty approach. The former is a characteristic of the human right to social security and 'built upon the notion that each individual is entitled to social security protection; it is then up to the states to take appropriate steps to realize this right'.[38] The State duty approach is applied in ILO's social security Conventions; 'they impose minimum requirements on a State, not for the sake of the individual, but for the project of social security itself'.[39]

Another train of thought could be that the human right to social security is not clear and accurate enough to establish an individual entitlement. For a person to invoke and consume the right, it should first be translated into a concrete norm, for example, the right to an old-age benefit amounting to USD 300 at the attainment of the age of 65. In this line of argument, a rights-based approach would simply mean that the State is obliged to prescribe social security benefits by law. From both points of view, the Recommendation adheres, or applies, a rights-based approach.

During the preparatory stage of the Recommendation, the importance of a rights-based approach was expressed.[40] It was feared that the Recommendation would contain just a policy framework and would thus depart from the rights-based approach by not providing a legal basis for individual entitlements. It has been argued in this respect that although the ILO emphasized in the different documents that a national social protection floor should involve entitlements to benefits, the examples of programmes given to illustrate the working of a social floor did not always involve rights-based benefits.[41]

Looking at the text of the adopted Recommendation, it seems that this concern has been taken into account. First, the rights-based approach is embedded in the term 'social security guarantees', relating to the four core elements of a social protection floor; this implies individual entitlements. Furthermore, the second of the principles set in Article 3 requires entitlements to benefits to be prescribed by national law.[42] In Part II, this obligation is further

---

38. G. Vonk, *The 2012 Recommendation Concerning National Floors of Social Protection (No. 202)*, 4 International Journal of Social Security and Workers Compensation 55 (2012-2013).
39. *Ibid.* Vonk underpins this distinction with reference to: ILO Committee of Experts, ILO, *Social Security and the Rule of Law* para. 159 (ILO 2011).
40. D. Mestrum, *Social Protection Floor: Beyond Poverty Reduction?* 9 Analysis for Global Social Justice.eu (4 Mar. 2012); M. Olivier, *Informality, Employment Contracts and Social Insurance Coverage: Rights-Based Perspectives in a Developing World Context* 27 The International Journal of Comparative Labour Law and Industrial Relations 422-425 (2011).
41. P. Arellano Ortiz, *Protection in Old Age in Chile* 425-426 (U. Becker, F. Pennings & T. Dijkhoff eds., Kluwer Law International 2013).
42. Recommendation 202, Art. 3(b).

specified by stating that 'basic social security guarantees should be established by law. National laws and regulations should specify the range, qualifying conditions and levels of the benefits giving effect to these guarantees' and provide for easily accessible complaint procedures.[43] The latter part is worded in a separate principle: '(o) Efficiency and accessibility of complaint and appeal procedures'. The challenge is, of course, to create laws that enable individual entitlements to be delivered in practice at the national and community level to, for example, informal workers.

If we accept that a rights-based approach means that entitlements must be based in laws, the question arises what law-based exactly means. Moser & Norton have analysed the different law regimes, which include not only international human rights law, regional law, constitutional law, and statutory law, but also 'living law'.[44] This last category would entail informal rights and norms of behaviour associated with localities and cultures. Living law operates at the micro level and is not incorporated into national legal systems; 'nonetheless, local elites may be able to co-opt elements of the state to help enforce elements of living law'.[45]

From this point of view, 'law-based' has a much broader scope and may include community-based social protection; the Self-Employed Women's Association (SEWA) in India is given as an example.[46] The various examples of initiatives within the framework of national social protection floors initially given by the ILO, which included local arrangements as established by SEWA, would suggest that the Recommendation was meant to adopt this wide interpretation of 'rights'. However, at the current ILO website dedicated to the Social Protection Floor, exclusively national schemes are included, which seems to indicate a changed view at this point.[47]

A narrow interpretation of 'law-based' – only involving the higher law regimes – is easy to defend in relation to social protection floors; it enhances legal certainty, transparency, and, eventually, access to social rights. This is all the more important in cases of weak administrative systems and widespread corruption. Informal arrangements are often characterized by discrimination, arbitrariness, and unsustainability and are difficult to combine with State responsibility. Still, grassroots initiatives such as local or regional small(er)-scale insurance schemes can make a significant difference, particularly in remote areas and for workers in the informal sector. Perhaps a new Recommendation on grassroots initiatives and micro-insurance could be developed in which Member

---

43. Recommendation 202, Art. 7.
44. C. Moser & A. Norton, *To Claim our Rights: Livelihood Security, Human Rights and Sustainable Development* 21-28 (Overseas Development Institute London 2001); L.H. Piron, *Rights-Based Approaches to Social Protection* 4-5 (Overseas Development Institute London 2004).
45. C. Moser & A. Norton, *To Claim Our Rights: Livelihood Security, Human Rights and Sustainable Development* 23 (Overseas Development Institute London 2001).
46. *Ibid.*, 23.
47. UNDP, *Sharing Innovative Experiences* vol. 18 (UNDP 2011).

States would be encouraged to support and facilitate such schemes, complementary to the rights-based social protection floor.

For the assessment of compliance with the principle of right-based benefits, the case studies may include an analysis of the legal framework of the scheme to establish whether or not all aspects of the benefits as set out in Article 7 are prescribed. This includes the question of the extent to which effective complaint and appeal procedures – which are inextricably entangled with individual entitlements – have been enacted and put in place.

2.4.5 Adequacy and Predictability of Benefits

Principle (c) requires benefits provided within the framework of a social protection floor to be adequate and predictable. Predictability is tightly linked with the previous principle; if the range, qualifying conditions, and levels of benefits are specified in laws and regulations, the benefits should be predictable. Predictability is also prerequisite for a benefit to be adequate. An uncertain benefit, either in terms of amount, point in time, or way of delivery, is never adequate since it lacks security.

Although adequacy is a key requirement for effective social security, it is not well elaborated in the Recommendation what this principle should involve. Article 4 says that the various benefits 'should together secure, over the life cycle, effective access to goods and services defined as necessary at the national level'. Article 5 specifies minimum requirements for child benefits, namely that they should provide access to nutrition, education, and care. These directions can hardly be called guidelines.

Most striking, the Recommendation is silent as to the concrete minimum levels of the benefits – these must be nationally defined. The Recommendation contains only few directions. Principle (f) reads: 'respect for the rights and dignity of people covered by the social security guarantees'. This can be interpreted in the sense of Article 8, which states that, at least, the benefits should allow life lived in dignity: 'The minimum income level to allow for a life in dignity may be defined as a set of necessary goods and services, or as a national poverty line, or income threshold for social assistance, or in any other way, and may take into account regional differences.' Still, the key issue of what a life lived in dignity is, is left open.

Adequacy also requires benefits to be actually accessible to the eligible persons. There may be many reasons for inaccessibility; for example, the application procedure is excessively complicated, specific documents are requested, the application office is too far away, or the benefit is not paid out because of practical reasons. This aspect of adequacy is included in Article 4 that also states that the benefit levels should be regularly reviewed through transparent procedures, that which not necessarily have to be laid down in laws; however, tripartite participation should be ensured.

All in all, the Recommendation gives disappointingly few guidelines as regards the adequacy of benefits. The absence of a clear statement that the benefits should ensure an income above the poverty line and of a universal definition of such poverty line makes the instrument less powerful and the application of the principle of adequacy difficult to assess.

It will be interesting to learn how different States deal with this undefined principle. Is some sort of minimum level applied in the country? Is the level of the benefit or benefits based on and/or connected with some sort of a poverty line or subsistence level? Are there other grounds for the set level of the benefit? Does the benefit allow for a life lived in dignity? Is it regularly being reviewed? Do eligible persons actually have access to the benefit and if not, what are the obstacles? And, of course, whether the benefits are predictable, which can be reviewed in connection with the previous principle.

2.4.6 Non-discrimination

Principle (d) reads 'non-discrimination, gender equality and responsiveness to special needs'. The remaining text of the Recommendation does not contain any explication of this principle. The only reference made to this principle is in the Preamble, stating that 'social security is an important tool to [...] promote equal opportunity and gender and racial equality'.[48]

Nevertheless, equal treatment has been addressed in length in various ILO documents and several Conventions and Recommendation,[49] and is intertwined with all the other principles. According to the fundamental Discrimination Convention, discrimination involves 'any distinction, exclusion or preference made on the basis of race, colour, sex, religion, political opinion, national extraction or social origin'.[50] Recommendation No. 204 on transition from the informal to the formal economy recommendation adds to these bases of discrimination, discrimination between formal and informal workers.[51] Considering the objectives and the broad scope of Recommendation 202, it is to be understood that this principle covers all forms of discrimination.

In the context of a social protection floor, the non-discrimination principle should not be understood as incompatible with measures in favour of particularly disadvantaged groups. On the contrary, with the additional phrase: 'and responsiveness to special needs', the Recommendation calls for affirmative

---

48. Recommendation 202, Preamble.
49. For example, Convention No. 111 concerning Discrimination in Respect of Employment and Occupation (Entry into force: 15 Jun. 1960), which has the status of a fundamental convention; Convention No. 118 concerning Equality of Treatment of Nationals and Non-Nationals in Social Security (Entry into force: 25 Apr. 1964).
50. Convention No. 111 concerning Discrimination in Respect of Employment and Occupation, adoption: Geneva, 42nd ILC session (25 Jun. 1958), Art. 1(a).
51. Recommendation No. 204 concerning the transition from the informal to the formal economy, adoption: Geneva, 104th ILC session (12 Jun. 2015), Art. 16(d).

actions of the part of the State in this respect. These actions may seek to enhance, for example, the participation of women and young/older people in the labour market; maternity protection; special schemes for low-paid workers; fictitious contribution periods for women raising children; etc. In fact, the ILO stated in 2001 that 'each society should consider introducing positive discrimination in favour of women where systematic discrimination is faced'.[52]

This gender aspect is particularly interesting with regard to conditional cash transfer schemes. In many cases, the benefits from these schemes are being paid to the mother, because she is supposed to be best placed to ensure that the conditions – mostly children's school attendance and doctors' visits – are being met. This practice, however, affirms the role of the woman as carer and housewife, and apparently counteracts any ambition to take part in economic activities, training programmes, or civil society activities. In fact, such systems may appoint the mother to sacrifice her own development and (possible) economic independency, while they may legitimate the father to distance himself from household and family tasks. Designing conditional benefits that do not hamper the development and participating power of women deserves special attention of policymakers and scholars.

It will be interesting to learn from the case studies how this gender aspect is taken into account in the different schemes: Is the benefit scheme non-discriminatory? Is the scheme equally accessible for women and men, or does it hamper earning power of women? Do women have a special position (e.g., as recipient of the benefit)? In case of conditions imposed: are these conditions equally addressed to women and men? Also, equal treatment of other often disadvantaged groups, such as immigrants, should be reviewed. Important is not only that the law stipulates equal treatment, but also that this right actually can be enjoyed in practice.

2.4.7 Financial Solidarity

The principle of financial solidarity is worded as follows: '(h) solidarity in financing while seeking to achieve an optimal balance between the responsibilities and interests among those who finance and benefit from social security schemes.' The Cambridge Dictionary defines solidarity as 'agreement between and support for the members of a group'. This is true for both financial and social solidarity.

Financial solidarity involves solidarity between generations, between economically active persons and those who are not able to work, the healthy and the sick, and between the poor and those who are well off. Additionally, with regard to informal workers, the ILO Conference concluded in 2001 that 'support for

---

52. ILO, *A New Consensus*, para. 10 (ILO 2001); C. Mesa Lago, *Reassembling Social Security. A Survey of Pensions and Health Care Reforms in Latin America* 9 (Oxford University Press 2007).

vulnerable groups in the informal economy should be financed by society as a whole'.

In the ILO report Social Security and the Rule of Law, it has been put forward that 'the principles of collective financing and social solidarity are inseparable. Social solidarity is a powerful weapon against poverty and an effective instrument for making societies more equal and just'.[53] Becker articulates that '[i]n social security law, solidarity is the fundamental requirement for the inclusion of certain persons in specific situations of need and subject to specific risks'.[54] In this sense, solidarity is prerequisite to universality and to the very concept of a basic floor.

During the discussion on the draft of the Recommendation, it was emphasized that '[I]t is essential that a rational balance is found between short- and long-term costs and benefits of social security systems for society and different groups of financiers and beneficiaries.'[55] Social security expenditure is a long-term investment in society, since it promotes social inclusion, a healthy and productive workforce, and economic security. At the same time, these investments require resources that have to be provided by society. Solidarity implies financial redistribution, but cannot exist without equivalence between contribution and benefit. In fact, financial solidarity limits the principle of equivalence and the other way around. Social dialogue is indispensable to defining the allocation of the financial burden between contributors and taxpayers and between generations.[56]

Solidarity in the form of collective financing is also incorporated as a main principle for social security in ILO Convention No. 102. This instrument requires that contributions or taxes for financing benefits should be charged on the basis of a person's ability to pay, and regardless of their individual risks. More specifically, the Convention provides that 'the cost of the benefits [...] and the cost of the administration of such benefits shall be borne collectively by way of insurance contributions or taxation or both in a manner which avoids hardship to persons of small means'.[57] The latter part is all important in the context of social protection floors.

---

53. ILO, *Social Security and the Rule of Law* 452 (ILO 2011).
54. U. Becker, *Introduction to the General Principles of Social Security Law in Europe* 15 (U. Becker et al. eds., Europe Law Publishing 2010).
55. ILO, *Conclusions Concerning the Recurrent Discussion on Social Protection* para. 15 Sixth item on the agenda: A recurrent discussion on the strategic objective of social protection (social security) under the follow-up to the 2008 ILO Declaration on Social Justice for a Fair Globalization (ILO 2011).
56. *Ibid.*, para. 25.
57. ILO Convention 102, Art. 71(1).

As regards the financing mechanism, it was reaffirmed that pay-as-you-go systems better comply with this principle than individual savings accounts.[58] Furthermore, the ILO Committee of Experts has stated that '[t]ax-financed schemes implicitly relying on solidarity should be promoted in developing countries, where the application of the principle of solidarity through social security has generally remained limited'.[59]

It will be informative to learn from the case studies how the respective schemes are financed and in which way these schemes apply the principle of financial solidarity. The same counts for equivalence between contributions and benefits: Are there groups that disproportionally contribute or benefit?

2.4.8 Good Governance

Good governance is a rather open term and not, as such, formulated as a principle in Article 3. However, several listed principles deal (also) with the management, administration, and supervision of social security measures; they can be clustered under the umbrella principle of good government. In a sense, each of the other principles could also be clustered under good governance, because good governance should ensure that all principles are being applied properly.

Explicitly recognizing the various elements of good governance as guiding principles is highly relevant in view of the Recommendation promoting innovative social protection measures. It does not advance specific designs or methods, but rather promotes the development of new sorts of measures in order to cover any protection gap. New techniques and innovative elements need to be even more carefully implemented and controlled than well-tested traditional insurance designs.

The principle also responds to the fact that a reliable and just administration is far from evident in most developing countries. Preparing the Recommendation, the ILO elaborated on this need for good governance of the social sector.[60] It has been stated that:

> there is a need of reinforcing basic governance principles, which convert moral and social values into the effective design and management of social security systems. [...] The Committee therefore suggests that future instruments should go beyond resonating the general responsibility of the State for

---

58. ILO, *Conclusions Concerning the Recurrent Discussion on Social Protection* para. 13 Sixth item on the agenda: A recurrent discussion on the strategic objective of social protection (social security) under the follow-up to the 2008 ILO Declaration on Social Justice for a Fair Globalization (ILO 2011).
59. ILO, *Social Security and the Rule of Law* 453 (ILO 2011).
60. *Ibid.*, paras 145-153; ILO, *Conclusions Concerning the Recurrent Discussion on Social Protection* paras 12, 16, 20, 22 Sixth item on the agenda: A recurrent discussion on the strategic objective of social protection (social security) under the follow-up to the 2008 ILO Declaration on Social Justice for a Fair Globalization (ILO 2011).

the due provision of benefits contained in Convention No. 102 (Article 71(3)) to address the issues of efficient administration, protection, supervision and inspection of social security funds.[61]

Special emphasis has been placed on the integration of policies, prudent investment of social security funds, the development of quality services and effective systems, setting and assessing objectives, efficiency in using resources, transparency, cooperation between administrative institutions, and active involvement of all stakeholders.

The Recommendation reaffirms good governance as a prerequisite for a functioning social protection system by formulating the following norms:

- (f) respect for the rights and dignity of people covered by the social security guarantees;
- (i) consideration of a diversity of methods and approaches, including of financing mechanisms and delivery systems;
- (j) transparent, accountable and sound financial management and administration;
- (k) financial, fiscal and economic sustainability with due regard to social justice and equity;
- (m) coherence across institutions responsible for delivery of social protection;
- (n) high-quality public services that enhance the delivery of social security systems; and
- (p) regular monitoring of implementation, and periodic evaluation.

In the remaining text of the Recommendation, some points recur in more detail. For example, attention should be paid to the prevention of fraud, tax evasion, and non-payment of contributions (Article 11(2)); funding should primarily come from national resources (Article 12); objectives should be set (Article 14(a)); appropriate monitoring mechanisms should be put into place and sufficient data, statistics, and indications should be collected, analysed, and published (Articles 19 and 21)); and data protection in view of the privacy of individuals should be secured (Article 23).

The case studies may reveal in what way the respective schemes reflect the different elements of good governance and what the particular problematic points are. Attention should also be paid to whether regular actuarial studies are performed in view of the sustainability of the scheme and whether the actual delivery of the benefits reflects the legal framework.

---

61. ILO, *Social Security and the Rule of Law* 618 (ILO 2011).

2.4.9 Coherence of Policies

Since different schemes protecting different categories of persons at different stages of their lives are meant to substantiate one comprehensive social protection floor, coherence of policies is crucial. This is expressed in the Recommendation through principle '(l) coherence with social, economic and employment policies' and further elaborated in several Articles. Article 10 stipulates that preventive, promotional and active measures, benefits and social services should be combined; productive economic activity and formal employment should be promoted through a variety of policies (such as public procurement, labour inspection, tax incentives, education, employability, etc.); and that coordination with other policies should be ensured. Similar wording is used in Articles 13(2), 14(d), and 15.

It is clear that the need for coherence of policies stretches further than to the context of benefits related to the four guarantees included in the Recommendation exclusively. There is a strong interdependency between social security measures and employment and economic strategies. A maximum synergy between the different fields of law can strengthen the social security part of a protection floor in the limited sense of the Recommendation, and extend its scope towards the broader social protection floor concept.

The need for coordinated strategies for the informal sector has been underpinned in various documents. In the ILO Report, 'The Rule of Law', it is expressed that:

> Virtuous cycle of coordinated economic, employment and social security policies enables to increase human capital, enhance employability, formalize employment, and provide feedback into higher economic growth, greater income security and better social services, which again enhance productivity and employability of the labour force.[62]

The necessity of a holistic approach to poverty reduction has also been stressed by Sepulveda and Nyst in their treatise 'The Human Rights-Based Framework for Social Protection':

> The interdependence, indivisibility and mutually reinforcing nature of human rights necessitate a holistic approach to poverty reduction. This approach requires that States establish a network of policies and programmes that collectively support the realisation of all human rights and the highest level of development possible.
> Social protection programmes must be not considered a panacea for all economic and social issues, but rather as one element within a broad development strategy aimed at overcoming poverty and realising human rights. To this end, States must complement social protection initiatives with

---

62. ILO, *Social Security and the Rule of Law* 520 (ILO 2011).

corresponding policies and programmes designed to maximise the effectiveness of the social protection programme in improving the lives of the beneficiaries.[63]

In essence, this principle forms a bridge between social security and all other forms of protection a comprehensive social protection floor should provide.

To learn how different countries deal with this principle, the case studies may examine in what way the schemes relate to other social security measures, to labour market policies, and to economic policies. Important in this respect is also the extent to which governments explicitly recognize the importance of an integral approach on poverty-reduction policies.

2.4.10 Social Participation

The Recommendation directly addresses social participation through two different principles: (q) full respect for collective bargaining and freedom of association for all workers; and (r) tripartite participation with representative organizations of employers and workers, as well as consultation with other relevant and representative organizations of persons concerned.

Subsequently, the Recommendation points out that participation and consultation should take place with regard to: the establishment and review of the levels of the different benefits (Article 8(d)); the formulation and implementation of social security extension strategies (Article 13(1)); promoting awareness of social protection floor strategies (Article 14(f)); and monitoring the progress in achieving agreed objectives (Articles 19, 20).

Participation and the freedom of association are inextricably bound up with each other – without freedom of association and collective bargaining, there is no representation. Only together, they can give substance to the principle of social participation, which is an essential element for the development of social protection. In fact, social participation, or representational security, is a key enabling right, as it facilitates access to a range of other rights.

The ILO noted in 2002, that '[e]verywhere in the world, people in the informal economy are excluded from or under-represented in social dialogue institutions and processes'.[64] Much more than the ILO social security Conventions, the Recommendation stresses the need for social participation at all stages and in all elements of a social protection floor. Moreover, the Recommendation stretches the scope of this principle by addressing not only employers' and workers' organizations, but also 'other relevant and representative organizations of persons concerned'. This is an important expansion of the traditional ILO concept of tripartism in view of the protection of informal workers. It also

---

63. M. Sepúlveda & C. Nyst, *The Human Rights Approach to Social Protection* 30 (Ministry for Foreign Affairs of Finland 2012).
64. ILO, *Decent Work and the Informal Economy* 71 (ILO 2002).

enables involvement of organizations that represent other non- or underrepresented groups such as immigrants, women, and disabled persons.

Of course, for civil society groups to officially represent their rank and file, they need the formal recognition and legal protection as a representative organization. In many countries, the legal framework only provides for the recognition of trade unions and employers' organizations. Governments should therefore safeguard and facilitate the freedom of association as well as the formal recognition of the various organizations representing different groups in society.

In spite of the great importance traditionally attached by the ILO to social participation, the involvement of these other organizations is limited to 'consultation', whereas for employers' and workers' representatives, the word 'participation' is used. Consultation seems to indicate that 'other organizations' should have the right to voice their opinions at a certain point in time rather than to be actually involved in policy- and decision-making. Although it is an improvement compared to traditional tripartism, it is difficult to understand that such a minor role is reserved for the majority of persons for whom the concept of a social protection floor has been invented.

During the discussion of the draft at the ILO Conference in 2012, it was proposed by Brazil and South Africa to change 'consultation' into 'involvement'. However, the established trade union social partners, supported by the employers, voted against the amendment.[65] This was not the first time that the alliance of the workers and employers acted out of self-interest by blocking more influence of NGO's in ILO matters.[66] The way of protecting their own power in the ILO decision-making process is certainly not beneficial to the development of social protection floors and goes against the spirit of the times.

Relevant issues to address for the case studies would be in what way and to what extent trade unions and civil society organizations have been recognized, have played, and still play, a role in both the formulation and implementation of the scheme as well as in the establishment of the levels of the benefits.

BIBLIOGRAPHY

Arellano Ortiz P., *Protection in Old Age in Chile* (U. Becker, F. Pennings & T. Dijkhoff eds., Kluwer Law International 2013).

Becker U., et al., *Security. A General Principle of Social Security Law in Europe* (Europe Law Publishing 2010).

Becker U., *Introduction to the General Principles of Social Security Law in Europe* (U. Becker et. al eds., Europe Law Publishing 2010).

Cichon M. & K. Hagemejer, *Changing the Development Policy Paradigm: Investing in a Social Security Floor for All* 60 International Social Security Review 169–196 (2007).

---

65. B. Deacon, *Global Social Policy in the Making* 88-89 (Policy Press 2013).
66. *Ibid.*, 89.

Deacon B., *Global Social Policy in the Making. The Foundation of the Social Protection Floor* (Policy Press 2013).

Dijkhoff T., *International Social Security Standards in the European Union. The Cases of the Czech Republic and Estonia* Social Europe Series vol. 28, 35 (Intersentia 2011).

Dijkhoff T., *Supervision of social security standards: Between Law and Politics* (F. Pennings & G. Vonk eds., Edward Elgar 2015).

Dijkhoff T., *The Introduction of Private Elements in National Social Security and the Role of International Standards* (K. Koldinska & M. Štefko eds., Auditorium 2010).

Fischer A.M., *Inequality and the Universalistic Principle in the Post-2015 Development Agenda* (Erasmus University Rotterdam, November 2012).

Humblet M. & R.Silva, *Standards for the XXIst Century, Social Security* 12 (ILO 2002).

Humblet M. & M. Zarka-Martres, *ILO Standards Policy* 447 (International Labour Office ed., ILO 2001).

ILO, *Minimum Standards of Social Security* International Labour Conference, 35th Session, Report V(a)(2) (ILO 1952).

ILO, *A New Consensus* (ILO 2001).

ILO, *Social Security: Issues, Challenges and Prospects* (ILO 2001).

ILO, *Decent Work and the Informal Economy* (ILO 2002).

ILO, *Setting Social Security Standards in a Global Society* (ILO 2008).

ILO, *Social Security for Social Justice and a Fair Globalization. Report VI* (ILO 2011).

ILO, *Social Security and the Rule of Law* (ILO 2011).

ILO, *Conclusions Concerning the Recurrent Discussion on Social Protection* Sixth item on the agenda: A recurrent discussion on the strategic objective of social protection (social security) under the follow-up to the 2008 ILO Declaration on Social Justice for a Fair Globalization (ILO 2011).

ILO, *Social Protection Floors for Social Justice and a Fair Globalization, Report IV(1)* (ILO 2012).

Mesa Lago C., *Reassembling Social Security. A Survey of Pensions and Health Care Reforms in Latin America* (Oxford University Press 2007).

Mesa Lago C., et al., *Re-reforms of Privatized Pension Systems*, 3 ZIAS (2012).

Mestrum D., *Social Protection Floor: Beyond Poverty Reduction?* Analysis for Global Social Justice.eu (4 March 2012).

Mikkola M., *Social Human Rights of Europe* (Bookwell Ltd. 2010).

Moser C. & A. Norton, *To Claim our Rights: Livelihood Security, Human Rights and Sustainable Development* (Overseas Development Institute London 2001).

Olivier M., *Informality, Employment Contracts and Social Insurance Coverage: Rights-Based Perspectives in a Developing World Context* 27 The International Journal of Comparative Labour Law and Industrial Relations (2011).

Pennings F., *Historical and Theoretical Background of Standard Setting in Social Security* (U. Becker et al. eds, Wolters Kluwer 2013).

Piron L.H., *Rights-Based Approaches to Social Protection* (Overseas Development Institute London 2004).

Schoukens P., *Social Security Law Instruments of the Next Generation* (F. Pennings & G. Vonk eds, Edward Elgar 2015).

Sepúlveda M. & C. Nyst, *The Human Rights Approach to Social Protection* (Ministry for Foreign Affairs of Finland 2012).

Tapiola K., *Global Standards: The Policy of the ILO* (U. Becker, F. Pennings, T. Dijkhoff eds., Kluwer International 2013).

Unni J. & U. Rani *Social Protection for Informal Workers: Insecurities, Instruments and Institutional Mechanisms* (ILO 2002).

Vonk G., *The 2012 Recommendation Concerning National Floors of Social Protection (No 202), The Human Rights Approach to Social Security in ILO Wrapping Paper*, 4 International Journal of Social Security and Workers Compensation (2012-2013).

UNDP, *Sharing Innovative Experiences* vol 18 (UNDP 2011).

Conventions, Recommendations, and Declarations

ILO Convention No. 102 concerning Minimum Standards of Social Security (1952).

ILO Convention No. 111 concerning Discrimination in Respect of Employment and Occupation (1960).

ILO Convention No. 118 concerning Equality of Treatment of Nationals and Non-Nationals in Social Security (1964).

ILO Recommendation No. 67 concerning Income Security (1944).

ILO Recommendation No. 69 concerning Medical Care (1944).

ILO Recommendation No. 202 concerning National Floors of Social Protection (2012).

ILO Recommendation No. 204 concerning the Transition from the Informal to the Formal Economy (2015).

UN, Declaration on Social Progress and Development, UN GA res. 2542 XXIV (1969).

UN, Universal Declaration of Human Rights (UDHR), UN GA res. 217A III (1948).

UN, International Covenant on Economic, Social and Cultural Rights (ICESCR), UN GA res. 2200A XXI (1966).

CHAPTER 3

Implementing the Principles of Social Protection Floors Recommendation, 2012 (No. 202)

Christina Behrendt, Emmanuelle Saint-Pierre Guilbault, Maya Stern-Plaza, Victoire Umuhire & Veronika Wodsak[*]

3.1 INTRODUCTION

Fifty years ago, the right of everyone to social security was laid down in the International Covenant on Economic, Social and Cultural Rights, 1966. This Covenant was to become one of the most widely ratified treaties of all time, substantiating the rights set out in the 1948 Universal Declaration of Human Rights. Yet, as the world celebrates the 50th anniversary of this landmark instrument, ILO research shows that more than 70% of the population – about 5.2 billion people – is not adequately covered by social protection. The human right to social security is ultimately largely unfulfilled for the majority. Deficits are apparent everywhere. Most notably, nearly 50% of all people over pensionable age do not receive a pension; 39% of the world's population lack any affiliation to a health system or scheme; and seventy-five countries have no child or family benefit programmes. Most of those insufficiently protected live in poverty, 800 million of them are working poor, and the majority work in the informal economy.[1]

---

[*] This contribution is written in a personal capacity and does not necessarily reflect the policy position of the ILO. Comments from Michael Cichon and Krzysztof Hagemejer are gratefully acknowledged.
[1] ILO, *World Social Protection Report 2014/15: Building Economic Recovery, Inclusive Development and Social Justice* (Geneva 2014).

With the adoption of the ILO Social Protection Floors Recommendation, 2012 (hereinafter Recommendation No. 202),[2] the world has taken a significant step towards the realization of the human right to social security by defining the basic social security guarantees that should be accessible to all through the social protection floor and committing to reaching higher levels of protection as soon, and to as many people, as possible. The 187 Member States of the ILO, represented by workers', employers' and government delegates, have given the world community a powerful tool for moving towards wider population coverage, higher levels and a more comprehensive protection. Its impact is expected to significantly increase in the years to come, as the 2030 Agenda for Sustainable Development comes into full motion.

This is because Recommendation No. 202 offers a roadmap to countries for the design and implementation of comprehensive social protection systems[3] and social protection floors (SPFs) as integral components of such systems. It guides Member States in extending social security, with the objective of reaching universal social protection in a progressive and sustainable way. In this way, it is not just a legal tool but also a policy tool.

Furthermore, its contents, in line with the preparatory works leading to its adoption, reflect the key role of social protection policies in reducing and preventing poverty, redressing inequality, and achieving more inclusive economic and social development. It is now largely recognized that social protection policies can stimulate inclusive growth by facilitating access to health and education, enabling workers to engage in more productive work; support domestic demand; and facilitate the structural transformation of national economies. As the repercussions of the 2008 global financial and economic crisis continue to be felt, social protection acts as an effective automatic stabilizer in such times of economic downturn by mitigating economic and social impacts, enhancing resilience and achieving faster recovery.[4]

The important role of social protection as a sound economic and social policy has been acknowledged by international, regional and multinational organizations, including the United Nations, the G20, ASEAN, the African Union and the European Union, and is now an important linchpin of the 2030 Agenda (see below). This represents an important paradigm shift in the role of social protection policies in a development context: while social protection was reduced to a marginal role in the 1980s and the 1990s, as a social safety net patching up the repercussions of structural adjustment policies, it was 'rediscovered' in pro-poor development approaches in the early 2000s as a key

---

2. See also: ILO, *Social Security for All: Building Social Protection Floors and Comprehensive Social Security Systems. The Strategy of the International Labour Organization* (Geneva 2012) and ILO, *Building Social Protection Systems: International Standards and Human Rights Instruments* (Geneva 2017).
3. We use the terms 'social security system' and 'social protection system' interchangeably.
4. ILO, *World Social Protection Report 2014/15: Building Economic Recovery, Inclusive Development and Social Justice* (Geneva 2014).

ingredient of economic and social policies that contribute to inclusive development and growth.[5]

More specifically, Recommendation No. 202 calls on Member States to establish and maintain comprehensive social security systems according to a progressive two-dimensional strategy to:

- achieve universal coverage by guaranteeing SPFs comprised of at least basic levels of income security and access to essential health care and;
- to ensure higher levels of protection guided by ILO social security standards.

The Recommendation complements other international labour standards, including the Social Security (Minimum Standards) Convention, 1952 (No. 102), by setting forth an integrated and coherent approach for social protection policies.[6] This approach is centred on the principle of universality of protection and the provision of social protection along the life cycle, with due consideration for disadvantaged groups and people with special needs. Recommendation No. 202 defines the social protection floor by laying out the basic social security guarantees that should be granted to all in need to ensure they can enjoy a life in health and dignity throughout their lives, and guides the progressive establishment of comprehensive social security systems to grant higher levels of social security to as many people as possible, as soon as possible.

In this regard, Recommendation No. 202 not only reinforces the guidance provided in the existing ILO social security standards, but also strengthens and broadens the international normative framework on the human right to social security as it sets out nineteen overarching/wide-ranging principles – from principles to guide the development and design of national social protection strategies, to financial and administrative principles to lead the implementation and transformation of national social protection systems. This framework continues to guide the reform of social protection systems and the gradual development of social security policies, strategies and law in many countries around the world, despite differences in levels of income and development; informs the development of regional social security instruments; and contributes to achieving the human right to social security for all.[7]

Giving effect to the Recommendation therefore brings countries closer to meeting their international human rights obligations. By securing persons'

---

5. C. Behrendt, *Investing in People: Implementing the Extension of Social Security Through National Social Protection Floors*, in *Beyond Macroeconomic Stability: Structural Transformation and Inclusive Development* pp. 228-261 (D. Kucera and I. Islam eds, Palgrave Macmillan UK 2013).
6. See, for example: U. Kulke and E. Saint-Pierre Guilbault, *The Social Protection Floors Recommendation, 2012 (No. 202): Completing the Standards to Close the Coverage Gap*, 66 International Social Security Review, 87-109 (2013).
7. See, for example: ILO, *Social Security and the Rule of Law: General Survey Concerning Social Security Instruments in the Light of the 2008 Declaration on Social Justice for a Fair Globalization* (Geneva 2011), Table 5 (p. 70).

enjoyment of their social security rights, States will also promote human development, political stability and inclusive growth, and in this way reduce and prevent poverty, redress inequalities and encourage the fair redistribution of economic wealth in line with the Sustainable Development Goals (SDGs).

In fact, social protection occupies a central role in the 2030 Agenda for Sustainable Development, cutting across several SDGs, emphasizing the multi-dimensional nature of social protection policies, which have an important 'bridging function'.[8] Most prominently, SDG 1 recognizes the critical contribution of social protection systems, including SPFs, in reducing and preventing poverty, in a specific target (1.3): 'Implement nationally appropriate social protection systems and measures for all, including floors, and by 2030 achieve substantial coverage of the poor and vulnerable.' This provides a bridge to the other goals which explicitly or implicitly relate to social protection, including goals on poverty reduction (1), health (3), gender equality (5), decent work and economic growth (8), reduced inequalities (10), and peace, justice and strong institutions (16). This is why the strengthening of social protection systems, and in particular SPFs, plays such an essential role in achieving the SDGs.

This chapter focuses on the implementation of SPFs at the national level, addressing, in particular, the guidance provided by the principles embodied in Recommendation No. 202 and its links to the 2030 Agenda. The starting point for this discussion is the role of SPFs for the realization of the human right to social security (section 2). This provides the background for the discussion of the implications of the principles set out in Recommendation No. 202 on the implementation of SPFs at the national level in section 3. Section 4 then concludes with an outlook on realizing the human right to social security.

3.2 SPFs AND THE HUMAN RIGHT TO SOCIAL SECURITY

The human right to social security is set out in the Universal Declaration of Human Rights (1948, Articles 22 and 25) and reiterated in the International Covenant of Economic, Social and Cultural Rights (ICESCR, 1966, Articles 9 and 11). As such, all 164 States Parties to the Covenant (as of November 2016) have a legal obligation to respect, protect and fulfil this right in law and practice.

In addition, the social protection rights of women, children, migrant workers and their families, indigenous and tribal peoples, persons with disabilities, and refugees have been specified in the Convention on Elimination of All Forms of Discrimination Against Women (1979, Articles 11(1)(e), 11(2)(b), 14(2)), the Convention on the Rights of the Child (1989, Articles 26, 27(1), 27(2) and (3)), the International Convention on the Protection of the Rights of All Migrant Workers and their Families (1990, Articles 27 and 54), the Convention on the Rights of Persons with Disabilities (2006, Article 28), the Convention

---

8. M. Kaltenborn, *Global Social Protection. New Impetus from the 2030 Agenda for Sustainable Development*, in *Global Governance Spotlight*, 7 (2015).

relating to the Status of Refugees (1950, Article 24), and the Convention on the Elimination of All Forms of Racial Discrimination (1965, Article 5(e)(iv)). This framework for the protection and promotion of the human right to social security and social protection informs a rights-based approach, in which policies and programmes are anchored in a system of rights and corresponding obligations established by international law.[9]

ILO social security Conventions and Recommendations complement this human rights framework. Human rights bodies, such as the Committee on Economic, Social and Cultural Rights (CESCR), have accordingly referred to these standards to substantiate the right to social security.[10] In particular, ILO Convention No. 102 is often cited by the CESCR in its observations concerning the compliance of State parties to the ICESCR with their obligation to implement the right to social security. This is owing to the fact that Convention No. 102, and other ILO social security instruments, provide detailed guidance that is intrinsic to the realization of the fundamental human right to social security.[11] Recommendation No. 202 is also put forward as a valuable reference in some of the CESCR's most recent concluding observations on the realization of the right to social security calling for 'the establishment of a social protection floor guaranteeing legal entitlements to individuals, as an initial element to be progressively developed into a universal and comprehensive social security system'.[12]

The concept of SPFs set out in Recommendation No. 202 further strengthens the approach taken by human rights instruments to social security (widely referred to, and hereinafter, as the rights-based approach). It does so, notably, by providing specific guidance to countries for guaranteeing that everyone enjoys at least a basic level of social security, which is considered by the CESCR as the minimum core content of the human right to social security under the ICESCR.[13] These minimum essential levels are those which are crucial to

---

9. See, for example: United Nations, *Guiding Principles on Extreme Poverty and Human Rights* (Geneva 2012); M. Sepúlveda and C. Nyst, *The Human Rights Approach to Social Protection* (Helsinki, Ministry for Foreign Affairs of Finland 2012). In addition, see the joint UN web platform on social protection and human rights (www.socialprotection-humanrights.org).
10. See, for example: CESCR, *General Comment No. 14: The Right to the Highest Attainable Standard of Health* (Geneva, United Nations 2000); *General Comment No. 19: The Right to Social Security* (2008); *General Comment No. 20: Non-Discrimination in Economic, Social and Cultural Rights* (2009); *General Comment No. 23: The Right to Just and Favourable Conditions of Work* (2016).
11. See: ILO, *Setting Social Security Standards in a Global Society – An Analysis of Present State and Practice and of Future Options for Global Social Security Standard Setting in the International Labour Organization*, (Geneva, 2008) and K. Markov, *Sécurité sociale*, in *Droit international social: Droits économiques, sociaux et culturels*, vol. 2 (J.-M. Thouvenin and A. Trebilcock eds, Bruylant 2013).
12. CESCR, *Statement on social protection floors: an essential element of the right to social security and of the sustainable development goals*, Doc. E/C.12/54/3, para. 2.
13. United Nations, *Report of the Special Rapporteur on extreme poverty and human rights, Philip Alston, on Social Protection Floors (A/69/297)* (New York 2016); CESCR, *Statement*

securing an adequate standard of living through basic subsistence, essential primary health care, basic shelter and housing, and basic forms of education for all members of society.[14]

SPFs therefore contribute not only to realizing the human right to social security but also to this set of other human rights. The realization of this broader set of rights follows from the commitment that 'these guarantees should ensure at a minimum that, over the life cycle, all in need have access to essential health care and basic income security which together secure effective access to goods and services defined as necessary at the national level' (paragraph 4).[15] Thus, for example, the fulfilment of the right to health or shelter may depend on the financial access that is provided through the realization of the right to social security. Social protection programmes that include a school feeding component or that are linked to school attendance are other examples of the interdependence and indivisibility of human rights. Overall, the provision of social protection to all can help ensure that individuals maintain a dignified standard of living and do not fall into poverty despite encountering contingencies which may deprive them of earning sufficient income. In the same vein, through the right to work, right to participation or the right to education, for instance, persons will be better informed and have improved access to social security systems that are better adapted to national needs and circumstances.

3.3 HOW DO THE PRINCIPLES OF RECOMMENDATION NO. 202 INFORM THE IMPLEMENTATION OF NATIONALLY DEFINED SPFs?

A major achievement of Recommendation No. 202 is the guidance it offers States to give effect to the right to social security by guaranteeing at least a basic level of social security to all and progressively move towards higher levels of coverage and protection by building and maintaining comprehensive social security systems. This is done through a set of principles that applies to the overall design and implementation of comprehensive and coherent social protection systems, reinforcing and further elaborating on the principles established in previous ILO social security standards, and notably Convention No. 102.[16] These guiding

---

on social protection floors: an essential element of the right to social security and of the sustainable development goals (UN 2015).

14. CESCR, *General Comment No. 19: The Right to Social Security*, para. 59(a) (Geneva 2008).
15. See: M. Cichon, *The Social Protection Floors Recommendation, 2012 (No. 202): Can a Six-Page Document Change the Course of Social History*, 66 International Social Security Review, 21-43 (2013).
16. U. Kulke and E. Saint-Pierre Guilbault, *The Social Protection Floors Recommendation, 2012 (No. 202): Completing the Standards to Close the Coverage Gap*, 66 International Social Security Review, 87-109 (2013).

principles echo fundamental human rights principles as well as good practices in the governance, delivery and financing of social security systems.[17]

Since the adoption of the Recommendation in 2012, many countries have followed the guidance it provides and have further stepped up their efforts in extending social protection. Some have undertaken national dialogues to define their social protection strategies, many have committed, explicitly or implicitly, to building SPFs in their national social protection strategies, and others are developing legal frameworks to anchor social protection entitlements in law and to govern the national social protection system, extend social security coverage, enhance adequacy and improve delivery structures.

The following sub-sections will discuss how the principles set out in Recommendation No. 202 are guiding country efforts to define and implement their national SPFs, and how they can contribute to achieving the SDGs by 2030.

3.3.1 State Responsibility

The greater role for social protection in development also implies that States fully assume their responsibility for guaranteeing at least a basic level of social security to all through a nationally defined social protection floor within the national social protection system.[18] This is part of the broader legal obligation of States to protect and promote human rights, and the rule of law, which is a prerequisite for any social protection system to operate successfully. The overall and primary responsibility of the State to establish and maintain social protection systems, including floors, is one of the key elements of institution-building highlighted in SDG 16 on promoting just, peaceful and inclusive societies, particularly with regard to developing effective, accountable and transparent institutions at all levels (target 16.6), and ensuring responsive, inclusive, participatory and representative decision-making at all levels (target 16.7).

In this regard, the Recommendation clearly sets out the overall and primary responsibility of the State to guarantee the proper administration of the social security system and the due provision of benefits (paragraph 3). This includes the realization of the right to social security without discrimination, the due provision of benefits according to clear and transparent eligibility criteria and entitlements, and the proper administration of the institutions and services. Where benefits and services are not provided directly by public institutions (e.g., in the case of private pensions), the effective enforcement of the legislative frameworks and oversight mechanisms are particularly important for the provision of benefits and services. Recommendation No. 202 therefore recognizes that

---

17. *See*, for example: CESCR, *General Comment No. 19: The Right to Social Security*, para. 59 (2008). For further discussion of the elements of a human rights framework for social protection, *see* http://socialprotection-humanrights.org/framework/.
18. This principle set out in Recommendation No. 202, paras 1 and 3, as well as in Convention No. 102, Arts 71 and 72.

there are a number of diverse methods and approaches available for implementing and delivering social protection (paragraph 3(i)), such as by way of private parties, but advocates that whichever the mechanism, the principles laid out be respected, including State oversight.

As part of their responsibility to guarantee a basic level of social security to all, the State should also ensure that sound legal frameworks and information systems are in place to raise awareness and ensure that persons are knowledgeable about their social security entitlements and are able to claim their rights, and that benefits are adequate and predictable.

Furthermore, in accomplishing this responsibility, States should follow the principle of progressive realization, both underlined in international human rights standards and Recommendation No. 202 (paragraph 3(f)). States therefore have a duty to satisfy, as a starting point, these minimum essential levels of the right to social security to the maximum of available resources with a view to providing protection to those who need it most, and to move quickly towards extending this protection (paragraph 13, 1(a)).[19] Moreover, the identification of national priorities should involve all stakeholders, in particular where resources are limited.

This does not mean, however, that States may use the notion of progressive realization as a justification for non-action. As previously mentioned, Recommendation No. 202 highlights that social protection extension strategies should not stop at SPFs but seek to establish comprehensive social protection systems for as many people, and as soon, as possible, in concert with economic and fiscal growth. In addition, States also have a clear obligation to demonstrate that every effort has been made to use all available resources to achieve minimum essential levels and protect the most disadvantaged, including in times of severe resource constraints.[20] Though national SPFs should be financed by national resources to the extent possible, this may also mean considering the availability of international assistance to guarantee the fulfilment of minimum essential levels of social protection (Recommendation No. 202, paragraph 12, *see also* below).

3.3.2 Universality of Protection, Comprising At Least a Basic Set of Social Security Guarantees for All

The principle of universality of protection is at the core of the social protection floor concept, reflecting the commitment to guaranteeing at least a basic level of social security for all. Social protection is one of the policy areas that States have at their disposal to reduce and prevent poverty, contain inequality and promote

---

19. ILO Convention No. 102 also sets out the principle of progressive realization in allowing States to initially accept obligations under three of the nine branches of social security as well as other exceptions including the scope of coverage, while providing that Members should subsequently accept other branches and move gradually towards the full achievement of the Convention (Art. 3).
20. CESCR, *General Comment No. 19: The Right to Social Security*, para. 60 (2008).

social inclusion, as part of their wider obligations in protecting and promoting human rights. In this context, it is essential to clarify the distinction between universality of protection and universality of benefits. Universality of protection means that everyone should be *protected* throughout the life course; this does not necessarily imply that everyone *receives* a benefit at every point in time. Universality of protection can be achieved through different means – universal benefits is one of them.

SDG target 1.3 also views the implementation of nationally appropriate social protection systems and measures for all – including floors – as central to reducing poverty (*see* above). The SDGs are, however, more ambitious than Recommendation No. 202, committing to achieve 'substantial coverage of the poor and vulnerable' by 2030. The role of social protection in containing inequalities is further addressed in SDG 10, which focuses on the capacity of social protection policies to channel redistribution (target 10.4) and as a means to achieve greater social cohesion (target 10.2).

Achieving substantial and sustainable reduction in poverty and inequality globally requires that social protection be universal. All members of society should be covered (paragraph 3(e)), in a way that respects their dignity (paragraph 3(f)) and by giving special attention to disadvantaged groups and people with special needs (paragraph 16). Protection therefore also needs to be extended to those in the informal economy (paragraph 3(e)) while supporting the transition towards formal employment (paragraph 15) and access to corresponding higher levels of protection. This is particularly relevant given that previous international standards were not sufficient to extend social protection coverage to the significant number of persons working in the informal economy.[21] In this regard, the ILO Recommendation on the Transition from the Informal to the Formal Economy, 2015 (No. 204) embeds the commitment of extending social security to workers in the informal economy within a larger policy framework to foster transition to the formal economy (paragraphs 18–20). For example, Niger's social protection system covers 3.4% of the working-age population for pensions on a mandatory basis – largely those in formal salaried employment.[22] In order to close coverage gaps, Niger has embarked on a reform, starting with the adoption of a new national Social Protection Policy, linked to the five-year National Social and Economic Development plan, based on the guidance of Recommendation No. 202.

To achieve universal protection, Member States should provide, at least, the basic social security guarantees to at least all residents and all children, subject to country's existing international obligations. While the Recommendation refers to national law and practice with regard to the definition of residents

---

21. U. Kulke and E. Saint-Pierre Guilbault, *The Social Protection Floors Recommendation, 2012 (No. 202): Completing the Standards to Close the Coverage Gap*, 66 International Social Security Review, 87-109 (2013).
22. ILO, *World Social Protection Report 2014/15: Building Economic Recovery, Inclusive Development and Social Justice*, Annex IV (Geneva 2014).

and children, it recalls existing international obligations, such as those under the ICESCR, which sets out 'the right of everyone to social security' (Article 9).

It can be noted that Recommendation No. 202 refers to the term 'guarantees' rather than 'benefits', which focuses on outcomes rather than means. According to the Recommendation, SPFs should at a minimum be composed of the following social security guarantees:

- access to a nationally defined set of goods and services, constituting essential health care, including maternity care, that meets the criteria of availability, accessibility, acceptability and quality;
- basic income security for children, providing access to nutrition, education, care and any other necessary goods and services;
- basic income security, for persons in active age who are unable to earn sufficient income, in particular in cases of sickness, unemployment, maternity and disability; and
- basic income security for older persons.

These guarantees aim at achieving universal coverage throughout the life course through a variety of benefits and schemes that best respond to national context, organizational structures and financial resources. States should use the most effective and efficient combination of contributory (e.g., social insurance), non-contributory (e.g., tax-financed schemes), negative income tax, and public employment or employment support schemes to ensure universal coverage, including of those in the informal economy. Whatever scheme or benefits chosen, whether in cash and/or kind, should secure effective access to essential goods and services.

The principle of universal coverage and the emphasis on outcomes contribute to eliminating poverty, containing inequality and promoting equity and social justice, and put in place effective and equitable redistribution mechanisms. The recent report by the UN Special Rapporteur on Extreme Poverty and Human Rights highlights the role of social protection systems, including SPFs, in this regard.[23] It is also highly relevant when it comes to ensuring adequate social protection coverage for workers in 'non-standard' forms of employment and extending social security to workers in the informal economy.[24] Where resource constraints force States to target the provision of social security benefits on specific groups of the population, generally the poorest, from a rights-based perspective, targeting mechanisms should be transparent, abide by the principles of equality and non-discrimination, and should be regularly reviewed to ensure the progressive realization of universal coverage. This implies that the

---

23. United Nations, *Report on Extreme Poverty and Human Rights* (A/HRC/29/31), submitted by the Special Rapporteur on extreme poverty and human rights, Philip Alston (New York 2015).
24. ILO, *Non-standard Forms of Employment: Understanding Challenges, Shaping Prospects* (Geneva 2016); ILO, *Extending Social Security Coverage to Workers in the Informal Economy: Lessons from International Experience* (under preparation).

eligibility criteria should be objective, reasonable and transparent, and that stigmatization of beneficiaries should be avoided.[25]

The new Global Partnership for Universal Social Protection, initiated by the World Bank and the ILO and supported by many other partners, highlights the significant progress made in many countries to achieve universal social protection coverage, ensuring that all those in need are adequately protected.[26]

3.3.3 Anchoring Social Protection Systems in Law

Recommendation No. 202 emphasizes the need to ground national social protection systems in a strong legal and institutional framework that clearly lays out entitlements, rights and obligations (paragraphs 3b and 7). This does not only contribute to realizing substantive rights but it also contributes to the rule of law, State-building and strengthening the 'social contract' in a society.[27] In this respect, SPFs also contribute to promoting just, peaceful and inclusive societies (SDG 16), particularly with regard to developing effective, accountable and transparent institutions at all levels (target 16.6), and ensuring responsive, inclusive, participatory and representative decision-making throughout (target 16.7).

A sound legal framework is one that includes: the scope of personal coverage; the type, level and range of benefits, as well as their duration; the conditions which people must meet for entitlement to a benefit and the causes which lead to the suspension of such entitlements; the financing mechanism and measures that need to be taken regularly to ensure the sustainability of social security schemes (e.g., actuarial reviews, audits, etc.) and the periodical adjustment of long-term benefits to increases in the costs of living; mechanisms and processes to give rise to people's right to complain and appeal, that are impartial, transparent, effective, simple, rapid, accessible and inexpensive and free of charge to the applicant; and the governance structure, including the roles and responsibilities of bodies and actors involved in administering, managing, delivering and enforcing social protection programmes under the overall responsibility of the State (paragraphs 3, 7, 8(d)).

Anchoring entitlements in law is key to guaranteeing the right to social security for all, including for the most disadvantaged and vulnerable groups. It ensures that beneficiaries are recognized as right-holders; that eligibility conditions, entitlements and obligations are clear and transparent; that authorities (duty-bearers) are accountable for their due provision; and that programmes are based on longer-term political and financial commitment.

---

25. E. Chase, E. and G. Bantebya Kyomuhendo, *The Shame of Poverty: Global Experiences* (Oxford 2014); R. Walker, *The Shame of Poverty: Global Perspectives* (Oxford 2014).
26. http://www.social-protection.org/gimi/gess/NewYork.action?id=34.
27. See, for example: ILO, *Social Contract and the Future of Work: Inequality, Income Security, Labour Relations and Social Dialogue*. Future of Work Issue Note No. 4 (Geneva 2016).

Moreover, by clearly setting out the main parameters of social protection programmes, the law can shed light on the linkages between the different components of the social protection system helping to reduce overlaps, duplications and gaps in protection. Furthermore, where the law establishes the mechanisms and rules (enforcement and compliance measures) that allow the persons protected to obtain redress in case these rights are violated, this can lead to strengthened accountability and prevention of fraud and corruption.

Finally, the enactment of law ensures the continuity and predictability of people's rights and entitlements through time and acts as a safeguard against arbitrary governance. For example, where parameters are established in law, following the necessary feasibility studies, the law can secure adequate protection and provide legal and financial foresight and sustainability. Financial sustainability can also be bolstered by establishing adequate financial management rules in the law, including as regards financing (e.g., establishing a stable and regular funding base), reserves and investments. This in turn contributes to building confidence in the system which can therefore act as an incentive to promote compliance with the law and the extension of coverage.

While many countries dispose of elaborate legal frameworks governing contributory social security schemes, it is not equally common to anchor non-contributory programmes in legal frameworks, which has contributed to a higher degree of instability and unpredictability in the implementation of these schemes, and a fragmented delivery of benefits and services. Countries which also have legal frameworks in place for tax-financed programmes benefit from more stability, transparency and accountability in the implementation of these programmes, which in turn contributes to enhancing their impact on reducing poverty and income inequality. Examples of good practices include South Africa's Social Assistance Act 13 of 2004 and its accompanying regulations that set out the main parameters for Child Support, Care Dependency and Foster Care Grants[28], as well as India's Mahatma Gandhi National Rural Employment Guarantee Act. Despite some implementation challenges, the latter represents an important step forward in strengthening transparency and accountability by establishing an entitlement for workers in rural areas to claim up to 100 days of employment per household.[29] Another example is Brazil's comprehensive social protection legal framework that guides the extension of social protection coverage in line with its Constitution, including through guaranteeing old-age,

---

28. *See*: ILO, *South Africa: Extending Social Protection by Anchoring Rights in Law*, Social Protection in Action: Building Social Protection Floors Series (Geneva 2016); Republic of South Africa, Report to the government: assessment of the South African legislation in view of a possible ratification of the Social Security (Minimum Standards) Convention, 1952 (No. 102) (Geneva and Pretoria, ILO 2014).
29. E. Ehmke, *Study on National Experiences in Building Social Protection Floors: The Indian MGNREGS* (Geneva, ILO 2015).

disability and survivors' pensions, as well as maternity, work injury and sickness benefits to workers in the agricultural sector.[30]

There is growing recognition of the importance of extending legal frameworks to social protection programmes that cannot rely on a stable financing source, create duplications, fragmentation and/or coverage gaps. Many low- and middle-income countries have acknowledged these challenges and are working towards strengthening their legal and institutional frameworks. Indeed, countries such as Cambodia, India and Zambia are reviewing their legal frameworks with the objective of creating more coherence and coordination across the social protection system and legal frameworks for social assistance programmes with the technical assistance of the ILO in line with international social security standards including Recommendation No. 202.

3.3.4 Adequacy and Predictability of Benefits (Accessibility, Responsiveness to Special Needs)

Ensuring adequate and predictable benefits is key to realizing the right to social security. This implies that the benefits provided should respond to needs, both in terms of their nature, their level and delivery mechanism, and should take into account national circumstances. Given the multidimensional nature of SPFs and the complementarity of cash benefits and access to services, the principle of adequacy does not only relate to the right to social security, but also to other rights, such as the right to food, health or education. This is why SPFs contribute not only to Goals 1 and 10, but also to a broad range of other goals, including Goals 2, 3, 4, 5, 6 and 8.

To ensure the adequacy and predictability of benefits, social protection floor guarantees should be defined at the national level, reflecting national circumstances. However, Recommendation No. 202 provides clear guidance on basic principles and possible benchmarks to ascertain the adequacy of benefits. Together, benefits in cash and in kind should be sufficient to secure effective access to essential goods and services, in a manner that can protect against poverty, vulnerability and social exclusion and enable a decent standard of living, and allow a life in dignity.[31] The complementarity of benefits in cash and in kind, including services, is important in defining the social protection floor guarantees. For example, basic income security for children is achieved when benefits are sufficient to ensure access to nutrition, education, care and other necessary goods and services (paragraph 5b).

More specifically, the basic income security guarantees should be defined in such a way that they provide beneficiaries with the means to live a life in dignity. Such minimum levels can be set in line with national poverty lines,

---

30. *See*: ILO, *Brazil: Extending Social Protection by Anchoring Rights in Law*, Social Protection in Action: Building Social Protection Floors Series (Geneva 2016).
31. Recommendation No. 202, paras 2 and 8b, and Convention No. 102, Art. 67.

income thresholds for social assistance, or other ways of setting a minimum monetary value of necessary goods and services. A regular review of these levels is important to ensure that benefit levels provide a meaningful level of income security over time, and these reviews should be conducted in a participatory process.[32] Benefit levels should not just be adequate, but also predictable. Where this is not the case, for example for defined-contribution pension schemes where the benefit levels are subjected to the performance of financial markets and other factors, measures should be taken to guarantee at least a basic level of social security. For example, Chile introduced a defined-benefit floor to complement the already existing defined-contribution scheme.

With regard to access to health care, Recommendation No. 202 refers to the principles of affordability, availability, accessibility and quality, and that those in need of health care should not face hardship or an increased risk of poverty due to seeking and accessing health care.[33] These principles are also highly relevant for the achievement of SDG 3 on good health and well-being, which includes a specific target on universal health coverage:

> Achieve universal health coverage, including financial risk protection, access to quality essential health-care services and access to safe, effective, quality and affordable essential medicines and vaccines for all (target 3.8).

This is one of the important factors for improving health outcomes (e.g., targets 3.1, 3.2, 3.4).

High-quality public services are essential for the delivery of adequate and predictable social protection benefits and the realization of human rights such as the right to social security housing, health, education and food. Such an integrated approach is essential for meeting people's needs throughout the life course in a comprehensive way, based on not only the principles of adequacy but also universal protection, non-discrimination and responsiveness to special needs. Practical guidance in this respect has been set out, for example, with regard to ensuring child-sensitive social protection.[34]

While the social protection floor guarantees set a basic level of protection, Recommendation No. 202 underscores the need to progressively ensure higher levels of protection to as many people as possible, as soon as possible, according to national economic and fiscal capacity, and guided by Convention No. 102 and more advanced standards. Recommendation No. 202 thus provides essential guidance with regard to achieving adequate levels of protection in the overall social protection system in the short, medium and long term.

---

32. Recommendation No. 202, paras 8b-d and Convention No. 102, Art. 65(10).
33. Recommendation No. 202, paras 5a and 8a; CESCR, *General comment No. 14: The right to the highest attainable standard of health* (Geneva, United Nations 2000).
34. UNICEF et al. *Joint Statement on Advancing Child-Sensitive Social Protection* (New York 2009).

3.3.5 Non-discrimination (Gender, Nationality and Status in Employment)

In building SPFs, States should avoid, and actively eliminate, direct and indirect discrimination in law and practice, while being responsive to special needs, and respect the dignity of those who are to be protected (paragraph 3d and 3f).[35] States should take special measures to protect the most vulnerable segments of the population as a matter of priority, and pay special attention to individuals who traditionally face difficulties in exercising this right when designing, implementing, and monitoring policies and programmes.[36] Such an approach can contribute to redressing various types of inequalities, as highlighted in SDG 10.

At the same time, States should promote gender equality, promote equal opportunities and address gender inequalities that hinder women's full realization of their right to social security (paragraph 3(d)). Addressing the structural inequalities that can have a direct impact on women's economic empowerment, including inequalities in the labour market and in employment, family responsibilities and the provision of care, requires a comprehensive approach that promotes gender equality and the empowerment of women. For example, cash transfer programmes can play a key role in promoting gender equality and empowering women, provided that they are designed in a way that does not reinforce traditional gender roles (which may be the case where responsibility for compliance with behavioural conditions in CCT programmes falls disproportionately on women)[37] and are embedded in a larger social protection framework ensuring adequate levels of protection (e.g., through the combination of non-contributory and contributory pensions).[38] The potential contribution of social protection to addressing the unequal distribution of unpaid care and domestic work is recognized in SDG target 5.4.

SPFs are an important tool for working towards substantial equality, which addresses structural inequalities and indirect discrimination. Equality should be understood in relation to outcomes as well as opportunities, and that universal protection does not necessarily mean uniform measures. 'Different' treatment may be required to achieve equality in practice.[39] In this regard, substantial equality therefore comprises the principle of responsiveness to special needs (paragraph 3d). Substantive equality differs from formal equality in that the

---

35. *See also*: ICESCR Art. 2(2) and CESCR, *General Comment No. 20: Non-Discrimination in Economic, Social and Cultural Rights* (2009).
36. CESCR, *General Comment 19: The Right to Social Security*, paras 29-31 (2008).
37. M. Molyneux, *Change and Continuity in Social Protection in Latin America: Mothers at the Service of the State?* (Geneva, UNRISD 2007).
38. ILO, Women at Work: Trends 2016 (Geneva, ILO 2016), particularly pp. 87-91; E. Fultz and J. Francis, *Cash Transfer Programmes, Poverty Reduction and Empowerment of Women: A Comparative Analysis: Experiences from Brazil, Chile, India, Mexico and South Africa* (Geneva, ILO 2013).
39. UN Women: *Progress of the World's Women, 2015-2016* (New York 2015).

latter refers to laws and policies that treat everyone equally, while substantive equality is concerned with the results and outcomes of these laws, policies and practices, in particular ensuring that they do not maintain, but rather alleviate, the inherent disadvantage that particular groups experience. Policy makers must take into consideration the specific needs of different groups, and work towards rectifying the effects of past discrimination, social norms and power dynamics that contribute to inequality.

For example, persons with disabilities face various impediments to the enjoyment of their human rights, and thus it is particularly important that the implementation of SPFs is fully inclusive of persons with disabilities, and responds to their specific needs in line with the Convention on the Rights of Persons with Disabilities (CRPD). Policies and programmes should be designed to take into account disability-related cost in a way that is non-discriminatory and responsive to special needs, as highlighted in a recent report of the UN Special Rapporteur on the Rights of Persons with Disabilities. Other concrete measures that States can take to transform traditional disability-welfare approaches into a rights-based model based on the CPRD include, for example, a review of eligibility criteria, targeting and disability determination mechanisms to ensure that people's rights and dignity are respected.[40]

3.3.6 Financial and Economic Management, and Financial Solidarity

Ensuring the sound, equitable and sustainable financing of national social protection schemes as a whole, and SPFs in particular, is one of the key implementation challenges. ILO Recommendation No. 202 sets out a number of financing principles to guide the design and implementation of social protection systems, including SPFs. These include ensuring transparent, accountable and sound financial management, financial, fiscal and economic sustainability with due regard to social justice and equity, and solidarity in financing (paragraphs 3j, k, h). These principles are closely linked to SDG 10, particularly target 10.4, as well as SDGs 16 and 17.

The best policy design and legal framework become meaningless if not backed by transparent, accountable and sound financial management, based on a sound overall regulatory and monitoring framework, including periodic actuarial valuations in line with international accounting and actuarial standards,[41] transparent fund management and investment rules, appropriate measures to address economic fluctuations, and effective accountability mechanisms.

Financial, fiscal and economic sustainability is also key to realizing the right to social security. States should explore ways to mobilize the necessary resources through a variety of different methods to progressively ensure the full

---

40. UN, *Report of the Special Rapporteur on the Rights of Persons with Disabilities*, A/70/297 (New York 2015).
41. ILO and ISSA, *Actuarial Guidelines for Social Security Administration* (Geneva 2016).

realization of the right to social security (paragraphs 11 and 12). In other words, the State must find fiscal space in the long run to guarantee the availability of resources when needed. There is an obvious tension between benefit level and sustainability. However, adequacy of transfer levels should never be compromised. The different financing methods could take into account demographic trends (increased longevity, declining fertility rates and increasing mobility), as well as structural changes in the labour market (labour force participation, structure of employment, levels of informality and casual work) and the changing needs of the population. The principle of progressive realization (*see* section 4.1) also implies that States should look to continuously improve conditions and avoid policies that lead to non-action or retrogressive measures that can obstruct the implementation of SPFs and higher levels of protection.[42]

This is also the reason why Recommendation No. 202 emphasizes the principle of financial solidarity, and the consideration of a diversity of financing mechanisms for social protection provisions through taxes and contributions, taking into account the contributory capacity of those with low and irregular incomes (paragraphs 3h, 3i). In fact, most countries combine financing through social security contributions and taxation, particularly when extending social coverage to larger groups of the population with a view to achieving universal protection. For example, China has nearly reached universal pension coverage by combining contributory and non-contributory provision of pensions in line with Recommendation No. 202.[43]

Seeking financial sustainability also requires looking at ways to expand fiscal space, which may involve the effective enforcement of tax and contribution obligations, reprioritizing expenditure, or a broader and sufficiently progressive revenue base, taking into account different types of taxes. Other possible options for expanding fiscal space for social protection include the earmarking of revenues from natural resources. For example, Bolivia expanded fiscal space and generated government revenues to support social and socio-economic development through taxation of natural resources, including also financial disclosure requirements and involving civil society in the monitoring.[44] Zambia offers a similar example.[45] Indonesia extended social protection coverage by gradually withdrawing fuel subsidies while at the same time introducing cash transfers to offset the adverse impact on the poor.[46] In applying such methods, Members should also consider the need to implement measures to prevent fraud, tax evasion and non-payment of contributions (paragraph 11).

---

42. UN OHCHR, *Report on Austerity Measures and Economic and Social Rights* (Geneva 2013).
43. ILO, *Universal Pension Coverage, People's Republic of China*, Social Protection in Action: Building Social Protection Floors (SPiA) Series (Geneva 2016).
44. ILO, *Bolivia: Financing Social Protection Through Taxation of Natural Resources*, SPiA Series (Geneva 2016).
45. ILO, *Zambia: Financing Social Protection Through Taxation of Natural Resources*, SPiA Series (Geneva 2016).
46. ILO, *Indonesia: Financing Social Protection Through Contributions and the Removal of Fuel Subsidy*; SPiA Series (Geneva 2016).

The extension of social protection programmes in many countries has shown that the necessary fiscal space can be secured if countries allocate the maximum of available resources to social protection, and the equitable and sustainable financing of social protection systems.[47] Many countries have found innovative ways to address such challenges.[48] For example, Ghana has expanded the fiscal space for its social protection system through various mechanisms, including by earmarking revenues from a value added tax on alcohol, cigarettes and luxury goods to fund the exemption from health insurance contributions for children, older persons, pregnant women and the most vulnerable.[49] Recent ILO costing studies provide new evidence that the extension of social protection is financial and fiscally attainable: for example, the cost of a minimum benefit package for Togo was projected at 13.5% of GDP in 2020 (5.3% of GDP in 2013).[50] Such investments in social protection will allow countries to progress towards achieving the SDGs.

The principle of solidarity in financing is also key in seeking financial sustainability. It aims at ensuring that all members of society have access to at least a minimum level of protection, irrespective of their contributory capacity, and that appropriate risk pooling and redistribution mechanisms are in place, which reflect solidarity between the healthy and the sick, between economically active age groups and elderly and children, between those with well-paying jobs or high incomes and those without employment or on very low incomes.

While the main emphasis is on resource mobilization from national resources for SPFs, Recommendation No. 202 also states that countries with insufficient economic and fiscal capacities may seek international cooperation and support which complement their own efforts.[51] In this regard, various proposals have been made to establish mechanisms of international financial support for the establishment of SPFs in countries with limited fiscal space.[52] Such considerations are highly relevant in the context of SDG 17 on global partnerships for sustainable development, particularly when it comes to the mobilization of resources (targets 17.1, 17.2 and 17.3).

---

47. ILO, *World Social Protection Report 2014/15: Building Economic Recovery, Inclusive Development and Social Justice* (Geneva 2014).
48. See, for example: I. Ortiz et al., *Fiscal space for social protection: options to expand social Investments in 187 countries*, ESS Discussion Paper No. 48 (Geneva 2015).
49. ILO, *Rationalizing social protection expenditure in Ghana (consolidated report)* (Geneva 2015).
50. OIT 2015. *Togo: un socle de protection sociale et des garanties pour l'emploi: pour une réduction de la pauvreté durable d'ici 2030* (Dakar 2015).
51. ILO, *World Social Protection Report 2014/15: Building Economic Recovery, Inclusive Development and Social Justice*, Chapter 6 (Geneva 2014).
52. O. de Schutter and M. Sepúlveda. *Underwriting the Poor: A Global Fund for Social Protection*. (New York, United Nations 2012); M Kaltenborn, *Global Social Protection. New Impetus from the 2030 Agenda for Sustainable Development*, in *Global Governance Spotlight* (2015).

3.3.7 Good Governance

Recommendation No. 202 recognizes that whatever the national institutional design and financing source for the implementation of social protection programmes and schemes, social protection systems need to be designed and implemented according to good governance principles. Recommendation No. 202 underlines a number of general principles that are recognized as leading to effective and efficient social protection systems. In addition to the principle of the overall responsibility of the State (*see* section 4.1), sound financial management and solidarity principles (*see* section 4.6), social protection systems should be built on an institutional framework, which considers a diversity of delivery mechanisms (paragraph 3(I)) that are not only sound, transparent and accountable (paragraph 3j) but also that have the administrative capacity, both as regards infrastructure and human resources, necessary to operate the schemes and deliver the benefits. An effective system to monitor progress in extending social security is essential for countries to evaluate their performance, and to provide the basis for a regular review and adjustment of policies (paragraphs 19–24) to adapt to evolving national circumstances and needs. All these elements of a good governance framework for social protection systems contribute to the strengthening of institutional capacities, and to achieving SDG 16 (particularly target 16.6).

Transparent and accountable financial and delivery mechanisms not only imply that the rules that govern the social protection system are clearly established and implemented, but that citizens are aware of their rights and responsibilities (paragraph 14f). For example, Uruguay has incorporated social security education in the curricula of schools from a very early age, raises public awareness through public information and communication campaigns, and builds the capacity of social security institution staff to respond efficiently to beneficiaries.[53]

Accountability is undeniably linked to effective enforcement and compliance mechanisms, including functioning complaints and appeal mechanisms that respect the principles of due process, as well as inspection mechanisms and other measures to encourage compliance (*see* section 3.3). Such mechanisms are key to minimizing corruption and fraud, contribution and tax evasion, and to making sure that people can trust that their rights are realized through effective and efficient governance and administration. In Qingdao city in the People's Republic of China, for example, social protection coverage was extended to 43,000 additional workers between 2012 and 2014, including self-employed workers, migrant workers and those working in small and rural enterprises, through effective inspection mechanisms using innovative technology-based tools.[54]

---

53. ILO, *Uruguay, Building a Culture of Social Protection*, SPiA Series (Geneva 2016).
54. ILO, *Extending Social Protection in Qingdao Through Labour and Social security inspection*; SPiA Series (Geneva 2016).

Given the challenge of extending social protection to previously uncovered groups, this also means using innovative administrative solutions to ensure effective access. For example, South Africa's Integrated Community Registration Outreach Programme (ICROP) reaches those in rural and semi-urban areas by using fully equipped mobile one-stop service units, or vehicles equipped with modern technology, facilities and personnel, to deliver social services.[55] In Brazil, the creation of a single national registry enhanced the outreach of social assistance programmes, eliminated duplication and mitigated the risks of data manipulation, fraud and clientelism.[56] The use of technology can also create greater efficiency and transparency if they are adapted to national circumstances and used in a manner that respects the dignity of the persons protected, including respect for protection of private information. India, for instance, has used new technologies to extend health protection to vulnerable and informal workers.[57]

Finally, good governance also includes effective mechanisms for coordination (*see* section 4) and the participation of relevant stakeholders, either directly or through consultation, in the design, management and governance of social protection schemes (paragraph 3(r), *see* section 4.9).

3.3.8 Coherence of Policies

Recommendation No. 202 strongly emphasizes the central role of social protection systems within the economic and social fabric of societies, and highlights the need to design and implement social security policies within the larger context of social, economic and employment policies (paragraph 3(l)) and, in particular, support the transition from informal to formal employment (paragraph 15). This reflects the bridging role that social protection plays in the 2030 Agenda.

The principle of policy coherence has two main dimensions. Internal coherence implies that the social protection system (including the floor) should be internally coherent, that is, the different schemes and programmes should be well coordinated under an overarching policy framework, ensuring protection along the life course in case of different contingencies while minimizing duplication, fragmentation and gaps. External coherence implies that social protection policies should be embedded in a wider policy context, and coordinated with other social and economic policies, including employment and labour market policies, macro-economic policies, rural development policies, as well as health, education and care policies.

---

55. ILO, *ICROP: Reaching out to Rural Poor Through Mobile Service Units*, SPiA Series (Geneva 2015).
56. ILO, *Cadastro Único – Operating a Registry Through a National Public Bank*; SPiA Series (Geneva 2014).
57. ILO, *RSBY: Extending Social Health Protection to Vulnerable Population by Using New Technologies*, SPiA Series (Geneva 2016).

Chapter 3: Implementing the Principles of Social Protection Floors

One of the key requirements for internal coherence is appropriate coordination mechanisms that link authorities responsible for implementing social protection schemes and programmes among each other, and with other relevant authorities, including those responsible for finance, health, education, agriculture and food security, public services, etc. Such coordination mechanisms can be achieved through different institutional arrangements. In the Dominican Republic, a new institutional framework was created to accompany the *Solidaridad* conditional cash transfer programme with the objective of ensuring inter-institutional and inter-sectoral decision-making. This new framework includes representatives from the Ministries of Health, Education, Planning and Finance.[58] In Niger, the Prime Minister's Office created in 2014 by decree, two steering committees, one political and the other technical, to bring all social protection stakeholders, national and international, together to coordinate all social protection actions, with a view to maximizing synergies and avoiding duplication.

Effective coordination between different social protection schemes and programmes, including social insurance and tax-financed schemes, is critical for achieving adequate social protection coverage for all. This should take into account labour mobility, including between different sectors of the economy, different types of employment (including self-employment), and international and internal labour migration.[59]

The responsibility to ensure programme and policy coordination also includes programmes funded by international assistance and private actors. This has important implications for national ownership and the strengthening of institutional frameworks, and resonates with commitments taken to improve aid effectiveness.[60] The emphasis on the national definition of the SPFs is closely linked to the responsibility of the State (*see* section 4.1) in ensuring its implementation in a way that is conducive to ensuring a coherent and appropriate social protection system, which is well coordinated with other social and economic policies.

With regard to external coherence, Recommendation No. 202 emphasizes the combination of preventive, promotional and active measures, benefits and services through an integrated and multidimensional approach (paragraph 10). These include policies that promote productive economic activity and formal employment through considering policies which include public procurement, government credit provisions, labour inspection, labour market policies and tax incentives, and which promote education, vocational training, productive skills

---

58. ILO, *Governance and Administration of Social Protection Floors in Southern Africa*, Module: Social Protection Floors Coordination (forthcoming).
59. ILO, *Non-standard Forms of Employment: Understanding Challenges, Shaping Prospects* (Geneva 2016); ILO, *Extending Social Security Coverage to Workers in the Informal Economy: Lessons from International Experience* (under preparation).
60. For example, Paris Declaration, the Accra Agenda for Action and the Busan Partnership Document.

and employability; and ensure coordination with other policies that enhance formal employment, income generation, education, literacy, vocational training, skills and employability, which reduce precariousness, and which promote secure work, entrepreneurship and sustainable enterprises within a decent work framework. Such policies (e.g., labour market and employment policies, wage policies, and skills development policies) are essential to enable people to engage in decent and productive employment, and to move out of poverty. Ensuring their continued social protection coverage is essential to prevent people from falling into poverty in the case of ill health, maternity, work injury, disability or other risks, and allowing for a sustained improvement of their standard of living and access to rights.

Furthermore, a stronger emphasis on policy coherence is important for reducing fragmentation, in particular with regard to coordination across institutions responsible for the administration and delivery of social protection, and with other social and economic policies (paragraphs 3m, 10c). By streamlining information and awareness raising activities, membership management, targeting, selection, registration and record-keeping, financial management, delivery of benefits, complaints and appeals procedures, or monitoring and evaluation, States can increase efficiency and accessibility and reduce costs through economies of scale. Chile uses an integrated information system that integrates both the *Chile Solidario* and *Chile Crece Contigo* as well as other programmes focused on health, education and employment, based on a single registry that links up to 43 State institutions and 345 municipalities.[61] Mongolia established one-stop shops as means to facilitate access to a broad range of services, including civil registration, social protection, employment counselling, notary and banking services, to address the challenge of providing social services within this large sparsely populated country.[62]

These linkages embodied in the social protection floor concept are essential to achieving a broad range of SDGs, including SDG 8 on decent work and economic growth, noting that social protection is one of the four pillars of decent work. Social protection can contribute to achieving full and productive employment and decent work for all women and men, including for young people and persons with disabilities, and equal pay for work of equal value (target 8.5); promoting education, skills and decent employment for young people (target 8.6); development-oriented policies that support productive activities, decent job creation, entrepreneurship, creativity and innovation, and encourage transition to the formal economy (target 8.3); and to eliminating child and forced labour (target 8.7). In addition, social protection can also contribute to achieving food security (SDG 2, targets 2.1, 2.2), access to education and care (SDG 4,

---

61. V. Barca and R. Chirchir, *Single Registries and Integrated MISs: De-mystifying Data and Information Management Concepts* (Barton ACT, Australian Department of Foreign Affairs and Trade 2014).
62. ILO, *Mongolia: A One-Stop Shop for Accessible, Transparent and Efficient Public Service Delivery*, SPiA Series (Geneva 2016).

targets 4.1, 4.2 and 4.5), and access to adequate, safe and affordable housing and basic services (SDG 11, target 11.1). Social protection systems are also one of the mechanisms that can help to strengthen resilience and adaptive capacity to climate-related hazards and natural disasters through a just transition (SDG 13, target 13.1).

3.3.9 Social Participation

The Recommendation places strong emphasis on the role of meaningful and effective social participation in building SPFs. The CESCR has noted that:

> the right of individuals and groups to participate in decision-making processes that may affect their exercise of the right to social security should be an integral part of any policy, programme or strategy concerning social security.[63]

The participation of stakeholders should be considered at all stages of social protection design, implementation and monitoring of policies. Effective participation allows for greater transparency and accountability, the sharing of information and knowledge, and the exchange of opinions and thus is one of the prerequisites for ensuring good governance of social protection schemes. Such participation also resonates with the 2030 Agenda, as reflected particularly in SDGs 16 and 17.

Recommendation No. 202 and other ILO social security standards provide for participation throughout the policy cycle, in particular with regard to national consultations on strategies and policies for the extension of social security, the periodic review of basic social security guarantees, the governance of social security schemes and in the monitoring of progress in extending social security. The Recommendation emphasizes the establishment of institutional structures, which render participation mechanisms more effective than ad hoc consultations. This approach follows the principles of social dialogue, envisaging the involvement of representative organizations of employers and workers as well as consultations with 'other relevant and representative organizations of persons concerned' to ensure the participation and representation of all stakeholders, including those in the informal economy.

In this context, it is important to take into account power relations such as patterns of marginalization and gender inequalities that exist within the household and the community. Efforts should be made to habilitate all stakeholders, through training and capacity building, for a more meaningful and effective participation. Moreover, specific measures should be adopted to ensure the inclusion of otherwise excluded categories of people, such as women, persons with disabilities, indigenous peoples, ethnic minorities, older persons and other groups that experience structural discrimination. Affirmative action measures

---

63. CESCR, *General Comment No. 19: The Right to Social Security,* para. 69 (2008).

could be considered to remediate the lack of participation of these categories through, for example, the establishment of quotas.

National consultations on strategies for the extension of social security should be based on 'consultations through effective social dialogue and social participation' (paragraph 13(1)). To facilitate such a national dialogue, the ILO has developed a guide[64] to assist countries to conduct effective consultation processes to build sustainable SPFs based on an assessment of policy and implementation gaps, priorities and policy options, supported by costing and other feasibility studies, as a first step towards the implementation of nationally defined SPFs. This process involves different line ministries, social partners and representatives of other stakeholders. A number of countries have successfully conducted such assessment-based national dialogues, including Indonesia, Malawi, Myanmar, the Philippines, Thailand, and Zambia.[65]

Participation should also be ensured in processes for the establishment and review of the social security guarantees (paragraphs 3r and 8d) and when monitoring progress in the extension of social security (paragraphs 19–24). In addition, Convention No. 102 establishes that when the administration of social security schemes is not entrusted to a public institution or regulated by public authorities, representatives of the persons protected by the scheme as well as employers and public authorities should participate in the management or be associated in a consultative capacity (Article 72 of Convention No. 102). The CESCR also recommends that beneficiaries participate in the administration of social protection programmes and that the system be established under national law. This is critical for strengthening public support, building trust and ensuring a sense of ownership and overall sustainability of the system.

Finally, social partners and civil society organizations can play a constructive role in contributing to national monitoring processes which are key to monitoring of progress in extending social security and to identify areas where policy adjustments are necessary.[66]

---

64. ILO, *Social Protection Assessment-Based National Dialogue: A Global Guide* (Geneva 2016).
65. ILO, *Social Protection Assessment Based National Dialogue: Towards a Nationally Defined Social Protection Floor in Indonesia* (Jakarta 2012); ILO, *Social Protection in Malawi, Assessment Based National Dialogue Brief* (Geneva 2016); ILO, *Social Protection Assessment Based National Dialogue: Towards a Nationally Defined Social Protection Floor in Myanmar* (Yangon 2015); ILO, *Social Protection Assessment Based national dialogue: Towards a Nationally Defined Social Protection Floor in Thailand* (Bangkok 2013).
66. FES, *Civil Society Guide to National Social Protection Floors* (Berlin 2015). This Guide was developed in the framework of the Global Coalition for Social Protection Floors, which brings together more than eighty civil society organizations advocating for social protection floors.

Chapter 3: Implementing the Principles of Social Protection Floors

3.4 THE WAY AHEAD: PROGRESS TOWARDS REALIZING THE RIGHT TO SOCIAL SECURITY FOR ALL

Since the adoption of Recommendation No. 202 in 2012, the world has seen substantial progress in the implementation of nationally defined SPFs. In many countries, this has further accelerated efforts in strengthening national social protection strategies, legal and institutional frameworks, better governance, administration and coordination of the social protection system, as well as expanding fiscal space, leading to the extension of existing or the introduction of new schemes and resulting in increased population coverage and more adequate benefit levels in some countries.

These developments reflect the growing importance of social protection systems as integral elements of sound economic and social policy. In effect, they contribute to stimulating inclusive growth by boosting the health and capacity of vulnerable segments of society, enhancing their productivity and enabling them to engage in decent work, supporting domestic demand and facilitating the structural transformation of national economies and labour markets. This has become particularly evident in the response to the 2008 financial and economic crisis, in which social protection systems have played a key role in containing negative social and economic impacts, increasing resilience and achieving faster recovery.[67]

Furthermore, by giving effect to the Recommendation, countries move towards greater compliance with their international human rights obligations. Any achievement in this sense contributes to human development, political stability and inclusive growth, and in this way to reducing and preventing poverty, redressing inequalities and encouraging the fair redistribution of economic wealth in line with the 2030 development agenda.

Regional bodies are embracing the role social protection can play and incorporating the guidelines of Recommendation No. 202 into their legal frameworks. This human rights-based approach to social protection is, for example, being witnessed on the African continent, where Regional Economic Communities have adopted, or are in the process of adopting, social security/social protection instruments.[68] At the continental level, Sectorial Ministers in charge of social development, labour and employment requested that the African Union Commission prepare an additional protocol to the African Charter on Human and People's Rights on the Rights of Citizens to Social Protection and Social Security that would be binding to all Member States. The development of this

---

67. ILO, *World Social Protection Report 2014/15: Building Economic Recovery, Inclusive Development and Social Justice*, Chapter 6 (Geneva 2014).
68. The Supplementary Act Relating to the General Convention on Social Security of Member States of ECOWAS, A/SA.5/'7/13 was adopted after Recommendation No. 202. The Protocol on Employment and Labour, 2014 adopted by Southern African Development Community (SADC), has a specific Article on the right of all to social protection regardless of their employment status, and references specifically Convention No. 102 and Recommendation No. 202.

Protocol aims to expressly set out, for the first time, the right to social security in a regional instrument. This is the first important step that can help ensure this right is guaranteed by the State in order to be made effective. It is notable, therefore, that the protocol follows many national socio-economic developments, and in particular social protection extension policies, strategies and national laws.[69]

At the national level, ILO Member States' progress in implementing Recommendation No. 202 will be analysed in 2018 as part of the ILO's supervisory system in the form of a 'general survey'. The Committee of Experts on the Application of Conventions and Recommendations, which is the ILO's supervisory body in charge of assessing the compatibility of Member States' law and practice with ILO standards, will present a report that will provide an in-depth account of the relevant law and practice in Member States and recommend further action to enhance States' application of Recommendation No. 202. It will subsequently be examined by the International Labour Conference in 2019.

This process will contribute to the broader efforts in monitoring 2030 Development Agenda. If taken seriously, the monitoring of the 2030 Agenda against the international social security legal framework will provide an effective platform to measure progress in realizing the right to social security and other human rights within the larger agenda of ensuring inclusive and sustainable economic and social development.

BIBLIOGRAPHY

Barca V. & R. Chirchir, *Single Registries and Integrated MISs: De-mystifying Data and Information Management Concepts* (Barton ACT, Australian Department of Foreign Affairs and Trade 2014).

Behrendt C., *Investing in People: Implementing the Extension of Social Security Through National Social Protection Floors* 228-261 (D. Kucera and I. Islam eds., Palgrave Macmillan UK 2013).

CESCR, *General Comment No. 14: The Right to the Highest Attainable Standard of Health* (Geneva, United Nations 2000).

CESCR, *General Comment No. 19: The Right to Social Security* (Geneva, United Nations 2008).

CESCR, *General Comment No. 20: Non-discrimination in Economic, Social and Cultural Rights* (Geneva, United Nations 2009).

CESCR, *General Comment No. 23: The Right to Just and Favourable Conditions of Work* (Geneva, United Nations 2016).

---

69. Pino A. and A. M. Badini Confalonieri, *National Social Protection Policies in West Africa: A Comparative Analysis*, 67 (3-4) International Social Security Review 127-152 (2014).

CESCR, *Statement on Social Protection Floors: An Essential Element of the Right to Social Security and of the Sustainable Development Goals*, Doc. E/C.12/54/3 (Geneva, ILO 2015).

Chase E. & G. Bantebya Kyomuhendo, *The Shame of Poverty: Global Experiences* (Oxford 2014).

Cichon M., *The Social Protection Floors Recommendation, 2012 (No.202): Can a Six-Page Document Change the Course of Social History*, 66 International Social Security Review, 21–43 (2013).

De Schutter O. & M. Sepúlveda. *Underwriting the Poor: A Global Fund for Social Protection* (New York, United Nations 2012).

Ehmke E., *Study on National Experiences in Building Social Protection Floors: The Indian MGNREGS* (Geneva, ILO 2015).

FES, *Civil Society Guide to National Social Protection Floors* (Berlin, FES 2015).

Fultz E. & J. Francis, *Cash Transfer Programmes, Poverty Reduction and Empowerment of Women: A Comparative Analysis: Experiences from Brazil, Chile, India, Mexico and South Africa* (Geneva, ILO 2013).

ILO & ISSA, *Actuarial Guidelines for Social Security Administration* (Geneva 2016).

ILO, *Bolivia: Financing Social Protection Through Taxation of Natural Resources*, SPiA Series (Geneva, ILO 2016).

ILO, *Brazil: Extending Social Protection by Anchoring Rights in Law*, Social Protection in Action: Building Social Protection Floors Series (Geneva, ILO 2016).

ILO, *Building Social Protection Systems: International Standards and Human Rights Instruments* (Geneva 2017).

ILO, *Cadastro Único – Operating a Registry Through a National Public Bank*; SPiA Series (Geneva, ILO 2014).

ILO, *Extending Social Protection in Qingdao Through Labour and Social Security Inspection*; SPiA Series (Geneva, ILO 2016).

ILO, *Extending Social Security Coverage to Workers in the Informal Economy: Lessons from International Experience* (under preparation).

ILO, *Governance and Administration of Social Protection Floors in Southern Africa*, Module: Social Protection Floors Coordination (forthcoming).

ILO, *ICROP: Reaching Out to Rural Poor Through Mobile Service Units*, SPiA Series (Geneva, ILO 2015).

ILO, *Indonesia: Financing Social Protection Through Contributions and the Removal of Fuel Subsidy*; SPiA Series (Geneva, ILO 2016).

ILO, *Mongolia: A One-Stop Shop for Accessible, Transparent and Efficient Public Service Delivery*, SPiA Series (Geneva, ILO 2016).

ILO, *Non-standard Forms of Employment: Understanding Challenges, Shaping Prospects* (Geneva, ILO 2016).

ILO, *Rationalizing Social Protection Expenditure in Ghana (Consolidated Report)* (Geneva, ILO 2015).

ILO, *Republic of South Africa, Report to the government: assessment of the South African legislation in view of a possible ratification of the Social Security (Minimum Standards) Convention, 1952 (No. 102)* (Geneva and Pretoria, ILO 2014).

ILO, *RSBY: Extending social health protection to vulnerable population by using new technologies*, SPiA Series (Geneva, ILO 2016).

ILO, *Setting Social Security Standards in a Global Society – An Analysis of Present State and Practice and of Future Options for Global Social Security Standard Setting in the International Labour Organization* (Geneva, 2008).

ILO, *Social contract and the future of work: Inequality, income security, labour relations and social dialogue*. Future of Work Issue Note No. 4 (Geneva, ILO 2016).

ILO, *Social protection assessment based national dialogue: Towards a nationally defined social protection floor in Indonesia* (Jakarta, ILO 2012).

ILO, *Social protection assessment based national dialogue: Towards a nationally defined social protection floor in Myanmar* (Yangon, ILO 2015)

ILO, *Social protection assessment based national dialogue: Towards a nationally defined social protection floor in Thailand* (Bangkok, ILO 2013).

ILO, *Social protection assessment-based national dialogue: A global guide* (Geneva, ILO 2016).

ILO, *Social Protection in Malawi, Assessment Based National Dialogue Brief* (Geneva, ILO 2016).

ILO, *Social Security and the Rule of Law: General Survey concerning social security instruments in the light of the 2008 Declaration on Social Justice for a Fair Globalization* (Geneva, ILO 2011).

ILO, *Social Security for All: Building social protection floors and comprehensive social security systems. The strategy of the International Labour Organization* (Geneva, ILO 2012).

ILO, *South Africa: Extending social protection by anchoring rights in law*, Social Protection in Action: Building Social Protection Floors Series (Geneva, ILO 2016).

ILO, *Universal Pension Coverage, People's Republic of China*, Social Protection in Action: Building Social Protection Floors (SPiA) Series (Geneva, ILO 2016).

ILO, *Uruguay, Building a culture of social protection*, SPiA Series (Geneva, ILO 2016).

ILO, *Women at Work: Trends 2016* (Geneva, ILO 2016).

ILO, *World Social Protection Report 2014/15: Building economic recovery, inclusive development and social justice* (Geneva, ILO 2014).

ILO, *World Social Protection Report 2017-19* (Geneva, ILO, forthcoming).

ILO, *Zambia: Financing social protection through taxation of natural resources*, SPiA Series (Geneva, ILO 2016).

Kaltenborn M., *Global Social Protection. New impetus from the 2030 Agenda for Sustainable Development*, Global Governance Spotlight (2015).

Kulke U. & E. Saint-Pierre Guilbault, *The Social Protection Floors Recommendation, 2012 (No. 202): Completing the standards to close the coverage gap*, 66 International Social Security Review, 87-109 (2013).

Markov K., *Sécurité sociale*, in *Droit international social: Droits économiques, sociaux et culturels*, vol. 2 (J.-M. Thouvenin & A. Trebilcock eds., Bruylant 2013).

Molyneux M., *Change and Continuity in Social Protection in Latin America: Mothers at the Service of the State?* (Geneva, UNRISD 2007).

OIT 2015, *Togo: un socle de protection sociale et des garanties pour l'emploi: pour une réduction de la pauvreté durable d'ici 2030* (Dakar 2015).

Ortiz I. et al., *Fiscal space for social protection: options to expand social Investments in 187 countries*, ESS Discussion Paper No.48 (Geneva, ILO 2015).

Pino A. & A. M. Badini Confalonieri, *National social protection policies in West Africa: A comparative analysis*, 67 International Social Security Review 127–152 (2014).

Sepúlveda M. & C. Nyst, *The Human Rights Approach to Social Protection* (Helsinki, Ministry for Foreign Affairs of Finland 2012).

UN OHCHR, *Report on austerity measures and economic and social rights* (Geneva, United Nations 2013).

UN Women, *Progress of the World's Women, 2015–2016* (New York, United Nations 2015).

UN, *Guiding principles on extreme poverty and human rights* (Geneva, United Nations 2012).

UN, *Report of the Special Rapporteur on extreme poverty and human rights, Philip Alston, on Social Protection Floors (A/69/297)* (Geneva, United Nations 2016).

UN, *Report of the Special Rapporteur on the rights of persons with disabilities*, A/70/297 (New York, United Nations 2015).

UN, *Report on extreme poverty and human rights* A/HRC/29/31 (New York, United Nations 2015).

UNICEF et al. *Joint statement on advancing child-sensitive social protection.* (New York, United Nations 2009).

Walker R., *The Shame of Poverty: Global perspectives* (Oxford 2014).

CHAPTER 4
Social Protection Floors and the Right to Food*

Stephen Devereux

4.1 INTRODUCTION

In June 2012, the International Labour Conference adopted Recommendation No. 202, 'concerning National Floors of Social Protection', a rights-based approach that calls on all Member States to ensure guaranteed universal access for everyone to essential services, especially health care, and to 'basic income security' throughout the life cycle, which should be defined 'at a nationally defined minimum level'. Proposed policy instruments include 'universal benefit schemes, social insurance schemes, social assistance schemes, negative income tax schemes, public employment schemes and employment support schemes'.[1]

Nutrition is mentioned only once in Recommendation No. 202: basic income security should provide 'access to nutrition, education, care and any other necessary goods and services' for children. Food and food security are not

---

* This chapter is based on an article commissioned by the ILO: Devereux, S. *Realising the right to social security and the right to food: The contribution of national social protection floors towards food security and the realisation of the right to adequate food for all*, Extension of Social Security (ESS) Working Paper, 51. Geneva: International Labour Office (2015) and a presentation at the international workshop, 'The ILO Recommendation on Social Protection Floors: Basic Principles for Innovative Solutions', organized by the Max Planck Institute for Social Law and the Centre for International and Comparative Labour and Social Security Law (CICLASS), at the University of Johannesburg in South Africa (12-13 Sep. 2016). The workshop and the writing of this chapter were supported by the National Research Foundation of South Africa (Grant Number: 98411) and the Newton Fund, administered by the British Council.
1. ILO, *Text of the Recommendation Concerning National Floors of Social Protection* (Geneva: International Labour Conference 2012).

mentioned at all. However, the implication of the phrase 'basic income security' is that social transfers and other components of the social protection floor should be sufficient to secure subsistence, which must include access to adequate nutrition. But the causal pathways from income security to food and nutrition security are complex. Income is a means to an end – or several ends, only one of which is securing access to food.

Food and nutrition security has four components or pillars:[2]

- *availability*: enough food to meet consumption needs at all levels, from global to individual – which is determined at national level mainly by food production and net food imports;
- *access*: well-functioning markets and adequate income or 'entitlements' to secure individual food needs – which is affected both by market prices and by poverty;
- *stability*: stable food supplies at all times, including during the 'hungry season' or after livelihood shocks – which can be compromised, *inter alia*, by conflict, bad weather and climate change; and
- *utilization*: biological absorption of nutrients consumed – which is determined more by a person's health status than their income.

A rights-based approach to food security focuses on availability ('adequate food'), access ('physical and economic access') and stability ('at all times'): 'The right to adequate food is realized when every man, woman and child, alone or in community with others, has physical and economic access at all times to adequate food or means for its procurement.'[3] Nutrition security focuses most attention on the utilization aspect.

It might seem that the Social Protection Floor and the right to adequate food are effectively congruent, since both concepts refer to public interventions to guarantee subsistence for all people at all times. While there are indeed many synergies, there are also some dissonances between income security and food security, which are explored in this chapter. It will be seen that universalizing the right to social protection is not necessarily sufficient to ensure the right to adequate food for all.

Ensuring that income security translates into food and nutrition security requires guaranteeing enough income to finance food purchases, for all people at all times. Operationalizing the 'basic income security' component of national social protection floors requires addressing both the horizontal dimension (coverage – how to ensure that everyone is income secure?) and the vertical dimension (adequacy – how much income do people need for food security?). Two additional questions relevant to food security are also considered in this chapter, concerning stability (How to allow for variability in needs over time?)

---

2. FAO, *Food Security*, ESA Policy Brief, Issue 2 (Rome: FAO 2006).
3. CESCR, *General Comment No. 12: The Right to Adequate Food (Art. 11)* para. 6, Document E/C.12/1999/5 adopted at the Twentieth Session of the Committee on Economic, Social and Cultural Rights, on 12 May 1999.

and intra-household issues (Is household food security sufficient for individual nutrition security?).

4.2 COVERAGE: HOW TO ENSURE THAT EVERYONE IS INCOME SECURE?

The only way to ensure that everyone in a country or territory is reached by a public intervention is to introduce a universal programme that benefits all citizens and residents. Applying the 'leave no one behind' principle, a programme that benefits everybody has zero exclusion errors, by definition. Examples of universal programmes include general food price subsidies, a 'basic income grant' (BIG), and fee-free social services (education, health care, etc.).

Consumer price subsidies have historically been preferred by governments in parts of the world such as North Africa and the Middle East, where subsidies absorbed close to 6% of Gross Domestic Product (GDP) until recently, compared to about 1% in other developing countries.[4] The main advantage – and disadvantage – of general price subsidies is that they not only benefit everybody, including all poor people, but also all people who are already food and income secure, and have more disposable income to spend on subsidized goods and services. In Egypt, over 80% of the value of food subsidies was captured by the non-poor, making this a very inefficient and cost-ineffective instrument. So, universal coverage leaves no one behind, but only at a heavy fiscal cost.

On the other hand, phasing out subsidies is politically costly, as influential and vocal middle classes and elites benefit most from them and often strongly resist losing these entitlements. Nonetheless, universal subsidies are being phased out in many countries, usually to be replaced with pro-poor targeted cash transfers. In several cases, such as in Sudan and Yemen, subsidy removal led to food price inflation that left poor people worse off than before, in the absence of effective and comprehensive compensatory mechanisms.[5]

There is a popular perception that universal benefits are rights-based and progressive, whereas targeted programmes are 'neoliberal' and incompatible with rights-based principles. Mkandawire, for instance, is a strident critic of targeting, which he believes either inadvertently excludes many needy people or is deliberately designed to ration access, by stigmatizing and shaming poor people (by forcing them to queue, for instance).[6] An alternative to subsidies that avoids these 'social costs' of targeting is to transfer income regularly and directly to everyone, in the form of a universal BIG. This idea seems entirely consistent

---

4. Silva, J., Levin, V. & Morgandi, M. *Inclusion and Resilience: The Way Forward for Social Safety Nets in the Middle East and North Africa* (Washington DC: World Bank 2012).
5. Devereux, S. *Social Protection and Safety Nets in the Middle East and North Africa*, IDS Research Report, 80 (Brighton: Institute of Development Studies 2015).
6. Mkandawire, T. *Targeting and Universalism in Poverty Reduction*, Social Policy and Development Programme Paper, 23 (Geneva: United Nations Research Institute for Social Development (UNRISD) 2005).

with the Social Protection Floor principle of universal access to basic income security.

Although a universal income transfer might appear to be just as expensive and inefficient as general price subsidies, BIG advocates argue that leakages to the non-poor could largely be recouped through a 'solidarity tax'. Nonetheless, in South Africa, the campaign for a BIG was defeated by the then Minister of Finance, Trevor Manuel, who argued that the idea was 'fundamentally flawed ... the country can't afford it'.[7] In neighbouring Namibia, the Basic Income Grant Coalition ran a BIG pilot project in 2008/2009, by delivering cash transfers worth about United States Dollars (USD) 12 each month for two years to all residents in two communities. Positive impacts were recorded on many economic and psychosocial indicators,[8] and a costing exercise concluded that scaling up to national level would be fiscally affordable, at 2%–3% of GDP or 5%–6% of the national budget.[9] However, the pilot project reached only 930 people, and it has not been implemented at scale in Namibia due to lack of political support.

Elsewhere, in 2010 Iran became the first country to implement a national BIG, paying cash transfers to all citizens to compensate them when subsidies were phased out. India implemented two BIG pilot projects in 2011, and the Netherlands and Finland are both running BIG experiments in 2017. On the other hand, voters in Switzerland rejected a proposal in 2016 for a universal BIG to all citizens.

If universal subsidies are inefficient and a universal BIG is deemed unaffordable at the level required to ensure food security for all, another option is to deliver regular cash transfers to designated vulnerable groups, such as children and older persons. This is also in line with the Social Protection Floor, which aims to guarantee basic income security for all children and for all older persons. Such 'demogrants' (social grants that target demographic categories) can reach high proportions of poor and food insecure people, though not all – economically active adults are usually excluded from categorical targeting, which favours demographic categories that are vulnerable because they are unable to work. Other provisions are needed to ensure that groups not covered by demogrants are reached. Options include mandatory social security schemes (e.g., unemployment insurance) for formally employed workers, complemented by voluntary social security contributions for informal and self-employed workers.

It is important to emphasize that it is possible to achieve income security for all without transferring income to all. In reality, a substantial proportion of any community or society is already income secure and has no need for social assistance from charities or the State. Even the rights-based Social Protection

---

7. Fin24, *Basic Income Grant 'Flawed'* 2015, http://www.fin24.com/Economy/Basic-income-grant-flawed-20050523 (accessed 20 Mar. 2017).
8. Haarmann, C. et al., *'Towards a Basic Income Grant for All': Basic Income Grant Pilot Project Assessment Report* (Windhoek: Basic Income Grant Coalition 2008).
9. BIG Coalition, *A Call for the National Implementation of the Basic Income Grant (BIG)* in Namibia, Press Release 25 June (Windhoek: Basic Income Grant Coalition 2015).

Floor implies that social assistance should be provided only to those who need it, while those who do not need it will achieve income security through their earnings plus savings, complemented by contributory social security schemes and private market-based insurance arrangements.

The logic behind targeted (rather than universal) social transfers is that identifying who needs income support, and redistributing income from wealthier taxpayers to poor people through social welfare programmes, is more equitable (because it reduces inequality) and cost effective (because it makes most efficient use of scarce public resources).[10] Another option, therefore, is to identify all poor and food insecure households through an individual assessment mechanism (e.g., a means test or poverty scorecard) and deliver regular cash transfers only to them. The challenge is that targeting is expensive and is never 100% accurate – some eligible people are invariably left out and some ineligible people are invariably included.[11] From a Social Protection Floor and a 'right to food' perspective, exclusion errors are more significant: in theory, for advocates of universal programmes, there are no inclusion errors. The risk of exclusion errors makes a powerful argument against targeting 'the poor' and in favour of universal programmes.[12]

4.3 ADEQUACY: HOW MUCH INCOME DO PEOPLE NEED FOR FOOD SECURITY?

Nationally defined poverty lines typically cover the costs of a basket of food and essential non-food goods and services, and social grants are often calibrated to the cost of a basic food basket, to enable recipients to meet their subsistence needs. This is important also for delivering the Social Protection Floor and its guarantee of 'basic income security for all'. However, these calculations are far from simple. Which items should be included in the food basket? Which prices should be used? (wholesale or retail? supermarket or village market?) How to allow for price variability and inflation? How to allow for differences in household size and age-sex composition?

The problem can be simplified if food transfers are delivered instead of cash transfers, because this eliminates the pricing issues. Giving food rations or commodity-denominated vouchers to poor and food insecure people ensures their access to food and contributes directly to achieving the human right to adequate food for all. India, for example, has a constitutional right to food which it upholds through large-scale programmes including the Public Distribution System (subsidized food for poor people through Fair Price Shops), the Midday

---

10. Devereux, S. *Is Targeting Ethical?* Global Social Policy, 16(2), 166-181 (2016).
11. Ellis, F. *'We Are All Poor Here': Economic Difference, Social Divisiveness, and Targeting Cash Transfers in Sub-Saharan Africa*, Journal of Development Studies, 48(2): 201-214 (2012).
12. Kidd, S. *The Political Economy of 'Targeting' of Social Security Schemes*, Pathways' Perspectives, no. 19 (Orpington: Development Pathways 2015).

Meal Programme (the national school feeding scheme), and the Mahatma Gandhi National Rural Employment Guarantee Act (demand-driven public works employment, available as a right to all rural households). Together these programmes deliver food or access to food to millions of Indian families, although they face implementation challenges and their effectiveness has been variable across States and over time. Rights on paper do not always translate into rights in practice. For example, in India, vulnerable groups such as older persons, women and Dalits face difficulties accessing benefits to which they are entitled.[13]

The Social Protection Floor is agnostic about whether income security should be delivered in the form of cash, vouchers, subsidies or food – it refers to 'social transfers in cash or in kind'. But increasingly the trend in social protection programmes is towards cash transfers, which are seen as less paternalistic and as offering more choice and flexibility to beneficiaries. Also, income security implies more than food security – the latter is a subset of the former. This raises the question of defining how much cash each individual or household needs to finance adequate food purchases and access to health care and other essential services (which is also a component of the Social Protection Floor), as well as other non-food basic needs (clothing, housing, etc.). The challenge of costing a nutritionally adequate food basket has already been noted. As for services, primary health and education are provided for free at the point of delivery in many countries, but even this is not sufficient to guarantee universal access, as there are other cost barriers (transport, medicines, school books) and non-cost barriers (time, distance, low uptake due to perceptions of poor service quality, etc.).

There are other challenges with attempting to guarantee the right to adequate food through subsidies or cash transfers. Even if the value of the transfer is sufficient to purchase adequate food, this cash is often diluted among different uses (not only food) and among secondary beneficiaries (child grants and social pensions are rarely spent exclusively on the designated child or pensioner). In South Africa, for example, an extensive social grants system now reaches 17 million people, almost one-third of the population. Social grants have been demonstrated to reduce poverty, inequality and food insecurity, but they have had a limited impact on malnutrition, which remains at very high levels. Three explanations have been offered for this: (1) the grants are not sufficient to purchase a nutritionally adequate diet, especially during periods of rapid food price inflation; (2) social grant income is fungible and is used for various needs (ranging from food and groceries to transport and airtime); and (3) social grants

---

13. Kabeer, N. *Can the MDGs Provide a Pathway to Social Justice? The Challenge of Intersecting Inequalities* (New York: United Nations Development Programme 2010).

are diluted among many household members, not just the designated beneficiary.[14]

One way to address the 'dilution' effect is to adjust the value of income transfers by household size and composition, so that larger households receive larger transfers, sometimes calibrated by adult equivalents (so children get less than adults). An example is 'full family targeting', as applied on Ethiopia's Productive Safety Net Programme (PSNP) – participants on the PSNP public works programme earn wages not only for themselves but also for their entire household, so a household of four earns twice as much as a two-person household. This ensures that all households, both large and small, receive similar benefits per capita, which is important in terms of the Social Protection Floor's objectives – income security and access to health care not for every household, but for every individual.

4.4 STABILITY: HOW TO ALLOW FOR VARIABILITY IN NEEDS OVER TIME?

Income security and food security both implicitly incorporate the time dimension – continuous access at all times to sufficient income to avoid poverty and to sufficient food to avoid hunger, respectively. There are at least three sources of threat to continuous access to sufficient income and food: income variability, food production variability and food price variability.

Social security is specifically designed to be sensitive to *income variability* throughout the life cycle. While economically active adults are formally employed, they are either encouraged to save or required by law to make payments (often deducted directly from their salaries) into social security schemes that will make payouts to them when they are not working and not earning income – during periods of unemployment, maternity leave, illness or disability, and in retirement. The primary function of social security is to stabilize income and smooth consumption over the life cycle, and in this sense, social security contributes to the three income-related objectives of the Social Protection Floor – to guarantee basic income security for all children, for all persons in active age unable to earn sufficient income and for all older persons.

However, social security does not provide complete protection against income variability. One issue facing pensioners, for instance, is the 'replacement ratio' (post-retirement income as a proportion of pre-retirement income). Social pensions are rarely generous enough to cover all of a pensioner's subsistence needs, and even contributory pensions replace only part of the pensioner's earnings before retirement, which leaves many pensioners living in poverty rather than enjoying income security in older age.

---

14. Devereux S. & Waidler, J. *Why Does Malnutrition Persist in South Africa Despite Social Grants?* Food Security SA Working Paper Series, No. 001 (South Africa: DST-NRF Centre of Excellence in Food Security 2017).

Of course, the people who are most income insecure and vulnerable to food insecurity are those who have no formal employment and no access to social security. In high-income highly urbanized countries, the majority of households have one or more members working in waged or salaried employment, earning regular, predictable and adequate income; they acquire food from markets that are strong, integrated and responsive to demand signals; and food prices are relatively stable and rise only slowly over time. By contrast, in rural areas of low-income countries, the majority of families are self-employed as smallholder farmers and agricultural labourers; they earn irregular, unpredictable and often inadequate income; they purchase food from markets that are weak, fragmented and respond slowly to demand signals; and food prices can fluctuate dramatically due to agricultural seasonality and supply failures.

When *food production* fails, small farmers are acutely exposed to food insecurity because they have lost their primary source of food. In extreme cases, humanitarian food aid might be needed to prevent famine. Food security can also be protected with emergency cash transfers, if markets are strong enough and local traders respond promptly to demand signals from affected communities. Even in 'normal' years, seasonal food insecurity is common in rural areas with a single rainy season, when farmers' granaries are depleted during the annual hungry season. Counter-seasonal measures to stabilize food consumption include public works projects and 'open market operations' – government agencies buying food after the harvest and releasing it during the hungry season, when local markets have limited supplies and prices start to rise.

Food price variability can be a significant contributor to food insecurity. During the global food price crisis of 2008, average food prices rose by 7% and the estimated number of malnourished people in the world increased by 44 million.[15] Regular cash transfer programmes are not designed to respond rapidly to dramatic food price rises. At best, social grants and social insurance payments might be index-linked to annual inflation rates, meaning they are adjusted once each year. Seasonal or emergency cash transfers can be adjusted more regularly – even monthly – to protect food security against variable food prices, but this requires too much administrative complexity for most social protection systems.

Instead of intervening on the demand side, to boost household income and stabilize household purchasing power as food prices rise, other mechanisms exist that intervene on the supply side, to boost food availability and minimize price rises. Food price subsidies and national grain reserve management were popular with governments throughout Africa and Asia until the 'Washington consensus' thinking of the 1980s, when State interventions in agricultural production and marketing were scaled down on the grounds that they interfered with private sector development and distorted local markets. Galtier has argued that these supply-side interventions are more effective than targeted cash transfers, and that variants on 'price banding' (regulation to maintain food

---

15. UNICEF, *The Right Ingredients: The Need to Invest in Child Nutrition* (London: UNICEF UK 2012).

prices between a minimum 'floor' for producers and a maximum 'ceiling' for consumers) and buffer stocks should be reintroduced, to assure food security.[16]

4.5 INTRA-HOUSEHOLD ISSUES: IS HOUSEHOLD FOOD SECURITY SUFFICIENT FOR INDIVIDUAL NUTRITION SECURITY?

Food security is often defined and measured at the household level, but nutritional outcomes are defined and measured at the individual level. This ambiguity makes 'food and nutrition security' a challenging concept to define and operationalize. Moreover, the Social Protection Floor is grounded in individual human rights, and is disaggregated to children, adults and older persons – not households. But there are many reasons why food security at household level might not translate into nutrition security for each and every household member. Analogously, income accrued by one household member – including social security payments or social cash transfers that accrue either to 'the household' or to a named recipient within the household – might not be distributed equitably among all household members. This leads to the possibility that a household can appear to enjoy income and food security, while at the same time some individuals within the household can be living in poverty, or can be 'nutrition insecure'. This section examines some plausible explanations for these apparently paradoxical outcomes.

4.5.1 Gender

In many societies, intra-household control over income, assets and food is gendered. As a generalization, in rural Africa men typically control major assets such as ploughs, bicycles and large livestock (e.g., cattle), while women control minor assets such as kitchen utensils and small livestock (e.g., poultry). Men also control cash crop production and income earned from cash crops, whereas women control (sometimes but not always) food crop production, especially kitchen gardens, and are responsible for storing food and feeding the family. In some parts of Africa, husbands are traditionally prohibited even from looking inside their wives' food granaries.

This gendered division of power and responsibilities within households can have implications – either positive or negative – for individual well-being. For instance, in southern Tanzania, the commercialization of maize marketing in the 1980s resulted in men in smallholder families taking control over white maize production away from women, as maize shifted from being cultivated mainly for household consumption to being cultivated mainly for sale. Although the profits earned from producing and selling maize as a 'cash crop' raised average household income overall, the nutritional status of children actually

---

16. Galtier, F. *Managing Food Price Instability: Critical Assessment of the Dominant Doctrine*, Global Food Security, 2: 72-81 (2013).

declined, because less of the maize harvest was consumed than before and only some of the earnings from maize sales was used to buy food for the family.[17] This is an unusual case in which household income security improved, but individual food security deteriorated as a consequence.

One factor that partly explains the paradoxical outcome in Tanzania is gendered differences in spending behaviour. In general, men have a higher marginal propensity to spend incremental income on personal consumption, whereas women spend more on the consumption needs of others, such as food for children. Also, men might be inclined to invest incremental income in productive assets for future income security, whereas women are responsible for domestic reproduction and therefore tend to spend a higher proportion of incremental income on current food security needs.

The implication of these gendered differences is that knowing total household income is not sufficient to establish whether all household members are likely to be food secure: it matters greatly who brings that income into the home. For this reason, social protection programmes that aim to promote the well-being of children and women often deliver social assistance directly to women, on the assumption that this will achieve bigger positive impacts on children than if this income is delivered to men in the same household. There is some empirical evidence for this assumption. In South Africa, social pensions given to women are associated with significant positive impacts on the anthropometric status of children in their care, but social pensions given to men registered no such impacts on children in their care.[18]

There are also risks associated with targeting social protection programmes at women, especially women living as wives, daughters or mothers in male-headed households. Illustrative examples come from microfinance, conditional cash transfers and public works programmes.

In patriarchal cultures, men might resent and resist the 'undermining' of their authority that is implicit in programmes that deliver benefits to women rather than to themselves. Men could take control over this income or even inflict gender-based violence against their partners. In Bangladesh, many women who received microfinance loans were forced to hand this cash over to their husbands, leaving these women indebted and responsible for repaying the loans, despite earning no income from them. Throughout Latin America, 'conditional cash transfer' programmes require caregivers to send their children to school and to health clinics for immunization and growth monitoring, as a condition for receiving the cash transfers. Critics have argued that the burden for adhering to these conditions falls mainly on women as primary caregivers,

---

17. Geier, G. *Food Security Policy in Africa Between Disaster Relief and Structural Adjustment: Reflections on the Conception and Effectiveness of Policies: The Case of Tanzania* (London: Frank Cass 1995).
18. Duflo, E. *Grandmothers and Granddaughters: Old Age Pension and Intrahousehold Allocation in South Africa*, NBER Working Paper, 8061 (Cambridge, MA: National Bureau of Economic Research 2000).

reinforcing stereotypical gender roles. Finally, the heavy manual labour requirements on most public works programmes in Africa and Asia effectively exclude many women who lack the physical strength needed – especially women who are sick, pregnant, elderly or time-stressed due to domestic responsibilities – which might result in men appropriating most of the workplaces and income available through public works.[19]

Gender bias within households can also explain differential outcomes for individuals. Pro-male bias in certain societies is reflected in a preference for sons rather than daughters, and in extreme cases, skewed sex ratios and demographic evidence of 'missing' girls and women. Less dramatically, pro-male bias can be seen in preferential access by sons to education, health care, even food in poor families. Again, income security at household level does not necessarily translate into food security for all household members. In such contexts, cash or food transfers to households are not enough. Complementary interventions are needed to tackle the sociocultural drivers of gendered poverty and food insecurity. In terms of social protection, options could include targeting girls to counteract anti-female bias, such as conditional cash transfers or take-home food rations only for girls who attend primary or secondary school.

4.5.2 Care

Cash transfers finance food purchases and increase food consumption, but food and nutrition security do not depend only on food intake. Mothers and young children need special care and attention to achieve good nutrition outcomes. For instance, it is well established that babies born to undernourished mothers will most likely have low birthweight, and will struggle to 'catch up' this deficit and achieve their full growth potential, even if their households enjoy income security and appear to be food secure in other respects. Providing cash or food transfers in this situation is too late to address this intergenerational transmission of malnutrition. A more effective approach is to focus on the nutritional status of pregnant and lactating women (PLW), with a package of support that could include nutrition education, fortified foods and iron supplements. A pre-emptive strategy is to target these packages at adolescent girls, to boost their nutritional status before they fall pregnant.[20]

Nutritional status also depends on access to health care, clean water and sanitation facilities. For children, a critical additional determinant is infant feeding practices. Specifically, children should be exclusively breastfed for the

---

19. Holmes R. & Jones, N. *Gender and Social Protection in the Developing World: Beyond Mothers and Safety Nets* (London: Zed Books 2013).
20. UNICEF, *The Right Ingredients: The Need to Invest in Child Nutrition* (London: UNICEF UK 2012).

first six months before complementary foods are introduced to the diet; otherwise, there is an elevated probability that the child will become malnourished.[21] Again, this pathway to good nutrition is not directly influenced by household income, but is determined mainly by mother's education and behaviour. In theory, a child could be malnourished in a non-poor household that is food secure, because of inappropriate childcare and feeding practices. Even after the child is weaned, good nutrition depends on a diversified diet that includes macronutrients (calories, protein, fats) as well as micronutrients (vitamins and minerals). And even if household members consume an adequate and diversified diet, unclean water and an unsanitary environment could cause illnesses that compromise nutritional status. Given these multiple pathways to (mal)nutrition, it follows that cash transfers might be an effective modality for achieving income security, but are either inadequate or – in some circumstances – inappropriate for achieving food and nutrition security.

4.6 CONCLUSION

The Social Protection Floor aims to provide comprehensive social protection, specifically income security as well as access to health care services, to all individuals, from infancy to old age. An implicit assumption is that income security is necessary and sufficient to guarantee food security. This chapter has identified several reasons why this assumption is questionable.

First, income security is difficult to define or measure, and even more difficult to deliver. 'Basic income security' is challenging to define and deliver because it implies that a minimum set of goods and services exists that everyone has a right to access and consume, that this set of goods and services can be accurately costed, that people's needs or deficits in relation to these goods and services can be accurately assessed, and that targeted individuals (or the entire population) can be given enough income to finance their acquisition of these goods and services, not only now but in perpetuity.

Each of these assumptions is heroic, but taken together they are arguably intractable. Has any society achieved basic income security, for all its citizens and residents, at all times? Prices of goods and services change constantly (food prices vary due to inflation, seasonality or food crises); different individuals (pregnant women, children, chronically ill people) have different nutritional needs; income – including cash transfers – might not be equitably distributed among household members (if women and men have differential control over income and divergent spending priorities); cash transfers might be 'diluted' among several unintended beneficiaries, and so on.

A national Social Protection Floor can make some allowances for these realities. For example: the 'basic income' line should be set higher than the cost

---

21. Save the Children Fund, *Superfood for Babies: How Overcoming Barriers to Breastfeeding Will Save Children's Lives* (London: Save the Children Fund 2013).

of a nutritionally adequate food basket, to allow non-food essentials to be purchased; cash transfers should be index-linked and adjusted as frequently as administratively possible, to compensate recipients for price rises; food assistance or commodity vouchers might be more appropriate than cash transfers in certain contexts; 'full family targeting' should be the norm, to ensure that all individuals are reached; and delivering transfers to women rather than men – even in male-headed households – can achieve better nutritional outcomes for children.

Second, the pathways from income security to food and nutrition security are complex and multiple, because nutritional outcomes are determined not by income alone. Achieving food security and adequate nutrition requires more than social transfers – well-functioning markets, accessible and good quality services, and nutrition-sensitive or nutrition-specific interventions are also needed. If these are lacking, then interventions to promote income security will be inadequate. Cash transfers stimulate the demand for goods and services, but this does not necessarily increase either the supply or quality of goods and services. For example, injecting cash transfers into food deficit communities where markets are weak will simply fuel food price inflation.[22] Similarly, if health services are of poor quality then making them fee-free will improve access but might have a negligible impact on health status, if the health care delivered does not address the health problems presented at clinics. In such situations, the Social Protection Floor objectives of income security throughout the life cycle and universal access to health care might be achieved, but food security and 'health security' for all will not.

Third, achieving comprehensive social protection, even at a minimum 'floor' level, requires an integrated and coordinated systems approach, not a single instrument or even a set of instruments. The Social Protection Floor is expected to make a positive difference at the micro-level of individuals and households, mainly by boosting their demand for basic goods and their access to essential services. But what about the macro-level, the supply side and the structural determinants of poverty, vulnerability and food insecurity? At the very least, social protection interventions must be complemented by linkages with other economic and social sectors, such as agriculture, trade and health (including sanitation and hygiene, even nutrition education), in order to enhance the availability, access, stability and utilization of food. It is also important to take the local sociocultural context into account, as some of the non-income drivers of food insecurity – social exclusion, political marginalization or gender discrimination – require sensitive analysis and tailored interventions.

Finally, achieving food security through the Social Protection Floor requires drawing on a wide range of social protection instruments, including cash transfers, food vouchers, public works and school feeding programmes. Since

---

22. Sabates-Wheeler R. & Devereux, S. *Cash Transfers and High Food Prices: Explaining Outcomes on Ethiopia's Productive Safety Net Programme*, Food Policy, 35(4): 274-285 (2010).

these interventions target individuals and households, they should be complemented by selected food security instruments that operate in the agriculture sector at food system level – a 'food security floor'[23] – including some instruments that have become unfashionable, such as farm input subsidies, food price subsidies and grain reserve management. Combining these two approaches has greater potential to achieve the human right to adequate food for all, rather than relying only on income security through cash or in-kind transfers.

BIBLIOGRAPHY

BIG Coalition *A Call for the National Implementation of the Basic Income Grant (BIG) in Namibia*, Press Release 25 June (Windhoek: Basic Income Grant Coalition 2015).

CESCR, *General Comment No. 12: The Right to Adequate Food (Art. 11)*, E/C.12/1999/5 adopted at the Twentieth Session of the Committee on Economic, Social and Cultural Rights, on 12 May 1999.

Devereux, S. & Waidler, J. *Why Does Malnutrition Persist in South Africa Despite Social Grants?* Food Security SA Working Paper Series, No. 001. South Africa: DST-NRF Centre of Excellence in Food Security 2017. http://foodsecurity.ac.za/working-papers (accessed 21 March 2017).

Devereux, S. *Realising the Right to Social Security and the Right to Food: The Contribution of National Social Protection Floors Towards Food Security and the Realisation of the Right to Adequate Food for All*, Extension of Social Security (ESS) Working Paper, 51. Geneva: International Labour Office (2015).

Devereux, S. *Is Targeting Ethical?* Global Social Policy, 16(2), 166-181 (2016).

Devereux, S. *Social Protection and Safety Nets in the Middle East and North Africa*, IDS Research Report, 80 (Brighton: Institute of Development Studies 2015).

Duflo, E. *Grandmothers and Granddaughters: Old Age Pension and Intrahousehold Allocation in South Africa*, NBER Working Paper, 8061 (Cambridge, MA: National Bureau of Economic Research 2000).

Ellis, F. *'We Are All Poor Here': Economic Difference, Social Divisiveness, and Targeting Cash Transfers in Sub-Saharan Africa*, Journal of Development Studies, 48(2): 201-214 (2012).

FAO, *Food Security*, ESA Policy Brief, Issue 2 (Rome: FAO 2006).

Fin24. *Basic Income Grant 'Flawed'* 2015, http://www.fin24.com/Economy/Basic-income-grant-flawed-20050523 (accessed 20 March 2017).

Galtier, F. *Managing Food Price Instability: Critical Assessment of the Dominant Doctrine*, Global Food Security, 2: 72-81 (2013).

---

23. HLPE, *Social Protection for Food Security*, A report by the High Level Panel of Experts on Food Security and Nutrition of the Committee on World Food Security (Rome: CFS 2012).

Geier, G. *Food Security Policy in Africa between Disaster Relief and Structural Adjustment: Reflections on the Conception and Effectiveness of Policies: The Case of Tanzania* (London: Frank Cass 1995).

Haarmann, C., Haarmann, D., Jauch, H., Shindondola-Mote, H., Nattrass, N., Samson, M. & Standing, G. *'Towards a Basic Income Grant for All': Basic Income Grant Pilot Project Assessment Report* (Windhoek: Basic Income Grant Coalition 2008).

HLPE, *Social Protection for Food Security*, A report by the High Level Panel of Experts on Food Security and Nutrition of the Committee on World Food Security (Rome: CFS 2012).

Holmes, R. & Jones, N. *Gender and Social Protection in the Developing World: Beyond Mothers and Safety Nets* (London: Zed Books 2013).

ILO, *Text of the Recommendation Concerning National Floors of Social Protection* (Geneva: International Labour Conference 2012).

Kabeer, N. *Can the MDGs Provide a Pathway to Social Justice? The Challenge of Intersecting Inequalities* (New York: United Nations Development Programme 2010).

Kidd, S. *The Political Economy of 'Targeting' of Social Security Schemes*, Pathways' Perspectives, no. 19 (Orpington: Development Pathways 2015).

Mkandawire, T. *Targeting and Universalism in Poverty Reduction*, Social Policy and Development Programme Paper, 23 (Geneva: United Nations Research Institute for Social Development (UNRISD) 2005).

Sabates-Wheeler, R. & Devereux, S. *Cash Transfers and High Food Prices: Explaining Outcomes on Ethiopia's Productive Safety Net Programme*, Food Policy, 35(4): 274-285 (2010).

Save the Children Fund, *Superfood for Babies: How Overcoming Barriers to Breastfeeding Will Save Children's Lives* (London: Save the Children Fund 2013).

Silva, J., Levin, V. & Morgandi, M. *Inclusion and Resilience: The Way Forward for Social Safety Nets in the Middle East and North Africa* (Washington DC: World Bank 2012).

UNICEF *The Right Ingredients: The Need to Invest in Child Nutrition* (London: UNICEF UK 2012).

PART II Implementation of the Basic
Principles: Case Studies

CHAPTER 5
The Child Support Grant in the Republic of South Africa

Letlhokwa George Mpedi

> 'There can be no keener revelation of a society's soul than the way in which it treats its children.'[1]

5.1 INTRODUCTION

The Republic of South Africa (hereinafter 'South Africa') has three children's grants, namely: the Child Support Grant (hereinafter 'the CSG'), the Forster Child Grant (hereinafter 'the FCG') and the Care Dependency Grant (hereinafter 'the CGD').[2] All these grants are part of the social assistance programme and, thus, non-contributory based. The CSG and CDG are means-tested. Unlike the other two children's grants, FCG is exempt from the means test. The CSG, which

---

1. N. Mandela, *Nelson Mandela Quotes on Children*, http://www.nelsonmandelachildrens fund.com/news/nelson-mandela-quotes-about-children (accessed 5 Jun. 2017).
2. The children's grants are flanked by other social grants, namely: the disability grant, grants for older persons and the war veteran's grant. All these grants are part of the South African social grant scheme and are administered by the South African Social Security Agency (hereinafter 'SASSA') (*see* s. 4 of the Social Assistance Act 13 of 2004 (hereinafter the Social Assistance Act). The total cost of the social grant system as percentage of Gross Domestic Product (GDP) is 3.2% (National Treasury (Republic of South Africa), *Budget Review 2017*, 59 (National Treasury (Republic of South Africa) 2017) and the total number of the social grant beneficiaries in South Africa stood at 17,241,409 as of 31 May 2017 (South African Social Security Agency (SASSA), *Fact Sheet: Issue no 5 of 2017 – 31 May 2017*, http://www.sassa.gov.za/index.php/knowledge-centre/statistical-reports (accessed 23 Jun. 2017)).

is the primary focus of this chapter, is payable once per month per eligible child and its value is ZAR 380.00 (approximately USD 29.15).[3]

The CSG succeeded the State Maintenance Grant in 1998.[4] Thus, the CSG predates the International Labour Organization (hereinafter 'the ILO') Social Protection Floors Recommendation 202 of 2012 (hereinafter 'the Recommendation'). Needless to say, the CSG, in combination with the other children's grants, plays an important role in South Africa's quest to fulfil the Recommendation's obligations. It should be recalled that the Recommendation directs that social protection floors should comprise, amongst other guarantees, basic income security for children.[5]

The Recommendation points out further that: '[s]ubject to their existing international obligations, Members should provide basic social security guarantees referred to in … [the] Recommendation to at least all residents and children, as defined in national laws and regulations'.[6] Interestingly, the Recommendation does not define a child and passes that task on to national laws and regulations. The question to be asked is who is a 'child' in terms of the relevant South African laws? Section 28(3) of the Constitution of the Republic of South Africa, 1996 (hereinafter 'the Constitution') defines a child as '… a person below the age of 18 years'.[7] It is, therefore, not surprising that the CSG is provided, subject to other qualifying conditions, to children from birth up to the age of 18 years.

This chapter provides a critical review of the CSG as provided in the South African social assistance system. It assesses the CSG on the basis of the following principles contained in the Recommendation: (a) State responsibility, (b) universality of protection, (c) entitlement based on law, (d) adequacy and predictability of benefits, (e) non-discrimination, (f) financial solidarity, (g) good governance, (h) coherence of policies, and (i) social participation. This is followed by a discussion on legislative deficits and implementation failures pertaining to the CSG. Last but not least, the chapter closes with some concluding observations.

---

3. USD 1 = ZAR 13.03 as of 22 Jun. 2017.
4. *Phasing Out of the Maintenance Grants*, Published under Government Notice R417 in Government Gazette 18771 of 31 Mar. 1998. See, for further reading, F. Lund, *Changing Social Policy: The Child Support Grant in South Africa* (Human Sciences Research Council Press 2008).
5. Article 5(b) of Social Protection Floors Recommendation 202 of 2012 (hereinafter the Recommendation).
6. Article 6 of the Recommendation.
7. It is worth noting that this definition is consistent with that contained in Art. 1 of the United Nations Convention on the Rights of the Child (Adopted and opened for signature, ratification and accession by General Assembly resolution 44/25 of 20 Nov. 1989) and Art. 5 of the African Charter on the Rights and Welfare of the Child (Adopted by the African Member States of the Organization of African Unity (now African Union), 11 Jul. 1990).

5.2 ASSESSMENT OF THE SCHEME ON THE BASIS OF THE PRINCIPLES

5.2.1 State Responsibility

The responsibility of the State as regards its social protection endeavours, including the provision of the children grants, is regulated by law. The Constitution, which is the supreme law of the country,[8] sets out a number of pertinent obligations with which the State must comply. First, the State has an obligation to, subject to the limitations contained in the Bill of Rights, respect, protect, promote and fulfil the rights in the Bill of Rights.[9] Second, the Bill of Rights recognizes every person's 'right to have access to (a) health care services, including reproductive health care; (b) sufficient food and water; and (c) social security, including, if they are unable to support themselves and their dependents, appropriate social assistance.'[10]

The State has a constitutional duty to take reasonable legislative and other measures to achieve the progressive realization of each of these rights.[11] This obligation is subject to the availability of resources.[12] In addition, every child in South Africa has a constitutional right to 'basic nutrition, shelter, basic health care services and social services'.[13] The realization of the foregoing children's rights is – unlike the right of access to health care, food, water and social security – not restricted by the availability of resources. In line with the supremacy of the Constitution principle,[14] law or conduct inconsistent with the Constitution is invalid and the obligations imposed by the Constitution must be fulfilled.[15]

Based on the preceding pronouncements, the State has a positive duty to act, i.e., to ensure that the legislative and other measures (such as an appropriate policy framework) are put in place to make certain that the relevant rights (e.g., right to social security) are realized. Furthermore, the State has a negative duty to comply with. That is, it must avoid or refrain from undermining the relevant rights entrenched in the Bill of Rights. These rights go beyond the right of access to social security and include fundamental rights such as the right to equality,[16] the right to human dignity,[17] the right to life,[18] the right to privacy,[19] the right of

---

8. Sections 1(c) and 2 of the Constitution of the Republic of South Africa, 1996 (hereinafter the Constitution).
9. Section 7(2)-(3) of the Constitution.
10. Section 27(1)(a)-(c) of the Constitution.
11. Section 27(2) of the Constitution.
12. *Ibid.*
13. Section 28(1)(c) of the Constitution.
14. For further reading on this principle, *see*: J. Limbach, *The Concept of the Supremacy of the Constitution*, 64 The Modern Law Review, 1 (2001).
15. Section 2 of the Constitution.
16. Section 9 of the Constitution.
17. Section 10 of the Constitution.
18. Section 11 of the Constitution.

access to information,[20] the right to just administrative action[21] and the right of access to courts.[22] It should be recalled, as acknowledged by the Constitutional Court, that the socio-economic rights contained in the Bill of Rights are intertwined and they reinforce one another.[23] In addition, the socio-economic rights are closely linked to the founding values of the Constitution, namely: human dignity, equality and freedom.[24]

It can thus be observed that the State has two key roles. First, the State is a *regulator* and an *administrator* in the sense that it has to ensure that the requisite social protection regulatory framework (i.e., social assistance law, regulations and policies) and administrative institutions are in place and functional. Second, the State functions as a *provider*. This role stems from the fact that the State has to appropriate requisite financial resources through the budgetary process[25] and avail them for the payment of social assistance benefits, including the CSG. It should be recalled that social assistance benefits are paid as a matter of right to qualifying beneficiaries. The State has to ensure that all qualifying beneficiaries who apply for the grant receive the grant. As a result, it could be said that the State guarantees the actual payment of the CSG.

Although the State does function as a regulator, administrator and provider, there are private actors involved in the social assistance administration process. This is particularly pronounced in the disbursement of social grants. The South African Social Security Agency (hereinafter 'SASSA') has, in the past partnered, with private providers such as the South African Post Office, private commercial banks, welfare organizations and private contractors, in its effort to ensure that the right social grant is paid to the right person at the right time and place. It is after all empowered by Regulation 21(1) of the Regulations Relating to the Application for and Payment of Social Assistance and the Requirements or Conditions in Respect of Eligibility for Social Assistance[26] (hereinafter 'the Regulations') to pay a social grant into a bank account of the beneficiary or institution where the beneficiary resides, or to use any payment method it deems appropriate. Another important point to note is that SASSA is an organ of state.[27]

---

19. Section 14 of the Constitution.
20. Section 32 of the Constitution.
21. Section 33 of the Constitution.
22. Section 34 of the Constitution.
23. *Khosa and Others v. Minister of Social Development and Others, Mahlaule and Another v. Minister of Social Development*, 2004 (6) SA 505 (CC) at para. 41.
24. Section 1(a) of the Constitution.
25. Section 9(1)(a) of the South African Social Security Agency Act 9 of 2004 (hereinafter 'the South African Social Security Agency Act').
26. Published under Government Notice R898 in Government Gazette 31356 of 22 Aug. 2008.
27. An 'organ of state' is defined by s. 239 of the Constitution as '(a) any department of state or administration in the national, provincial or local sphere of government; or (b) any other functionary or institution – (i) exercising a power or performing a function in terms of the Constitution or a provincial constitution; or (ii) exercising a public power or performing a public function in terms of any legislation, but does not include a court or a judicial officer'.

Chapter 5: The Child Support Grant in the Republic of South Africa

In line with this status, it can, within the confines of the law,[28] contract for goods and services.[29] At the moment, the disbursement of social grants has been outsourced to Net1. Net1 has been described as a private entity '...which owns the companies that pay out the grants (Cash Paymaster Services), facilitate grant payments through retailers (Easypay) and provide loans targeted at grant recipients (Moneyline)'.[30] Nonetheless, it should be noted that there are discussions underway towards the insourcing of the social grant payment function.[31]

5.2.2 Universality of Protection

The CSG is a targeted benefit in the sense that it is provided subject to a means test.[32] The Minister of Social Development is empowered by law to prescribe an income threshold that would assist in determining eligibility for social assistance in South Africa.[33] The income threshold for 2016 was set as follows:

Table 5.1 Income Threshold 1 April 2014-1 April 2016

Child Grants		1 April 2014	1 October 2014	1 April 2015	1 October 2015	1 April 2016
Child Support Grant	Single person	ZAR 37,200	ZAR 38,400 (3,200)	ZAR 39,600 (3,300)	-	ZAR 42,000
	Married person	ZAR 74,400	ZAR 76,800	ZAR 79,200 (6,600)	-	ZAR 84,000

---

28. For instance, as required by s. 217(1) of the Constitution, it must procure services goods and services 'in accordance with a system which is fair, equitable, transparent, competitive and cost-effective'.
29. SASSA has discretion to 'with the concurrence of the Minister enter into an agreement with any person to ensure effective payments to beneficiaries' (s. 4(2)(a) of the South African Social Security Act 9 of 2004). Such an agreement is required to include provisions to ensure: '(a) the effective, efficient and economical use of funds designated for payment to beneficiaries of social security; (b) the promotion and protection of the human dignity of applicants for and beneficiaries of social security; (c) the protection of confidential information held by the Agency ...; (d) honest, impartial, fair and equitable service delivery; (e) mechanisms to regulate community participation and consultation; and (f) financial penalties for non-compliance with the provisions of the agreement'(s. 4(3) of the South African Social Security Act 9 of 2004).
30. Department of Social Development (Republic of South Africa), *Comprehensive Report in the Review of the White Paper for Social Welfare, 1997*, 231 (Department of Social Development (Republic of South Africa) 2016).
31. See: *Black Sash Trust v. Minister of Social Development and Others* [2017] ZACC 8.
32. See, for an interesting discussion on targeting, S. Devereux, *Is Targeting Ethical?* 16 Global Social Policy, 166 (2016).
33. Section 5(2)(a) of the Social Assistance Act.

Child Grants		1 April 2014	1 October 2014	1 April 2015	1 October 2015	1 April 2016
Forster Child Grant	Child	No means test				
Care-Dependency Grant	Parent/PCG: Single	ZAR 162,000	-	ZAR 169,200	ZAR 170,400	ZAR 180,000
	Parent/PCG: Married	ZAR 324,000	-	ZAR 338,400	ZAR 340,800	ZAR 360,000
	Child	No means test				

The CSG covers qualifying indigent children from birth up to the age of 18 years.[34] In addition, a person is eligible for the CSG if he or she is the primary caregiver (hereinafter 'the PCG')[35] and must be a South African citizen,[36] a permanent resident[37] or a refugee.[38] Furthermore, the PCG qualifies for the CSG if, amongst other eligibility requirements, 'he or she is not formally or informally employed to take care of the child, the child in question is not resident in an institution funded by the State and he or she or any other person is not already in receipt of a social grant in respect of that child'.[39] In the final analysis, it should be pointed out that the CSG is needs based. Thus, the PCGs engaged in the informal sector are eligible for the grant if they comply with the prescribed requirements and conditions.

---

34. Reg. 9(2) of the Regulations Relating to the Application for and Payment of Social Assistance and the Requirements or Condition in Respect of Eligibility for Social Assistance, Government Notice R898 in Government Gazette 313 of 22 Aug. 2008 (as amended) (hereinafter the Regulations). It should be noted that there are plans to extend the age of eligibility for the CSG from 18 to 21 years of age. The aim is, among others, to align the CSG with the Forster Care Grant which continues up to the age of 21 years if the child continues with their studies.
35. Section 6 of the Social Assistance Act. The primary caregiver may apply for a CSG in respect of his or her biological or legally adopted child. However, a caregiver can apply for the CSG for a maximum of six legally adopted children (reg. 9(2)(b) of the Regulations).
36. Seciton 5(1)(c) of the Social Assistance Act.
37. Section 5(1)(b) of the Social Assistance Act. The inclusion of persons with a permanent residence status is with effect from 16 Sep. 2010 when the Social Assistance Act was amended by the Social Assistance Amendment Act 4 of 2010 following the seminal Constitutional Court decision of *Khosa and Others v. Minister of Social Development and Others, Mahlaule and Another v. Minister of Social Development*, 2004 (6) SA 505 (CC). See, for further reading, L.G. Mpedi, *Charity Begins – but does not End – at Home: Khosa v Minister of Social Development; Mahlaule v Minister of Social Development* 2004 6 BCLR 569 (CC), 26 Obiter 173, (2005); and L. Jansen van Rensburg, *The Khosa Case – Opening the Door for the Inclusion of All Children in the Child Support Grant?*, 20 South African Public Law 102, (2005).
38. Reg. 6(1)(g) of the Regulations.
39. Reg. 6(1)(d)-(f) of the Regulations.

According to the SASSA, South Africa had slightly over 12 million CSG recipients as of 31 May 2017.[40] This makes the CSG the largest social grant in the country in terms of the number of beneficiaries it covers. As noble as this may be, the CSG is not universal in nature. There have been calls for scrapping of the means test in the case of the CSG.[41] These stem from concerns pertaining to the cost of administering and effectiveness of the means test in the South African social grant system. It is correctly argued that: 'The means test…assumes that incomes are stable, whereas earnings are often erratic, and poor households may fall in and out of "poverty" as defined by the poverty line.'[42] Second, it has been argued that means testing has cost implications on both the CSG applicant (e.g., travel costs) and the government (i.e., administrative costs).[43] It is, therefore, pleasing to note that there are serious considerations to universalize the CSG.[44]

5.2.3 Entitlements Based on Law

The CSG is rooted in law. Entitlement to the CSG is regulated by the Social Assistance Act 13 of 2004 (hereinafter 'the Social Assistance Act') and the Regulations Relating to the Application for and Payment of Social Assistance and the Requirements or Conditions in Respect of Eligibility for Social Assistance.[45] The Social Assistance Act and Regulations have been enacted and promulgated respectively to give effect to the right of access to social security which is contained in the Constitution.[46]

The social assistance institutional and administrative framework, which is also applicable to the CSG, is set out in the SASSA Act 9 of 2004. The South

---

40. South African Social Security Agency (SASSA), *Fact Sheet: Issue no 5 of 2017 – 31 May 2017*, http://www.sassa.gov.za/index.php/knowledge-centre/statistical-reports (accessed 23 Jun. 2017).
41. J.D. Triegaardt, *The Child Support Grant in South Africa: a Social Policy for Poverty Alleviation?* 14 International Journal of Social Welfare, 249, 253 (2005); and P. Proudlock, *Weighing Up the Policy Proposals: Some Considerations*, in *South African Child Gauge 2016*, 95 (A Delany, S. Jehoma & L. Lake eds., Children's Institute, University of Cape Town 2016).
42. S. Jehoma & E. Guarnieri, *Universalisation of Child Support Grant*, in *South African Child Gauge 2016*, 80, 81 (A Delany, S. Jehoma & L. Lake eds., Children's Institute, University of Cape Town 2016).
43. S. Jehoma & E. Guarnieri, *Universalisation of Child Support Grant*, in *South African Child Gauge 2016*, 80, 82 (A Delany, S. Jehoma & L. Lake eds., Children's Institute, University of Cape Town 2016); and *Extending Social Security Coverage to the Excluded and Marginalized: Perspectives on Developments in South Africa*, in *Social Security Coverage Extension in the BRICS: A Comparative Study on the Extension of Coverage in Brazil, the Russian Federation, India, China and South Africa*, 135, 146 (International Social Security Association ed., International Social Security Association, Geneva 2013).
44. Department of Social Development (Republic of South Africa), *Comprehensive Report in the Review of the White Paper for Social Welfare, 1997*, 241 (Department of Social Development (Republic of South Africa) 2016).
45. Published under Government Notice R898 in Government Gazette 31356 of 22 Aug. 2008.
46. Section 27(1)(c) of the Constitution.

African Social Security Agency Act has been enacted solely to 'provide for the establishment of the South African Social Security Agency as an agent for the administration and payment of social assistance; to provide for the prospective administration and payment of social security by the Agency and the provision of services related thereto; and to provide for matters connected thereto'.[47]

The fact that entitlement to the CSG is based in law entails that the right to the CSG is to be respected, protected, promoted and fulfilled by, among others, the State and persons.[48] Alongside the aforementioned right, there are duties which must be complied with. Such duties may be in the form of an act[49] or an omission.[50] By virtue of the fact that the entitlement to the CSG is set in law, failure to respect and comply with the relevant rights and duties could result in a 'sanction imposed by a competent authority and in a fair manner'.[51]

5.2.4 Adequacy and Predictability of Benefits

The value of the CSG was ZAR 100 (about USD 7.67) at the inception of the grant in 1998. This has been adjusted annually and its value as of 1 April 2017 is, as noted earlier, ZAR 380 (about USD 29.17). Despite the aforementioned inflation motivated adjustments, the question that begs attention is whether the grant is adequate. An answer to this question depends on the angle from which one looks at the value of the grant. On the one hand, the grant is provided to qualifying individuals in need. Thus, it is income which would have not been available to the targeted recipients otherwise. This is along the viewpoint that the glass is 'half full' and not 'half empty', or 'half a loaf is better than nothing'. Accordingly, the grant is a poverty alleviation scheme.[52]

On the other hand, it should be recalled that the grant is a human right which is meant to provide a dignified existence. Viewed from a variety of determining factors such as the cost of living, the CSG stands accused of being

---

47. Preamble of the South African Social Security Agency Act 9 of 2004.
48. 'Persons' in this case refers to both natural and juristic persons.
49. For example, reg. 6(5) of the Regulations Relating to the Application for and Payment of Social Assistance and the Requirements or Conditions in Respect of Eligibility for Social Assistance published under Government Notice R898 in Government Gazette 31356 of 22 Aug. 2008 (hereinafter 'the Regulations') requires the primary caregiver to ensure that a child between the ages of 7 and 18 in his or her care is enrolled at, and attends, school.
50. For instance, the CSG recipient should refrain from defrauding the South Africa Social Security Agency.
51. L.G. Mpedi, *Pertinent Social Security Issues in South Africa*, 9 (Community Law Centre (University of the Western Cape) 2008).
52. *See*: A. Delany & P. Proudlock, *Expanding Social Assistance for Children: Considering Policy Proposals*, in *South African Child Gauge 2016*, 75 (A Delany, S. Jehoma & L. Lake eds., Children's Institute, University of Cape Town 2016); L. Hye-Young, *Alleviating Child Poverty in South Africa: The Role of Social Assistance Grants*, 7 ESR Review: Economic and Social Rights in South Africa. 2 (2006); and L. Kgamphe, *The Government's Budgeting for Children's Right to Social Assistance*, 5 ESR Review: Economic and Social Rights in South Africa, 8 (2004).

insufficient to meet the daily needs of the child.[53] The CSG falls short of the national poverty line proposed by Statistics South Africa of ZAR 1,077 (about USD 82.69) per month.[54] This buttresses the conclusion reached by some academics that the value of the CSG does not appear to be set with the actual needs of children in mind,[55] and should thus be increased.[56] The grant is largely criticized on the basis that it is spread thinly. In other words, it is so little, yet it is expected to do so much for the child. For instance, in reality, it is expected to meet the child's other needs that are meant to be free of charge, such as education and primary health care.

Notwithstanding the debates around the (in)adequacy of the grant, it must be acknowledged that the CSG is predictable. This is informed by the fact that it is paid on a monthly basis as an entitlement and not a privilege. Furthermore, the CSG is paid in a manner determined by the beneficiary in accordance with the applicable regulations and policies.[57] Moreover, any increase in the value of the social grants, inclusive of the CSG, is publicized in a Government Gazette with an implementation date.[58]

5.2.5 Non-discrimination

Unfair discrimination is legally prohibited in South Africa. Every person in South Africa is equal before the law and has the right to equal protection and benefit of

---

53. A. Delany & P. Proudlock, *Expanding Social Assistance for Children: Considering Policy Proposals*, in *South African Child Gauge 2016*, 75 (A Delany, S. Jehoma & L. Lake eds., Children's Institute, University of Cape Town 2016).
54. D. Van Rensburg, *SA Poverty Lines Rise Faster than Inflation*, http://city-press.news24.com/Business/sa-poverty-lines-rise-faster-than-inflation-20160719, (accessed, 20 Jun. 2017).
55. *See*, for instance, L. Jansen van Rensburg & D. Horsten, *The Inadequacy of the Social Grant System available to Children in South Africa*, 29 Journal of Juridical Science, 52, 64 (2004).
56. A. Delany & P. Proudlock, *Expanding Social Assistance for Children: Considering Policy Proposals*, in *South African Child Gauge 2016*, 75 (A Delany, S. Jehoma & L. Lake eds., Children's Institute, University of Cape Town 2016); D Budlender, *Increasing the Amount of the Child Support Grant*, in *South African Child Gauge 2016*, 78 (A Delany, S. Jehoma & L. Lake eds., Children's Institute, University of Cape Town 2016); and P. Proudlock, *Weighing up the Policy Proposals: Some Considerations*, in *South African Child Gauge 2016*, 95 (A Delany, S. Jehoma & L. Lake eds., Children's Institute, University of Cape Town 2016).
57. In accordance with reg. 21(1) of the Regulations: 'The [South African Social Security] Agency shall pay a social grant – (a) into a bank account of the beneficiary or institution where the beneficiary resides; provided that, (i) the beneficiary of the social grant consents to payment in accordance with subregulation 21(1) (a) in writing and has submitted such consent in person to the Agency; (ii) where a beneficiary is unable to submit the consent contemplated in subparagraph (i) in person, alternative arrangements must be made with the Agency; or (b) by the payment method determined by the Agency.'
58. *See*, for example, Increase in Respect of Social Grants published under Government Notice R305 in Government Gazette 40754 of 31 Mar. 2017.

the law.[59] The State may not, in its social assistance provisioning endeavours, 'unfairly discriminate directly or indirectly against anyone on one or more grounds, including race, gender, sex, pregnancy, marital status, ethnic or social origin, colour, sexual orientation, age, disability, religion, conscience, belief, culture, language and birth'.[60] In respect of children and access to the CSG, it has been acknowledged in *Khosa and Others v. Minister of Social Development and Others, Mahlaule and Another v. Minister of Social Development* that: '…as a matter of law, children who are South African citizens should not be denied access to child-support grants and that a provision in legislation which denies such children access because their primary caregiver or their parents are not South African citizens would be unconstitutional'.[61]

The Social Assistance Act, which was enacted to give effect to the right of access to social security in the Constitution, specifically social assistance, does not distinguish between men and women when it comes to the provision of the CSG. The CSG is provided to the PCG. The PCG refers to 'a person older than 16 years, whether or not related to a child, who takes primary responsibility for meeting the daily care needs of that child'.[62] The PCG concept, as defined in the Social Assistance Act, is gender neutral. Nonetheless, in practice, women are the main recipients of the CSG.[63] This may, it is opined, underscore the role of women in the society as caregivers. Furthermore, it has been established that a majority of men tend to pursue a solitary existence pursuant to the breakdown

---

59. Section 9(1) of the Constitution.
60. Section 9(3) of the Constitution. It should be noted that the right to equality is not absolute and can be limited in accordance with s. 36 of the Constitution. Section 36 of the Constitution provides for the limitation of fundamental rights, including the right to equality as follows: '(1) The rights in the Bill of Rights may be limited only terms of law of general application to the extent the limitation is reasonable and justifiable in an open and democratic society based on human dignity, equality and freedom, taking into account all relevant factors, including – (a) the nature of the right; (b) the importance of the purpose of the limitation; (c) the nature and extent of the limitation; (d) the relation between the limitation and its purpose; and (e) less restrictive means to achieve the purpose. (2) Except as provided in subsection (1) or in any other provision of the Constitution, no law may limit any right entrenched in the Bill of Rights.' It should mentioned that the State's duty to achieve the progressive realization of the right of access to social security is subject to the availability of resources (s. 27(2) of the Constitution).
61. 2004 (6) SA 505 (CC) at para. 33.
62. Section 1 of the Social Assistance Act.
63. B. Goldblatt, *Developing the Right to Social Security – A Gender Perspective*, 116-117 (Routledge 2016); L. Patel, *Poverty, Gender and Social Protection: Child Support Grants in Soweto, South Africa*, 11 Journal of Policy Practice, 106, 107 (2012); L. Patel, T. Hochfeld & J. Moodley, *Gender and Child Sensitive Social Protection in South Africa*, 30 Development Southern Africa, 69 (2013); and B. Goldblatt & S. Liebenberg, *Giving Money to Children: The State's Constitutional Obligations to Provide Child Support Grants to Child Headed Households*, 20 SAJHR. 151, 161 (2004).

of a relationship.[64] Women, unlike men, have been found to be generally inclined to live with children following the collapse of a relationship.[65]

5.2.6 Financial Solidarity

The CSG is financed through general taxation on year-by-year basis.[66] General taxation is the main source of government revenue.[67] It largely comprises company income tax, personal income tax, and value-added tax.[68] The funds used by the SASSA to pay social grants are appropriated by Parliament for that purpose.[69] In light of the preceding pronouncements, it is observed that the financing of the CSG is in line with the financial solidarity rule. It must be remembered that in accordance with this rule '...taxes for the financing of benefits are charged on the basis of the members' ability to pay, regardless of their risks or circumstances...'[70] In conclusion, it can be argued that the CSG plays a role in redistributing income from the wealthy to the needy.[71]

5.2.7 Good Governance

The SASSA falls under the policy and regulatory jurisdiction of the Department of Social Development. It is, as an organ of state, subject to the Constitution. The Bill of Rights has a number of rights germane to good governance[72] with which

---

64. Statistics South Africa, *Vulnerable Groups Series I: The Social Profile of the Youth, 2009 – 2014*, 23 (Statistics South Africa 2016).
65. *Ibid.*
66. A. Asher, *Finance and Tax*, in *Social Security: A Legal Analysis*, 595, 597 (M.P. Olivier, N. Smit & E.R. Kalula eds., LexisNexis Butterworths 2003).
67. Department of Social Development (Republic of South Africa), *Comprehensive Report on the Review of the White Paper for Social Welfare, 1997*, 85 (Department of Social Development (Republic of South Africa)).
68. *Ibid.*
69. Section 9(1)(a) of the South African Social Security Agency Act 9 of 2004.
70. M. Cichon, et al., *Financing Social Protection*, 226 (International Labour Organization and International Social Security Association 2004).
71. M. Sadan, *Social Assistance for Children: Looking Back, Thinking Forward*, in *South African Child Gauge 2016*, 99 (A Delany, S. Jehoma & L. Lake eds., Children's Institute, University of Cape Town 2016).
72. The concept of good governance, within the social protection framework, has been elucidated by McKinnon (R. McKinnon, *Good Governance in Social Security Administration*, 64 International Social Security Review, 3, 5-6 (2011)) as follows: 'Most commonly, the concept of governance as it is practiced in many national social security systems speaks to efforts geared to support and foster improvements in all aspects of the internal management of social security administrations. However, it may relate also to grass-roots/ civic-society action to monitor social security rights and entitlements. It may cover formalized and inclusive processes of tripartite social dialogue – legitimizing processes that seek to build and maintain broad-based consensus in support of social security programmes and regulatory frameworks with the strategic objective of satisfying the needs of citizens and residents may contribute to strengthening existing systems of national

SASSA must comply. These rights include the right to equality,[73] the right to privacy,[74] the right of access to information,[75] the right to just administrative action,[76] the right of access to courts[77] and the enforcement of rights.[78] The Constitution makes provision for basic values and principles governing public administration which public social security institutions should respect and uphold. In accordance with section 195(1) of the Constitution:

> Public administration must be governed by the democratic values and principles enshrined in the Constitution, including the following principles: A high standard of professional ethics must be promoted and maintained. Efficient, economic and effective use of resources must be promoted. Public service must be development-oriented. Services must be provided impartially, fairly, equitably and without bias. People's needs must be responded to, and the public must be encouraged to participate in policy-making. Public administration must be accountable. Transparency must be fostered by providing the public with timely, accessible and accurate information. Good-human resource management and career-development practices, to maximise human potential, must be cultivated. Public administration must be broadly representative of the South African people, with employment and personnel management practices based on ability, objectivity, fairness, and the need to redress the imbalances of the past to achieve broad representation.

The preceding principles apply to administration in every sphere of government, organs of state and public enterprises. Accordingly, SASSA has a duty to abide by these principles in the administration of social grants.

---

governance and, furthermore, support the process of democratization and nation building. This perspective encapsulates notions of trusteeship or stewardship, to protect and advance common interest. At a higher level, in support of global governance agendas, national social security systems represent integral institutional mechanisms for rights-based and inclusive approaches to social and economic development and, thus, are essential for well-being, stability and cohesion.' See, for further reading, on the concept 'good governance', S. de la Harpe, C. Rijken & R. Roos, *Good Governance*, 2 Potchefstroom Electronic Law Journal, 1 (2008); and M.H. Kanyane, *Exploring and Developing a Culture of a Good Governance*, in *Norms and Institutional Design: Social Security in Norway and South Africa*, 95 (M. Olivier & S. Kuhnle eds., Sun Press 2008).
73. Section 9 of the Constitution.
74. Section 14 of the Constitution.
75. Section.32 of the Constitution.
76. Section 33 of the Constitution. The Promotion of Access to Justice Act 3 of 2000 (hereinafter 'PAJA') was enacted to give effect to the provision of this section of the Constitution. PAJA, together with the Promotion of Access to Information Act 2 of 2000, is geared at the 'promotion of *efficient administration* and *good governance*, as well as the *creation of accountability*, openness and *transparency* in the public administration or in the exercise of a public power or performance of a public function...' (italics in the original) (L.G. Mpedi, *Administration and Institutional Framework*, in *Social Security: A Legal Analysis*, 149, 152 (M.P. Olivier, N. Smit & E.R. Kalula eds., LexisNexis Butterworths 2003).
77. Section 34 of the Constitution.
78. Section 38 of the Constitution.

Second, SASSA is subject to the Public Finance Management Act 1 of 1999. Chapter 6 of the Public Finance Management Act, which deals with public entities, makes provision for the accounting authorities, the fiduciary duty of accounting authorities, the general responsibilities of accounting authorities, the annual budget and corporate plan, information to be submitted by accounting authorities, and the annual report and financial statements. Furthermore, SASSA is bound by pertinent provisions contained in the SASSA Act.

In addition, the South African Social Security Act has been enacted so as to 'assist in securing the well-being of the people of the Republic and to provide effective, transparent, accountable and coherent governance in respect of social security for the Republic as a whole'.[79] It provides for the appointment of the Chief Executive Officer of SASSA who is responsible for the management of the Agency, subject to the direction of the Minister of Social Development and the compilation of a business plan and reports in terms of the Public Finance Management Act. The Chief Executive Officer of SASSA has a duty to 'ensure that the Agency's annual budgets, corporate plans, annual reports and audited financial statements are prepared and submitted in accordance with the Public Finance Management Act'.[80] In addition, SASSA has a duty to submit an annual report on its activities and a statement of income and estimated expenditure for the following financial year to the Minister of Social Development for approval.[81] SASSA's books, records of account and financial statements must be audited annually by the Auditor-General.[82]

5.2.8 Coherence in Policies

As pointed out earlier, the CSG falls under the policy domain of the Department of Social Development. However, there are other policies that intersect with the provisioning of the CSG which fall under the regulatory framework of other government departments. These policies concern pertinent social protection matters such as access to primary education and access to primary health services.[83] There is a lack of collaboration between departments, and this results

---

79. Preamble of the South African Social Security Agency Act 9 of 2004.
80. Section 10(2) of the South African Social Security Agency Act.
81. Section 11(1)(a) of the South African Social Security Agency Act.
82. Section 11(2) of the South African Social Security Agency Act.
83. This challenge has been succinctly outlined by Sadan (M. Sadan, *Social Assistance for Children: Looking Back, Thinking Forward*, in *South African Child Gauge 2016*, 99, 100 (A Delany, S. Jehoma & L. Lake eds., Children's Institute, University of Cape Town 2016)) as follows: 'Social grants support multiple positive outcomes for children's development they need to be integrated with other services and interventions. This includes accessible, high quality education and healthcare, and responsive social welfare services; as well as other policies aimed at supporting vulnerable children and families such as free schooling and health care, nutrition programmes, and access to subsidised housing and basic services, amongst others. An ongoing challenge is that programmes and services tend to operate in isolation. Greater effort is needed to increase coordination and synergies between social

in disjointed policy-making which invariably undermines the government's capacity and efforts to deliver an integrated and effective social protection service. The ineffective implementation of applicable laws and policies has been identified by the Committee on the Rights of the Child as one of the areas of concern in South Africa.[84] Greater collaboration between the departments is of utmost importance and is required.

Another crucial point, which requires attention, is that the current social protection policy framework pertaining to children, which involves the CSG, is mainly focussed on the awarding of a cash benefit. In so doing, it neglects measures aimed at the prevention of destitution and the (re-)integration of caregivers into the labour market. It is therefore crucial that the social protection policy loop be closed by striking an appropriate balance between policy measures aimed at compensation, prevention and integration in South Africa.

5.2.9 Social Participation

The apartheid era social protection legislative process was characterized by a lack of consultation. As summarized by the White Paper for Social Welfare, 1997:[85]

> legislation was seldom developed in an inclusive, consultative process and there was no mandatory involvement of stakeholders in either the evaluation of legislative needs or the drafting process. It is therefore based to a great extent on the preferences and values of an elite group of politicians, public servants and opinion makers. Some aspects of the laws consequently do not have the support of the public as a whole. Their appropriateness for the South African context can rightly be questioned. The lack of consultation also applies intersectorally. Legislation was generally drafted in isolation, by the welfare sector alone, without taking sufficient cognisance of broader issues in the socio-economic environment, dealt with by other departments or sectors. This, together with the lack of trust between departments, and vested interests, arrested the potential to develop a meaningfully integrated approach which in turn could consolidate efforts towards self-reliance in communities. Legislation was not effectively co-ordinated at the inter-departmental level, which caused legislation which impacted on welfare issues to be relatively unsympathetic to welfare causes, hindering rather than promoting services.

> grants and other services to reinforce and strengthen their positive impacts on children. Access to social grants from birth; adequate nutrition; quality learning opportunities and health care from a young age; and community –based support for vulnerable families and care givers will go some way to addressing childhood disadvantage and the poverty and inequality it perpetuates.'

84. Committee on the Rights of the Child, *Concluding Observations on the Second Periodic Report of South Africa*, 19 (United Nations 2016).
85. Republic of South Africa, *White Paper for Social Welfare, August 1997: Principles, Guidelines, recommendations, Proposed Policies and Programmes for Developments for Developmental Social Welfare in South Africa*, http://www.gov.za/sites/www.gov.za/files/White_Paper_on_Social_Welfare_0.pdf, (accessed, 20 Jun. 2017).

The current set-up is different in the sense that the basis for social participation in the social protection legislative process[86] can be found in the Constitution.[87] Section 59 of the Constitution makes provision for public access to, and involvement in, National Assembly as follows:

> (1) The National Assembly must – (a) facilitate public involvement in the legislative and other processes of the Assembly and its committee; and (b) conduct its business in an open manner, and hold its sittings, and those of its committees, in public, but reasonable measures may be taken – (i) to regulate public access, including access of the media, to the Assembly and its committees…(2) The national Assembly may not exclude the public, including the media, from a sitting of a committee unless it is reasonable and justifiable to do so in an open and democratic society.

In addition, section 72 of the Constitution regulates public access to, and involvement in, National Council in a similar manner to that of the National Assembly as outlined above. It is a common practice in South Africa for Bills to be publicized with a request for comments from the general public and any other interested stakeholders. In addition, as the CSG falls within the regulatory purview of the Departments of Social Development, the Minister of Social Development publicizes regulations for comments and input from the public before such regulations are adopted. Another important point to note is that draft social policy documents are generally shared with the public and interested organizations for input before adoption.[88] Furthermore, committees and commissions are duly established to investigate and/or review any aspects of the social protection system to encourage social participation by soliciting submission by the general public. In addition, such committees and commissions hold the so-called stakeholder engagements or public hearings at which the public can make verbal submissions.[89]

At an institutional level, the National Economic Development and Labour Council (hereinafter 'NADLEC') is one of the key institutions through which social participation is fostered in South Africa. NADLEC is a legal person established in terms of the National Economic, Development and Labour Council Act.[90] NADLEC comprises members who represent organized business,

---

86. *See*, for further reading on the legislative process, Parliamentary Monitoring Group, *The Legislative Process*, https://pmg.org.za/page/legislative-process#Green_and_White_Papers (accessed 19 Jun. 2017).
87. *See*, for an interesting discussion on participation, S. Liebenberg, *Social Rights and Transformation in South Africa: Three Frames*, 31 South African Journal on Human Rights, 446, 466–470 (2015).
88. However, *see*: P.A. Brynard, *Civic Engagement and Public Policy Implementation: The Child Support Grant*, 44 Journal of Public Administration 312 (2009).
89. *See*, for example, Parliamentary Monitoring Group, *A Comprehensive Social Security System for South Africa: Hearing*, https://pmg.org.za/committee-meeting/2551/ (accessed 19 Jun. 2017).
90. Act 35 of 1994.

organized labour organizations and development interests, and the State.[91] It is required to '(a) strive to promote the goals of economic growth, participation in economic decision-making and social equity; (b) seek to reach consensus and conclude agreements on matters pertaining to social and economic policy; (c) consider all proposed labour legislation relating to labour market policy before it is introduced in Parliament; (d) consider all significant changes to social and economic policy before it is implemented or introduced in Parliament; (e) encourage and promote the formulation of co-ordinated policy on social and economic matters'.[92]

It should also be noted that the Advisory Board on Social Development Act 3 of 2001 was assented to on 16 May 2001. The purpose of the Advisory Board on Social Development Act is '[t]o provide for a national advisory structure in the social development sectors with the aim of building and consolidating partnership between government and civil society...'[93] The objectives of the Advisory Board on Social Development envisaged by the Act are as follows:

> (a) to advise the Minister on – (i) measures to promote the transformation and continuous improvement of (ii) measures to promote social development initiatives; (iii) measures to include local government in the provision of integrated (iv) proposals for new legislative frameworks for the social development (v) the introduction of local and international best practices in social (b) to act as a consultative forum for the Minister to discuss social development matters, including- (i) improving the quality of provincial and national social development; (ii) the introduction of new policy and successful policy implementation in the government and non-governmental environment; (iii) facilitating consultation between stakeholders and government regarding the implementation of social development; (iv) ensuring effective review of formulation, implementation and evaluation of social development policies, programmes and legislation, as informed by the needs and priorities of society; (v) inputs from the social development sector to international forums and protocols. Although the Advisory Board on Social Development Act has been assented to by the President over 15 years ago, it is regrettable that the Act has not yet been put into operation.

The consultative process, which was ushered in by the new constitutional dispensation, has yielded some positive results. For instance, meaningful and effective participation in the social protection policy and legislative making process has increased significantly in South Africa.[94] As a result, it is foreseen that this consultative approach will yield social protection legislation and policy that is appropriate and embraced by the affected stakeholders[95] than was

---

91. Section 3(1) of the National Economic, Development and Labour Council Act 35 of 1994.
92. Section 5(1) of the National Economic, Development and Labour Council Act 35 of 1994.
93. Preamble of the Advisory Board on Social Development Act 3 of 2001.
94. Department of Social Development (Republic of South Africa), *Comprehensive Report in the Review of the White Paper for Social Welfare, 1997*, 50 (Department of Social Development (Republic of South Africa) 2016).
95. As rightly pointed out by Kumitz (D. Kumitz, *Nothing About Us Without Us: Self-representation in Social Protection in Southern Africa*, 16 Global Social Policy, 215, 217

previously the situation under the apartheid regime.⁹⁶ This should not be construed to imply that the resultant policy or legislation is welcomed by all South Africans. As can be expected in any democracy, not all members of the population can be consulted. Furthermore, not all those that have been consulted will agree with the final legislation and/or policy. As appositely explicated by the Department of Social Development:

> The consultative process typically involves consultation in all provinces, as well as with representatives of all relevant government and related agencies. With a diverse population of about 55 million people, and the attendant diverse interests; needs and opinions, any legislation or policy will inevitably not satisfy everyone. Further, those who are less 'connected' are less likely to be reached by consultations. In addition, realistically, many people may not have the knowledge, inclination or time necessary for meaningful participation.

5.3 LEGISLATIVE DEFICITS

The inequitable apartheid social protection laws and policies had to be repealed or amended so as to streamline them with democratic dispensation which is characterized by constitutional supremacy, the rule of law and a human rights-based approach to social security provisioning. In addition, the social protection legislation that existed during the apartheid era had to be reviewed so as to craft a comprehensive and coherent legislative framework. New social protection laws were enacted. These laws include the Social Assistance Act 13 of 2004 which repealed the Social Assistance Act 59 of 1992.⁹⁷

Despite the much-needed repeal and/or amendment of apartheid social protection laws, which is to be welcomed, it is regrettable to point out that a few challenges have emerged. First, there is a proliferation of laws and regulations and as a result, it is generally difficult to know with great certainty which version of the law is in force.⁹⁸ This problem was alluded to by the Court in *Cele v. South African Security Agency and 22 Related Cases*⁹⁹ as follows:

(2016)): 'When those who are affected by decisions are actively engaged in the *negotiation* of policy, the outcomes will actively belong to them as citizens with the right *and* duty to participate in the policy process. Then, they are able to formulate and advocate positions, organise themselves (in non-discriminatory ways that protect minority concerns) and provide oversight and monitoring – in short to articulate a voice, the voice of those policy interventions are about' (italics in the original).

96. Department of Social Development (Republic of South Africa), *Comprehensive Report in the Review of the White Paper for Social Welfare, 1997*, 50 (Department of Social Development (Republic of South Africa) 2016).
97. Section 33(1) of the Social Assistance Act 13 of 2004.
98. L.G. Mpedi, *Pertinent Social Security Issues in South Africa*, 14 (Community Law Centre (University of the Western Cape) 2008).
99. 2008 (7) BCLR 734 (D) at para. 11.

in the field of social assistance in South Africa the primary and secondary legislation is as labyrinthine as it apparently is in the United Kingdom and the entitlement of any applicant to relief flowing from a failure on the part of the Minister of Social Development or SASSA may well be complex. All this can only serve to emphasise the necessity for those lawyers who practise in this area of the law to be thoroughly familiar with the applicable legislation, both primary and secondary, and to ensure that it is properly placed before the Court in a coherent form when the need for litigation arises.

The social security laws, inclusive of social assistance laws, are not consolidated. Furthermore, each social protection statute in South Africa makes provision for the dispute resolution mechanisms applicable to its provisions. This has resulted in a plethora of dispute resolution mechanisms that can be invoked to resolve a social protection dispute. There is a dire need for the systematization of the various laws regulating social security in South Africa.[100] This should be accompanied by efforts to develop a coherent social protection system for the country.[101]

Another challenge that can be distilled from the current social protection legislative framework is that it is not accessible to the general public. There are a variety of reasons for this state of affairs. Chief amongst them is that the social protection laws are legalistic for lay persons and not published in all the official languages.[102] Furthermore, there is no direct legal duty to inform the public about social protection rights imposed on the South Africa Social Security Agency and Department of Social Development.

5.4 IMPLEMENTATION FAILURES

The CSG covers the largest number of social grant beneficiaries in South Africa. However, it is characterized by the so-called exclusion errors.[103] That is to say, there are persons who do not draw the grant to which they are in effect

---

100. L.G. Mpedi, *Pertinent Social Security Issues in South Africa*, 15 (Community Law Centre (University of the Western Cape) 2008).
101. See, for further reading, M.A.T. Nyenti, *Reforming the South African Social Security Adjudication System: Innovative Experiences from South African Non-Social Security Jurisdictions*, 19 Potchefstroom Electronic Law Journal, 1, (2016); and M.A.T. Nyenti, *Dispute Resolution in the South African Social Security System: the Need for more Appropriate Approaches*, 33 Obiter, 27 (2012).
102. South Africa has thirteen official languages, namely: Sepedi, Sesotho, Setswana, siSwati, Tshivenda, Xitsonga, Afrikaans, English, isiNdebele, IsiXhosa and isiZulu (s. 6(1) of the Constitution).
103. Department of Social Development (Republic of South Africa), et al., *Review of the Child Support Grant: Uses, Implementation and Obstacles*, 19 (United Nations Children's Fund 2008).

entitled.[104] It is estimated that there are 2.1 million eligible children who are not in receipt of the CSG.[105] There is a multiplicity of factors which contribute to this situation and they include the following: supporting documents, the urban-rural divide, minor PCGs, children living on the streets and other impediments to access to the CSG.

5.4.1 Supporting Documents

The Regulations require that an application for a social grant be accompanied by original documents or certified copies of an identity document of the applicant and his or her spouse, and an identity document or a valid birth certificate of each child in respect of whom an application for a social grant is made.[106] They prescribe that an application for a CSG must be made on the relevant form and, in addition to the aforementioned documents, must be accompanied by the following documents:

> (a) a sworn statement or an affidavit in a format prescribed by the Agency, indicating the income of the applicant, together with any supporting documents that may be deemed necessary and in the case of a spousal relationship, that of his or her spouse. In the absence of supporting documents an applicant may submit a sworn statement or an affidavit in a format prescribed by the Agency, stating that the applicant does not have supporting documents;
> (b) proof that the applicant is the primary care-giver of the child, which may take the form of any of the following- (i) an affidavit from a police official; (ii) a report from a social worker; (iii) an affidavit from a biological parent of the child; or (iv) a letter from the principal of the school attended by the child.[107]

In practice, the requisite supporting documents have proved to be problematical for some potential beneficiaries. Acquiring the required documentation is a burden for many indigent South Africans.[108] The Committee

---

104. National Planning Commission (Republic of South Africa), *National Development Plan 2030: Our Future – Make it Work*, 259 (National Planning Commission (Republic of South Africa)), http://www.nationalplanningcommission.org.za/Pages/NDP.aspx (accessed, 23 Jun. 2017).
105. *Ibid.*
106. Reg. 11(1) of the *Regulations Relating to the Application for and Payment of Social Assistance and the Requirements or Conditions in Respect of Eligibility for Social Assistance*, Published under Government Notice R898 in Government Gazette 31356 of 22 Aug. 2008.
107. Reg. 11(3) of the *Regulations Relating to the Application for and Payment of Social Assistance and the Requirements or Conditions in Respect of Eligibility for Social Assistance*, Published under Government Notice R898 in Government Gazette 31356 of 22 Aug. 2008.
108. National Planning Commission (Republic of South Africa), *National Development Plan 2030: Our Future – Make it Work*, 259 (National Planning Commission (Republic of South Africa)), http://www.nationalplanningcommission.org.za/Pages/NDP.aspx (accessed, 23 Jun. 2017).

on the Rights of the Child has recently expressed its concerns on this matter as follows:

> (a) administrative and practical obstacles in obtaining birth registration, including punitive measures for late registration under the Births and Deaths Registrations Act (Act No. 51 of 1992), may have negative and discriminatory impacts; (b) The South African Citizenship Act (Act No. 88 of 1995) sets disproportionately strict conditions for granting the nationality of the State party to certain groups of children, and also allows for deprivation pf nationality from children on the basis of the loss of nationality of their parents; (c) There are reportedly many children, who either migrated to or were born in the State Party, in child and youth care centres who are undocumented and /or whose births have not been registered; (d) Possession of one's birth certificate is a rigid requirement for accessing social and child protection services.[109]

It recommended, amongst others, that South Africa should '[e]nsure that a lack of birth registration does not hinder access to child protection services and basic social services, while enhancing its efforts for universal birth registration'.[110]

Delay in the processing of the applications for the prescribed documentation has the propensity of indirectly impeding access to the grant. It is true that, pursuant to the *Alliance for Children's Entitlement to Social Security (ACESS) v. Minister of Social Development*,[111] the CSG applicant experiencing delays in obtaining the required official documents is empowered to produce alternative forms of identification.[112] As helpful as this may be, it has the disadvantage of opening the CSG up to abuse by charlatans. To address this problem, it is proposed that the CSG be universalized.[113]

5.4.2 The Urban-Rural Divide

Social grants are more accessible for those persons who live in urban areas than those in rural settings.[114] This is largely due to the fact that services are predominately located in urban areas much to the neglect of those who leave in rural locations.[115] The problem is aggravated by the high illiteracy rates and poor

---

109. Committee on the Rights of the Child, *Concluding Observations on the Second Periodic Report of South Africa*, 7 (United Nations 2016).
110. Committee on the Rights of the Child, *Concluding Observations on the Second Periodic Report of South Africa*, 8 (United Nations 2016).
111. Unreported High Court judgment (Case No. 5251/2005).
112. L.G. Mpedi, *Pertinent Social Security Issues in South Africa*, 25 (Community Law Centre (University of the Western Cape) 2008).
113. *See*: the discussion above on the need for the universalization of the CSG.
114. L.G. Mpedi, *Pertinent Social Security Issues in South Africa*, 25 (Community Law Centre (University of the Western Cape) 2008).
115. *Ibid*.

information sharing mechanisms which are prevalent in rural areas.[116] The poor rural dwellers are often short of resources to travel to urban areas to apply for the social grants including the CSG.[117] To address this problem, SASSA has introduced the so-called Integrated Community Registrations Outreach Programme (hereinafter 'ICROP'). This programme entails reaching out to the rural poor through mobile service units. A total of 570 ICROP interventions were conducted during the 2015/2016 financial year.[118] ICROP is to be welcomed, particularly when one notes that 320,000 applications for the CSG have been completed since its introduction in 2007.[119] However, ICROP should not be romanticized as a panacea for the above-mentioned problem. The point is that it has its own imperfections. For instance, it has been reported that '[t]he mobile units and services in farms do not have the same level of automation and sophistication as those offered at regular SASSA offices...'[120] Furthermore, ICROP is blamed for depleting the human resource capacity at local offices for the reason that existing staff members are deployed to mobile offices.[121] A more permanent solution should be found to ensure easy access to the social grant system by the impoverished rural members of the society. This should include the establishment of permanent offices staffed by well-trained personnel.

5.4.3 Minor PCGs

As noted earlier, the CSG is provided to PCGs. The fact that the CSG applicant must produce an identity document betrays the fact that the applicant must be 16 years or older. The point is only persons who are South African citizens and persons who are lawfully and permanently resident in the Republic[122] and who are 16 years or older can qualify for an identity document in South Africa.[123] The

---

116. L.G. Mpedi, *Pertinent Social Security Issues in South Africa*, 25 (Community Law Centre (University of the Western Cape) 2008); G. Mirugi-Mukundi, *Reaffirming the Social Security rights of Children in South Africa with Particular Reference to the Child Support Grant*, 11 Economic and Social Rights in South Africa Review, 7, 8 (2010); and L. Jansen van Rensburg & D. Horsten, *The Inadequacy of the Social Grant System available to Children in South Africa*, 29 Journal of Juridical Science, 52, 67 (2004).
117. L. Jansen van Rensburg & D. Horsten, *The Inadequacy of the Social Grant System Available to Children in South Africa*, 29 Journal of Juridical Science, 52, 67 (2004).
118. South African Social Security Agency, *Annual Report 2015/16*, 15 (Department of Social Development (Republic of South Africa) 2016).
119. International Labour Organization, *ICROP: Reaching Out to Rural Poor through Mobile Service Units*, http://www.social-protection.org/gimi/gess/RessourcePDF.action?res source.ressourceId=51861 (accessed, 23 Jun. 2017).
120. Department of Social Development (Republic of South Africa), *Comprehensive Report in the Review of the White Paper for Social Welfare, 1997*, 230 (Department of Social Development (Republic of South Africa) 2016).
121. South African Social Security Agency, *Annual Report 2007/ 2008*, 17 (South African Social Security Agency 2008).
122. Section 3 of the Identification Act 68 of 1997.
123. Section 15 of the Identification Act 68 of 1997.

problem is that these invariably exclude minor PCGs from applying for the CSG for children in their care. The situation is compounded by the prevalence of the child-headed households largely due to the HIV/AIDS pandemic in South Africa.[124] It is highly debatable whether this exclusion will survive a constitutional challenge on the basis that it unfairly discriminates against PCGs on the basis of age.[125] On the other hand, it is undesirable and morally questionable to allow children to raise children. Alternative solutions must be found to address this situation which invariably prevents children from accessing the CSG. Thus, the proposal by the South African Law Commission (hereinafter 'the SALC') for legal recognition to be accorded to 'household mentors' is to be welcomed. The SALC recommended that 'legal recognition be given to schemes in terms of which one or more appropriately selected and mandated adults are appointed as "household mentors" over a cluster of child-headed households by the Department of Social Development, a recognized NGO or the court'.[126] The Committee on the Rights of a Child recommended that South Africa should:

> while keeping its focus on family-like alternatives care: (a) Expedite actions to resolve systemic challenges in the foster care system and come up with sustainable arrangements for alternative care and for monitoring the arrangements, based on wide consultation with children, parents and extended families as well as with civil society organisations and professionals working on alternative care; [and] Expedite the revision of the Social Assistance Act with the aim of introducing an extended support grant for families caring for orphans while ensuring an adequate and feasible monitoring mechanism.[127]

5.4.4 Children Living on the Streets

Children living on the streets are deprived of a family environment. They inevitably lack an adult caregiver. This excludes them from accessing the CSG even if they qualify.[128]

---

124. *See*: Committee on the Rights of the Child, *Concluding Observations on the Second Periodic Report of South Africa*, 11 (United Nations 2016); H. Meintjes. et al., *Children 'In Need of Care' or In Need of Cash? Social Security in the Time of AIDS'*, 36 South African Review of Sociology, 238 (2005); and B. Goldblatt & S. Liebenberg, *Giving Money to Children; The State's Constitutional Obligations to Provide Child Support Grants to Child Headed Households*, 20 South African Journal on Human Rights, 151 (2004).
125. *See*: B. Goldblatt & S. Liebenberg, *Giving Money to Children; The State's Constitutional Obligations to Provide Child Support Grants to Child Headed Households*, 20 South African Journal on Human Rights, 151, 160-162 (2004).
126. South African Law Commission, *Project 110: Review of the Child Care Act Report*, 169 (South African Law Commission 2002).
127. Committee on the Rights of the Child, *Concluding Observations on the Second Periodic Report of South Africa*, 11 (United Nations 2016).
128. L. Jansen van Rensburg & D. Horsten, *The Inadequacy of the Social Grant System Available to Children in South Africa*, 29 Journal of Juridical Science, 52, 63 (2004).

5.4.5 Other Impediments to Access

Other obstacles to access to the CSG include corruption and fraud, poor levels of service (which at times lead to litigation) and abuse of the social grant payment system by some of the service providers (e.g., illicit deductions from unsuspecting beneficiaries' social grants).[129],[130]

5.5 CONCLUSION

The CSG is one of the key social protection interventions that have been put in place to alleviate child poverty in South Africa. As shown in this chapter, the CSG is built on a strong legal foundation which is spearheaded by the Constitution. The fundamental rights and constitutional values that undergird the CSG unashamedly point at a rights-based approach towards the provisioning of a tax-financed basic income security for children in South Africa. Benchmarked against the principles contained in the Social Protection Floors Recommendation, it goes without saying that the CSG is an appropriate mechanism through which South Africa can strive towards the realization of its obligations pertaining to children as outlined in the Recommendation. This is the case despite the fact that the CSG was in place long before the Recommendation was adopted. Notwithstanding the foregoing observation, there are a few 'last mile' challenges that require attention. These include the implementation failures that have been highlighted in this chapter. In the final analysis, the CSG is one of those success stories of the post-apartheid South African social protection system which carries valuable lessons for other countries, especially in the developing world, that desire to introduce a tax-financed basic income scheme targeted at children.

BIBLIOGRAPHY

Asher, A., *Finance and Tax*, in *Social Security: A Legal Analysis* (M.P. Olivier, N. Smit & E.R. Kalula eds., LexisNexis Butterworths 2003).

Brynard, P.A., *Civic Engagement and Public Policy Implementation: The Child Support Grant*, 44 Journal of Public Administration 312 (2009).

---

129. *See*: Department of Social Development (Republic of South Africa), South African Social security Agency and United Nations Children's Fund, *Removing Barriers to Accessing Child Grants: Progress in Reducing Exclusion from South Africa's Child Support Grant*, 64 (United Nations Children's Fund 2016); and N.T. Vally, *Insecurity in South African Social Security: An Examination of Social Grant Deductions, Cancellations, and Waiting*, 42 Journal of Southern African Studies, 965 (2016).

130. *See*: L.G. Mpedi, *Pertinent Social Security Issues in South Africa*, 18-19 (Community Law Centre (University of the Western Cape) 2008); and G. Mirugi-Mukundi, *Reaffirming the Social Security Rights of Children in South Africa with Particular Reference to the Child Support Grant*, 11 Economic and Social Rights in South Africa Review, 8 (2010).

Budlender D., *Increasing the Amount of the Child Support Grant*, in *South African Child Gauge 2016*, 78 (A Delany, S. Jehoma & L. Lake eds., Children's Institute, University of Cape Town 2016).

Cichon, M. et al., *Financing Social Protection* (International Labour Organization and International Social Security Association 2004).

Committee on the Rights of the Child, *Concluding Observations on the Second Periodic Report of South Africa* (United Nations 2016).

Delany A. & P. Proudlock, *Expanding Social Assistance for Children: Considering Policy Proposals*, in *South African Child Gauge 2016* (A Delany, S. Jehoma & L. Lake eds., Children's Institute, University of Cape Town 2016).

Department of Social Development (Republic of South Africa), *Comprehensive Report in the Review of the White Paper for Social Welfare, 1997* (Department of Social Development, Republic of South Africa 2016).

Department of Social Development (Republic of South Africa), et al., *Review of the Child Support Grant: Uses, Implementation and Obstacles* (United Nations Children's Fund 2008).

Department of Social Development (Republic of South Africa), South African Social security Agency and United Nations Children's Fund, *Removing Barriers to Accessing Child Grants: Progress in Reducing Exclusion from South Africa's Child Support Grant* (United Nations Children's Fund 2016).

Devereux, S., *Is Targeting Ethical?* 16 Global Social Policy, 166 (2016).

Goldblatt B. & S. Liebenberg, *Giving Money to Children: The State's Constitutional Obligations to Provide Child Support Grants to Child Headed Households*, 20 SAJHR. (2004).

Goldblatt, B., *Developing the Right to Social Security – A Gender Perspective* (Routledge 2016).

Hye-Young, L., *Alleviating Child Poverty in South Africa: The Role of Social Assistance Grants*, 7 ESR Review: Economic and Social Rights in South Africa, 2 (2006).

International Labour Organization, *ICROP: Reaching Out to Rural Poor through Mobile Service Units*, http://www.social-protection.org/gimi/gess/RessourcePDF.action?ressource.ressourceId=51861 (accessed, 23 June 2017).

ISSA, *Extending Social Security Coverage to the Excluded and Marginalized: Perspectives on Developments in South Africa*, in *Social Security Coverage Extension in the BRICS: A Comparative Study on the Extension of Coverage in Brazil, the Russian Federation, India, China and South Africa* (International Social Security Association ed., International Social Security Association 2013).

Jansen van Rensburg L. & D. Horsten, *The Inadequacy of the Social Grant System available to Children in South Africa*, 29 Journal of Juridical Science (2004).

Jansen van Rensburg, L., *The Khosa Case – Opening the Door for the Inclusion of all Children in the Child Support Grant?*, 20 South African Public Law 102 (2005).

Jehoma S. & E. Guarnieri, *Universalisation of Child Support Grant*, in *South African Child Gauge 2016* (A Delany, S. Jehoma & L. Lake eds., Children's Institute, University of Cape Town 2016).

Kgamphe L., *The Government's Budgeting for Children's Right to Social Assistance*, 5 ESR Review: Economic and Social Rights in South Africa, 8 (2004).

Khosa and Others v. Minister of Social Development and Others, Mahlaule and Another v. Minister of Social Development, 2004 (6) SA 505 (CC).

Kumitz, D., *Nothing About Us Without Us: Self-representation in Social Protection in Southern Africa*, 16 Global Social Policy, 215, 217 (2016).

Liebenberg, S., *Social Rights and Transformation in South Africa: Three Frames*, 31 South African Journal on Human Rights, 446 (2015).

Limbach, J., *The Concept of the Supremacy of the Constitution*, 64 The Modern Law Review, 1 (2001).

Lund, F., *Changing Social Policy: The Child Support Grant in South Africa* (Human Sciences Research Council Press 2008).

Mandela, N., *Nelson Mandela Quotes on Children*, http://www.nelsonmandelachildrensfund.com/news/nelson-mandela-quotes-about-children (accessed 5 June 2017).

McKinnon, R., *Good Governance in Social Security Administration*, 64 International Social Security Review, 3, 5–6 (2011)).

Meintjes, H., et al., *Children in Need of Care' or in Need of Cash? Social Security in the Time of AIDS*, 36 South African Review of Sociology, 238 (2005).

Mirugi-Mukundi, G., *Reaffirming the Social Security rights of Children in South Africa with Particular Reference to the Child Support Grant*, 11 Economic and Social Rights in South Africa Review (2010).

Mpedi, L.G., *Administration and Institutional Framework*, in *Social Security: A Legal Analysis* (M.P. Olivier, N. Smit & E.R. Kalula eds., LexisNexis Butterworths 2003).

Mpedi, L.G., *Charity Begins – but does not End – at Home: Khosa v Minister of Social Development; Mahlaule v Minister of Social Development* 2004 6 BCLR 569 (CC), 26 Obiter 173, (2005)

Mpedi, L.G., *Pertinent Social Security Issues in South Africa* (Community Law Centre, University of the Western Cape 2008).

National Planning Commission (Republic of South Africa), *National Development Plan 2030: Our Future – Make it Work* (National Planning Commission (Republic of South Africa)), http://www.nationalplanningcommission.org.za/Pages/NDP.aspx (accessed, 23 June 2017).

National Treasury (Republic of South Africa), *Budget Review 2017* (National Treasury Republic of South Africa 2017).

Nyenti, M.A.T., *Dispute Resolution in the South African Social Security System: the Need for more Appropriate Approaches*, 33 Obiter, 27 (2012).

Nyenti, M.A.T., *Reforming the South African Social Security Adjudication System: Innovative Experiences from South African Non-Social Security Jurisdictions*, 19 Potchefstroom Electronic Law Journal, 1, (2016).

Parliamentary Monitoring Group, *A Comprehensive Social Security System for South Africa: Hearing*, https://pmg.org.za/committee-meeting/2551/ (accessed 19 June 2017).

Parliamentary Monitoring Group, *The Legislative Process*, https://pmg.org.za/page/legislative-process#Green_and_White_Papers (accessed 19 June 2017).

Patel L., T. Hochfeld & J. Moodley, *Gender and Child Sensitive Social Protection in South Africa*, 30 Development Southern Africa, 69 (2013).

Patel, L., *Poverty, Gender and Social Protection: Child Support Grants in Soweto, South Africa*, 11 Journal of Policy Practice, 106 (2012).

Proudlock, P., *Weighing Up the Policy Proposals: Some Considerations*, in *South African Child Gauge 2016* (A Delany, S. Jehoma & L. Lake eds., Children's Institute, University of Cape Town 2016).

Sadan, M., *Social Assistance for Children: Looking Back, Thinking Forward*, in *South African Child Gauge 2016* (A Delany, S. Jehoma & L. Lake eds., Children's Institute, University of Cape Town 2016).

South African Law Commission, *Project 110: Review of the Child Care Act Report* (South African Law Commission 2002).

South African Social Security Agency (SASSA), *Fact Sheet: Issue no 5 of 2017 – 31 May 2017*, http://www.sassa.gov.za/index.php/knowledge-centre/statistical-reports (accessed 23 June 2017)).

South African Social Security Agency, *Annual Report 2007/ 2008* (South African Social Security Agency 2008).

South African Social Security Agency, *Annual Report 2015/16* (Department of Social Development Republic of South Africa 2016).

Statistics South Africa, *Vulnerable Groups Series I: The Social Profile of the Youth, 2009 – 2014* (Statistics South Africa 2016).

Triegaardt, J.D., *The Child Support Grant in South Africa: a Social Policy for Poverty Alleviation?* 14 International Journal of Social Welfare, 249 (2005).

Vally, N.T., *Insecurity in South African Social Security: An Examination of Social Grant Deductions, Cancellations, and Waiting*, 42 Journal of Southern African Studies, 965 (2016).

Van Rensburg, D., *SA Poverty Lines Rise Faster than Inflation*, http://city-press.news24.com/Business/sa-poverty-lines-rise-faster-than-inflation-20160719, (accessed, 20 June 2017).

CHAPTER 6

Conditional Cash Transfers for Families and Children under Mexico's PROSPERA Programme

Gabriela Mendizábal Bermúdez

6.1 INTRODUCTION

6.1.1 Social Security in Mexico

Social security in Mexico has been characterized by the creation of social securities that protect workers and their families in the formal economy and its expansion through assistance programme that aim at achieving two objectives:

(1) to alleviate the poverty of a large part of the population (46.2% of the total population currently);[1] and
(2) the inclusion of benefits granted to workers in the informal economy, who unfortunately make up almost 60% of the economically active population. However, official statistics indicate[2] that both objectives have not been met with much success.

---

1. CONEVAL, *Pobreza en México*, http://www.coneval.org.mx/Medicion/Paginas/PobrezaInicio.aspx, (accessed 12 Jul. 2016). CONEVAL is the acronym for the National Council for the Evaluation of Social Policy Development (*Consejo Nacional de Evaluación de la Política de Desarrollo Social*).
2. INEGI, *Estadísticas a propósito del día internacional del trabajo* (2015). INEGI, an acronym for the *Instituto Nacional de Estadística y Geografía* (National Institute for Statistics and Geography), is an autonomous public body in charge of regulating and coordinating the National Statistics and Geographical Information System in Mexico.

The high poverty rates and the continued existence of a large informal economy demonstrate that without a real sustainable social security system, the key elements needed to generate productive economic growth evenly and to mitigate the economic and social impact of economic crises are absent.

Thus, the implementation of ILO Social Protection Floors Recommendation 202 is very important for both the Mexican government and the population in poverty since the Recommendation is believed to embody the expansion of social security coverage and the extension of the scope of social assistance programmes.

6.1.2 PROSPERA as a Means to Combat Poverty

One of the most emblematic social programmes is PROSPERA, which has been in place for nineteen years. Its name and objectives have changed according to the expectations and needs of the population – from the perspective of each administration – but the cash transfers and benefits for families that mainly consist of food aid, scholarships and basic health care have continued. This programme was originally introduced in small rural communities covering 300,705 families in 1997 and has since expanded to cover over 6,043,824 families.[3] PROSPERA was the first nationwide cash transfer programme that targeted poor and extremely poor households.[4]

There is no literature corroborating that the ILO was motivated by its successor programmes (PROGRESA or OPORTUNIDADES) to develop social protection floors, but the ILO's evaluation of this programme considered it a successful social protection floor experience and the period of analysis begins in 2008.

To put the problem of poverty into context, in 2014 Mexico had 55.3 million poor (46.2% of its total population), 11.4 million (9.5%) of which were living in extreme poverty.[5] At this point, it should be noted that Mexico was the first country to introduce an official multidimensional poverty[6] measurement consisting of an index that, in addition to considering the lack of economic resources, includes other aspects that social policy also needs to address.[7]

According to the Mexican legal framework, the CONEVAL identifies the population living in poverty based on an analysis of their economic conditions

---

3. SEDESOL, *Padrón de beneficiarios*, SEDESOL (Mexico 2016). SEDESOL is the acronym of the Ministry of Social Development in Mexico.
4. Francesca Lamanna, *A Model from Mexico for the World* (World Bank 19 Nov. 2014).
5. Enrique Provencio Durazo, *Situación actual y reforma de la seguridad social en México* (Jesuswaldo Martínez Soria ed., Instituto Belisario Domínguez del Senado de la República, 2015).
6. The multidimensional poverty measurement typifies the population with the highest number of disadvantages, in addition to presenting their situation in terms of different dimensions of poverty.
7. CONEVAL, *Multidimensional Measurement of Poverty in Mexico: An Economic Wellbeing and Social Rights Approach*.

Chapter 6: Conditional Cash Transfers for Families

(an income below the minimum wellbeing line – LBMa) and social deprivation. One or more of the following indicators define whether an individual is considered as being socially deprived:

- Low education attainment.
- Lack of access to health services.
- Lack of access to social security.
- Housing with inadequate quality or insufficient space.
- Lack of basic housing services.
- Lack of access to food.

Based on these measurement criteria, those in poverty are the ones that suffer from at least one social deprivation and receive an income below the LBMa (*see* Footnote 29),[8] equivalent in value to the joint cost of both food and non-food baskets. Meanwhile, people in extreme poverty are those who have three or more social deprivations and earn an income below the LBMa – that is, their total income is lower than the cost of the basic food basket.

PROSPERA was also the first social programme to incorporate three basic social rights: health, education and food. Therefore, the social protection floor was readily implemented in Mexico. The legal framework that regulates the PROSPERA programme is made up of decrees and rules of operation:

(1) The Decree for the Creation of the National Coordinating Office for the PROSPERA Social Inclusion Programme (*Decreto por el que se crea la Coordinación Nacional de PROSPERA Programa de Inclusión Social*) was issued by the President of the United Mexican States on behalf of the Federal Executive branch.

(2) The Agreement to Issue the Rules of Operation of the PROSPERA Social Inclusion Programme for the 2016 Tax Year (*Acuerdo por el que se emiten las Reglas de Operación de PROSPERA Programa de Inclusión Social, para el ejercicio fiscal* 2016) was released by the Federal Executive branch with the following ministries: the Ministry of Finance and Public Credit; the Ministry of Social Development; the Ministry of Economy; the Ministry of Agriculture, Livestock, Rural Development, Fisheries and Food; Ministry of Public Education; the Labour Ministry; the National Coordinating Office for the PROSPERA Social Inclusion Programme; and the Mexican Social Security Institute.

It should be noted that the Ministry of Social Development is the main body in charge of implementing PROSPERA policies.

---

8. The monthly price of the basic food basket per person stands 2016 at MXN 1,346.46 (USD 65.97).

The above-mentioned Decree and Agreement are based on the Social Development Act, which does not expressly mention the PROSPERA programme. The Act simply states that the national social development policy must include social security and assistance programmes as one of its components (Article 14) and that priority should be given to programmes aimed at people living in poverty, exclusion or vulnerable situations (Article 19). This gives PROSPERA little legal stability. Since it is not explicitly included in a law directly approved by Congress, a unilateral presidential decision can result in a decree to change or discard the programme in its entirety.

6.1.3 Mexico and the ILO

Mexico's relationship with the International Labour Organization (ILO) has been a constant one. It has been a member since 1931, and has ratified seventy-nine Conventions, sixty-eight of which are in force. Among these Conventions, Convention 102 was ratified on 12 October 1961, with reservations on Parts IV on Unemployment Benefits and VII on Family Benefits. This relationship led to the signing of a collaboration agreement between the ILO Office for Mexico and Cuba and the PROSPERA National Coordination in February 2014.

This agreement aimed at establishing the bases and exchange of information on research and good practices used in the design of the change of OPORTUNIDADES to PROSPERA and its correlative implementation. The main objective of this change was to move from a conditional cash transfer programme for improving education attainment to promoting incorporation into the labour market.

6.1.4 The Structure of This Chapter

In this setting, this chapter analyses the principles included in Article 3 of the above-mentioned ILO Recommendation – as discussed in Chapter 2 of this volume – from a legal point of view and with regard to PROSPERA. Based on the literature on the fundamental right to social security, these principles are considered 'umbrella principles'.

It should be noted that this chapter only analyses how and to what degree the principles contained in Recommendation 202 have been effectively implemented within a legal framework for granting conditional cash transfers (CCTs) to families and children in the PROSPERA programme. The objectives of PROSPERA are much more far-reaching than this. It strives to implement and coordinate the available institutional social policy programmes and actions, including those that promote productivity, income generation, economic well-being, financial and labour inclusion, education, food and health. These actions aimed at the population living in extreme poverty are joint responsibility schemes; that is, several assistance programmes are used together to give benefits in cash and in kind.

Therefore, this chapter is composed of five sections: the background of the PROSPERA programme; a detailed analysis of nine principles of Recommendation 202 and their effectiveness in the PROSPERA programme; a discussion of legislative deficits; and lastly, the conclusions and research sources.

6.2 PROSPERA'S BACKGROUND

In order to understand the Mexican context and the way the PROSPERA programme is currently operating, it is necessary to briefly present two aspects of the situation in the country. The first focuses on PROSPERA's historical development and the second deals with the social problems this programme is trying to solve, as summarized below.

6.2.1 Social Security Through Social Security and Assistance Programmes

In Mexico, labour and social security rights are protected by Article 123 of the 1917 Political Constitution of the United Mexican States. In terms of social security, this Article ordered the enactment of social security laws, which in turn gave rise to the federal laws that created three national institutions that manage the most important social insurances in the country: the Mexican Social Security Institute (*Instituto Mexicano del Seguro Social* – IMSS), the Institute for Security and Social Services for State Workers (*Instituto de Seguridad y Servicios Sociales de los Trabajadores del Estado* – ISSSTE) and the Social Security Institute of the Mexican Armed Forces (*Instituto de Seguridad Social para las Fuerzas Armadas Mexicanas* – ISSFAM), as well as State pension institutes.

Over time, this has meant that only formal workers who meet the requirements established in the said social security laws receive comprehensive social security protection, leaving informal workers who do not meet the requirements of membership or citizens excluded by law (domestic workers, prisoners, priests, orphans, migrants, single mothers who are not formal workers, etc.) unprotected. Several social assistance programmes have been established to give coverage to those excluded from social securities. Therefore, insurance in Mexico can be illustrated as follows.

Table 6.1 Insured Population and Open Population

Total population: 121,168,094										
Insured population 71,489,175 59%						Open population 49,678,919 41%				
						PROSPERA				
PRIVATE INSURANCE	SEMAR	SEDENA	PEMEX	ISSSTE	IMSS	SEGURO POPULAR DE SALUD (People's Health Insurance)			SOCIAL PROGRAMS	NOT PROTECTED

Source: Tercer informe de gobierno, agosto 2015. Cifras preliminares al mes de junio del 2015; INEGI.

The Federal Executive branch can create social assistance programmes without them having to be approved by the legislative branch. These programmes can be replaced by other programmes depending on social needs and the vision of the current government.

The most important social programme at the moment is PROSPERA as it clearly gives coverage to the population in conditions of poverty and to informal workers. Although PROSPERA's most remote precursor is the COPLAMAR programme that dates back to 1977,[9] the PROGRESA programme is recognized as the first conditional cash transfer programme since then.

The Programme for Education, Health and Food (*Programa de Educación, Salud y Alimentación* – PROGRESA) under the Mexican Federal Executive and the Ministry of Social Development (SEDESOL) from 1997 had the attribute of being the first programme ever to incorporate three elements identified as priorities in the fight against poverty:

(1) Food: consisting of food supplements for children under 5 and pregnant women, as well as a cash transfer for each member of the protected family.
(2) Health: limited to a basic preventive health care package consisting of family planning, pregnancy and childbirth.

---

9. COPLAMAR is the acronym for the General Coordinating Office of the National Plan for Depressed Areas and Marginalized Groups.

(3) Education: consisting of encouraging regular school attendance and improving children's performance, beginning in third grade and continuing over the next six years of school (to 9th grade), through the use of scholarships.[10]

Although the programme was developed long before the introduction of social protection floors and the formulation of Recommendation 202, the priorities are partly congruous with the first two 'guarantees' laid down in this Recommendation – mainly aiming at the social protection of children.

In 2000, the scope of the programme was extended by adding scholarships for middle school education and improving adolescent health care programmes. The programme's name was changed to OPORTUNIDADES and was in place for twelve years. The beneficiaries of this programme were families who were marginalized, living in poverty and unable to meet the needs of education, health care and food. One of the features of this programme was that it prioritized households with members under the age of 22 and women of reproductive age. Its activities were managed by various ministries: of Health, of Education, of Finance and Public Credit and of Social Development.

The OPORTUNIDADES programme offered health care through the 'Basic Guaranteed Package' that consisted of new measures for prevention, the promotion of health and the early diagnosis of illnesses.[11] Financial aid was also granted for food, ranging from MXN 130 to MXN 450 (USD 6.37 to USD 22.00)[12] as additional food support to MXN 345 (USD 16.90) per older adult in the family. In terms of education, the programme gave scholarships to purchase school supplies. These CCTs were well below the family minimum income for that year (2000). Calculations were based on the official minimum wage, which in that period was set at MXN 1,137 (USD 55.70). By introducing financial support, an element of basic income security as is included in Recommendation 202 was added to the programme.

6.2.2 PROSPERA and Its Scope of Application

In 2014 and under a new administration, OPORTUNIDADES became what is now known as the PROSPERA programme. Its objectives are to contribute to skills development, access to social rights, and social welfare for those living in poverty in four main areas:

---

10. José Gómez de León Cruces, *Progresa*, https://archivos.juridicas.unam.mx/www/bjv/libros/3/1397/39.pdf (accessed 22 Jun. 2016).
11. SEDESOL, *Programa de Desarrollo Humano Oportunidades* http://www.sedesol.gob.mx/work/models/SEDESOL/Transparencia/TransparenciaFocalizada/Programas_Sociales/pdf/oportunidades.pdf (accessed 9 May 2016).
12. The exchange rate used in this chapter is USD 1 = MXN 20.41. All exchange rates were based on the Banxico rate of 9 Dec. 2016, available at http://www.banxico.org.mx.

(1) Food, by delivering monetary support directly to beneficiary families so as to help them improve the amount, quality and diversity in their diets, as well as benefits in kind through a programme called the Crusade against Hunger (See Table 6.2).
(2) Health, by implementing health promotion measures to prevent illnesses, as well as access to the health care services provided by the People's Health Insurance (Seguro Popular de Salud).
(3) Education, by offering greater educational coverage and granting scholarships as an incentive to stay in school and for student progression (See Table 6.2).
(4) Liaison services. This element establishes a liaison between the institutions and beneficiaries in order to further the comprehensive programme through counselling and information, as well as by enabling the beneficiary families to have access to the programmes or actions that promote productivity, income generation, training and employment, financial education, access to saving schemes, life insurance and loans through inter-agency coordination.[13]

One of the most important changes in the PROSPERA programme is that it is expanding its field of action. However, in this chapter, the analysis will solely centre on the CCTs it gives and which can be summarized in the following table.

Table 6.2 *PROSPERA Conditional Cash Transfers*

Cash Transfer	Amount	Benefits	Conditions for Receiving the Benefit
Food support	USD 16.41 monthly	To improve the nutrition of the members of the families, with emphasis on children, as well as pregnant and lactating women.	Be enrolled in the program opportunities PROSPERA Use the cash support of the food component to improving food and the nutritional status of family members. Voluntarily participate in the information and activities on the institutional offer

---

13. PROSPERA, *Reglas de Operación de PROSPERA Programa de Inclusión Social, para el ejercicio fiscal 2016* (Mexico, 2016).

Chapter 6: Conditional Cash Transfers for Families

Cash Transfer	Amount	Benefits	Conditions for Receiving the Benefit
Food support			sessions on production and employment Inclusion that will be offered by the staff PROSPERA
Food additional support	USD 6.87 monthly	In cash and by delivery food supplements.	
Additional support for Children	USD 5.87 monthly	Additional support to strengthen the development of children from 0 to 9 years of age as well as to compensate families for the increases in the cost of food and energy.	Receive and consume food supplements that are delivered in the health unit every two months for children aged 6 to 59 months It is the responsibility of the mother, father or person responsible for a child under five years, with some degree of malnutrition, assist to medical appointments
Adults 70 years old and over	USD 18.12 monthly	Support for adults without income.	Not receive income from some type of retirement pay
School Supplies	From USD 11.51 to USD 21.55 yearly by Grade Level	Bonuses for scholastic achievement.	Allocate resources of educational component to improving the education of their children
Scholarships for elementary school	From USD 8.59 to USD 17.14 bimonthly	For students of elementary and high schools, who remain in school and complete these educational levels.	Support to the family members of school age for to attend regular classes and improve their utilization To be a student of a school of basic education recognized by the SEP

Cash Transfer	Amount		Benefits	Conditions for Receiving the Benefit
	Men	Women		
Scholarships for high school first 3 years	From USD 25.23 to USD 27.92 bimonthly	From USD 26.45 to USD 32.33 USD bimonthly	For students of elementary and high schools, who remain in school and complete these educational levels.	The delivery of the scholarships of primary and secondary are subject to the certification of the inscription. Support to the scholars of average top education in order that they be present in form to regulate both to the school and to the community workshops
Scholarship for high school second and three years	From USD 42.38 to USD 48.01 bimonthly	From USD 48.50 to USD 54.877 bimonthly		

Source: Developed by author, based on the Rules of Operation for the PROSPERA Social Inclusion Programme.

It should be noted that the text of the General Social Development Act, the agreements and decrees that give PROSPERA its legal foundation, as well as the rules governing the establishment of the CONEVAL,[14] do not directly mention the International Labour Organization or Recommendation 202. Nevertheless, their analyses show that (1)reference is made to the objectives of national institutions and international bodies in general (CEPAL, FAO, Mexican State ministries) and (2) that while Recommendation 202 is not expressly cited, the changes made to the PROSPERA programme in 2014 can be seen as a form of alignment with the recommendation.

For instance, PROSPERA and its predecessor programmes already included CCTs for education, health, food and so on. But this programme extended its activities to promote the social and productive inclusion of its beneficiaries. To achieve this, PROSPERA enables beneficiaries to access additional social and productive programmes, expanding training opportunities for young people through scholarships for technical education and job training, and fostering job placement through the National Employment Service. It also sponsors financial inclusion by offering the poor access to savings, micro-credits and insurance.

The concept of an SPF can also be observed in the CONEVAL since it establishes the parameters for measuring poverty in accordance with the basic social security guarantees contained in Recommendation 202. The poverty indicators established by the CONEVAL are income, educational lags, access to

---

14. CONEVAL is the acronym for the National Council for the Evaluation of Social Policy Development (*Consejo Nacional de Evaluación de la Política de Desarrollo Social*).

health services, access to social security, access to food, housing quality and space, and access to basic services. Thus, the measurement considers income and six dimensions under a social rights approach.

Finally, to better understand the analysis, it is necessary to know that:

- The minimum wage for a formal worker is MXN 2,191.20 (USD 107.35) a month while the maximum amount of all the CCTs a family can receive is MXN 2,945.00.[15]
- The price of the basic food basket in Mexico is MXN 1,346.46 (USD 65.97) per person.[16]
- According to the CONEVAL, the amount needed to cover a person's basic needs for a month (food, education, housing, clothing, and recreation as stated in Article 4 of the CPEUM) stands at MXN 2,717.81 (USD 133.16).[17] Therefore, even with a minimum salary, a CCT or even a guaranteed income that covers the minimum amount a person needs, it is difficult to speak of universal coverage in real terms.

6.2.3 PROSPERA's Impact on Poverty

The PROSPRERA programme has served as a model for fifty-two countries.[18] This was mainly due to – among other factors – the positive results the actions have had in the areas where these were implemented impact as evidenced in the assessments made by academics from other countries. Although it represents progress made in the process of securing universal access to health care or income security for children, it has yet to be fully attained.

The following results stand out:

- Between 2006 and 2012, the overall fertility rate of women between the ages of 15 and 49 dropped by 15% among OPORTUNIDADES programme beneficiaries, while the rate increased by 10% for those who were not programme beneficiaries.[19]
- During the OPORTUNIDADES programme implementation (2000 to 2006), there was an 11.8% decrease in the number of cases of anaemia in children under the age of 2.[20]

---

15. CONASAMI, *General and Professional Minimum Wages* (Mexico 2016). CONASAMI is the acronym of National Commission of Minimum Wages in Mexico.
16. CONEVAL, *Evolution of Welfare Lines and Food Basket* (Mexico 2016).
17. *Ibid.*
18. Francesca Lamanna, *A Model from Mexico for the World* (World Bank 19 Nov. 2014).
19. ENSANUT, *El programa Oportunidades ¿promueve nacimientos?* ENSANUT is the acronym of Mexico's National Health Survey (*Encuesta Nacional de Salud*), which updates the information collected by the National Health Survey System in place since 1986.
20. Francesca Lamanna, *A Model from Mexico for the World* (World Bank 19 Nov. 2014).

- The Food and Agriculture Organization of the United Nations recognized Mexico's effort in achieving the first of the Millennium Goals (MDG-1) for having reduced the prevalence of undernourishment from 6.9% between 1990 and 1992 to 4.6% between 2012 and 2014.[21]
- From 2012 to 2013, the OPORTUNIDADES programme showed improvement in the job placement of young people beneficiaries of the programme. Likewise, a salary increase between 12% and 14% was observed, although this figure was higher for men than for women.[22]

PROSPERA has 25,128,194 registered beneficiaries. However, poverty and inequality persist, which is highly questionable. It calls for further consideration of the relevance and the effect of public policy instruments and the social policies that have been implemented. Although thousands of Mexicans show notable improvement in their quality of life with these social programmes, it has not been possible to curtail the dependence on these programmes for maintaining a better quality of life and millions of people are still living in poverty and extreme poverty; without government cash transfers and benefits, these people would perish.

For instance, since effective poverty measurements began to be carried out in Mexico by the National Council for the Evaluation of Social Development Policy (*Consejo Nacional de Evaluación de la Política de Desarrollo Social* – CONEVAL), poverty data for recent years read as follows:

Table 6.3 Poverty in Mexico, According to the CONEVAL, 2008–2014

Year	Total Population in Millions	Poor Inhabitants in Millions	Percentage of the Total Population Living in Poverty	Inhabitants Living in Extreme Poverty in Millions	Percentage of the Total Population Living in Extreme Poverty
2008	109.6	48.8	44.5%	11.7	10.6%
2012	117.3	53.3	45.5%	11.5	9.8%
2014	119.9	55.3	46.1%	11.4	9.5%

Source: Developed by author based on CONEVAL indicators.[23]

---

21. SEDESOL, *Reconoce la FAO a México por reducir la subalimentación un año antes de lo previsto*, (Mexico 2015).
22. CONEVAL, *Informe de la Evaluación Especifica de Desempeño 2012-2013 del Programa Oportunidades* (Mexico 2013).
23. CONEVAL, CONEVAL informa los resultados de la medición de pobreza 2014 (Mexico 2015) and CONEVAL, CONEVAL informa los resultados de la medición de la pobreza 2010 (Mexico 2011).

Recent years have seen a drop in extreme poverty among the Mexican population. The PROSPERA programme has exerted a significant positive influence because CCTs give the programme's beneficiaries the opportunity to acquire basic food basket products. However, this does not allow them to escape from poverty; on the contrary, poverty is on the rise.

It should also be mentioned that Recommendation 202 points out that when implementing SPFs, productive economic activity and formal employment should be promoted.

6.3 ASSESSMENT OF PROSPERA ON THE BASIS OF THE PRINCIPLES

6.3.1 State Responsibility

On examining the legal rationale of the PROSPERA programme, it can be said that the Mexican government is both the supplier and the administrator of the benefits. Even the CCTs are given directly and in cash to the families beneficiaries through a debit card issued by a public institution: BANSEFI.[24]

State responsibility is acknowledged in the General Social Development Act, a federal law implemented nationwide. The Act includes the objective to 'bring about the conditions that ensure the enjoyment of social rights, and access to social development and equal opportunity programmes'.[25] This Act is complemented by the Decree for the Creation of the National PROSPERA Coordinating Office for the Social Inclusion Programme (*Coordinación Nacional de PROSPERA Programa de Inclusión Social*) of 5 September 2014, stipulating that this programme is to administrate and establish social policies and programmes offered through the collaboration of various ministries, such as the Ministry of Social Development, of Economy, of Finance and Public Credit, of Health, of Agriculture and of Labour and Social Security, in order to 'improve the education, health, nutrition, income generation of the sector of the population living in extreme poverty through joint responsibility schemes'.[26] To give an example, people living in extreme poverty have 'priority access to 15 federal productivity programmes to increase productivity and encourage the generation of independent and sustainable income'.[27]

PROSPERA funding is approved annually by the Chamber of Deputies at the request of the Federal Executive. This programme has no set budget, but Article 23 of the General Social Development Act states that the budget for social

---

24. BANSEFI is the acronym for the National Savings and Financial Services Bank, National Credit Society (*Banco del Ahorro Nacional y Servicios Financieros, Sociedad Nacional de Crédito*), a public Mexican institution under the authority of the federal government, Cfr, *Ley Orgánica del Banco del ahorro Nacional y Servicios Financieros*.
25. Chamber of Deputies, *Ley de desarrollo social*, Congreso de la Unión (Mexico 2016).
26. Federal Official Gazette, *Decreto por el que se crea la Coordinación Nacional de PROSPERA Programa de Inclusión Social* (Mexico 2014).
27. To view the programmes, *see*: PROSPERA, *Preguntas frecuentes* (Mexico 16 May 2016).

expenditure cannot be less than that approved for the previous tax year. PROSPERA falls under this category as long as it is not replaced by another programme. As to the total federal budget for 2017, MXN 82.15 million (USD 4.02 million) have been earmarked for this purpose.

The CONEVAL is a public institution with technical and administrative autonomy, whose mission is to regulate and coordinate the evaluation of social development policies and programmes. This institution is responsible for evaluating the development and results of the PROSPERA programmes.

It can be concluded that PROSPERA complies with the principle of State responsibility, since the State provides the legislative framework, formulates and implements strategies, earmarks and distributes the necessary funds, and supervises the programme. No private actors are involved in the implementation of the scheme.

6.3.2 Universality of Protection

The first thing that should be pointed out in the analysis of the principle of the universality of social security is that universal coverage does not yet exist in Mexico. This justifies the need for social protection floors and stresses importance of adopting such measures. Around 40% of the population does not have social insurance (*see* Table 6.1), including people who can be described as societal groups living in precarious conditions because they do not meet the basic requirements to access social security: (1) to be a worker in the formal economy or a beneficiary of this type of worker; or (2) to have the necessary means and the desire to join the compulsory regime as an independent professional, but without the right to enjoy all the benefits.

These groups of people without social insurance include informal workers, children, older adults, women, indigenous people, homosexuals, regular or irregular migrants without formal employment, prisoners and people with disabilities. Each one of these groups is in a vulnerable position for different reasons. For example, women are vulnerable to gender discrimination when gaining access to formal employment or having to take care of children, older adults, sick people and people with disabilities; prisoners are vulnerable because Mexico does not have regulations that provide them social security benefits, and even though some of them do work for private companies from detention facilities, inmates do not contribute to pensions; homosexuals are vulnerable because although many are formal workers and the Supreme Court of Justice has declared the Articles of certain laws – including those in the Social Security Act – unconstitutional, these Articles have not been amended and continue to rule out insurance for their partners as the Act only recognizes traditional marriages or heterosexual couples as workers' beneficiaries; and so on.

Despite the above, under the terms of SPFs, it should be stressed that formally employed workers have income security and access to social security.

Those who do not, as in the case of informal workers, receive social assistance (through programmes like PROSPERA) to attain income security.

Specifically, the requirements to be a PROSPERA beneficiary are not established per beneficiary, but per family to thus minimize the possibilities of discrimination. The families chosen to enter or re-enter the programme are those whose estimated monthly per capita income is less than the minimum wellbeing line (LBMa). Moreover, the legal framework adheres to the fact that in the case of foreigners, they must prove their regular immigration status. In addition, one requirement for the process is that the person designated as the head of the family certifies their identity with official identification, which is something not all poor people have.

Family income is determined based on the information the family itself provides in a questionnaire supplied by PROSPERA officials. Therefore, the decision of who is a beneficiary and what CCTs they are entitled to depends on what is established in the law and how it is directly applied by the Mexican government. For example, a formal worker's family with an income below the LBMa is entitled to CCTs for each family member (scholarships, nutritional supplements for pregnant women, the elderly, etc.), but not to health services because they are provided by the social insurance to which he is entitled as a formal worker. Meanwhile a family with a higher income, but without social insurance, would not be entitled to CCTs, but can receive social benefits for health services. This could lead us to prematurely conclude that universal coverage exists under this parameter.

According to Recommendation 202, SPFs guarantee income security for three age cohorts: children, working-age adults and older persons. From this perspective, it can be noted that PROSPERA is not a universal programme since it includes specific CCTs for the specific needs of only two age groups:

- For children, scholarship opportunities linked to school enrolment, as well as monthly financial benefits in order to help purchase and diversify foodstuffs.
- For older adults, a monthly cash support is given to persons over the age of 70 who are members of beneficiary families. Support is given as long as the beneficiaries are not being assisted by the SEDESOL Pension Programme for Older Adults (*Programa de Pensión para Adultos Mayores*).[28]

It should be noted that in addition to the above requirements for granting the family support, additional support for children is given through the requirement of medical consultations that determine whether there is any level of malnutrition. In this case, the CCT is contingent upon attendance to the medical appointments deemed necessary for control purposes.

---

28. PROSPERA, *Reglas de Operación de PROSPERA Programa de Inclusión Social, para el ejercicio fiscal 2016* (Mexico, 2016).

For poor adults (regardless of whether they are formal, informal or unemployed workers), CCTs only consist of food assistance and supplementary foodstuffs, as long as they are part of a family with an estimated monthly per capita income less than the adjusted LBMa.[29] This includes regular migrants since they are required to provide evidence of their legal stay with the corresponding migration documents.[30] This means that it goes against Recommendation 202 because it discriminates against families of irregular migrants.

The goal of the PROSPERA CCT is to provide benefits to all children and families living below the LBMa. This universality is not achieved because:

- The benefit depends on being enrolled in school.
- Families made up of illegal immigrants are not covered.
- Many people do not apply because they do not have official identification.

6.3.3 Entitlements Based on Law

Each of the programmes coordinated by PROSPERA establishes who shall benefit from them and what requirements must be met, based on the decrees or rules of operation issued by the Federal Executive. The process begins with a socio-economic survey, which uses the family's responses to determine whether they are eligible to become beneficiaries. However, on analysing the legal right to claim benefits, three issues must be addressed.

First, the Mexican legal framework is structured as follows. First of all, there are instruments of constitutionality and conventionality consisting of the Political Constitution of the United Mexican States, and, as of 2011, the international human rights treaties ratified by Mexico as a means to offer persons broader protection. Then, there are the general international treaties Mexico has signed with the Senate's approval, followed by federal laws, organic and special laws, State constitutions and State laws. Lastly, there are administrative regulations and the executive decrees (ministries), which are rules that are not issued by the legislative branch.

Second, a widespread feature of social programmes managed under PROSPERA is that they do not have any direct legal mechanisms for claiming benefits (administrative remedies). In other words, mechanisms are established in decrees and rules that, while specifying the scope, the qualification conditions, and benefit levels, do not include impartial, transparent, effective, simple, fast, accessible, and low-cost complaint and appeal procedures.[31]

---

29. This will be discussed in depth in section 8.3.4 Adequacy and predictability of benefits.
30. PROSPERA, *Reglas de Operación de PROSPERA Programa de Inclusión Social, para el ejercicio fiscal 2016* (Mexico 2016) 13.
31. *See* s. 8.4 Legislative deficits and implementation failures 1. Legality.

Third, despite the above, if a person who meets the requirements for becoming a PROSPERA CCT beneficiary is not included as a programme beneficiary or is not granted the benefits according to the established amount or frequency, he or she has the following legal options:

(a) a grievance can be lodged before Human Rights Commissions; or
(b) the PROSPERA programme has an inbuilt mechanism consisting of two avenues that help beneficiaries voice their objections to the programme. The first is complaints and claims, and the second is the right to a hearing, although it should be noted that the hearing is just with the local administration in the State of residence, as explained below.

Regarding the first avenue mentioned in paragraph (b) above, Item 12 of the PROSPERA Programme, entitled 'Complaints and Claims Regarding the Rules of Operation of the PROSPERA Programme', establishes that 'complaints and claims regarding the operation of the programme are channelled to the competent authorities, under the legal, administrative and regulatory provisions applicable to each case'.[32] The purpose of this point is to establish the procedures for complaints and claims so that beneficiaries or applicants can use this mechanism in the event of any violation to or omission concerning their rights. It specifies how these complaints or claims should be submitted (in writing, via electronic means, courier or telephone) and the institutions to which they should be addressed. However, it does not provide an actual administrative remedy because the programme is not established in the Federal Law on Administrative Proceedings (*Ley Federal de Procedimientos Administrativos*), but on rules of operation that can vary according to the will of the government in power. In 2014, 920 complaints or claims regarding the PROSPERA programme were submitted, 541 in 2015 and 579 in 2016.[33]

As regards the second avenue in paragraph (b) above, the right to be heard is established to ensure that the assistance given by PROSPERA is not taken away from any family without just cause, giving families a way to reassert their rights if the assistance has been suspended temporarily or indefinitely. This measure seeks to avoid discretionary practices and contributes to greater transparency in the procedures for enrolling and remaining in the programme. However, the right to be heard in PROSPERA simply consists of the beneficiary families being called to appear before the programme administration in their States of residence so they can avail themselves of their rights. Families can also be notified through personalized official letters.

---

32. *Ibid.*
33. Information provided by the Transparency Unit (*Unidad de Transparencia*) through an official letter dated 6 Dec. 2016, No. 200010001151516 from Julio Antonio Sarabia Gallardo, Head of the Transparency Unit.

Compliance with the principle of Entitlements Based on Law is partial, because it depends on whether the benefits are framed in legal rules, and whether the right of audience is really accessible to the beneficiaries who have been discharged from the programme. Furthermore, the programme might disappear or change drastically from one year to the next because it is based on legal norms issued by the Federal Executive and not by the Mexican Congress.

In addition to this negative point, in case of non-fulfilment in granting the CCT or the amounts given, there is no real mechanism accessible to beneficiaries other than being included as a beneficiary.

Due to the above, a family could be beneficiary of PROSPERA and nevertheless not receive CCTs due to some irregularity. However, even though the family has the right to such a benefit, the family's poverty would hinder them in claiming CCTs. This poverty implies a lack of economic resources to pay for legal counsel or transportation, living in remote villages far from the institutions that administer and impart justice, and ignorance.

6.3.4 Adequacy and Predictability of Benefits

Taking into account that (1) every year the Agreement to Issue the Rules of Operation of the PROSPERA Social Inclusion Programme is issued by the various State Ministries (Social Development, Finance, Health, etc.) in charge of the social programmes managed by PROSPERA, and (2) this agreement clearly stipulates the requirements to qualify as a PROSPERA beneficiary, the types of CCTs, the specific amount of each transfer, the method of payment and the requirements for obtaining each type of CCT, PROSPERA CCTs can thus be regarded as predictable.

As regards adequacy, PROSPERA benefits used together ensure a decent standard of living since they are awarded to families and not individuals. Moreover, it grants benefits both in kind and in cash in the fields of health, education and food. Specifically, PROSPERA CCTs give each family a package of benefits throughout their lifetime. In other words, the focus is on children, adults and older adults. CCTs make it possible to gain genuine access to goods and services deemed necessary nationwide, specifically established as part of the basic food basket, although the programme does not monitor beneficiaries' expenses.

In Mexico, a single poverty measurement system was established and outlined by the CONEVAL. This system uses the LBMa[34] as the basis for measurement. This is equivalent to the monthly price of the basic food basket

---

34. The minimum wellbeing line is based on the methodology proposed by the Economic Commission for Latin America and the Caribbean (ECLAC) that uses household spending patterns as a reference point to estimate the thresholds of energy and micronutrient consumption consistent with the different levels of income. This and the poverty rates serve as the basis for establishing social policy measures and actions to be implemented nationwide. CONEVAL, *Preguntas frecuentes*.

per person: MXN 1,346.46 (USD 65.97). The maximum amount provided by PROSPERA CCTs is MXN 2,945.00 (USD 144.29). However, this benefit is granted on a family basis. To this amount, MXN 370.00 (USD 18.12) can be added for each older adult living with the beneficiary family.

In this way, CCTs do not always cover the minimum level of income needed to allow for a decent standard of living because the amount granted by CCTs depends on the particularities of each household. In other words, households are actually given financial support for food and energy, but increments to the transfers depend on having children in elementary, middle or high school; the existence of older adults in the family; and any other income the family may receive. This does not make it possible for beneficiaries to lift themselves out of poverty completely, rather, just out of extreme poverty. They continue to be poor (see Table 6.3).

In conclusion, it can be stated that the principle of Adequacy and Predictability of Benefits is not fulfilled from several perspectives. CCTs and their amounts may vary from year to year, depending on their distribution as decided by the Secretaries of State involved in the annual operating rules. The budget for social programmes cannot be reduced by law, but there can be changes in the programmes that will receive funding.

The lack of flexibility towards the beneficiaries, such as in the case of those who do not have official identification, is also to be criticized considering the fact that they are living in extreme poverty.[35]

Finally, CCTs do not guarantee that each family sits above the LBMa. It is only a requirement to be a beneficiary, but the particularities of each family, such as the number members and their ages, determine the amount to be granted and not the amount they require to genuinely sit above the LMBa.

6.3.5 Non-discrimination

The principle of non-discrimination forms part of the basic rules of PROSPERA. Therefore, any family has the right to be a beneficiary of PROSPERA CCTs based on their level of income and regardless of formal or informal economic activity, citizenship status (national or foreigner with legal residence in the country), health or illness, and certainly of gender. The programme's only restriction for receiving CCTs is that families contain children, youngsters or older adults. In particular, No. 11 on Focus on the Rules of Operation states that:

> The public servants involved in the operation of the programme are encouraged to promote, respect, protect and guarantee the effective exercise of the beneficiaries' human rights, according to the principles of universality, interdependence, indivisibility and progressivity, offering at all times dignified and respectful treatment of the target population, in compliance with the criteria of equality and non-discrimination.

---

35. See: s. 8.3.2 Universality of Protection.

The importance of positive discrimination actions that give CCTs to women gain significance, especially in the form of the following:

- Scholarships. While scholarships are awarded to both men and women, the amounts of educational support are higher for women with the aim of contributing to narrowing the gender gap in education.[36]
- The Life Insurance Programme for Female Heads of Families offers children, who have lost their mothers, economic support until the age of 23 (or the day before their 24th birthday).[37]
- PROSPERA gives priority to the inclusion of its women beneficiaries through fifteen SEDESOL programmes to achieve the empowerment of women through start-ups of their own projects or options for working.[38]

The financial benefits given to women are affirmative actions against gender discrimination. As the changes implemented in the programme begin to empower women in their family units by gradually bringing them in an income simply for being female members of the productive and work productivity programmes, it is expected that the wide gender gap will be closed.

In conclusion, it can be said that, in terms of the principle of non-discrimination, the rules are very clear and specific to combating non-discrimination. However, this principle is not entirely fulfilled and certain challenges can be observed, for example, incorporating irregular migrants, and, of course, the promotion of productive and labour inclusion through recent reforms to PROSPERA, as well as the elimination of gender discrimination through CCTs.

6.3.6 Financial Solidarity

All the benefits provided by PROSPERA are fully funded by federal taxes.[39] Because of this, CCT beneficiaries do not make any contribution themselves. The benefits are granted to assist vulnerable groups in society living in poverty. These benefits are mainly funded through taxes on production and services, value added tax and income tax. Different percentages of this revenue are then distributed among the entire population.

---

36. PROSPERA, *Educación*.
37. The first quarter of 2016 reported the death of 14,520 female heads of families. Datos de SEDESOL, *Programa Seguro de Vida para Jefas de Familia cifras al primer trimestre de 2016* (Mexico 2016).
38. PROSPERA, *Es prospera un programa social de vanguardia a nivel mundial* (Mexico 15 Mar. 2016).
39. This budget is determined on a year-by-year basis at the request of the Federal Executive as part of the federal expenditures budget and is approved by the Congress.

Providing cash directly to families encourages beneficiaries' participation through the requirement to send their children to school[40] and to attend health centres for medical check-ups. It eases extreme restrictions on income used to cover food expenses. Meanwhile, the latest change to PROSPERA aims to strengthen policies and programmes that give young people an opportunity to enter the formal labour market; to bring rural development, financial inclusion and microcredit programmes to PROSPERA families so they can lift themselves out of poverty; to increase their income and buying power, and thereby also enabling them to pay taxes.

In conclusion, the CCTs comply with the principle of solidarity as laid down in the Recommendation.

6.3.7 Good Governance

In its introduction, the PROSPERA Rules of Operation set out the objective of ensuring the effective, efficient and transparent use of public funds allocated for its operation, which complies with Article 3, paragraph j) of Recommendation 202.

As regards the indispensable evaluation criteria for contributing to compliance with the principle of good governance, Item 6 of these rules includes the criteria for establishing evaluations that lead to accountability in resource management,[41] specifying the forms of evaluations and the periods during which they are to take place, while focusing on the resources used, the actions performed and the objectives fulfilled, among others. Meanwhile, Item 8 Operation Monitoring, Control and Auditing states that an Operation Monitoring Model approved by the sectors involved is to be implemented.

As can be seen in the above paragraph, from a legal perspective there are some elements that show an attempt has been made to make the application of financial resources and the impact of the benefits granted more transparent.

One very positive factor in complying with the principle of good governance has been the creation of the CONEVAL in 2005. This is an autonomous public body whose mission is to evaluate social development policy for the purpose of improving outcomes. In short, it ensures that the money invested in each programme delivers the desired results.

Despite the above, various studies highlight the common problems associated with social aid programmes like PROSPERA:[42] the lack of transparency in the procedures, in resource management and in the granting of benefits;

---

40. It should be noted that the requirement for school scholarships is simply to be enrolled in school. No attendance record is required nor are minimum school achievement scores obtained.
41. PROSPERA, *Reglas de Operación de PROSPERA Programa de Inclusión Social, para el ejercicio fiscal 2016* (Mexico, 2016) 13.
42. Anavel Monterrubio, *Integración y concatenación de padrones de beneficiarios como factores de transparencia y rendición de cuentas*, Reporte CESOP, No. 77 (CESOP, July

irregular acts and the corruption of public servants, and no enforcement regarding the fulfilment of obligations on the part of the public servants who implement the programmes; the use of social programmes for electoral gain; and the lack of financial and actuarial reports. These studies include the following:

- María Marván, a researcher at the UNAM Institute for Legal Research, documented one case of corruption in which a SEDESOL official would school female PROSPERA beneficiaries on the specific responses to give in the surveys.[43]
- Bracamontes and Camberos, documented that the low impact the OPORTUNIDADES – now PROSPERA – programme has had on levels of poverty is due to errors of omission, the exclusion of poor households and the inclusion of households that are not poor.[44]
- Madrid and Ladrón de Guevara concluded that the objectives of social programmes are not actually achieved 'due to the mismanagement of the programmes'.[45]

6.3.8 Coherence of Policies

The coherence of policies with the country's development, especially in terms of the fight against poverty and the implicit establishment of SPFs, ranges from the design to the implementation and evaluation of the public policies by the different political actors. As evidenced, it includes legal provisions issued by Congress and decrees approved by the Executive, which are compatible with the current 2012-2018 National Development Plan. The legal frame of reference for the coherence of social policies takes into account the following important points:

(1) The identification of vulnerable groups in respect of poverty in the country, while also addressing the age groups of children, adults and older adults established in Recommendation 202. Also included are gender-based programmes and benefits, i.e., benefits are targeted at vulnerable groups.

2014), and María del Rosario Ruiz Moreno, *El seguro popular, un penoso engaño social para los pobres* (Ángel Guillermo Ruiz Moreno ed., Mexico, Porrúa 2007).
43. María Marván Laborde, *No, no, no tienen hambre* (No, no, not hungry), Magazine Facts and Rights, No. 32 (March-April 2016).
44. Joaquín Bracamontes Nevárez, Mario Camberos Castro & Luis Huesca Reynoso, *The Impact in the Early Years of the Oportunidades Program by Type of Poverty in Mexico and Baja California, 2002-2006*, 15, No. 30 Estudios Fronterizos, nueva época (July-December 2014) 150.
45. The aforementioned text is by Joaquín Bracamontes Nevárez & Mario Camberos Castro, *Poverty in Mexico and Its Regions: An Impact Analysis of the Oportunidades Program in the Period 2002-2006*, Center for Research in Food and Development, population papers No. 67 (January/March 2011) 169-170.

(2) Tax incentives exist that contribute to job creation and social insurance for vulnerable groups, including:
   (a) A tax incentive shall be granted to whosoever hires older adults, consisting of 25% of the salary effectively paid to persons aged 65 or older.[46]
   (b) The employer who hires persons with a motor disability and who require the permanent use of prosthetics, crutches or wheelchairs; a mental disability; hearing or language impairment of 80% or more than the normal capacity or in the case of the blind, may deduct from their income an amount equal to 100% of the income tax of these workers, as long as the employer fulfils the obligation of registering them with the Mexican Social Security Institute *(Instituto Mexicano del Seguro Social)*.[47]
(3) In education, the large number of scholarships granted range from PROSPERA programmes to State programmes, such as the scholarship salary in the State of Morelos, scholarships for higher and postgraduate education including those granted by the National Council for Science and Technology *(Consejo Nacional de Ciencio y Tecnología* – Conacyt), and so on. Unfortunately, a pertinent issue is the specific lack of policies linking education and the job market.
(4) In terms of employment, PROSPERA includes fifteen productive programmes,[48] but most of them are aimed at self-employment, which do not meet the characteristics of decent employment by a long chalk. Although self-employment does add to the family income, it will not help informal workers become formal workers.

It could be concluded that the PROSPERA child benefit is part the National Development Plan that aims at social protection of the most vulnerable groups in society and covers a variety of needs and different periods during the lifecycle. The incorporation of the CCT in a larger programme under the umbrella of the National Development Plan is a good example of the coherence of policies as meant by Recommendation 202. The main challenge in this regard is that the policies together may prevent people from falling into extreme poverty, but policies to help them escape from poverty and build up their own independent lives are lacking.

6.3.9 Social Participation

Social participation in PROSPERA centres on the beneficiaries themselves. The federal government points out that social participation takes place through

---

46. Federal Official Gazette, *Ley del Impuesto Sobre la Renta*, Art. 186.
47. *Ibid.*
48. PROSPERA, *Preguntas frecuentes*.

planning community development, gathering citizen opinion, claiming rights and accountability, all of which are elements that contribute to human development and social cohesion within a framework of rights.[49]

In addition, there exists the Agreement to Issue the Rules of Operation of the PROSPERA Social Inclusion Programme for the 2016 Tax Year and the Operational Guidelines for the PROSPERA programme. The following:

- Community protection committees and individual committee members that are 'organizations composed of PROSPERA forms of social participation are present:beneficiaries who have been democratically elected by the beneficiaries of a district or neighbourhood'.[50] All PROSEPRA programme beneficiaries have the right to assume this role voluntarily and in an honorary capacity.
- Private institutions. When establishing the PROSPERA State Technical Committees,[51] which are the inter-agency coordinating bodies (between authorities from the three levels of government: federal, State and municipal), representatives of private institutions and representatives of social sector organizations can participate as honorary contributors when their contributions are deemed appropriate and useful due to the affinity of objectives. Some such institutions are non-governmental organizations and non-profit civil associations aimed at helping youth, children, vulnerable social groups and so on.

However, legislation does not determine how many institutions should be established, how they are selected or whether there is an obligation to participate. Therefore, participation is discretionary:

- Members of the academic community, whose most important contribution is the evaluation of the programme.[52] It should be pointed out that the evaluations are carried out independently of the programme and the results are published in literature that can be consulted. However, the evaluation results have no direct connection to PROSPERA decision-making processes.
- Tripartism. Only in the case of IMSS-PROSPERA is there a Mexican Social Security Institute governing body with the participation of the government, workers and employers.
- Non-governmental organizations and labour unions representing informal workers. The involvement of these groups in the implementation of PROSPERA is limited. Their participation mainly lies in counselling and helping beneficiaries receive different types of support.

---

49. PROSPERA, *Reglas de Operación de PROSPERA Programa de Inclusión Social, para el ejercicio fiscal 2016* (Mexico, 2016).
50. *Ibid.*
51. PROSPERA, *Lineamientos Operativos del Programa Prospera.*
52. *Ibid.*

Despite the above, one cannot definitively state that there is actual social participation that makes it possible to redirect or extend the scope of the programme because all the decisions depend on the incumbent government.

6.4 LEGISLATIVE DEFICITS AND IMPLEMENTATION FAILURES

The first thing to note in this analysis is that there are legal instruments that support PROSPERA. The PROSPERA legal framework is an important part of the regulation of social protection in Mexico for vulnerable social groups. The legal reforms that gave rise to PROSPERA allow the current government to accomplish several objectives: to continue with the CCTs given under the previous programme, OPORTUNIDADES; to correct their deficiencies; to give the programme greater scope by establishing the productive inclusion component; and thereby to bring it closer to the objectives of Recommendation 202. Nonetheless, the following legal challenges exist:

- Legality. The legal framework that supports PROSPERA is composed of decrees and operational guidelines, which establish the benefits, characteristics, beneficiaries, requirements and conditions for receiving CCTs. These agreements and guidelines find their legitimacy in federal law, namely the General Social Development Act. It should be mentioned that the PROSPERA programme is not specifically mentioned in this law, which simply determines the general objective, characteristics and organization all social development programmes in Mexico should have.

  This gives PROSPERA little legal stability because the most important rules of its legal framework (Decree for the Creation of the National Coordinating Office for the PROSPERA Social Inclusion Programme and the Agreement to Issue the Rules of Operation of the PROSPERA Social Inclusion Programme) are not approved by Congress or any legislative body, but only approved by the Executive branch, i.e., the President of Mexico and his cabinet (ministers). Therefore, the President can take the unilateral decision to change or even eliminate the programme.
- Progressivity. PROSPERA's legal framework does not include a specific plan of action on an agenda, or long-term goals that allow the extension of beneficiary coverage to either escape poverty or advance to the second step of the social protection ladder: social insurance.
- Direct mechanisms to claim benefits. PROGRESA is a social assistance programme and therefore, (like all social programmes in Mexico) it does not have a mechanism to make it easy for beneficiaries to receive benefits without having to take recourse to the Court.
- Transparency in reporting. Not all State ministry programmes that form part of PROSPERA have the obligation to regularly report their registry of beneficiaries and/or the support given.

- Anti-corruption shield. The beneficiaries' lack of information on the PROSPERA rules allows corruption. It is necessary that the beneficiaries of PROSPERA know their rights and demand them to avoid clientelism,[53] to contribute to guaranteeing their social rights, and to force the State to fulfil its responsibilities.
- Dissemination of information about rights. The basis for claiming any right is knowledge, and the programme does not have suitable mechanisms for disseminating information about the programme.

6.5 CONCLUSIONS

Some of the factors contributing to social problems in Mexico are an unmistakable period of slow economic growth, the persistence of poverty and inequality, growing insecurity, a lack of credibility in public institutions (largely due to corruption), large migratory fluxes and a high prevalence of people without social insurance. This justifies the implementation of social protection floors.

Mexico's history of social programmes that provide CCTs were implemented long before the creation of Recommendation 202. However, the PROSPERA programme has adapted its objectives in such a way that they implicitly conform to the Recommendation.

The analysis of the principles of this Recommendation in terms of CCTs for families and children shows that the programme complies – to different extents – with a number of principles, notably with the principles of State responsibility, financial solidarity, coherence of policies and non-discrimination.

Some principles urgently need much better implementation in order for CCTs to comply with Recommendation 202, in particular, the universality of protection, entitlements based on law, adequacy, and good governance are far below the standards set by the Recommendation. These incompliances result in a failure to distribute the benefits to eligible persons and in misallocation, which undermines the overall objectives of the PROSPERA programme. Furthermore, the benefits are not adequate. Although the cash transfers may prevent extreme poverty, they do not enable the beneficiaries to escape poverty and live their lives in dignity.

Looking at the PROSPERA programme overall, it is striking that these benefits extend social security to the poor, but do not contemplate specific cash benefits for informal workers. In other words, CCTs are given to families and only those with children, young people and older adults. No cash transfers for unemployment or low income are given to informal workers as such. These workers only benefit from CCTs given to the family for food.

The reforms made to the PROSERA programme in 2014 envisage the inclusion of informal workers in the formal labour market by strengthening their

---

53. Clientelism is the exchange of goods and services for political support.

productive capacities, mainly through scholarships for students in higher education and for professional training. Since 2014, PROSPERA objectives have included short-term results associated with productive development, income generation, financial well-being and the employability of programme beneficiaries. Nevertheless, these objectives are limited to the incorporation of labour or an increase in beneficiaries' income, but so far, the goals have not proposed an increase in the number of programme beneficiaries affiliated to social insurance.

It should be noted that the approach to be used for this would be the implementation of a bi-dimensional floor (horizontal/vertical), in order to comply with the SPF as envisages by Recommendation 202.[54] However, the regulations governing PROSPERA do not include mechanisms for the inclusion of informal workers in formal employment, or any link to obtain benefits characterized by social insurance schemes, in accordance with ILO Convention 102 on social security.

The principles analysed have been traced back to the legal framework governing the PROSPERA programme, which consists of decrees and operational rules. However, although these decrees and rules are based on the National Development Act, they do not guarantee the continuance of the programme. The decrees and operational rules are renewed each year, according to the federal expenditure budget and the direction chosen by the government for the country's social policy. Thus, PROSPERA has been in place for almost twenty years, albeit with changes to its name and restructured objectives. Nonetheless, the programme could disappear or change from one year to the next. It is evident that regulations need to be transferred into laws in order to fully comply with Recommendation 202. Moreover, these laws must provide measurable and progressive results.

For PROSPERA, to protect informal workers the most important principles are clearly State responsibility, universal protection with horizontal and vertical coverage, and good governance, because these are the building blocks for the efficient granting of non-discriminatory, coherent and adequate CCTs to Mexico's poor. As the analyses show, these principles need to be much better implemented, both in laws and practice.

Lastly, it can also be concluded that it is necessary to create a comprehensive evaluation agenda that particularly focuses on the priority aspects that would make it possible for the population to find a way out of poverty and take steps toward social insurance within a time frame that allows for coherent and measurable progress in the attainment of objectives because assessments only measure achievements without having a parameter of measureable objectives.

---

54. Fabio Durán-Valverde, *Articulando los programas de protección social en el contexto de la construcción de los pisos de protección social* (ISSA 2012) 4.

BIBLIOGRAPHY

Bracamontes Nevárez, Joaquín & Mario Camberos Castro, *Poverty in Mexico and its Regions: An Impact Analysis of the Oportunidades Program in the Period 2002–2006*, Center for Research in Food and Development, population papers No. 67 (January/March 2011) 169–170.

Bracamontes Nevárez, Joaquín, Mario Camberos Castro & Luis Huesca Reynoso, *The Impact in the Early Years of the Oportunidades Program by Type of Poverty in Mexico and Baja California, 2002–2006*, 15, No. 30 Estudios Fronterizos, nueva época (July–December 2014) 150.

CONASAMI, *General and Professional Minimum Wages* (Mexico, 2016). http://www.gob.mx/conasami/articulos/salarios-minimos-generales-y-profesionales?idiom=es (accessed 18 November 2016).

CONEVAL, *CONEVAL informa los resultados de la medición de la pobreza 2010* (Mexico 2011). http://www.coneval.org.mx/informes/Pobreza%202010/COMUNICADO_PRENSA_MEDICION_DE_POBREZA_2010.pdf.

CONEVAL, *CONEVAL informa los resultados de la medición de pobreza 2014* (Mexico 2015). http://www.coneval.org.mx/SalaPrensa/Documents/Comunicado005_Medicion_pobreza_2014.pdf (accessed 18 November 2016).

CONEVAL, *Evolution of Welfare Lines and Food Basket* (Mexico 2016). http://www.coneval.org.mx/Medicion/MP/Paginas/Lineas-de-bienestar-y-canasta-basica.aspx (accessed 14 November 2016).

CONEVAL, *Informe de la Evaluación Específica de Desempeño 2012-2013 del Programa Oportunidades* (Mexico 2013). https://www.gob.mx/cms/uploads/attachment/file/45145/Ejecutivo.pdf (accessed 18 November 2016).

CONEVAL, *Multidimensional Measurement of Poverty in Mexico: An Economic Wellbeing and Social Rights Approach*. http://www.coneval.org.mx/InformesPublicaciones/FolletosInstitucionales/Documents/Multidimensional-Measurement-of-poverty-in-Mexico.pdf (accessed 28 January 2017).

CONEVAL, *Pobreza en México*. http://www.coneval.org.mx/Medicion/Paginas/PobrezaInicio.aspx (accessed 18 November 2016).

CONEVAL, *Preguntas frecuentes*. http://www.coneval.org.mx/Medicion/Paginas/Preguntas-frecuentes.aspx (accessed 18 November 2016).

Decreto por el que se crea la Coordinación Nacional de PROSPERA Programa de Inclusión Social, Federal Official Gazette (Mexico 2014).

Durán-Valverde, Fabio, *Articulando los programas de protección social en el contexto de la construcción de los pisos de protección social* (ISSA 2012) 4.

ENSANUT, *El programa Oportunidades ¿promueve nacimientos?* https://evaluacion.prospera.gob.mx/es/wersd53465sdg1/otrainfo/oport_fecundidad_insp.pdf (accessed 6 July 2016). http://www.gob.mx/cms/uploads/attachment/file/87896/Registro_de_fallecimientos_primer_trimestre_2016.pdf (accessed 18 November 2016).

INEGI, *Estadísticas a propósito del día internacional del trabajo (1 de mayo)*. http://www.inegi.org.mx/saladeprensa/aproposito/2015/trabajo0.pdf (accessed 22 June 2016).

Lamanna, Francesca, *A Model from Mexico for the World* (World Bank 19 November 2014).

Ley de desarrollo social, Cámara de Diputados, Congreso de la Unión, México, 2016. http://www.diputados.gob.mx/LeyesBiblio/pdf/264_010616.pdf (accessed 18 November 2016).

Ley del Impuesto Sobre la Renta, artículo 186, Diario Oficial de la Federación, http://www.diputados.gob.mx/LeyesBiblio/pdf/LISR_301116.pdf (accessed 18 December 2016).

Marván Laborde, María, *No, no, no tienen hambre* (No, no, not hungry), No. 32 Magazine Facts and Rights (March–April 2016).

Monterrubio, Anavel, *Integración y concatenación de padrones de beneficiarios como factores de transparencia y rendición de cuentas*, No. 77 Reporte CESOP (July 2014).

PROSPERA, *Educación* https://www.prospera.gob.mx/swb/es/PROSPERA2015/Educacion (accessed 18 November 2016).

PROSPERA, *Es prospera un programa social de vanguardia a nivel mundial* (Mexico 15 March 2016). http://www.gob.mx/prospera/prensa/es-prospera-un-programa-social-de-vanguardia-a-nivel-mundial-23264 (accessed 18 November 2016).

PROSPERA, *Lineamientos Operativos del Programa Prospera*. https://www.gob.mx/cms/uploads/attachment/file/139143/LINEAMIENTOS_OPERATIVOS_2016._APROBADOS_CT__9_DE_SEPTIEMBRE_2016.pdf (accessed 18 November 2016).

PROSPERA, *Preguntas frecuentes*. https://www.prospera.gob.mx/swb/es/PROSPERA2015/Preguntas_frecuentes (accessed 18 November 2016).

PROSPERA, *Reglas de Operación de PROSPERA Programa de Inclusión Social, para el ejercicio fiscal 2016* (Mexico, 2016). https://www.prospera.gob.mx/swb/work/Web2015/documentos/Rop_para_ejercicio_fiscal%202016.pdf (accessed 9 May 2016).

Provencio Durazo, Enrique, *Situación actual y reforma de la seguridad social en México* (Jesuswaldo Martínez Soria ed., Instituto Belisario Domínguez del Senado de la República, 2015).

Reglas de Operación de PROSPERA Programa de Inclusión Social, para el ejercicio fiscal 2016, Federal Official Gazette (Mexico, 2016), https://www.prospera.gob.mx/swb/work/Web2015/documentos/Rop_para_ejercicio_fiscal%202016.pdf (accessed 9 May 2016).

Rosario Ruiz, Moreno María del, *El seguro popular, un penoso engaño social para los pobres* (Ángel Guillermo Ruiz Moreno ed., Mexico, Porrúa 2007).

SEDESOL, *Oportunidades.* http://www.sedesol.gob.mx/work/models/SEDESOL/Transparencia/TransparenciaFocalizada/Programas_Sociales/pdf/oportunidades.pdf (accessed 18 November 2016).

SEDESOL, *Padrón de beneficiarios,* (Mexico, 2016). http://pub.sedesol.gob.mx/spp (accessed 11 November 2016).

SEDESOL, *Programa Seguro de Vida para Jefas de Familia cifras al primer trimestre de 2016* (Mexico 2016).

SEDESOL, *Reconoce la FAO a México por reducir la subalimentación un año antes de lo previsto,* (Mexico 2015). http://www.gob.mx/sedesol/prensa/reconoce-la-fao-a-mexico-por-reducir-la-subalimentacion-un-ano-antes-de-lo-prevists.

CHAPTER 7
Argentina: From an Emblematic Case to Its Institutionalization – An Analysis of the Universal Child Allowance for Social Protection

*Laura Pautassi**

7.1 INTRODUCTION

The Argentine Republic, as a Federal State comprised of twenty-three provinces and an autonomous city (Buenos Aires), has distinguished itself in the context of Latin American countries for having developed early on a welfare system with 'hybrid' characteristics. From mid-1945 onwards, the foundation was laid for a protectionary system which combined different social risk insurance principles based on the contributory capacity of formal salaried workers, mainly men, with coverage for health care, old-age and disability insurance, protection for work-related accidents or illnesses and a system of allowances aimed at guaranteeing the growth and expansion of the nuclear family of the workers. That is to say, a broad social security scheme that was based on a strong legal framework related to the right to work and to social security.

In the Latin American tradition, the international human rights treaties – both from the international system and the Inter-American human rights system – and the ILO Conventions have a significant influence on specific legislative systems, particularly as regards the right to work and social security, as guidelines for the law. According to a 1994 constitutional amendment, international treaties take precedence over ordinary law without having constitutional

---

* I am very grateful for the assistance from Lorena Balardini and Laura Royo. I also appreciate the translation by Jane Scott. A special thank you to Tineke Dijkhoff for the commentary.

rank. However, a list of international human rights declarations and international covenants on human rights are declared part of the constitution.

Argentina, which has been a Member of the ILO since 1919, has ratified eighty-two ILO Conventions and two Protocols, of which sixty-one are in force, eighteen have been denounced and two have been ratified in the last twelve months.[1] Among the fundamental Conventions ratified are C29, C87, C98, C100, C105, C111, C138 and the most recent technical Conventions Argentina has ratified – C184, C186 and C189 – are all in force. By Law No. 26.678, Argentina adopted Convention No. 102 concerning Minimum Standards of Social Security, ratified in 2016 and it will enter into force in July 2017.

In this way, the constituent basis for social security presumes a protection dynamic which is connected to the relationship with the formal labour market. This dynamic has significant gender bias as the allowance is based on the male being the main provider of family income and social services, and the woman being in charge of household tasks.

These institutional arrangements based on the recognition of paid work as the only way to access services and at the same time the transfer of responsibilities of care in an exclusive and excluding manner to women, introduced a dynamic that gave hierarchy to paid work and entitlement to the social security right to the men of the household, leaving women unprotected, and allowing access only to social services through their husbands. In other words, entitlement to the main core of social risk coverage is given to the male and is extended to their wives and children who access the social benefits not through their own rights but rather as a derivative of their relationship with the salaried worker.[2]

This institutional scheme, based mainly on the contributory capacity of the workers, was complemented by two universal institutions, education and health. Under this scheme, the State guaranteed the supply subsidy at all levels, in the education system (from primary education to university) as well as the health system with a wide institutional network (including primary care to tertiary care) ensuring that services were free at the point of access and coverage was universal.

The economic base for this 'hybrid' regimen was purely Keynesian with a strong intervening role of the State in the economy which strengthened the contributory system which was maintained, including after the wave of neoliberal reforms of the 1990s. These reforms implied a dismantling of the State's regulatory capacity of the economy which had a strong impact on the regional

---

1. Source: http://www.ilo.org/dyn/normlex/es/f?p=NORMLEXPUB:11200:0::NO::P11200_COUNTRY_ID:102536.
2. Pautassi, Laura ¿Bailarinas en la oscuridad? Seguridad social en América Latina el marco de la equidad de género. Paper presented in the Thirty-Eighth Meeting of the General Committee of the Regional Conference on Latin American and Caribbean Women (Mar del Plata, 7 and 8 Sep. 2005).

economies and involved a transfer of responsibilities for public provision from the national government to the provinces.[3]

Meanwhile, the functioning of the labour market was to show signs of structural change, with an increase in female labour force participation, but mostly on an informal basis, and with high unemployment rates, underemployment with marked gender gaps and an ongoing process of regulatory change, mainly at the level of the individual employment relationship, in labour regulations among others. Nevertheless, the 'contributory' matrix continues to be the main basis for redistribution of social benefits, even despite the significant increases in non-contributory services and allowances.

In fact, the Argentine case demonstrates a growing gap between the basis of the formulation of a welfare regime established during the second half of the twentieth century, that remained stable, and the structure of social risks inherent to the intense economic and social transformations occurring at the beginning of the twenty-first century, producing strong inconsistencies between the institutions and the solutions provided to citizens.[4] It is since the turn of the new millennium, that the importance of the non-contributory systems, especially through income transfer programmes, has begun to take a turn in terms of coverage, impact and increase in resources for non-contributory services.

In this context, the Argentine government created the first Decent Work Programme (2004-2007) as the central nucleus of inclusion and social protection policies, followed by a second (2008-2011), and the third 'Decent Work Programme per Country 2012-2015', which was launched in July 2012.[5] In the latter, the signatories set out the fourth priority objective: 'Consolidate the extension of social protection coverage and promote the culture of prevention of occupational risks', in which policies were framed according to the principles of ILO Convention No. 102 and Recommendation No. 202, establishing results to be achieved and indicators of compliance. Moreover, to achieve these objectives, the ILO assumes the commitment of technical assistance to the government, social actors and other social organizations.

The experience in Argentina presents with characteristics of a Federal State, with local peculiarities and relevant institutional fragmentation. Within

---

3. The 'hybrid' concept is attributed to Rubén Lo Vuolo and Alberto Barbeito: Lo Vuolo Rubén & Alberto Barbeito, *La Nueva oscuridad de la política social* (Miño & Dávila eds, Buenos Aires, 1998); while Aldo Isuani (2014) refers to it as 'enduring and resistant': A. Isuani, *The Argentine Welfare State: Enduring and Resisting Change*, International Journal of Social Welfare 19 Issue 1, 104-114 (2014); and Laura Pautassi and Gustavo Gamallo (2015) identify the welfare gaps that this dynamic has produced: Pautassi Laura & Gustavo Gamallo, *El bienestar en brechas. Las políticas sociales en la Argentina de la postconvertibilidad* (Buenos Aires, Editorial Biblos 2015).
4. Pautassi Laura & Gustavo Gamallo, *El bienestar en brechas. Las políticas sociales en la Argentina de la postconvertibilidad* (Buenos Aires, Editorial Biblos 2015).
5. The agreements were signed by the Argentine government, representatives of employers and workers' organizations, and the ILO Office for Argentina. Available at: http://www.ilo.org/buenosaires/lang--es/index.htm.

this framework, both Convention No. 102 and Recommendation No. 202 are inserted into a protective structure with strong contributory components, but with an insufficient level of formality and economic development, coupled with a significant gap in income distribution.[6]

7.2 THE PROCESS OF INCORPORATING A SOCIAL PROTECTION FLOOR

7.2.1 Background

During the 1990s, approximately twenty transitory employment programmes were implemented for those who were unemployed, consisting of the provision of a 'non-remunerative economic assistance' in exchange for four hours a day of mandatory work for the beneficiaries. These programmes had limited coverage and although their names were changed several times, large changes to their dynamic and the benefits provided were not made.[7]

The Plan for Unemployed Household Heads (*Plan Jefes y Jefas de Hogar Desocupados* (PJJHD)) was the first conditional cash transfer programme which was implemented on a large scale. Later, in 2003–2004 the State implemented new social programmes that continued, to a large extent, the logic of assistance programmes as tools for alleviating extreme poverty. One such programme is the Programme for the Social Inclusion of Families (*Programa Familias por la Inclusión Social* (IDH)). These programmes are aimed at resolving social conflict and at preventing the exacerbation of poverty and inequality caused by the serious political and institutional crisis that occurred in Argentina in December 2001.

In September 2006, there were 1,271,886 beneficiaries of PJJHD, each receiving an allowance of about Argentine Pesos (ARS) 150 (about United States Dollars (USD) 42),[8] according to data from the Ministry of Labour. The amount of the benefit, which was a single benefit per household and incompatible with a minimum wage, was fixed directly by the Executive Branch without establishing criteria for any increase. In the six-year duration of the programme, it was never modified, being completely misaligned given the levels of inflation and insufficient to meet needs and at least access to the essential institutions that guarantee a minimum standard of living. In the case of the programme for

---

6. Bertranou, Fabio et al., *Performance of Social Protection in Argentina. Assessment of Two Decades of Reforms* (Buenos Aires, ILO Country Office for Argentina 2016).
7. Pautassi Laura, *Social Security Standards in Latin America*, in *International Standard-Setting and Innovations in Social Security* 73-88 (U. Becker, F. Pennings and T. Dijkhoff eds., Kluwer Law International, 2013). In addition to that, they had a policy logic of 'until' they join the formal economy. In general, execution was mainly handled by the Ministry of Work and the Ministry of Social Development: Arcidiácono, Pilar. *La política del 'mientras tanto'. Programas sociales después de la crisis 2001-2002* (Biblos 2012).
8. In 2001, the subsidy was equivalent to 75% of the minimum wage. In July 2005, it represented only 23.8% of the minimum wage.

families, the allowance for each family was ARS 150 per beneficiary with two children, plus an additional ARS 25 per child, up to a maximum of six children, and ARS 275. This programme had 323,138 beneficiaries in September 2006, most of whom were women.

In spite of the magnitude of the social plans implemented in the country during the recession, the reduction in the poverty rate in 2002–2006 can hardly be attributed to them, as they were designed to alleviate rather than to overcome poverty. The PJJHD was responsible, in 2004, for a reduction of about three percentage points in the indigence rate and less than one percentage point in the poverty rate (from 18.2% to 15%, and from 40.9% to 40.2%, respectively according to the National Institute of Statistics and Censuses). The existence of a large population excluded from the formal labour market and the stability of the very high levels of poverty call for the implementation of reduction strategies and effective mechanisms to overcome poverty. The intensity of indigence and poverty is not uniform: there are significant differences by region, gender and age.[9]

These measures quickly revealed their limitations. In the first place because although they included an important increase in coverage and they were extremely relevant for 'containing' a crisis of the magnitude that had occurred in Argentina, they proved to be insufficient, *inter alia*, because the PJJHD was a self-targeted transitory measure whose request period lasted for less than two months and whose inscription closed on 17 May 2002. This short period left a large number of potential beneficiaries without the possibility of being able to request the benefit, many of whom took legal action.[10] Something similar happened with IDH, in addition to the fact that the transfers were not increased, which diluted their purchasing power due to inflation.[11]

7.2.2 Universal Child Allowance for Social Protection (AUH)

From the ILO office in Argentina, there is recognition of the existence of previous work done from the mid-1990s to 2003, identifying the application of the Social Protection Expenditure Review (SPER) methodology to the case of Argentina. In this context, the terminology 'social protection' broadly refers to the set of policies, schemes and programmes that involve not only social security but also other cash and in-kind transfer programmes, usually not covered as part of

---

9. Faur, Eleonor et al., *Rights Questioned. Limitations of Poverty-Reduction Policies in Argentina*, 60 Issue 197-198 International Social Science Journal (2010).
10. Center for Legal and Social Studies (*Centro de Estudios Legales y Sociales* (CELS), *Las pensiones por vejez frente al derecho a la seguridad social* (Buenos Aires 2010).
11. Arcidiácono, Pilar. *La política del 'mientras tanto'. Programas sociales después de la crisis 2001-2002* (Biblos 2012); Center for Legal and Social Studies, *Programa Familias por la Inclusión Social. Entre el discurso de derechos y la práctica asistencial* (Buenos Aires 2007).

traditional social security. That is to say, the concept had already been introduced, and was then taken up within the framework of the application of Recommendation No. 202.

In 2009, in the context of economic recovery, the Universal Child Allowance for Social Protection (AUH) was implemented by decision of President Cristina Fernández, commencing a new implementation process with a minimum social protection floor that two years later in 2011 was extended to transfers to pregnant women or Universal Allowance for Pregnant Women (AUE).[12]

Both programmes, still in force, have become the third component of social security in Argentina. In the first place, they recognize the informal labour situation and expand the formal Family Allowances (AAFF) regime to include those who have historically been excluded. Second, this measure absorbs the previous programmes by declaring them incompatible and transfers the responsibility of execution to the National Social Security Administration (ANSES) that up to now has only handled the management of the social security contributory system. Finally, with the AUH, children and adolescents are the ones entitled to the transfer with the obligation that they regularly attend school and have periodic health checks.

The two allowance schemes (AUH and AAFF) have mechanisms for access, requirements, amounts and demands which are different. In addition to this, there are also other transfer options such as deductions for 'family expenses' from income tax and non-contributory pensions for mothers of more than seven children administered by the Ministry of Social Development. The fragmentation – and in many cases the disintegration – constitutes a structural characteristic of the social security system in Argentina from its beginning.

On the other hand, and also as a characteristic of the welfare system, new inequalities within the system have been generated amongst the people covered by these social protection measures and that do not necessarily relate to their informal labour status, but rather are inequalities inherent to the system.

The AUH programme is dealt with in depth throughout this chapter, which presents its main characteristics, its connection with the standards established in ILO Recommendation No. 202, its conditionalities and current modifications and concludes with the main impacts of the measure. The methodological approach is from a rights and gender focus, based on official information sources and secondary studies.

---

12. Bertranou, Fabio et al., *Desempeño y financiamiento de la protección social en Argentina: consideraciones a partir de la Recomendación núm. 202 sobre pisos de protección social*, Oficina de País de la OIT para Argentina (ILO 2015).

Chapter 7: Argentina: From an Emblematic Case to Its Institutionalization

7.3 ASSESSMENT OF THE AUH ON THE BASIS OF THE PRINCIPLES

7.3.1 State Responsibility

As was previously mentioned, from 2003, the government began to focus on two types of measures:

(1) Reforms with regards to formal salaried employment, in the context of the implementation of the three Decent Work Programmes, particularly: the recomposition of salaries, the repeal of labour flexibilization reforms, the limitation of employer's powers, the reopening of collective bargaining processes and reforms related to the welfare system and to family allowances.[13] Likewise, two tranches of the programme were implemented for the registration of employment, with the creation of the Integral System of Labour Inspection and Social Security (Law No. 25,877) and the National Employment Regularization Plan (PNRT) with results below expectations.[14]

(2) Measures for the informal and excluded sectors: with a large set of social assistance programmes such as transfers related to the PJJHD, IDH as well as in the health (e.g., *Plan Nacer-Sumar*), education and social assistance areas. These measures are framed in the floors of social protection and the overall strategy of decent employment for Argentina.[15]

At the legislative branch level, the debate deepened regarding the possibility of universalizing the family allowance system. In Argentina, there were various records of Bills that were presented by different social sectors regarding citizens' income (Basic or Citizen Income) to guarantee benefits for all children and adolescents, and other Bills that contemplated more limited transfers. That is to say, there was a specific demand by various political and social sectors (social organizations, labour unions, academic institutions, and the Catholic Church) to modify the family allowance system and extend the services.[16] However, it should be noted that the creation of the AUH is framed within the general guidelines of the Social Protection Floors. Instead, proposals like 'Citizen

---

13. Pautassi, Laura et al., *Asignación Universal por Hijo para Protección Social de la Argentina. Entre la satisfacción de necesidades y el reconocimiento de derechos*. División de Políticas Sociales, CEPAL, Number 184 (Santiago de Chile 2013).
14. In Argentina in 2012, 44.3% of workers worked in the formal private market while 43.2% worked in the informal market, and 12.5% in government administration (Lindemboin and Salvia 2012), these trends have yet to be reversed.
15. Bertranou, Fabio et al., *Desempeño y financiamiento de la protección social en Argentina: consideraciones a partir de la Recomendación núm. 202 sobre pisos de protección social*, Oficina de País de la OIT para Argentina (ILO 2015).
16. Bestard, Ana María et al., *El Poder Legislativo Nacional y los programas sociales en el período 2002-2009* (L. Pautassi and G. Gamallo eds. Biblos 2012).

Income' are part of the logic of guaranteeing a right to income and not a right to work, marking a significant difference with the measure adopted. Thus, point 5(c) of Recommendation No. 202 indicates as a guarantee the 'basic income security, at least at a nationally defined minimum level, for persons in active age who are unable to earn sufficient income, in particular in cases of sickness, unemployment, maternity and disability'. The difference with the proposals for citizen income was that they extended the unconditional transfer to all the children and adolescents, irrespective of the employment situation of their parents. Instead, the AUH relates the perception of the cash transfer to the employment situation of the child's parent.

In relation to the AUH, Argentina satisfies its primary responsibility of establishing and maintaining a social protection floor comprising basic income security, at least at a nationally defined minimum level. Moreover, some years after being implemented, the AUH was enshrined in law so this minimum standard was firmly established.

7.3.2 Universality of Protection

With regards to entitlement to access, it was established that only one of the parents would receive the benefit, giving priority to the mother,[17] which explains why 94.4% of people who receive AUH are women who are mothers or guardians aged between 30 and 34 years. It requires at the same time, that the children and adults who are recipients are Argentinian, naturalized or legal residents for a period of no less than three years. That is to say, it excludes migrant workers, which provoked criticism by the Committee on the Protection of the Rights of All Migrant Workers and the Members of their Families, and the Committee on Economic, Social and Cultural rights – both Committees of the United Nations.[18]

Considering the recipients of the measure, there is no doubt that there will be an increased risk of problems relating to documentation since a high percentage of children and adolescents do not have documents due to various circumstances including their migratory status. This type of requirement, especially for migrants, contrasts with important regulatory changes made since the approval of Law 25,871 in 2004, which considerably broadened the rights of migrant workers in Argentina.

Likewise, in 2015 the new government's 'zero poverty' objective falls within its plan, whose main strategy is to strengthen the AUH by extending the benefits to those who have been previously excluded, such as self-employed

---

17. In accordance with Art. 10 of Res. 393/09, which states: 'when the custody of the child, adolescent or disabled person is shared by both parents, the mother shall have preference over the father with regard to the entitlement to the benefit'.
18. Ceriani, Pablo et al., *Migración, derechos de la niñez y Asignación Universal por Hijo: las fronteras de la inclusión social*, http://conti.derhuman.jus.gov.ar/2011/10/mesa_2/ceriani_cyment_morales_mesa_2.pdf (Accessed 21 Mar. 2017).

workers.[19] The Decree 593/16 incorporates self-employed workers[20] into the Family Allowance system, which is an expansion of the AAFF, and not of the AUH, which covers the rest of the informal workers, unemployed workers and domestic employees. That is to say, the benefit has been incorporated into the formal allowance,[21] but these benefits are lower in amount than those of the AUH and are not the same benefits as those of the AAFF.

Even though the AUH exists through the discursiveness, and its classification as universal, it is not a universal benefit. Although there have been several modifications to expand coverage, groups of children still remain without access to any social protection.

In the case of AUH, conditionalities are called 'considerations' and involve the continual certification of school attendance and periodic health checks, in particular in respect of vaccinations and the monitoring of pregnant women. However, not only are beneficiaries required to present documents of proof, but the element of control is greater. Mechanisms were established by which 20% of the benefit is retained on a monthly basis until compliance is demonstrated on an annual basis. Currently, each beneficiary receives the monthly sum of ARS 1,100 (USD 74) for each child, but by retaining 20%, this amount is reduced to ARS 882.40 (USD 58.50) and the remaining ARS 220.60 (USD 14.50) is paid upon presentation of a properly completed and certified form. In the case of AUE, the same amount is received as for AUH. In the case of a child with a disability, without any age limit, the amount is ARS 3,597 (USD 240) with the same retaining mechanism. There are cases of regionally disadvantaged areas where the amount of the AUH is higher.

In accordance with ANSES reports, the following numbers of suspensions were made between 2011 and 2014: 221,836, 541,222, 691,443 and 665,632, respectively. These suspensions are evidence of supply problems in terms of health services and education insofar as the beneficiaries have not been able to comply with the respective requirements or that they received an income above the minimum salary.[22]

Without doubt, the impact in terms of coverage is notable and after almost seven years of implementation, is irrefutable. Only by way of example, and in

---

19. This plan is a simplified tax regimen where contribution categories relating to a presumed income are assumed. The services covered relate to health insurance and pension contributions, and do not cover access to family allowances. In the case of those in the lowest categories or single taxpayers in a situation of vulnerability, they were not eligible to receive AUH.
20. Self-employment is earning a living through doing something by oneself. The informal sector or informal economy is the part of an economy that is neither taxed, nor monitored by any form of government.
21. Pilar Arcidiácono 2016, *La asignación Universal en su laberinto* (Buenos Aires, Revista Bordes June 2016).makes a detailed analysis of the regulation and official communicative action to identify what was incorporated and what was left out.
22. Cited by Arcidiácono, Pilar *La asignación Universal en su laberinto* (Buenos Aires, Revista Bordes June 2016).

the absence of other records, approximately 75% of children and adolescents in Argentina would be entitled to some type of transfer.[23]

7.3.3 Entitlements Based on Law and Non-discrimination

In October 2009, President Cristina Fernández created by decree the Universal Child Allowance for Social Protection (Decree 1602/09) (AUH), as a non-contributory subsystem within the regimen of formal family allowances, under jurisdiction of the National Social Security Administration (ANSES), for informal and unemployed workers that do not receive any insurance as a result of their informality. A year and a half later, during the opening of the legislative sessions, the creation of the Universal Allowance for Pregnant Women (Decree 446/11) (AUE) was announced. Both initiatives are now in force. Those interested can approach the offices of the ANSES that are located throughout the country and, if they comply with the requirements stipulated by the policy, can begin to collect the benefit. This implies that the programme is 'self-targeting'. There is no information on the existence of particular complaint mechanisms.

In both cases, and contrary to Article 7 of Recommendation No. 202, the implementation of these measures did not follow the suggested legislative path, but rather it was based on the use by the head of the executive branch of a regulated exceptional measure at a moment, as was stated, when there were already Bills that proposed similar measures. From the former executive power, there was no explanation as to why it was decided to create the AUH by decree and not to take any of the parliamentary initiatives that were to be debated before the National Congress. At the time of signing the decree, various civil organizations and academics regretted that it had been established as a government decision and not through a State law that transcended the current government.

The AUH is for children and adolescents (up to 18 years of age except in the case of children with disabilities have no age limit) whose mothers and fathers or guardians or tutors are unemployed or work in the informal economy with a salary below the minimum living wage, or for pregnant women up to 18 years of age. According to the Law on Employment Contracts, the Adjustable Minimum Living Wage is defined as 'the lowest remuneration that a worker without family dependents should receive in cash for a legal work day, in such a way as to ensure adequate food, decent housing, education, clothing, health care, transportation and leisure, vacations and planning for future'. The minimum wage value is determined in a tripartite manner by the National Board of Employment, Productivity and Minimum Wage. Currently it is ARS 8,060 (USD 538).

---

23. In 2011, 42.5% of children and adolescents younger than the age of 18 received AAFF while 24.9% received AUH. Pensions and other social benefits were received by 4%, deductions for income tax were received by 3.2%, meanwhile 12.4% did not have any coverage, and 13.1% were excluded from the regulations that provide access to benefits. Ministry of Work, Employment and Social Security (2014).

Moreover, the expansion of AAFF to self-employed workers in 2016 did not authorize the receipt of AUH but rather strengthened a structure of different exceptions to the common rule that implies leaving them unprotected from contingencies related to the growth and expansion of the family nucleus.

7.3.4 Adequacy and Predictability of Benefits

If we consider that currently 3,897,334 children and adolescents currently receive AUH, of which 24,822 have a disability and there are 77,203 pregnant women who are covered by AUE,[24] the importance of the programme is clear. It must be taken into account that the amount of the AUH only helps to avoid falling into indigence and far from guarantees an adequate standard of living; it is not designed as a policy that seeks to articulate or give comprehensive answers to poverty issue.

The following table presents a comparison of formal family allowances (contributory) with the AUH (non-contributory) in accordance with official ANSES data from 2015.

Table 7.1 Coverage by Type of Allowance, Argentina, 2015

Type of Allowance/Date	Formal Family Allowance	Universal Child Allowance
June 2015	1,866,287	3,385,490
December 2015	1,687,480	3,723,763

Source: prepared by the author based on ANSES http://www.transparencia.anses.gob.ar/anses-numeros/asignaciones-universales (accessed 29 November 2016).

Regarding the access to information by the potential beneficiaries, it is unequal. On one hand, many have difficulties with understanding and accessing the different protectionary schemes, or in any case, with being able to process why one system protects them and another system or service does not. From the perspective of the children and adolescents, even though they are the ones entitled to the benefit and this is how they internalize it, the scope, characteristic and dynamic of this benefit is inseparable from the labour status of their parents. The migratory status or criminal record also prevents the exercise of each child or adolescent of their right to receive this benefit.

In other words, the 3,897,334 beneficiaries of AUH demonstrate that the non-contributory component is far from being residual within the system. The main question is regarding the continuity of these institutional responses that should have made progress in increasing minimum social protection floors.

---

24. ANSES, http://www.transparencia.anses.gob.ar/anses-numeros/asignaciones-universales (accessed 29 Dec. 2016).

To summarize, the relationship between the entitlement to the AUH and the labour status of the adults presents particular problems in an unstable job market. Due to this, the ANSES Resolution No. 532/11 established a one-time payment of two extra months to those people that move from unemployment or the informal market to the formal market as a way to ensure continuity of the benefit. This measure demonstrates the problems of a measure that conditions the transfer meant for children and adolescents upon the labour status or career path of the adult because it guarantees the continuity of the perception regardless of whether the parents of the children work in the formal or informal sector.

7.3.5 Non-discrimination

The AUH programme depends primarily on women, the 'mothers' for the purposes of the programme, who must guarantee obligatory and regular attendance at educational establishments and periodic health checks. This direct transfer of responsibilities however has not been accompanied by an investment in the care infrastructure that would reduce the burden responsibility on women and redistribute the care tasks. That is to say, strategies to promote the distribution of care between both parents have not been contemplated, creating an important gender bias in the welfare system that presumes the mothers to be the only ones responsible for children and adolescents.

The lack of consideration for the burden of responsibility for care of these programmes has not been considered in any of the transfer programmes that have been implemented in the region. This only strengthens the traditional and 'naturalized' concept that those who should provide care are the mothers. In this sense, both the AUH as well as the AUE give privilege to the women as beneficiaries, because the ANSES during the implementation of the programme presume that they will make 'better use of the resource', and the regulations do not include within the State responsibilities the provision of services and the infrastructure of care, or mechanisms aimed at improving articulation between the programme and the demands for care that exist in each one of the areas involved.

For example, efficient mechanisms to avoid women having to spend hours waiting with children in public hospitals were not considered and in many cases, no thought was given as to how women will get to the health care centres, especially those who live in remote or rural areas. The relationship between transfer programmes and public transportation policies should be a central concern. Likewise this issue in the context of the female responsibility for care and of the workload that this represents for the beneficiaries of the transfer programme is also not addressed in Recommendation No. 202, remaining once again silent on the matter.

On the other hand, since the demand for care is so important without there being any means and tools available to address the issues; added to the fact that that there is a regulation establishing the termination of the transfer if the beneficiary assumes paid tasks that represent an income equivalent or higher than the minimum salary, there is a large disincentive for women to seek work.

In other words, the responsibility for care of various generations has been transferred via these programmes without anyone taking note of the living situation of those who take on this unpaid work. At the moment, they are active middle-aged women, with an average of three to five children, with a low educational level and without development of a sustained work history. We should ask ourselves what will the future bring once their children become adults? They will not receive AUH or AUE nor have they been encouraged to finish school or professional training or take any other type of action promoting independence.[25] They do not tend to enter the social security system given the most contributory character of the system other than the permanence in the informal labour market, and the lack of educational qualifications and a sustained history of inclusion in the labour market mean that the system will not be of help in the future, indeed, on the contrary. The fact that entitlement to the social benefit has been given to the children and adolescents do not exempt the State from the responsibility to take urgent measures and actions that include women with care responsibilities.

At the same time, if the women do not prove that they care for the children or adolescents, they no longer receive the benefit, and in fact, a percentage of the amount of the benefit is retained until the 'mother' certifies that she has carried out her duties. That is to say, the exercise of the right to health and education of the children and adolescents which is given a 'co-responsibility' treatment by the welfare system is directly dependent on the work of the women. A large part of the success attributed to the increase in school registration and vital statistics is not from the programme in and of itself, which is undoubtedly a significant stimulus, but rather from the commitment of the women to compliance. That is to say, universality is guaranteed because of the ongoing and unseen work of the mothers. In fact, it is 'preferred' that they be the beneficiaries because they know how to make 'good use' of the benefit.

If we return to Recommendation No. 202, Article 3, paragraph a), which states: 'a) universality of the protection, based on social solidarity', the unpaid task of care should not be included in this concept, since far from being an evaluative activity, it is a job that contributes to the generation of economic value.[26] This is one of the main aspects that should be evaluated in light of

---

25. In 2013, a programme for vulnerable women with at least three children who are victims of domestic violence and are beneficiaries of AUH was implemented by the Ministry of Social Development, which includes them in a cooperative work dynamic and establishes a component of mandatory completion of school studies. This programme, called *Ellas Hacen* (*Women they do it*), is still in force and is an attempt at a more comprehensive response for women.
26. Just as the feminist economists in the region asserted: Razavi, Sheila *The Political and Social Economy of Care in a Development Context Conceptual Issues, Research Questions and Policy Options* (UNRISD, 2007) and Rodríguez Enríquez, Corina *La cuestión del cuidado ¿el eslabón perdido del análisis económico?* 109 Revista Cepal, 23-36 (2012).

Recommendation No. 202 and the rest of the framework of the transfer programme.

On the other hand, the AUH covers a maximum of five children per family, without regard, for example, as to whether, when there is a family with six children, the sixth child is left without coverage. Families with seven children are covered by another programme which is the non-contributory pension for mothers with seven children, administered by the National Ministry of Social Development.[27]

The first point to highlight based on Recommendation No. 202 is the exclusion of the sixth child that had already existed under the IDH Plan that established the same limit. In this case, there are no arguable ways for the ANSES to justify the discrimination against the sixth child leaving him/her out of the perceived benefit.

A second point is that the AUH decree requires sons and daughters of beneficiaries to attend school in the national public education system, leaving aside approximately 30% of children and adolescents who attend private schools. However, at the moment of putting the system into place, controls were not put in place, so this did not act as an excluding factor (private schools). Hence, the discrimination appears in the regulation and not during the implementation of the AUH because the exception was made.

During the implementation of the programme, allowances for children of temporary registered workers from the agricultural sector and of domestic employees were also implemented. In this last case, and given that in 2013 an employment regimen for domestic employees was approved (Law 26,844/13) that repealed discriminatory rules that placed them below other employees, these employees are now entitled to the maternity leave of the contributory system, at the same that they receive the AUE and AUH corresponding to the 'non-contributory' sub-component. That is to say, a sort of 'mix of services' between both systems was produced.

Likewise, and in addition to the aforementioned restrictions, during the course of the implementation of AUH, groups began to emerge that had not been included despite being vulnerable. In this case, I am referring specifically to the people deprived of their liberty and within this group, a group of mothers with children younger than 4 years of age in an incarcerated setting. This case deals specifically with approximately thirty women deprived of liberty who are involved in a prison labour programme who have filed for legal action after ANSES refused to grant them the social benefit. The National Prisoner's Ombudsman Office of Argentina filed a collective corrective habeas corpus for this group in order to request their inclusion, and obtained by the end of 2015 a favourable judgment in the Federal Criminal Cassation Chamber.[28] However, ANSES has filed an appeal with the National Supreme Court of Justice. Taking a

---

27. http://www.desarrollosocial.gob.ar/pensiones.
28. Case 58330/2014, *Internas Unidad 31 s/ Habeas Corpus*, cited by Pilar Arcidiácono 2016, *supra* n. 22.

case to the highest State court in order to claim a benefit from a transfer programme is a unique precedent in the region.

7.3.6 Financial Solidarity

As already mentioned, another one of the distinctive features of this measure was its placement with ANSES (traditional institute for contributory social security) in an attempt to consolidate the contributory benefits (associated with formal work) and the extension to informal employment sectors and to a lesser degree, the unemployed (non-contributory). This change in institutional structure is in line with the framework of Recommendation No. 202, which explicitly recognizes informal labour and extends benefits for formal workers to informal workers.

ANSES's funding scheme has historically been based on the contributions of workers and employers and as such the introduction of AUH, extending the benefit to those who have not contributed in the context of a salaried relationship, marked a positive step forward in terms of financial solidarity. Furthermore, since the benefit does not come from exclusively contributory funds, but rather it is diversified, those who access its benefits participate indirectly in its funding by means of a consumption tax (value added tax and other tax resources). This is one of the newest characteristics of the AUH, since the State is taking responsibility for the absence of or lower level of contributions due to the informality of the labour market. This point marks an important difference with the other transfer programmes. In order for informal workers and the unemployed to access the AUH, the State assumes the contribution that is not made from the economy. That is to say, that the State assumes responsibility in some way for the contribution that the employers do not make for the informals.

In addition to the recognition of the informal labour market, other distinctive features of the AUH with respect to other income transfer programmes in force in Latin America are: (a) the permanent and open access for people selected as beneficiaries (unlike previous conditional transfer programmes that established a programme end date); (b) the increase in the amounts of the benefits;[29] and (c) the means of funding it, which in contrast to other programmes, did not come from an international credit assistance institution but rather from social security resources (ANSES).

---

29. Since its implementation, increases in the value of the monthly allowance were established by the executive branch, and following the approval of Law 27,160 in July 2015 increases in the amounts of the allowance as well as the ranges of income for entitlement to the benefit have been regulated.

7.3.7 Good Governance

According to data from 2014, the AUH accounts for 0.8% of Gross Domestic Product (GDP) and covers approximately 15% of households (1.8 million households with 3,500,000 children and teenagers).[30] The AUH is one of the programmes that uses more resources in the region. Its sources of financing come from the pension system and the resources generated by the Sustainability Guarantee Fund (FGS). This fund is part of the national budget that must be used for social security. In the case of formal Family Allowances, they are financed with contributory resources. According to ILO, in 2013 the amount allocated to the social protection of children and adolescents was 0.99% of GDP, with the main components being the AUH with 0.47%, and the AAFF, with a 0.44%. Family allowances of provincial governments and tax credits are excluded.[31]

In relation to Article 3(j) of Recommendation No. 202, financial and non-contributory funds are applied. Hence, it is reiterated that the key information is that the administration of the AUH is undertaken by the ANSES and not the Ministry of Social Development, institutionalizing a strategy of social protection in the same management entity. In this sense, it is important to add that the AUH is part of this social floor protection, and it is not considered as a classic cash transfer programme.

7.3.8 Coherence of Policies

The Universal Child Benefit co-exists with an older system called Social Security Inclusion Programme created to guarantee a minimum social protection floor for older adults. In 2005, this Social Security Inclusion Programme was implemented, which is in reality a pension fund moratorium.[32] Generally speaking, it consisted of all those people who had not made the required number of years of contributions applying for a debt repayment plan, and all the periods (months declared in the repayment plan) had to fall under the category of self-employed workers. They could declare through an affidavit for up to a maximum of seven years of contributions for work carried out as an employee or a self-employed worker. That is to say, the procedure was relatively simple.

Up to the last quarter of 2010, more than 2.5 million people were incorporated into the national pension system under the framework of this mechanism. This, together with the increase in the number of non-contributory pensions, has

---

30. Maurizio Roxana & Gustavo Vázquez, *Argentina: efectos del programa Asignación Universal por Hijo en el comportamiento laboral de los adultos* in *Revista de la CEPAL, N° 113*, Comisión Económica para América Latina y el Caribe (Santiago de Chile, August 2015).
31. Bertranou, Fabio et al., *Performance of Social Protection in Argentina. Assessment of Two Decades of Reforms* (Buenos Aires, ILO Country Office for Argentina 2016).
32. The programme was included within the laws that contained the pension system (Laws 25,994; 24,476; and 24,241), in addition to Law 25,994 (2015) that allowed for registration up to April of 2007. Subsequently, a second moratorium was offered (2014).

had a strong impact on ANSES at the operative as well as budgetary level. The results of this pension moratorium are a striking example of how the gender gaps in the labour market are reproduced in the pension system: 87% of the people that requested it were women with an average age of 72, and three-quarters of them did not have any prior pension benefit. For these reasons, this moratorium is commonly referred to as the 'pension for housewives'.[33]

These were measures that had a time frame for the request and that allowed an increase in the pension coverage of about 100%. A notable characteristic of the moratorium was that it did not act as a separate programme but rather it incorporated the requestors into the contributory social security system, with the applicable resultant rights.

Currently, as part of the announcements of the current government administration, the creation of the Universal Pension for Senior Adults has been announced within a programme of 'historical reparation for pensioners'. It involves a lifelong pension that is paid monthly at the equivalent of 80% of the minimum pension (approximately USD 265) for people older than 65 years of age who are Argentines or naturalized citizens with ten years of continual residence in the country and who do not receive any other social security benefit or receive a benefit for a lesser amount, in which case they must choose between one or the other.

This Universal Pension will be tied to the adjustment law, and consequently will be increased twice a year, in March and September, and will allow the beneficiaries to continue with their labour activities in order to obtain a regular retirement pension. Once again and contrary to the established precepts in terms of migration, it establishes as a prerequisite for foreigners, twenty years of continual residence in Argentina, a provision which has been declared unconstitutional in other cases. In addition to the amount transferred, access is given to health services of the National Institute of Social Services for Retirees and Pensioners (PAMI). This is a recent development and there is no information available regarding its implementation.

It is necessary to add that the AUH and the universal pension are a necessary result of the disconnection between social policies of social protection and the labour market. Or they are the result of the inability of the labour market to include informal workers, particularly women who share the burden of responsibility for care. There are no comprehensive policies, and the AUH does not liaise with the Ministry of Education, Health, Housing, or any other area.

Taking into account the different benefits in place that complement each other (e.g., the AUH and AUF; the hybrid scheme covering formal and informal workers; the universal pension), it could be said that there has been an attempt

---

33. Pautassi, Laura et al., *Sistema previsional en Argentina y equidad de género. Situación actual (2003-2010) y perspectivas futuras*, Series of Working Documents from Latin American Justice and Gender Team (2011).

to create a coherent system of different benefit schemes. However, the connection with labour market policies is missing which is necessary to prevent the existence of a poverty trap, particularly for women.

7.3.9 Social Participation

The design and implementation of the AUH did not establish a mechanism for social participation. Only a web page was made available to access information about the programme, which has resulted in being significantly limited due to the restricted access to the Internet in the country. By not providing mechanisms for involvement of trade unions and other representative organizations, it is clear that the AUH does not comply with the principle of social participation.

7.4 LEGISLATIVE DEFICITS AND IMPLEMENTATION FAILURES[34]

After a decade of a policy of continuity between President Néstor Kirchner and the subsequent terms of Cristina Fernández, in December 2015 a candidate from a centre-right political alliance called *Cambiemos* ('Let's change') led by the then Head of the Government of the City of Buenos Aires, Mauricio Macri, won the Presidential election. One of the main questions was whether the AUH was going to continue to remain in force. During the electoral campaign, its continuity was not only reaffirmed but also announcements about its universalization were made.

At the same time, the new administration announced a single payment of ARS 800 (USD 53) to those entitled to the family allowance to encourage the purchase of school supplies. This was not a new measure, but rather it has already existed since 2015 under the name 'school assistance' and was meant for the beneficiaries of AUH with the objective of it being comparable to the transfer that formal workers receive.

In 2016, by means of Decree 591, a single payment of ARS 500 was established (USD 34) for those who receive AUH. Another one of the measures adopted was the increase in the amount, in March 2016, from ARS 837 to ARS 933 (USD 56 to USD 64 respectively). The communicative action was presented as a political decision of the executive branch, but in reality, the calculation was required to be made based on Law 27,160 of 2015, which established that family allowances and AUH will be regularly adjusted.

With regard to the four last provisions of the decree of necessity and urgency of the executive branch:

(1) The incompatibilities between AUH and other social benefits are eliminated although restricted to some transitory employment programmes

---

34. A special thank you to Pilar Arcidiácono and Mora Straschnoy for the substantial contributions they made to this section.

such as Training and Employment Insurance, among others in place. The possibility of ANSES resolving future cases of incompatibility between national, provincial and municipal benefits is authorized.

(2) Decree 492 of 2016, increased the upper limits for receiving formal family allowances, that for ten years had been subject to upper limits in remuneration in order to access the allowances by rule of Law 24,714 of 1996. This increase had an impact on the AAFF system by incorporating in it 1.2 million more children. Once again, in a context of inflation and significant salary devaluation, the impact of this measure is clear and noteworthy. However, this type of measure is palliative. It allows the transfer to be made according to salary fluctuations but does not check their background which means that the recognition of the family responsibilities of formal salaried employees is made according to the level of income. On the other hand, the amount of the formal transfer which has remained at ARS 199 (USD 14) has not increased.

(3) The dissemination in public opinion with regard to the AUH and associated measures has been headed by the Social Development Ministry and not by ANSES, who is in charge of the execution of social security. This again stresses, worryingly, the supposed universality of the programme thus marking a return to an assistance perspective. Clearly, a change can be seen in the framework for addressing the problem and in the course that this administration is taking with its 'zero poverty' plan.

(4) Finally, the presidential announcement about promoting a 'basic citizen income for childhood' was very noteworthy, in light of the history of Bills presented from the 1990s onward which were never subject to legislative scrutiny. The expectation of this government is to achieve its implementation within the next three years, and to date they have only advanced with Decree 593/16 which establishes the creation of a committee created to analyse the viability of its implementation. Initially, the proposal would receive funding from international credit assistance institutions, specifically the World Bank.

In summary, the new administration has shown signs of strengthening the social protection matrix however, as was analysed, the supposed universality in light of the measures adopted to date and interpreted in accordance with the legal commitments contained in international treaties and agreements and in Recommendation No. 202 is a sum of actions that increase the coverage but are far from being universal measures.

In any case, the current administration has demonstrated a political willingness to continue with the dynamic of transfers established from AUH onwards; however, the incorporation within the framework of the zero poverty plan, the diversification of measures to 'include' new beneficiaries and an assistance-based halo that floats around the 'social' does not mean there will be better results with regards to human rights standards.

Although a year has passed since President Macri took office, and any analysis may be premature, what is certain is that an increase in coverage should not be confused with universality, nor incorporation with non-discrimination or institutionalism with welfare assistance. In short, social security should not be confused with social protection.

7.5 CONCLUSIONS

The analysis of the Argentine case is quite significant for various reasons. In comparison to other countries in the region, and in relation to Recommendation No. 202, the social protection component has significantly increased, incorporating the main policy of transfer of income, such as the Universal Child Allowance, to the centre of the administration of social security. Although the gap between contributory and non-contributory benefits remains clearly established, the AUH is not part of the typical transfer programmes but rather it is part of a type of hybrid response to the situations of labour and social vulnerability.

This is the case particularly because it is not about a programme, or at least its origins, aimed at resolving questions of poverty, but rather part of the State acknowledgement of the existence of the informal labour market and therefore formal salaried employee benefits being extended to informal workers. Up to this point, progress has been made with regards to the State responsibilities for the lack of registration of employment. However, the stimulus measures for registration have had a low impact and employer inspection mechanisms have not been activated. That is to say, a State effort has been consolidated but sanctions have not been established for the business people that do not register their employees.

In accordance, the existence of conditionalities imposed on the children and adolescents of practices that comprise the exercise of the right to education and to health go against the guarantee that the State should provide for those entitled to those rights. That is to say, the conditionalities scheme is asymmetrical for the beneficiaries and not for the State who must guarantee protected employment opportunities.

But what is even more significant is the transfer of the responsibilities of care to women, along with conditionalities and penalties, since the payment of the transfer is directly related to 'adequate care', that requires women to do things but does not facilitate them. Not only has no investment been made in care infrastructure, or in actions that distribute a little more equally the responsibilities of care between men and women, but also quite to the contrary, this income depends on them providing evidence of this care. Furthermore, this proof is required only for AUH and not for AAFF, establishing discriminatory treatment between the origin of one benefit and the other.

If we contextualize this situation with the fact that children, adolescents and women are overrepresented in poverty, after seven years of implementation of this measure, current data on poverty by income that shows that 23% of urban homes live in conditions of income poverty which covers 32.2% of the population, which demonstrates that the measure has been extremely important but still not enough.[35]

The eloquence of this evidence is incomparable because there has been an economic recovery in the interim and therefore it makes it very clear that poverty cannot be eradicated with money transfers alone. The limits of this type of intervention and the need to revise and mainstream the State's responses need to be urgently debated.

As long as this multidimensional complex phenomenon is not addressed in its entirety and comprehensive measures are adopted which are respectful of the universality principle and indivisibility and inalienability of human rights, without gender bias or other types of discrimination, we will not move forward with sustainable solutions.

In terms of Recommendation No. 202, in Article 5, it can be noted that the AUH complies with the basic social security guarantees. That is, coverage of the transfer, access to health and education of children, and adolescents and pregnant women. However, the other guarantees established – linked to the criteria of availability, accessibility, acceptability and adequacy – have not yet been met. Thus, the social protection floor aims present to a greater extent for children but ignores, for example, the health of their parents, especially women, the extensive network of care infrastructure or instances of educational termination that are outside the social protection floor minimum. The challenge and the immediate action of the State is to broaden the bases of the social protection floor so as not to concentrate efforts only on programmes such as the AUH or AUE, but to advance in providing comprehensive protection for older adults, people with disabilities and the population in general. The challenge is that the floor does not become the roof, but social protection advances towards integral policies based on rights.

In other words, proposals such as the minimum social protection floor (Recommendation No. 202, ILO) have an impact if they really are a floor as a basis for progressive protection towards inclusive rights based arrangements. A social protection floor should not become a ceiling that at the same time results in the compartmentalization of benefits and beneficiaries – those who are entitled, excluded or conditioned – and formal salaried employees. It is, furthermore, necessary to place emphasis on guaranteeing for each person, independent of their age, education level or gender, the autonomous exercise of their rights. Coherence of policies, particularly including labour market policies, is necessary for the social protection floor in Argentina to remain a floor that enables people to escape from poverty and build a better life.

---

35. Third quarter of 2016, Statistics and Census Institute (*Instituto de Estadísticas y Censos* (INDEC)), 2016, http://www.indec.gob.ar/uploads/informesdeprensa/eph_pobreza_01_16.pdf.

BIBLIOGRAPHY

Arcidiácono, Pilar, *La política del 'mientras tanto'. Programas sociales después de la crisis 2001–2002* (Biblos 2012).

Arcidiácono, Pilar, *La asignación Universal en su laberinto.* (Buenos Aires, Revista Bordes June 2016) available at http://revistabordes.com.ar/la-asignacion-universal-en-su-laberinto/ (accessed 21 March 2017).

Bertranou, Fabio, Oscar Cetrángolo, Luis Casanova, Alejandra Beccaria & Julián Folgar, *Performance of Social Protection in Argentina. Assessment of Two Decades of Reforms* (Buenos Aires, ILO Country Office for Argentina 2016).

Bertranou, Fabio, Oscar Cetrángolo, Luis Casanova, Alejandra Beccaria & Julián Folgar, *Desempeño y financiamiento de la protección social en Argentina: consideraciones a partir de la Recomendación núm. 202 sobre pisos de protección social* (Buenos Aires, ILO Country Office for Argentina 2015).

Bestard, Ana María, Maximiliano Carrasco & Mora Kantor, *El Poder Legislativo Nacional y los programas sociales en el período 2002–2009* (L. Pautassi & G. Gamallo eds, Biblos 2012).

Center for Legal and Social Studies (*Centro de Estudios Legales y Sociales* (CELS)), *Las pensiones por vejez frente al derecho a la seguridad social* (Buenos Aires 2010).

Center for Legal and Social Studies (*Centro de Estudios Legales y Sociales* (CELS)), *Programa Familias por la Inclusión Social. Entre el discurso de derechos y la práctica asistencial* (Buenos Aires 2007).

Ceriani, Pablo, Paola Cyment, & Diego Morales, *Migración, derechos de la niñez y Asignación Universal por Hijo: las fronteras de la inclusión social.* Available at http://conti.derhuman.jus.gov.ar/2011/10/mesa_2/ceriani_cyment_morales_mesa_2.pdf (Accessed 21 March 2017).

Faur, Eleonor Luis Campos, Laura Pautassi & Silvina Zimerman, *Rights Questioned. Limitations of Poverty-Reduction Policies in Argentina*, 60 Issue 197–198 International Social Science Journal (2010).

Isuani, Aldo. *The Argentine Welfare State: Enduring and Resisting Change*, 19 Issue 1 International Journal of Social Welfare, 104–114 (2014).

Lo Vuolo, Rubén & Alberto Barbeito, *La Nueva oscuridad de la política social* (Miño & Dávila eds, Buenos Aires, 1998).

Maurizio, Roxana & Gustavo Vázquez, *Argentina: efectos del programa Asignación Universal por Hijo en el comportamiento laboral de los adultos* in *Revista de la CEPAL, Nº 113*, Comisión Económica para América Latina y el Caribe, (Santiago de Chile, August 2015).

Ministry of Work, Employment and Social Security, *Resultados de la Encuesta Nacional de Protección y Seguridad Social 2011* (ENAPROSS. – 1a ed. Ministry of Work, Employment and Social Security 2014).

Pautassi Laura & Gustavo Gamallo, *El bienestar en brechas. Las políticas sociales en la Argentina de la postconvertibilidad* (Buenos Aires, Editorial Biblos 2015).

Pautassi, Laura ¿*Bailarinas en la oscuridad? Seguridad social en América Latina el marco de la equidad de género*. Paper presented in the Thirty-Eighth Meeting of the General Committee of the Regional Conference on Latin American and Caribbean Women, Social Protection and Gender Panel, Economic Commission for Latin America and the Caribbean (Mar del Plata, September 7th and 8th of 2005).

Pautassi Laura, *Social Security Standards in Latin America*, in *International Standard-Setting and Innovations in Social Security* 73–88 (U. Becker, F. Pennings and T. Dijkhoff eds, Kluwer Law International, 2013).

Pautassi, Laura, Claudia Giacometti & Natalia Gherardi, *Sistema previsional en Argentina y equidad de género. Situación actual (2003–2010) y perspectivas futuras*, Series of Working Documents from Latin American Justice and Gender Team (2011).

Pautassi, Laura, Pilar Arcidiacono & Mora Straschnoy, *Asignación Universal por Hijo para Protección Social de la Argentina. Entre la satisfacción de necesidades y el reconocimiento de derechos*. División de Políticas Sociales, CEPAL, Number 184 (Santiago de Chile 2013).

Razavi, Sheila *The Political and Social Economy of Care in a Development Context Conceptual Issues, Research Questions and Policy Options* (UNRISD 2007).

Rodríguez Enríquez, Corina *La cuestión del cuidado ¿el eslabón perdido del análisis económico?* 109 Revista Cepal, 23–36 (2012).

CHAPTER 8
Tunisian National Programme for Assistance to Families in Need

Tania Abbiate

8.1 INTRODUCTION

The adoption in June 2012 of Recommendation No. 202 (R202) by the International Labour Conference has promoted the enactment of social protection floors (SPFs) at the national level. These are 'nationally defined sets of basic social security guarantees which secure protection aimed at preventing or alleviating poverty, vulnerability and social exclusion'.

The R202 provides guidelines in this regard and the objective of this study is to investigate if certain already existing national programmes on the provision of social and income security to vulnerable groups of the population are in line with the principles expressed in it.

The present contribution focuses on the Tunisian National Programme for Assistance to Families in Need (*Programme National d'Aide aux Familles Nécessiteuses* – PNAFN) which is a nationwide cash transfer programme that aims to provide income security to vulnerable families. This scope makes the programme close to the SPFs' goal of providing a basic income security for children, for persons in active age and older persons.

The present case study is divided into four sections. The first section provides an overview of the PNAFN by framing it within the broader context of Tunisian social protection sector, as well as within the constitutional framework introduced after the 'Tunisian Revolution' of 2011.

The second section provides an assessment of the PNAFN based on the principles expressed in the R202, namely State responsibility, universality of protection, entitlement based on law, adequacy and predictability of benefits, non-discrimination, financial solidarity, good governance, coherence of policies and social participation. The third section deals with the legislative deficits of the scheme, and the fourth contains the concluding remarks.

8.1.1 Overview of Tunisian Social Protection Schemes

Tunisia has one of the most comprehensive social protection systems in Africa, comprising contributory and non-contributory schemes. It provides for health care, retirement pensions, widows' allowances, allowances for orphans and the elderly, family allowances and work injury benefits. This system is complemented by social assistance for persons in need.

The development of social security dates back to the beginning of the twentieth century and was influenced by the French Protectorate (1881–1956). However, it was only in the 1960s that social security was extended to cover a greater proportion of workers.[1] Since then, the Tunisian social security system has progressively extended its coverage,[2] and it currently covers most of the workforce engaged in the formal sector (85.6%–100% of the public sector and 81.5% of the private sector).[3]

This extension has corresponded to the adoption of vast legislation dealing with social security. Since the 1980s, Tunisian lawmakers have adopted a variety of acts: considerable improvements were introduced through the adoption of Act No. 2002-32 of 12 March 2002, which extended social insurance to home-based workers, household employees, fishermen and peasants, as well as artisans. In the same year, Act No. 2002-104 of 30 December 2002 extended social security to artists, while in 2004, two Decrees (No. 2004-3018 of 19 November and No. 2004-167 of 20 January) extended social security coverage to self-employed persons.

The insurance-based schemes are State-run and are presided over by three public agencies. The CNRPS (National Pension and Social Insurance Fund) covers the public sector and the CNSS (National Social Security Fund) is the equivalent for the private sector. Moreover, in 2004, the CNAM (National Health Insurance Fund) was created to cover sickness, accident and occupational disease for both public and private sector contributors.

With special regard to social assistance, several legal interventions were made in the 1980s and 1990s, in correspondence with the adoption of Structural Adjustment Programmes (SAPs) in the country.[4] In particular, Circular No. 5 of

---

1. Remarkably, in 1960, Act No. 60-30 was adopted. The Act introduced the National Social Security Fund for the private sector.
2. In particular in the period from 1989 to 1999, social security coverage rose from 60% to 84%. Cf. M. Chaabane, *Towards the Universalization of Social Security: The Experience of Tunisia*, ILO, Extension of Social Security, 4 ESS Paper (2002).
3. OECD, *Investing in Youth: Tunisia Strengthening the Employability of Youth during the Transition to a Green Economy*, 114 (2015).
4. The first SAP in Tunisia was adopted in 1986. In line with the other economic reform packages prescribed by the International Monetary Fund and the World Bank to developing

the Ministry of Social Affairs of 16 May 1986 introduced the Tunisian National Programme for Families in Need (PNAFN), while Decree No. 98-1812 of 21 September 1998 and Decree No. 98-409 of 18 February 1998 introduced two programmes providing access to public medical institutions, either free of charge (*Assistance médicale gratuite –AMG*) or at a reduced rate (*Assistance médicale à tarifs réduits –AMGII*).[5] These programmes are supported by ad hoc social assistance programmes, such as social aid programmes available in the Ramadan period.[6]

The development of Tunisia's social protection system benefits also from the long collaboration with the International Labour Organization (ILO). In fact, Tunisia has been a State Member of the ILO since independence in 1956, and by 2016, it had ratified sixty-two Conventions and one Protocol, fifty-six of which are in force.[7] The ratification of these treaties, however, has not prevented the existence of national legislation which contradicts the Conventions, as was the case with Decree Law No. 62-17 of 15 August 1962 on re-educative work and Act No. 78-22 of 8 March 1978 on civil service, which were considered by the ILO Committee of Experts on the Application of Conventions and Recommendations to be in contravention with Conventions No. 29 and No. 105 which ban forced labour. The Acts in question were indeed amended by the entry into force of Act No. 95-9 of 23 January 1995.[8]

Despite this progress, it has to be noted that Tunisia has not ratified any social security Conventions. Not even the engagement of post-revolutionary Governments with ILO obligations has promoted changes in this regard.[9] Despite the development of significant contributory schemes and the enactment of several social assistance programmes, about 15.2% of the population lived

---

countries, it was structured along three axes: the reduction of the borrowing country's fiscal imbalances, the adoption of appropriate pricing policies, and the adjustment of exchange rate. This policy had negative effects on vulnerable social groups, because of the cut in public spending and the reduction in subsides: in particular there was an increase of public healthcare fees, as well as in public education, and in unemployment. See S. Chaker, *Impacts sociaux de l'ajustement structurel: cas de la Tunisie*, 10 Nouvelles pratiques sociales, 151, 152 (1997).

5. These regulations have sub-legislative status, being issued by the government or Ministries; thus they can be overridden by superior legislation or subsequent decisions of the government.
6. These programmes had already been introduced by the 1980s and continue to operate today. *See* R. Ben Amor, *Politique sociale et pauvreté en Tunisie*, 49 Cahier de la Méditerranée 211-212 (1994).
7. For details about the conventions ratified by Tunisia, *see* below s. 8.1.3.
8. N. Mzid, *Les Droits fondamentaux au travail en Tunisie a la lumière des normes de l'Oit*, 11 Etudes Juridiques, 36 (2004). *See also* A. Abdeljaouad, *The Influence of International Labour Conventions on Tunisian Legislation*, 91 International Labour Review, 191 (1965).
9. Since the Revolution, the country has ratified three ILO Conventions on labour standards (No. 144, No. 151 and No. 154) and has expressed its commitment to establishing national social protection floors, as assessed by the inclusion of this objective with the Governmental Plan of Major Reforms 2016-2020. *See* Présidence de Gouvernement, Conseil d'Analyse Economique, *Programme National Des Réformes Majeures 2016–2020* (2016).

below the poverty line in 2015, with extreme variation across regions: while in Tunis, the percentage of people living below the poverty line was 5.3%, in the Centre-West, it was 30.8%.[10]

There is a severe regional disparity, with a lower rate of poverty in cities, particularly in greater Tunis (9.1%), and a higher rate in rural areas, especially in the Centre-West area (32.3%).[11] This variation depends on the labour market situation and, more generally, on the economic situation in the geographical areas: the Tataouine Governorate,[12] for example, had an unemployment rate of 51.7% in 2012, while the national average was 17.6%.[13] Another salient issue to be considered is the high percentage of workers in the informal sector (about 37%)[14] who are not covered by contributory schemes.

This paints a gloomier picture of social protection's effectiveness, reflecting that in reality more than 50% of the active population is not covered by social insurance.[15]

8.1.2 Socio-Economic Rights Guarantees in the 2014 Constitution

The adoption of the 2014 Constitution represents a significant improvement in terms of protection of socio-economic rights and this is not surprising if we consider that the demand for social justice was one cornerstone of the revolution. The new constitutional framework reserves a special protection for the right to social security, which is expressed in Article 38 paragraph 3, which states:[16]

> [...] the State shall ensure free health care for those without means and those with limited income. It shall guarantee the right to social assistance in accordance with the law.

---

10. Institut National de la Statistique, Enquête *nationale sur le budget, la* consommation *et le niveau de vie des ménages (2015)*.
11. Institut National de la Statistique, *Mesure de la pauvreté des inégalités et de la polarisation en Tunisie 2000-2010*, 23 (2012).
12. A governorate is an administrative division corresponding mainly to a region administered by a regional committee. The governorate is headed by the Governor. Before the adoption of the new Constitution, governors were not directly elected by the people, but nominated by the President of the Republic, while the regional committees were administered by the Ministry of Interior Affairs. The 2014 Constitution provides for the direct election of local and regional committees. Finally, it is worth mentioning that Tunisia is comprised of 24 governorates which are in turn articulated in 264 delegations.
13. Ministère de l'Equipement, de l'Aménagement du Territoire et du Développement Durable, Agence Nationale de Protection de l'Environnement, *Les* indicateurs de développement *durable en Tunisie*, 23 (2014).
14. OECD, *Investing in Youth: Tunisia Strengthening the Employability of* Youth *during the Transition to a Green Economy*, 115 (2015).
15. *Rapport Alternatif de la Société Civile Tunisienne au Pacte International Relatif aux Droits Économiques, Sociaux et Culturels*, 13 (2016).
16. Translation by UNDP.

Besides this clause, there are socio-economic guarantees throughout the whole constitutional text. The Preamble asks the State to strive for equality among the regions and social justice, and to preserve a healthy environment. Moreover, the Preamble recognizes the socio-economic dimensions of the foundations of the Revolution, notably work and employment as fundamental dimensions of human dignity. Article 7 sets out the principle of family protection; Article 8 underlines the value of youth and the State's commitment to provide the necessary conditions for developing the capacities of young citizens and realizing their potential, through their participation in social, economic, cultural and political development.

Article 10 is dedicated to the fight against tax evasion, fraud and corruption, and stresses the duty of each citizen to pay taxes and contribute to the public office under a fair and equitable system. It is for the State to set and define the management and operation mechanisms. Article 12 urges the State to be responsible for social justice, regional development and maintaining a balance among the regions as part of affirmative action. Article 14 tackles the unequal distribution of wealth among regions and is devoted to decentralization as the preferred mode of governance, urging the State to implement it.

The distribution of powers to local authorities is further described and prescribed in Chapter 7, which is devoted to local power. With reference to this, it has to be noted that the introduction of the principle of devolved government represents an absolute novelty in the Tunisian legal framework, because up to now the State has always been characterized by centralist management and has never known real decentralization. Moreover, Article 21 also reflects a socio-economic consideration, expressing the State's commitment to 'ensure the conditions for a dignified life' for all citizens.

Article 36 provides for trade union rights and the right to strike; Article 38 enshrines the right to health and the State's role as guarantor of free health care and social assistance for those without means and those with limited income; Article 39 expresses the right to free public education; Article 40 states that work is a right of every citizen, that working conditions have to be decent, and that work is to be done in return for a decent wage; Article 44 explicitly recognizes the right to water; Article 45 states the right to a healthy and protected environment; Article 46 expresses the protection of women from violence and the State's commitment to eradicate violence against them; Article 47 states the protection of children; and Article 48 enshrines the rights of persons with disability.

Remarkably, these clauses, deliberately, do not make explicit reference to the fact that the implementation of these rights must be subordinated to the availability of financial resources, as is the case with other constitutions, notably that of South Africa.

Furthermore, it is relevant to note that the constitutional framework concerning socio-economic rights provides for the direct enforceability of socio-economic rights. These rights are indeed collocated in Chapter 2 with civil and political rights. Article 49, which contains the limitation of rights clause, clearly states: 'Judicial authorities ensure that rights and freedoms are protected from all violations'.

The adoption of the 2014 Constitution with its broad constitutional recognition of socio-economic rights supports the development of a more coherent and efficient social protection system. In order to achieve this objective, the implementation of SPFs can make a significant contribution, and in fact some steps have already been taken in this direction.

In January 2013, the main Tunisian trade union, *Union Génerale des Travailleurs Tunisiens* (UGTT); the main Tunisian employers' union, *Union Tunisienne de l'Industrie, du Commerce et de l'Artisanat* (UTICA); and the government, signed a new social contract which provides for social protection and foresees the establishment of a National Social Dialogue Council, which will be in charge of evaluating all bills concerning economic and social rights.[17]

Moreover, in 2014, a Decree was passed creating a management unit within the Ministry of Social Affairs to develop a data bank on needy families with limited income,[18] and the intention to reform the social protection system is clearly stated in the 2016-2020 National Plan of Major Reform issued by the Presidency of the Government.[19]

8.1.3 Tunisian Compliance with ILO and Steps Towards the Implementation of SPFs

Tunisia has ratified all ILO fundamental Conventions, namely the Forced Labour Convention 1930 (No. 29), the Freedom of Association and Protection of the Right to Organize Convention 1948 (No. 87), the Right to Organize and Collective Bargaining Convention 1949 (No. 98), the Equal Remuneration Convention 1951 (No. 100), the Abolition of Forced Labour Convention 1957 (No. 105), the Discrimination (Employment and Occupation) Convention 1958 (No. 111), the Minimum Age Convention 1973 (No. 138), and the Worst Forms of Child Labour Convention 1999 (No. 182). However, it has never ratified ILO Convention No. 102, which sets the benchmark for social security.

The commitment expressed since 2014 to the adoption of national social protection floors is therefore to be welcomed as a first step towards the establishment of basic social security standards. In the process of implementing a national set of goods and services and a basic income security, the Tunisian

---

17. The process of creating the National Social Dialogue Council began in 2015 and the bill concerning its establishment is currently under discussion in the Tunisian Parliament. See N. Adhadhi, *Vers la création Conseil National du Dialogue Social*, http://www.realites.com.tn/2015/05/vers-la-creation-conseil-national-du-dialogue-social/ (accessed 4 May 2015).
18. Decree n° 2014-1526 dated 30 Apr. 2014, creating a management unit in the Ministry of Social Affairs to develop a data bank on needy families with limited income.
19. Présidence du Gouvernement Conseil des Analyses Economiques, *Programme National Des Réformes Majeures 2016–2020* (Janvier 2016).

government is supported by external actors, namely the ILO and the World Bank; and by internal actors, such as the main trade union (UGTT) and the employers' organization (UTICA).[20]

The first action of the Minister of Social Affairs in order to make Tunisia's commitment effective has been to create a team of national experts in charge of undertaking a feasibility study for the establishment of a national social protection floor. Moreover, the government has created a division within the Ministry of Social Affairs in charge of developing a data bank of families in need and has started a process of reviewing social benefit eligibility criteria.

In fact, at first sight the PNAFN's aim of providing a basic income security to children, to persons of active age who are unable to earn sufficient income and to older persons seems to be in line with R202, although the programme has several shortcomings and needs to be reformed.

8.1.4 Background of the PNAFN

The PNAFN is a direct cash transfer programme providing a social safety net for vulnerable households. It was introduced in 1986 – before the adoption of the ILO Recommendation on SPFs – by the Minister of Social Affairs and the Tunisian Union of Social Solidarity[21] in order to counterbalance the negative effects of the Structural Adjustment Programmes. It is managed by the Department of Social Promotion of the Ministry of Social Affairs (MAS) and aims to provide direct financial assistance to families below the poverty line. It entails an unconditional cash transfer, as well as free access to public health care (*Assistance médicale gratuite –AMG*), or cost reductions to indigent or low-income families that are not registered with the social insurance system (*Assistance médicale à tarifs réduits –AMGII*). Moreover, since 2007, it has worked together with an educational support programme (*Programme d'allocations scolaires*), which in 2014 covered nearly 80,000 children from more than 40,000 families.[22]

Eligibility criteria are listed in Circular No. 5 of the MAS of 16 May 1998, which states that the programme addresses families that meet a certain set of criteria: first, their income must fall below the poverty line as assessed by the Tunisian Institute of Statistics; second, some additional socio-economic conditions are taken into account, namely:

---

20. Ministère des Affaires Sociaux, *Rapport général de la conférence nationale sur le système de la protection sociale: 'pour la mise en place d'un socle de protection sociale'* (Tunis -Hôtel le Palace 11-12 Sep. 2014).
21. The Tunisian Union of Social Solidarity is a local NGO created in 1964 committed to providing social assistance for the poor and vulnerable persons.
22. Ministry of Social Affairs, UNICEF, *Evaluation of Tunisia's Education Benefit Programme of PNAFN*, http://socialprotection.org/discover/publications/evaluation-education-benefit-programme-pnafn-tunisia (accessed on 30 Jan. 2017).

- household size;
- the number of household members with a disability and/or chronic health condition;
- household living conditions, such as dwelling and assets; and
- the inability for the head of household to work due to a physical or mental impairment.

Public benefits are awarded on the basis of declarations made by families and they involve several actors. The process generally flows as follows:

(a) the family claims for the cash transfer declaring that its household income falls below the poverty threshold;
(b) social workers carry out an investigation into the household income, considering the aforementioned additional criteria;
(c) subsequently, a list of eligible families is drawn up and sent to local and regional commissions;
(d) the regional commissions prepare the final list of beneficiaries and excluded families, taking into consideration the regional budget allocated by the MAS.

Up until 2015, the poverty line used to determine the eligibility to the PNAFN was fixed at TND 585 per year (equivalent to USD 256.42),[23] but an increase is currently under discussion.[24]

The amount of the monthly cash transfer increased gradually over the years: TND 7.7 in 1987, TND 15 in 1990, TND 36.3 in 2000, TND 56.7 in 2010, TND 120 in 2014, and TND 150 (equivalent to USD 64.66) in 2015, with an addition of TND 10 (equivalent to USD 4.50) for each child (up to a maximum of three children), and TND 30 (equivalent to USD 13.51) at the beginning of the new school year.[25] Remarkably, before 2011, the benefit was provided every three months.

The overall increase in the amount of the cash transfer has been considerable and has more than compensated for inflation, and therefore the buying power of beneficiaries has increased.[26] According to the estimates of the MAS, in 2013 the scheme benefited approximately 235,000 families across Tunisia

---

23. This eligibility condition is fixed in the joint circular No. 2011-17 of 27 May 2011 issued by the Ministry of Interiors and of the Ministry of Social Affairs, which fixes the eligibility conditions for the AMGI.
24. CRES, BAD, Enquête d'évaluation de la performance des programmes de lutte contre la pauvreté en Tunisie. Résultat de la phase 1 de l'étude. Résumé exécutif 3 (2015).
25. In addition, the Tunisian Union of Social Solidarity grants TND 30 for every dependent child, up to a maximum of three children.
26. It is remarkable that on the contrary, the guaranteed minimum income (*salaire minimum interprofessionnel garanti* – SMIG) has declined and this could represent a disincentive to seek employment. See CRES, BAD, Enquête d'évaluation de la performance des programmes de lutte contre la pauvreté en Tunisie. Résultat de la phase 1 de l'étude. Résumé exécutif, 6 (2015).

Chapter 8: Tunisian National Programme for Assistance

(approximately 7.3% of the population). This marks a considerable extension of cover compared to its launch in 1986 when it covered 74,000 families, and even compared to the more recent estimates of 2009, when it covered only 115,000 families.[27] One of the main shortcomings of the programme is the fact that, despite having been established for more than thirty years, the programme has not been subject to continuous monitoring, and just recently an investigation into the targeting of the programme has been completed, which will be discussed later in section 8.2.2.

Finally, it is particularly deplorable that a survey has not been undertaken on the impact of the programme on poverty reduction. However, according to a study carried out in 2013, had the PNAFN not been in place, the poverty rate would have been higher – 16.5% instead of 15.5% – and the extreme poverty rate would have been 5.3% instead of 4.6%.[28] The overall limited increase in poverty anticipated in the absence of the programme seems to support the argument of the World Bank that the major contribution to poverty reduction in Tunisia comes from economic growth rather than social programmes.[29]

However, it has to be noted that the PNAFN was not conceived as a poverty reduction programme, but as a social assistance scheme initially aimed at alleviating the negative social effects of SAPs. Later on, it evolved in a political instrument used by the autocratic regime to ensure its legitimacy. This political diversion considerably reduced its capacity to contribute to poverty reduction, and as a consequence, social assistance for poor families has been rather complex and limited. The Tunisian revolution has introduced the possibility of reform in the social protection sector and improvement to the PNAFN.

8.2 ASSESSMENT OF THE SCHEME ON THE BASIS OF PRINCIPLES

8.2.1 State Responsibility

The analysis of compliance with the principle of State responsibility regarding PNAFN has to take into account the fact that the introduction of this programme preceded the adoption of the SPFs initiative both at international level, and at national level. Therefore, the assessment of the programme's compliance with the principle of State responsibility has to be carried out from an *ex post* perspective.

Through Circulars No. 5 of 16 May 1986 and No. 18 of 4 June 1986, the Tunisian government introduced the PNAFN to alleviate poverty caused by the SAPs, and this State initiative has to be evaluated positively, with evidence of the

---

27. T. Abdessalem, H. Nemsia and A. Benhamida, *Objectives du Millénaire pour le Développement, Rapport National de Suivi*, 48 (2013).
28. INS, CRES, AfDB, *Analyse de l'impact des subventions alimentaires et des programmes d'assistance*, Tunis: Institute Nationale de la Statistique 8 (2013).
29. Banque Mondiale, *Tunisie. Diagnostic-pays systématique*, 23 (2015).

State as initiator and main actor of the social assistance scheme (Article 13 of R202).

Since its adoption, the programme has always remained under the direction of the MAS and, over time, has progressively extended its coverage and increased the benefit levels. The PNAFN could in principle ensure the basic guarantees expressed in ILO R202, entailing: (i) a national set of goods and services, including essential health care; (ii) basic income security for children; (iii) a basic income security for older persons; and (iv) basic income security for persons in active age.

Indeed, cash transfers are meant to provide a minimum subsistence to families living below the poverty line, and the programme also includes free access to health care. However, the real capacity of the programme guaranteeing this basic income is undermined by the fact that the funds for the programme are not secured and their allocation depends on regional social budgets, thus undermining the State responsibility in guaranteeing basic income security to people in need.

Moreover, the State has not continuously monitored the programme, thus resulting in cases of the misallocation of grants. The only monitoring carried out in more than thirty years of the programme focused on high-level indicators, such as the number and type of beneficiaries. This represents a serious incompliance with the principle of State responsibility in monitoring social protection floor strategies (Article 19 of R202).

To address this significant failing, the MAS has recently established a new framework for monitoring and evaluation that is in the early stages of development. This effort comes alongside with the project of establishing a new single registry for all social benefits and an integrated system for information management jointly funded by the government and the World Bank.[30]

8.2.2 Universality of Protection

The PNAFN addresses all families in need, giving priority to families with children and/or family members with chronic diseases and disabilities. The programme, however, is not in line with the principle of universality of protection as set out in the R202 for two reasons: first of all, it addresses only Tunisian families thus excluding other nationals living in the country; second, not all families who meet the eligibility requirements of the programme receive benefits from this scheme.

With regard to the former reason, the exclusion of non-citizens is problematic because the country is transforming from a transit country of migration to a destination country, and migrants are excluded from all social assistance

---

30. Banque Mondiale, *Consolidation de la Politique de Protection Sociale et d'Emploi en Tunisie Renforcer les Systèmes, Connecter à l'Emploi*, xiv (2015).

programmes. The PNAFN could theoretically provide them with a minimum subsistence.

With regard to the exclusion of potential beneficiaries, this is a serious incompliance with the R202. This is mainly due to the fact that the social benefit allocation depends on the regional quotas allocated by the MAS. These quotas are defined yearly by the MAS and are not available to the public, thus demonstrating a serious lack of transparency. Besides the problem of the quotas, the mismanagement of the programme has contributed to a breach of the principle of universality of protection, because, while some families are illegitimately excluded from the programme, about 15% of the beneficiaries have been enrolled in the programme since at least 1989.[31] According to the latest estimates the programme covers almost 7.3% of the population (4.38% of elderly people and 2.92% of persons in active age),[32] a percentage that is not high enough because as much as 15.5% of the population is living below the poverty line.

Moreover, the programme has severe targeting problems as revealed by a survey published in 2015 commissioned by the MAS. Additionally, some data on the targeting of PNAFN are contained in a report published in 2013 by the World Bank. The figures in the two studies differ slightly, especially because the MAS report uses original data collected in 2013,[33] while the World Bank report uses data from a 2005 survey.[34] Nonetheless, both studies report a significant degree of mistargeting: according to the World Bank study, 42% of Tunisia's poorest quintile do not receive any form of assistance, either from PNAFN or from AMGII;[35] the figure is only slightly lower (38.2%) in the MAS report, which is based on more recent data.[36]

The latter report underlines that the poorest half of the lowest quintile (i.e., the poorest decile of the overall population) is targeted better since the percentage excluded is only 10.1%.[37] However, this does not mitigate the issue of severe mistargeting, and as the same MAS report notes elsewhere,[38] if the PNAFN was better targeted at the poorest households, 25% of the current beneficiaries would not be entitled to any cash transfer at all.

---

31. CRES, BAD, Enquête d'évaluation de la performance des programmes de lutte contre la pauvreté en Tunisie. Résultat de la phase 1 de l'étude. Résumé exécutif, cit. 4.
32. La lettre du CRES, Les socles nationaux de protection sociale: émergence du concept, meilleures pratiques internationales et pertinence pour la Tunisie, No. 7, 4 (2015).
33. CRES, BAD, Enquête d'évaluation de la performance des programmes de lutte contre la pauvreté en Tunisie. Résultat de la phase 1 de l'étude. Résumé exécutif, cit. 4-6.
34. Banque Mondiale, Vers une meilleure équité: les subventions énergétiques, le ciblage et la protection sociale en Tunisie, 24 (2013).
35. Ibid.
36. CRES, BAD, Enquête d'évaluation de la performance des programmes de lutte contre la pauvreté en Tunisie. Résultat de la phase 1 de l'étude. Résumé exécutif, cit. 8.
37. Ibid.
38. Ibid. 10.

In conclusion, the programme appears to be unfairly balanced with regard to the needs of poorer households and is not in conformity with the Recommendation as far as universality of protection is concerned. Unfortunately, the implementation of this principle does not seem to be one of the main targets of the government, which is more committed to limiting the misallocation of funds and promoting better governance of the programme, than guaranteeing that all families who meet the programme's requirements receive benefit.

8.2.3 Entitlements Based on Law

The PNAFN was implemented through two governmental circulars: Circular No. 5 of the MAS of 16 May 1998 and Circular No. 18 of the First Minister of 4 June 1986. Circular No. 5 of the MAS of 16 May 1998 sets out the eligibility criteria already listed in section 8.1.4, and the functions of the local and regional commissions.

Circular No. 18 of the First Minister of 4 June 1986 essentially deals with the implementation of the regional commission in charge of developing the list of PNAFN beneficiaries, as well as with the first determination of cash transfer amounts and their delivery. Remarkably, the regulation foresees a periodical evaluation of the programme, which however has been lacking for many years, mainly because of lack of political will. At the same time, the Circular itself does not set out how often these evaluations have to take place, save stating that the list of eligible beneficiaries has to be amended in the continuous monitoring of the programme.

Moreover, it is worth mentioning that definition of the poverty line used for the allocation of the social benefit has been updated in subsequent circulars, such as the joint Circular No. 2011-17 of 27 May 2011 issued by the Ministry of Interiors and the MAS, which also sets out the eligibility conditions for the AMGI. This overlapping of sources might create difficulties for potential beneficiaries in informing themselves about the programme.

According to the R202, the programme is not based on law, because it has not been introduced by legislation, but rather by governmental regulation. This means that it can be easily repealed by a subsequent ministerial decision even if, to date, this has never occurred.

Indeed, the fact that the programme is based on ministerial regulation is itself an infringement of the principle of certainty of law because the circulars are not easy to access for the public: for instance, they are not available online in the legislation database.

Further, a serious incompliance with the principle of entitlement based on law is the fact that the circulars make no reference to complaint and appeal procedures. From the information I could collect, there are no formal, documented mechanisms of redress or accountability for responding to grievances, aside from informal complaints to the Bureaus of Citizen Relations.[39] These organs were created by Decree No. 93-1549 of 26 July 1993 within each Ministry and Governorate and are tasked with facilitating the relationship between public administration and citizens. Although these offices could provide a minimum form of redress in matters of social assistance, in practice they have been judged to be dysfunctional.[40]

In 2008, the Tunisian government in a written answer to the UN Special Rapporteur on human rights and extreme poverty declared that the PNAFN provides for two forms of complaint: one at the administrative level, before the local and regional commissions, the General Director of Social Affairs, the MAS or other public institutions such as the administrative Ombudsman; and another at the judicial level, before the Administrative Tribunal.[41] However, recent research on the issue does not confirm the existence of these redress mechanisms.[42] The absence of complaint and redress mechanisms represents a serious infringement of Article 7 of R202, according to which the principle of entitlements prescribed by national law is inextricably bound to the principle of effectiveness and accessibility of legal remedies.

Nonetheless, the adoption of the 2014 Constitution has opened the way for general justiciability mechanisms. According to Article 49, judicial authorities are entitled to ensure that all rights and freedoms are protected from all violations, and this clause also applies to the right to social assistance, enshrined in Article 38. It is however questionable whether PNAFN's beneficiaries enjoy a subjective right since the ministerial regulations establishing the programme do not make explicit reference to such a right.

Besides, it must be noted that the entire judiciary is currently under review because it has to be updated on the new constitutional framework, which for example provides for its independence (Article 102); and states that it is composed of the Court of Cassation, Appellate Courts and Courts of First Instance; and that the law will regulate the organization of the judicial system, its mandate, procedures, and the statute of its judges (Article 115).

This legal framework is promising in terms of improvement of the rule of law, demonstrating a political will to establish a democratic state. However, these provisions have to be implemented, and in particular, it is necessary that the Constitution is converted into laws and practice. In the first three years of the new Constitution's adoption, the first steps in the implementation process have

---

39. C. Harfa and H. Elgazzar, *Consolidation and Transparency: Transforming Tunisia's Health Care for the Poor*, 7 (2013).
40. *Ibid.*
41. Ministère des Affaires Etrangères, *Réponse du Gouvernement tunisien au 'questionnaire relatif aux programmes de transferts financiers adressé aux gouvernements par l'Experte indépendante sur la question des droits de l'homme et l'extrême pauvreté'*, 6 (2008).
42. M. Ben Braham, *L'approche basée sur les droits de l'homme du système de sécurité sociale tunisien*, Etude du Bureau des Droits de l'Homme des Nations Unies en Tunisie, Tunis, 27 (2013).

been taken; however, the progress to date in the judicial system is rather limited and the road appears long and rocky.

With regard to PNAFN, it is desired that proper legislation is adopted. This should establish adequate complaint procedures, ensure protection from rights violations and enshrine redress mechanisms. Currently, the absence of these has to be regarded as a serious infringement of the R202.

8.2.4 Adequacy and Predictability of Benefits

The assistance programme targets persons living below the (absolute) poverty line, the latter being defined by the Institute of National Statistics taking into account a mixture of basic food basket costs and a minimum of non-alimentary costs calculated per household. These data are collected and updated every five years, and the poverty line is adjusted accordingly.[43] Currently, the poverty line used to determine PNAFN eligibility is an annual income of TND 585 (equivalent to USD 256.42) and the system does not account for differences between the rural and urban areas, even though in reality the difference is quite relevant.[44]

The cash transfer is provided not only on the basis of the household's income, but also on the basis of other criteria, such as the family members' inability to work, the absence of the head of the household, the lack of other forms of family support, the presence of a disabled and/or a chronically ill person, and the size of the family.

The procedure for allocation of benefit involves different actors and is very much dependent on the declared income of families and subjective assessment of social workers and/or the decision of the regional commissions, as already mentioned in section 8.1.4.[45]

This procedure is in contrast with the principle of adequacy and predictability of benefits because the assessment of the regional commission is not transparent and because the quota system finally determinates who will benefit from the cash transfer and who will not. It appears therefore that the enjoyment of the social benefit depends ultimately on the funding available and not on the eligibility criteria as such.

As far as the adequacy of the benefit is concerned, on the one hand, the social benefit has been considered inadequate for living a life in dignity as

---

43. PNUD, *Stratégie de réduction de la pauvreté. Etude du phénomène de la pauvreté en Tunisie*, 6 (2004). R. Béchir, *Pauvreté et niveau de vie de la population rurale en Tunisie*, 67 Les notes d'alerte du CIHEAM, 2 (2010).
44. Banque Africaine de Développement, *Subventions alimentaires et aides sociales directes: vers un meilleur ciblage de la pauvreté monétaire et des privations en Tunisie*, (2013) 78.
45. An inquiry carried out by the Ministry of the Woman and the Family in 2013 assessed that only one person in ten interviewed had received a visit from a social assistant in the previous twelve months, and only four in ten had received a visit upon request. *See* M. Ben Braham, *Effectivité des droits économiques et sociaux en Tunisie*, in, *Report of the Workshop 'Transparency and the rule of law as* pre-conditions of equitable and sustainable development', 45 (European Commission Through Law ed. 2014).

prescribed by Article 8 of the R202, as well as by Article 21 of the Tunisian Constitution,[46] and on the other hand the recent evaluation of the programme has highlighted that sometimes the families cumulate social benefits and live in more than one household together in order to maintain a dignified standard of living.

In fact, the level of benefits has increased over the years, and its buying power has increased by about 6% each year.[47] This rise is linked to the instrumental political role played by the programme: the government passed the increase in order to gain the support of the most disadvantaged and vulnerable people, and recently, after the revolution, the increase was motivated by the socio-economic popular claims.[48]

By considering its adequacy, it is worth noting that the PNAFN also provides access to public medical institutions either free of charge (AMG) or at a reduced rate (AMGII), thus providing essential health care as prescribed by the R202. Furthermore, the PNAFN pays special attention to children, as demonstrated by the increased cash transfers for families with children providing an additional TND 10 (equivalent to USD 4.50) for each child (up to a maximum of three children), and TND 30 (equivalent to USD 13.51) at the beginning of the new school year. In this regard, the programme gets close to the prescription of guaranteeing basic income security for children. However, as noted above, it is questionable whether this amount of money is sufficient to provide access to nutrition, education care and any other necessary goods and services. The very fact that households resort to cumulating benefits in order to survive proves that the programme itself is not sufficient.

In conclusion, the PNAFN is not adequate in terms of: (i) predictability, since the allocation of the cash benefit is not based on transparent criteria and depends on the subjective assessment of local and regional commissions, as well as on regional quotas defined by the MAS; (ii) level of the benefit, since if not combined with other sources of income it is sufficient to live a life in dignity; and (iii) effectiveness, since eligible persons do not have access if the quota has been reached. Thus, it can be argued that the PNAFN is not in conformity with the R202.

8.2.5 Non-discrimination

The principle of non-discrimination aims at guaranteeing equality of treatment, but in order to achieve this, differentiations in scope are allowed and encouraged. This means that affirmative action in favour of particularly disadvantaged groups is more than welcome.

---

46. M. Ben Braham, *L'approche basée sur les droits de l'homme du système de sécurité sociale tunisien*, cit., 35.
47. CRES, BAD *supra* n. 24, 7.
48. M. Ben Braham, *L'approche basée sur les droits de l'homme du système de sécurité sociale tunisien*, cit., 35.

Women can be considered to be one of these groups, because of their lower rate of engagement in formal labour market and their fundamental role as caregivers.

In fact, the MAS boasts that PNAFN pays special attention to women, reserving privileged access to benefits allocated to single mothers;[49] however, according to the latest estimates, just 51% of those who received cash assistance under PNAFN were women.[50] This percentage does not prove a genuine affirmative action, since it does not seem adequate to provide a governmental response to the phenomenon of the 'feminization of poverty'.[51]

More relevant is the fact that the programme presents a geographically unequal distribution of social benefits, since most households that benefit from the PNAFN are located in the north-west and centre-west areas (42%)[52] which are among the poorest regions in the country.[53] These areas have also been subject to a considerable increase in the awarding of benefits. The number of families covered by the programme has increased all over the country, but the most disadvantaged areas have been particularly affected by the increase: as a matter of fact, the number receiving cash benefits in the Governorates of Kasserine has tripled, while in Sidi Bouzid it has multiplied by 2.5.[54]

---

49. Ministère des Affaires de la Femme, de la Famille, de l'Enfance, Direction Générale de la Communication et de l'Information, *Réponse du Gouvernement tunisien au questionnaire adressé aux gouvernements sur la mise en œuvre du programme d'action du Beijing (1995) et les textes issus de la 23eme session extraordinaire de l'assemblée générale (2000)*, 13.
50. C. Arfa and H. Egazzar, *Consolidation and Transparency: Transforming Tunisia's Health Care for the Poor*, 8 (2013).
51. S. Bessis, *La situation des femmes en Tunisie aujourd'hui*, https://nawaat.org/portail/2012/03/08/interview-sophie-bessis-la-situation-des-femmes-en-tunisie-aujourdhui/ (accessed on 2 Mar. 2017).
52. T. Abdessalem, H. Nemsia and A. Benhamida, *Objectives du Millénaire pour le Développement, Rapport National de Suivi*, cit., 49.
53. In 2010, 41.3% of the people living below the poverty line were residing within this area. See Banque Mondiale, *La Révolution Inachevée. Créer des opportunités, des emploisde qualité et de la richesse pour tous les Tunisiens*, 303 (2014).
54. T. Abdessalem, H. Nemsia and A. Benhamida, *Objectives du Millénaire pour le Développement, Rapport National de Suivi*, cit., 50.

Figure 8.1 Comparison of Number of PNAFN's Beneficiaries in 2011 and 2005

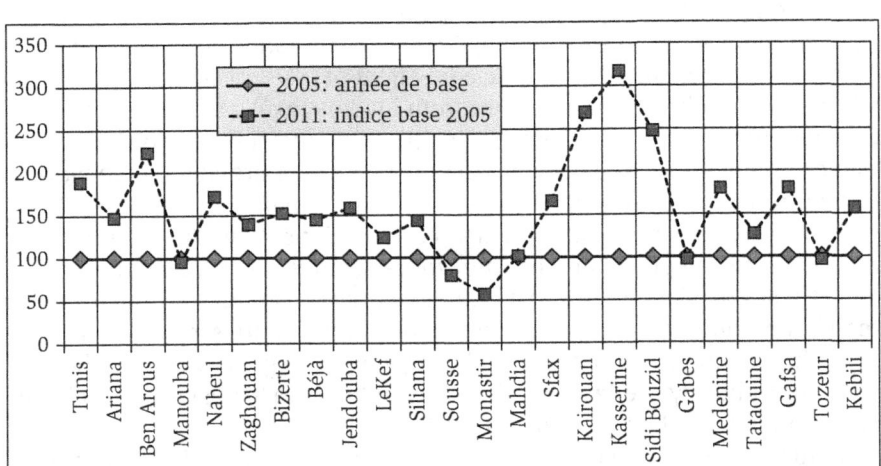

Source: Tunisian MAS. retrieved from République tunisienne, PNUD, *Objectifs du Millénaire pour le Développement. Rapport national de suivi* 2013, (2014) 50.

Moreover, it is worth mentioning that since 2009, the programme has included an affirmative action scheme in terms of access to the labour market, providing preferential access to the public sector for young graduates belonging to families who benefit from the PNAFN, according to criteria such as the duration of the unemployment status.[55]

To sum up, it is possible to argue that although the PNAFN is not inherently discriminatory, its implementation raises some concerns with regard to non-discrimination: the enjoyment of the public benefit depends ultimately on the decision made by the regional commission taking into account the regional quota assigned by the MAS. This mechanism can result in discrimination by excluding families who meet the requirements of the programme and should benefit from the cash transfer. This concern is increased by the fact that the procedure at the regional commissions is not transparent, and therefore it is not unlikely that arbitrary decisions are taken. Finally, the fact that the programme addresses only households tends to exclude those who live alone, however limited in numbers.

---

55. Ministère des Affaires Sociales, Bureau des Etudes, de la Planification et de la Programmation, *Les programmes sociaux de lutte contre la pauvreté et d'amélioration des conditions de vie*, 3 (2011).

8.2.6 Financial Solidarity

The PNAFN is financed out of the annual budget allocated to public spending and, according to the estimates of the World Bank, during the period 2012-2015 the government spent approximately TND 420 million (corresponding to USD 189 million) per year on PNAFN, the equivalent of 0.4% of GDP.[56] The allocated funds come from the State's revenues from income taxes and therefore it can be argued that the scheme respects the principle of financial solidarity, according to which economically active persons finance those who are not able to work and the amount of tax depends on each one's ability to pay.

However, in terms of workers' contributions there is a considerable imbalance between public and private workers, since according to the estimates of the Ministry of Finance, in 2010, public workers paid 80% of the total direct taxes in the country, while the amount of public salaries represents 37% of GDP;[57] this inequality is not justified by generally higher wages in the public sector, but rather by the fact that the self-employed in Tunisia are less likely to declare and pay all their personal taxes.[58]

Actually, this can be understood as a general flaw in Tunisia's contribution system, where everyone is required to pay relatively high rates of income tax,[59] but while the well off have the instruments and capability to evade or avoid taxes, low-income households do not have the means to 'work the system', and therefore generally pay their taxes in full, resulting in a de facto inequality. Beneficiaries of PNAFN are not required to pay taxes on the cash benefit they receive, but the tax burden on low-income families can affect their buying power and therefore push them towards and across the poverty line.

Moreover, the high rate of unemployment and the relevance of the informal sector represent a serious challenge in terms of public revenue, which in turn is reflected in State spending on social aid.

As a consequence, the fiscal reform started in 2012 is very much welcomed, since it aims, among others, to limit tax evasion, increase local budgets in order to promote regional development, and promote financial transparency. However, it has been argued that the measures adopted in the immediate aftermath of the revolution have been in continuity with previous regimes and have been

---

56. World Bank, *Implementation Completion and Result Report on a Trust Fund to the Republic of Tunisia for a State and Peace Building Fund. Participatory Service Delivery for Reintegration Project*, http://documents.worldbank.org/curated/en/812131467992782272/text/ICR3568-P127212-Box393228B-OUO-9.txt (accessed on 30 Jan. 2017).
57. *Rapport Alternatif de la Société Civile Tunisienne au Pacte International Relatif aux Droits Économiques, Sociaux et Culturels*, cit., 5.
58. J. Alm, *Analyzing and Reforming Tunisia's Tax System*, Tulane Economics Working Paper Series No. 1515, 25 (2015).
59. N. Jouini, N. Lustig, A. Moummi, and A. Shimeles, *Fiscal Incidence and Poverty Reduction: Evidence from Tunisia*, CEQ Working Paper No. 38, 3, 21 (2016).

lacking in any coherent long-term vision of economic reform; in particular, they do not focus enough attention on equity and wealth redistribution.[60]

These aspects have necessarily to be improved in order for the PNAFN to be in line with the R202, since presently, the programme does not comply with the principle of financial solidarity.

8.2.7 Good Governance

The Circulars establishing the programme do not make explicit reference to the principle of good governance, and they stop at referring to the need for regular monitoring of the programme. Nonetheless, the State has not even undertaken a constant monitoring of the programme and as a consequence, PNAFN has serious shortcomings in terms of management and implementation.[61]

The recent assessments of the cash transfer programme have highlighted numerous cases of misallocation of funds, as well as a lack of transparency. The number of beneficiaries of the programme is defined at the discretion of the Minister of Social Affairs and the local and regional commissions; additionally, this number is not available to the public. Finally, the whole procedure of developing the list of beneficiaries is not transparent.[62] This alarming report confirms the general Tunisian pattern with reference to good governance.

Indeed, according to Transparency International's index, which measures the perceived levels of public sector corruption, Tunisia ranked 76th out of 176 countries assessed in 2015.[63] The awareness of the high incidence of corruption pushed the Constitution makers to give special recognition to the principle of good governance in the 2014 Constitution: it figures among the founding principles of the Republic in the Preamble.

Moreover, Article 130 of the Constitution foresees the creation of the Constitutional Commission for Good Governance and Fight against Corruption. This body will be in charge of contributing to policies of good governance, preventing and fighting corruption, as well as monitoring cases of corruption within the public and private sectors. The constitutional provision of this commission is promising and demonstrates the public authorities' commitment to tackle the shortcomings of the system.

Although the creation of this Constitutional Commission is still ongoing, in 2011, the National Authority for the Fight against Corruption was created and in

---

60. M.C. Paciello, *Delivering the Revolution? Post-uprising Socio-economics in Tunisia and Egypt*, 48 The International Spectator, 19 (2013).
61. Remarkably, the only evaluation carried out by the Ministry of Social Affairs in the period 1986-2011 dates back to 1993 and it had envisaged an evaluation of the programme every five years. Cf. CRES, BAD, Enquête *d'évaluation de la* performance des programme *de lutte contre la pauvreté en* Tunisie., cit. 6.
62. M. Ben Braham, *L'approche basée sur les droits de l'homme du système de sécurité sociale tunisien*, Etude du Bureau des Droits de l'Homme des Nations Unies en Tunisie, 27 (2013).
63. Transparency International, *Corruption Perception Index 2015*, http://www.transparency.org/cpi2015 (accessed on 27 Nov. 2016).

2016, a specific Ministry with the task of fighting corruption was established. These bodies are charged with the difficult task of tackling the widespread corruption and poor governance in the public sector.[64]

As far as the PNAFN is concerned, some efforts to improve the targeting of beneficiaries have been carried out: in 2016, a unique social identification number was introduced and it should limit the misallocation of funds. Moreover, it is worth mentioning that the Parliament has passed the Organic Law No. 2016-22 of 24 March 2016 concerning the right to access information, which should allow interested people access to the decisions of the regional commissions as well as the MAS. At the time of writing, it is, however, too early to evaluate its effectiveness.

These legislative developments are welcoming but several other steps have to be taken in this regard because the PNAFN is not in conformity with the R202 as far as good governance is concerned.

8.2.8 Coherence of Policies

A national social protection floor may consist of different schemes and measures and consequently, the coherence of policies is crucial. The PNAFN fits within a broader spectrum of social policies, whose adoption dates back to the final decades of the last century.

The most relevant policies are the Free Medical Assistance Programme (AMG), the Medical Assistance Programme at a reduced rate (AMGII), both established in 1998; and the National Solidarity Fund created in 1992 in order to promote and finance development initiatives in the so-called shadows areas corresponding to the most disadvantaged in the population. This Fund was strengthened in 1999 with the creation of the National Employment Fund, which aimed at reducing unemployment among the most vulnerable categories of job seekers.

These two Funds were financed through quasi-mandatory donations and the State budget, and are considered to be representative of the instrumental social policy of the authoritarian regime.[65] Although the regime's legitimization function of the Funds and their clientelistic management cannot be ignored, they have been successful in reducing poverty and have served as models for other countries.[66]

Moreover, the State runs supplementary programmes providing financial assistance on an ad hoc basis, such as the social benefit allocated for religious

---

64. I. Atif, *Lutte anticorruption: Une multitude d'instances et zéro résultat*, in http://www.businessnews.com.tn/impression/519/62572/ (accessed on 2 Feb. 2017).
65. M. Catusse, *Les temps des entrepreneurs. Politique et transformations du capitalisme au Maroc*, Institut de recherche sur le Maghreb contemporain: Rabat, 159 (2008).
66. L. Sadiki, *Tunisian National Solidarity Fund as an Alternative Model*, http://carnegieendowment.org/sada/22473 (accessed 2 Mar. 2017).

holidays. A further contribution to the fight against poverty is made by the General Compensation Fund, which subsidizes food products.[67]

Through the establishment of all these schemes, Tunisia has demonstrated its dedication to social development and the principle of coherence of policies is one of the better-respected ones. Without underestimating this, it can be noted that it could be better implemented: the policies are not in fact integrated into a national programme for the fight against poverty and this represents the major shortcoming. If harmonized and better coordinated, these schemes would be more effective in alleviating poverty. Moreover, while the existence of various programmes is a positive, it is questionable whether potential beneficiaries excluded from PNAFN have access to the other social benefits.

Finally, it is particularly deplorable that in general these programmes have been distorted by politics, and it is a reform of the social policies in order to prioritize their scope is desired.

8.2.9 Social Participation

As far as the social participation principle is concerned, the PNAFN provides for the participation of civil society representatives within the local and regional commissions in charge of evaluating the eligibility of beneficiaries. These commissions comprise members of the Tunisian League of Human Rights and the Tunisian Union of Social Solidarity.

The involvement of these members has to be praised since it is in line with the principles laid down in R202. However, the participation of these actors is not without criticism: first of all, it is not transparent, because it is not possible to find information about the role actively played by these organizations within the commissions; second, they can only participate in compiling the lists of beneficiaries, but do not have a part in the establishment of the benefit levels, or in the definition of regional quotas, since these are defined by the MAS; third, they are not involved in the evaluation assessment of the programme.

As a consequence, within the frame of the envisaged reform of the programme in line with the SPFs, a greater inclusion of these actors and more transparency in their activity is necessary.

It is remarkable that in this context trade unions do not seem particularly engaged in supporting the programme, despite their claims about their engagement in promoting social protection for informal workers. This could be explained by the fact the PNAFN mainly supports families of non-working members or persons engaged in informal work, providing them with a minimum income. This aspect however should not be a reason for uninterest on the part of trade unions, and on the contrary, the protection of these workers should be a matter of concern.

---

67. The General Compensation Fund was created by Act No. 26/1970 of 29 May 1970.

This disengagement does not seem provoked by a restrictive legal framework as far as freedom of association is concerned. In the aftermath of the Tunisian revolution of 2011, the freedom of association was re-established through the adoption of Decree No. 2011-88 of 24 September 2011, and the new Constitution establishes the right to organize in trade unions and associations (Article 35). As a consequence, the number of associations has mushroomed:[68] new trade unions have been created, as have associations specifically dealing with informal workers.

These developments, however, have not prevented cases of intimidation and threats to the trade unions and their leaders, as documented by the observations of the International Trade Union Confederation to the ILO Committee of Experts.[69]

In my opinion, these deficiencies are not so serious as to have limited social participation. The main problem seems to be the rather weak engagement of trade unions in this sector, as witnessed by the fact that the social contract signed between the government, the UGTT and the UTICA in 2013 has not dedicated so much attention to the reform of social benefit schemes.

To sum up, it is possible to say that the PNAFN's design respects the principle of social participation. In its implementation, however, some deficiencies are present and the involvement of representative organizations of persons concerned is missing, because of a lack of engagement on the part of trade unions and other civil society organizations, which are more active in other fields, such as civil and political rights.

8.3 LEGISLATIVE DEFICITS

The analysis of the PNAFN reveals several legislative shortcomings. First of all, the social assistance programme finds its normative basis in governmental circulars which are not available in the online legislative database, thus undermining the principle of certainty of law. These circulars, moreover, can be easily repealed and therefore the programme does not have a secure legal basis.

Second, the programme's implementation is very much dependant on the role of regional and local commissions in a situation where these bodies are

---

68. Remarkably, a survey carried out in 2013 highlighted that after the Revolution the number of Tunisian associations increased rapidly: from January 2011 to December 2012, about 4,997 new associations were created. *See* Fondation pour le futur, *Etude sur les organisations de la société civile en Tunisie. Rapport final*, in Foundation for futur, 10 (2013), http://foundationforfuture.org/en/Portals/0/Publications/Etude%20OSC%20Tunisie-Rapport%20Final%20v%204.pdf (accessed on 24 Feb. 2017).
69. Observation (CEACR) – adopted 2015, published 105th ILC session (2016) concerning the Freedom of Association and Protection of the Right to Organise Convention, 1948 (No. 87): http://www.ilo.org/dyn/normlex/en/f?p=NORMLEXPUB:13100:0::NO::P13100_COMMENT_ID,P11110_COUNTRY_ID,P11110_COUNTRY_NAME,P11110_COMMENT_YEAR:3254961,102986,Tunisia,2015 (accessed on 24 Feb. 2017).

rarely accountable to the citizens. This deficiency is witnessed also by the fact that their decisions are not available to the public.

Third, the programme performs badly in terms of targeting poor families, since 38.2% of Tunisia's poorest quintile do not receive any form of assistance, and if the PNAFN was better targeted towards the poorest households, 25% of the current beneficiaries would not be entitled to any cash transfer at all.

As a consequence of this misallocation of the social benefit, it is not surprising that the PNAFN has not succeeded in eradicating social injustice, or in alleviating the difficulty in accessing the labour market or in diminishing regional inequalities.[70]

Moreover, it is deplorable that, despite having been operational for three decades, the programme has not been subject to periodic evaluation.[71]

In addition, beneficiaries are totally excluded from the process of cash transfer allocation: they are responsible for applying for the social benefit but then they do not participate at all in the decision-making process of local and regional commissions and they do not even know the procedure for allocation.[72]

Finally, the number of social assistants in charge of verifying the eligibility conditions of households is largely insufficient (1 per 7,000 inhabitants).[73]

8.4 CONCLUSIONS

Tunisia boasts a comparatively well-developed and long-established social protection system, which also has a non-contributory component. The PNAFN belongs to this category and guarantees social assistance to families in need. The programme was designed and implemented before the adoption of R202, and currently does not qualify as a social protection floor as defined by it.

As previously highlighted, the programme has several shortcomings and thus proves itself unable to respond to the many needs of poor and vulnerable households. This inability to promote a reduction of regional inequality and poverty has to be linked to the ultimate cause of the 2011 Revolution, which indeed had the purpose of dignity at its core.[74] In fact, the popular upheaval paved the way for a political and constitutional transition that resulted in breaking a fifty-year reign of authoritarianism and established a constitutional democracy; however, an improvement in the socio-economic situation has been more difficult to achieve.

---

70. T. Abdessalem, H. Nemsia and A. Benhamida, *Objectives du Millénaire pour le Développement, Rapport National de Suivi*, cit., 50.
71. M. Ben Braham, *L'approche basée sur les droits de l'homme du système de sécurité sociale tunisien*, cit., 35.
72. M. Ben Braham, *L'approche basée sur les droits de l'homme du système de sécurité sociale tunisien*, cit., 27.
73. *Ibid.* 39.
74. N. Ben Cheik, *L'extension de la protection sociale à l'économie informelle à l'épreuve de la transition en Tunisie*, CRES Working Papers, 4 (2013).

Indeed, Tunisia faces serious problems in terms of its high unemployment rate (above 15%) and a high rate of informal employment (37% of the overall economy). These problems are exacerbated by the strong regional differences that characterize the country. Due to this, social assistance programmes should be in a position to play a fundamental role in mitigating poverty and vulnerability, and consequently in stabilizing the troubled political situation.

So far, the PNAFN has not been capable of meeting this challenge, but it could constitute a basis for the establishment of a national social protection floor. However, in order to be properly set up, the programme would need some major reforms, since currently, it does not comply with the majority of principles set out by R202.

In this sense, the recent legislative measures adopted to improve the social protection system have to be praised, and it is highly desirable that the PNAFN is interested in reform to further strengthen its potential and to address its shortcomings. In particular, major measures to help the people in need have to be taken. First, all families who comply with the eligibility criteria of the scheme should receive the social benefit; second, the funds for financing the programme should be secured and increased in order to guarantee a decent standard of living; third, it is necessary to continuously monitor the programme and introduce improved management and a complaints mechanism; and fourth, reform of the programme should tackle the geographical imbalances.

With regard to this latter point, it has to be noted that the constitutional objective of decentralization in order to promote regional development may also have an impact on the PNAFN's management. The 2014 Constitution in fact has given more relevance to local authorities and has created a new level of government, that of districts. As a consequence, the role of local and regional commission, as far as PNAFN is concerned, could be reformed.

In conclusion, the Tunisian Legislator should take the opportunity of the constitutional transition, started in 2011, to reform its social assistance system, which can be improved considerably, basing on the foundations already in place.

BIBLIOGRAPHY

Abdeljaouad, A. *The Influence of International Labour Conventions on Tunisian Legislation*, 91 International Labour Review, 191 (1965).

Abdessalem, T. & Nemsia, H. & Benhamida, A. *Objectives du Millénaire pour le Développement, Rapport National de Suivi*, Tunis: PNUD (2013).

Adhadhi, N. *Vers la création Conseil National du Dialogue Social*, http://www.realites.com.tn/2015/05/vers-la-creation-conseil-national-du-dialogue-social/ (accessed 20 November 2016).

Alm, J. *Analyzing and Reforming Tunisia's Tax System*, in Tulane Economics Working Paper Series No. 1515, (2015).

Arfa, C. & Egazzar, H. *Consolidation and Transparency: Transforming Tunisia's Health Care for the Poor*, Washington DC: World Bank (2013).

Atif, I. *Lutte anticorruption: Une multitude d'instances et zéro résultat*, in http://www.businessnews.com.tn/impression/519/62572/ (accessed 20 November 2016).

Destremau, B. *La protection sociale en Tunisie. Nature et cohérence de l'intervention publique*, in M. Catusse & E. Verdier (eds.), L'Etat face aux débordements du social au Maghreb. Formation, travail et *protection sociale*, Paris: IREMAM/ Karthala, 129-171 (2009).

Banque Africaine de Développement, *Subventions alimentaires et aides sociales directes: vers un meilleur ciblage de la pauvreté monétaire et des privations en Tunisie* (2013).

Banque Mondiale, *Consolidation de la Politique de Protection Sociale et d'Emploi en Tunisie Renforcer les Systèmes, Connecter à l'Emploi*, Washington DC: Banque Mondiale (2015).

Banque Mondiale, *La Révolution Inachevée. Créer des opportunités, des emplois de qualité et de la richesse pour tous les Tunisiens*, Washington DC: Banque Mondiale (2014).

Banque Mondiale, *Tunisie. Diagnostic-pays systématique*, Washington DC: World Bank, (2015).

Banque Mondiale, *Vers une meilleure équité: les subventions énergétiques, le ciblage et la protection sociale en Tunisie*, Rapport n. 82712-TN, Washington DC: Banque Mondiale (2013).

Béchir, R. *Pauvreté et niveau de vie de la population rurale en Tunisie*, 67 Les notes d'alerte du CIHEAM, 2 (2010).

Ben Amor, R. *Politique sociale et pauvreté en Tunisie*, 49(1) Cahier de la Méditerranée 189, 227 (1994).

Ben Braham, M. *Effectivité des droits économiques et sociaux en Tunisie*, in European Commission Through Law (eds), *Report of the Workshop 'Transparency and the rule of law as pre-conditions of equitable and sustainable development'*, 41,52 (2014).

Ben Braham, M. *L'approche basée sur les droits de l'homme du système de sécurité sociale tunisien*, Tunis: Etude du Bureau des Droits de l'Homme des Nations Unies en Tunisie, (2013).

Ben Chaabane, T. *Social Rights in Post-Revolutionary Tunisia: Is a Consensus-Driven Policy Still on the Table?*, EU Spring (2016).

Ben Cheik, N. *L'extension de la protection sociale à l'économie informelle à l'épreuve de la transition en Tunisie*, Tunis: CRES Working Papers (2013).

Bessis, S. *La situation des femmes en Tunisie aujourd'hui*, https://nawaat.org/portail/2012/03/08/interview-sophie-bessis-la-situation-des-femmes-en-tunisie-aujourdhui/ (accessed 2 March 2017).

Catusse, M. & Verdier E. (eds), L'Etat face aux débordements du social au Maghreb. Formation, travail et *protection sociale*, Paris: IREMAM/ Karthala (2009).

Catusse, M. *Les temps des entrepreneurs. Politique et transformations du capitalisme au Maroc*, Institut de recherche sur le Maghreb contemporain: Rabat (2008).

Centre de Recherches et d'Etudes Sociales (CRES), Banque Africaine de Développement (BAD), Enquête *d'évaluation de la* performance des programmemes *de lutte contre la pauvreté en* Tunisie. Résultat de la phase 1 de l'étude. Résumé exécutif, 1, 10 (2015).

Chaabane, M. *Towards the Universalization of Social Security: The Experience of Tunisia, ILO, Extension of Social Security*, ESS Paper No. 4, 1, 29 (2002).

Committee of Experts on the Application of Conventions and Recommendations, *Observation concerning the Freedom of Association and Protection of the Right to Organise Convention, 1948 (No. 87)*, http://www.ilo.org/dyn/normlex/en/f?p=NORMLEXPUB:13100:0::NO::P13100_COMMENT_ID,P11110_COUNTRY_ID,P11110_COUNTRY_NAME,P11110_COMMENT_YEAR:3254961,102986,Tunisia,2015 (accessed 24 February 2017).

Committee on Economic, *Social and Cultural Rights Reviews Third Report of Tunisia*.

Committee on Economic, Social and Cultural Rights, *Concluding Observations to the 3rd periodical report*.

Fondation pour le futur, *Etude sur les organisations de la société civile en Tunisie. Rapport final*, in *Foundation for futur*, 10 (2013), http://documents.worldbank.org/curated/en/812131467992782272/text/ICR3568-P127212-Box393228B-OUO-9.txt (accessed 25 November 2016).

INS, CRES, AfDB, *Analyse de l'impact des subventions alimentaires et des programmemes d'assistance*, Tunis: Institute Nationale de la Statistique (2013).

Institut National de la Statistique, Enquête *nationale sur le budget, la* consommation *et le niveau de vie* des ménages (2015).

Institut National de la Statistique, *Mesure de la pauvreté des inégalités et de la polarisation en Tunisie 2000-2010*, Tunis: Institute Nationale de la Statistique (2012).

Jouini, M. & Lustig, N. Moummi, A. Shimeles, A. *Fiscal Incidence and Poverty Reduction: Evidence from Tunisia*, CEQ Working Paper No. 38 (2016).

La lettre du CRES, *Les socles nationaux de protection sociale: émergence du concept, meilleures pratiques internationales et pertinence pour la Tunisie*, No. 7 (2015).

Ministère des Affaires de la Femme, de la Famille, de l'Enfance, Direction Générale de la Communication et de l'Information, *Réponse du Gouvernement tunisien au questionnaire adressé aux gouvernements sur la mise en œuvre du programmeme d'action du Beijing (1995) et les textes issus de la 23eme session extraordinaire de l'assemblée générale (2000)*.

Ministère des Affaires Etrangères, *Réponse du Gouvernement tunisien au « questionnaire relatif aux programmemes de transferts financiers adressé aux gouvernements par l'Experte indépendante sur la question de droits de l'homme et l'extrême pauvreté »* (2008).

Ministère des Affaires Sociales, Bureau des Etudes, de la Planification et de la Programmemation, *Les programmemes sociaux de lutte contre la pauvreté et d'amélioration des conditions de vie* (2011).

Ministère des Affaires Sociales, *Rapport général de la conférence nationale sur le système de la protection sociale: 'pour la mise en place d'un socle de protection sociale'* (2014).

Ministry of Social Affairs, UNICEF, *Evaluation of Tunisia's Education Benefit Programme of PNAFN*, http://socialprotection.org/discover/publications/evaluation-education-benefit-program-pnafn-tunisia (accessed 20 November 2016).

Mzid, N. *Les Droits fondamentaux au travail en Tunisie a la lumière des normes de l'Oit*, 11 Etudes Juridiques, 36 (2004).

OECD, *Investing in Youth: Tunisia Strengthening the Employability of Youth During the Transition to a Green Economy*, http://www.oecd-ilibrary.org/social-issues-migration-health/investing-in-youth-tunisia_9789264226470-en (accessed 20 November 2016)

Paciello, M.C. *Delivering the Revolution? Post-uprising Socio-economics in Tunisia and Egypt*, 48 The International Spectator, 19 (2013).

PNUD, *Stratégie de la réduction de la pauvreté en Tunisie. Etude du phénomène de la pauvreté en Tunisie*, Tunis: PNUD (2004).

Présidence du Gouvernement, Conseil des Analyses Economiques, *Programme National Des Réformes Majeures 2016–2020* (2016).

Société Civile Tunisienne, Rapport Alternatif de la au Pacte International Relatif aux Droits Économiques, Sociaux et Culturels, http://tbinternet.ohchr.org/_layouts/treatybodyexternal/Download.aspx?symbolno=INT%2fCESCR%2fCSS%2fTUN%2f24946&Lang=en (accessed 20 November 2016).

République tunisienne, PNUD, *Objectifs du Millénaire pour le Développement. Rapport national de suivi 2013*, (2014).

S. Chaker, 'Impacts sociaux de l'ajustement structurel: cas de la Tunisie', 10(1) *Nouvelles pratiques sociales* 151 (1997).

Sadiki, L. *Tunisian National Solidarity Fund as an Alternative Model*, http://carnegieendowment.org/sada/22473 (accessed 2 March 2017).

Transparency International, *Corruption Perception Index 2015*, http://www.transparency.org/cpi2015 (accessed 20 November 2016).

World Bank 2016, *Tunisia Poverty Assessment 2015*, https://openknowledge.worldbank.org/handle/10986/24410 (March 2016).

World Bank, *Chapter 5: Social and Economic Inclusion*, in World Bank, *Tunisia Country Programme Evaluation*, Washington DC: World Bank, 97-126 (2014).

World Bank, *§ Report on a Trust Fund to the Republic of Tunisia for a State and Peace Building Fund. Participatory Service Delivery for Reintegration Project* (2015), http://documents.worldbank.org/curated/en/812131467992782272/text/ICR3568-P127212-Box393228B-OUO-9.txt (accessed on 30 January 2017).

CHAPTER 9
Chile Solidario CCT Programme: New Logic Behind Chilean Social Protection Programmes

Pablo Arellano Ortiz

9.1 BACKGROUND FROM CHILE SOLIDARIO PROGRAMME TO OPORTUNIDADES Y SEGURIDADES PROGRAMME

Chile is known worldwide for various aspects of its history and in the matter of protection of social risks by its controversial private pension fund system.[1] Despite this constant criticism of the way, it protects old-age pensions, social security in Chile has a long standing[2] and an acceptable level of coverage. The Chilean social protection system is solid, with various sub-systems and programmes that provide protection to the most vulnerable people, regardless of their sex, nationality or migratory situation. Today, the social protection systems in Chile provide coverage through sixty-nine social programmes that are implemented through the Ministry of Social Development. As part of this system of social protection, the Chile Solidario programme existed, which has been

---

1. About this *see*: Pablo Arellano Ortiz, *Protection of Old Age in Chile*, 415-427 (Ulrich Becker, Frans Pennings and Tineke Dijkhoff eds, Kluwer 2013); Pablo Arellano Ortiz, *Universalism and Individualism in Chilean Pension Law: An Example of Extension of Coverage for Eastern Europe*, 219-231 (Roger Blanpain, William Bromwich, Olga Rymkevich & Iacopo Senatori eds.), Bulletin of Comparative Labour Relations Vol. 80, Labour Markets, Industrial Relations and Human Resources Management, Kluwer 2012); Pablo Arellano Ortiz, *The Private Pension System. Critic Study Base on the Chilean Case*, 363 (Roger Blanpain & Michele Tiraboschi eds, Bulletin of Comparative Labour Relations 65, Global Labour Market: From Globalisation to Flexicurity, Kluwer 2008).
2. In this regard *see*: ILO, *El seguro social y la protección social*, Conferencia Internacional del Trabajo, 80a reunión, Memoria del Director General (Parte I), 9 (Ginebra 1993).

transformed into the Securities and Opportunities programme. The Chile Solidario programme achieved a certain level of recognition for the innovative nature of its conditional cash transfer policies in the Latin American region and also for having been considered by the ILO in the preparatory work for Recommendation No. 202.[3] Today the mechanism no longer exists and it has been reformulated, nevertheless, the protected group continues to exist.

The work begins with an explanation of what we have named as the key factors in social protection in Latin America; this in order to be able to situate the Chilean context. Then we will refer to the discussion of the origin of the Chile Solidario programme, its evolution and transformation to its current version: Securities and Opportunities. A final point that we consider necessary to analyse is the determination of the beneficiary. The change of focus on this point is of prime importance when analysing social protection mechanisms.

9.1.1 Key Factors in the Latin American Context

The difficulties involved in social protection are present in Chile as in its neighbouring countries. Thus, we can see serious problems of inequality and also in the structure of the labour market where the main obstacle to social protection is the high rate of informal employment, although it is low when compared to the regional figures.[4]

In terms of inequality, the Economic Commission for Latin America and the Caribbean (ECLAC) has recently published a study[5] that shows that the average Gini coefficient for the countries with recent information available fell from 0.497 in 2013 to 0.491 in 2014. When the most recent figures are compared with those from the start of the 2010s, a more substantial reduction is found. The regional index stood at 0.507 in 2010, so by 2014, there had been a cumulative fall of 3.2%, equivalent to 0.8% a year. There were statistically significant changes in the Gini coefficient in nine of the sixteen countries considered during this period. The largest reductions were in Uruguay (-2.7% a year), Argentina (-2.3% a year) and Ecuador (-2.2% a year).

---

3. For example see: ILO OMS, *Social Protection Floor for a Fair and Inclusive Globalization*. Report of the Social Protection Floor Advisory Group (Geneva, International Labour Office 2011) and ILO, *Extending Social Security to All, A Guide Through Challenges and Options* (International Labour Office, Social Security Department, Geneva 2010).
4. For an explanation of these problems in relation to old age risk, see: Pablo Arellano Ortiz, *Reto actual de las pensiones de vejez: ¿Fin de las AFP?¿Regreso a reparto?* (Santiago, Librotecnia 2015).
5. See: ECLAC, *Social Panorama of Latin America 2015* (Social Development Division and the Statistics Division of the Economic Commission for Latin America and the Caribbean (ECLAC), 2016).

Chapter 9: Chile Solidario CCT Programme

Figure 9.1   Annual Rate of Change in the Gini Coefficient, 2002-2010 and 2010-2014

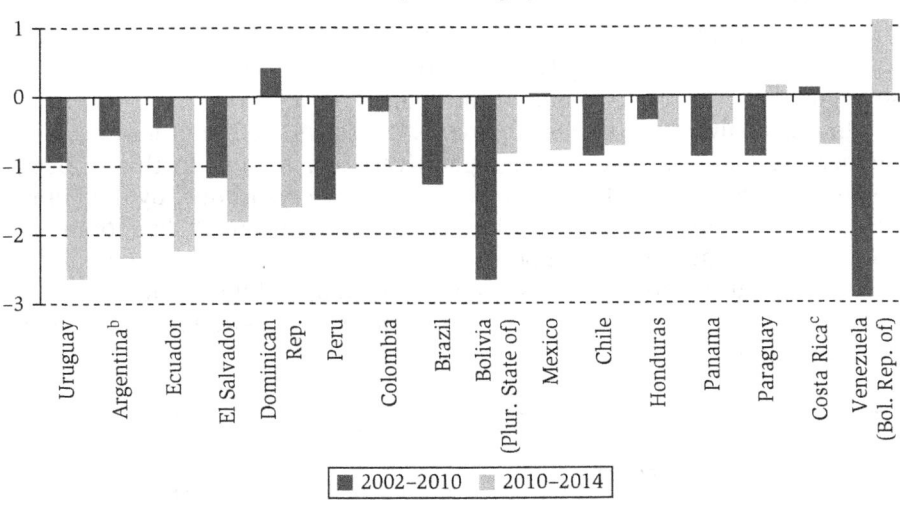

Source: ECLAC 2016, p. 13.

However, when analysing the presence of Latin American countries in the context of the OECD, the true reality of inequality in the region can be seen. The data show that Mexico and Chile are the most unequal countries of the OECD.

Figure 9.2   Gini Coefficient of Disposable Income Inequality in 2007-2014

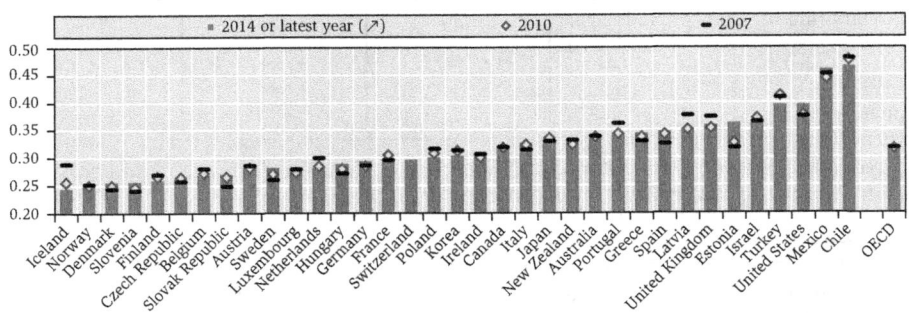

Source: OECD, November 2016.

199

In addition to the above, it should be mentioned that according to ECLAC and OXFAM, income and wealth concentration are at the heart of inequality in the region. The richest 10% in Latin America and the Caribbean own 71% of the wealth and their tax rate is only 5.4% of their income.[6]

As the data show, Chile is a country whose internal reality shows great inequality. This is shown above all by the levels of wages. The minimum wage in Chile reaches CLP 264,000[7] (USD 393),[8] and according to the *Fundación Sol*, 50% of Chilean workers earn less than CLP 340,000 (USD 506), and seven out of ten workers earn less than CLP 500,000[9] (USD 744). A very small percentage of the population has all the wealth of the country.

In this analysis, the poverty line must be considered in order to establish whether the minimum wage is comparatively low or not. In this respect, it should be pointed out that according to information distributed by the Ministry of Social Development, one must take into account one poverty line for the poor and another for the extremely poor. In the table that follows, we will take into account the figures and consider a family group of up to four members. This will be done following the classic family model of the bread-winning male, female and two children.

Table 9.1 Poverty Line in Chile

	One Family Member	*Two Family Member*	*Three Family Member*	*Four Family Member*
Poverty line in CLP	155.620	252.806	335.777	410.684
Poverty line in USD	231	376	499	611
Poverty line in CLP, for extreme poverty	103.747	168.537	223.851	273.790
Poverty line in USD, for extreme poverty	154	250	333	407

Source: Ministerio de Desarrollo Social, *Valor de la Canasta Básica de Alimentos y Líneas de Pobreza, Informe Mensual*, November 2016, p. 4.

---

6. See the information at http://www.cepal.org/en/pressreleases/income-and-wealth-concentration-are-heart-inequality-region-according-eclac-and-oxfam (accessed 23 Jan. 2017).
7. Chilean Pesos.
8. The minimum wage is readjusted periodically this value is the effective one as of 1 Jan. 2017.
9. See: Fundación Sol, *Los Verdaderos Sueldos de Chile, Panorama Actual del Valor de la Fuerza de Trabajo Usando la NESI 2015*, Documento de trabajo área Salarios y Desigualdad (Estudios de la Fundación SOL August 2016).

Thus, when comparing income and poverty line, it can be easily concluded that a significant portion of the population lives on incomes that limit poverty or are directly poor. However, this considers exclusively declared income. An obligatory reference must therefore be made to those groups of people who de jure or de facto have been excluded from the formal labour market and whose income does not feature in official statistics. We refer without a doubt to the informal economy, which is a phenomenon with a strong presence in the Latin American region. In Chile, it is present with significant numbers, although not in as high a level as in other countries.

It has been argued[10] historically that the rate of informality in Chile has remained below the levels observed in the Latin American region. Taking the period 2010-2014, based on data from the NENE survey, there was a continuous decrease until the end of 2012, from 39.4% to 35.7%, while in 2014 there was a slight increase during the first half of the year. However, on the other hand, it can be observed that as of June 2016, there were 8,056,676 employed workers, of which 64.0% were in formal employment (5,159,707) and the remaining 36.0% were informally employed (2,896,969).[11] From these figures, it is concluded that after a period in which the informal sector suffered a slight decrease, it has increased in the last two years, making up a 36% of the Chilean labour market.

The figures expose the complex reality of the Chilean population. It is very similar to that of neighbouring countries in terms of inequality and informality but the numbers are not so stark. However, the most recent poverty rates show that poverty has not been prevented. The poverty rate today in Chile is 26.9%, taking into account those who do not receive any help from the State; if the subsidies and benefits are taken into consideration, the rate drops down to 11.7%.[12] These are the ways to measure the poverty that is considered to exist in Chile – to take into consideration those who receive benefits from the State or those who do not.

These factors were taken into account for the creation of the Chile Solidario programme. The current figures do not show a great improvement but they demonstrate an important State activity of protection. This idea of innovative State activity is what has led to the Chilean Solidarity Programme being considered to be an example of conditional transfers of money as contained in international reports.[13] This is the reason why Chile Solidario programme has

---

10. *See*: CIEDESS, *Análisis y propuestas para incentivar la cotización de los trabajadores al sistema de pensiones chileno*, informe final (Santiago, 29 Jan. 2015).
11. CIEDESS, *Boletín de Informalidad Laboral: Situación de la Informalidad en el Mercado Laboral Chileno, Cifras a junio de 2016* (Gerencia de Estudios, Santiago, November de 2016).
12. *See* the opinion on these figures in http://www.fundacionsol.cl/2017/01/pobreza-chile-la-luz-la-casen-2015-peor-lo-se-piensa/ (accessed 23 Jan. 2017).
13. For example, *see*: ILO OMS, Social protection floor for a fair and inclusive globalization. Report of the Social Protection Floor Advisory Group (Geneva, International Labour Office

been highlighted as an example of CCT in the previous discussion of ILO Recommendation No. 202, and because it is relevant to this research.

Before advancing to the origins of the programme, we must point out that this programme existed prior to the approval of the ILO Recommendation No. 202, so it can be pointed out that Chile already had a social protection floor when it was approved. The transformation of the programme was made as part of a restructuring of Chilean public policies with the intention of better protecting the poorest in society. In this transformation, the role of the ILO Recommendation No. 202 was minimal, and in our opinion, almost non-existent, since the motives for the transformation were purely of a national character.

9.1.2 Origin and Evolution: From Chile Solidario to Securities and Opportunities

At this stage, let us take a step back and see how the programme was implemented. The origins of the programme lie in the activity of the Ministry of Planning. In 2002, President Lagos introduced an innovative programme called Chile Solidario. The objective of this programme was to incorporate the families living in extreme poverty into the State's network of social protection in a guaranteed and/or preferential manner, meaning that the linkages, interaction and manner of the existing programmes were adapted. According to this programme, the family was viewed as the new focus of social intervention, based on information that demonstrated the greater effectiveness of social programmes when they are centred on the family, and on the women within the family as the main victims of poverty. Plus, the need to provide psychological and social services to families living in extreme poverty was emphasized in the programme. In sum, this support allowed families to achieve concrete results and to maintain these results over time, thus improving their quality of life and not just their incomes.

The Chile Solidario system comprised three main components in order to benefit the targeted population:

- psycho-social support and a family protection vouchers;
- guaranteed monetary subsidies; and
- preferential access to social development programmes.

All these components reflected a will to link institutions, to coordinate public assistance, as well as to coordinate between private and public sectors. For example, in 2006 the Chile Solidario programme covered about 240,000 families, as can be seen in the following chart.

2011); ILO, *Extending Social Security to All, A Guide Through Challenges and Options* (Geneva, International Labour Office, Social Security Department 2010).

Table 9.2   Coverage of Households in Chile Solidario (Puente Programme)

	Total at Beginning of Year	Accumulated	Accumulated as % of Total Households
2002	40,741	40,741	1.01
2003	50,827	91,568	2.22
2004	51,545	143,113	3.41
2005	54,806	197,919	4.64
2006	50,936	248,855	5.74
2007	39,931	288,786	6.49
2008	48,273	337,059	7.38
2009	48,291	385,350	8.23
2010	45,535	430,885	8.93
2011	57,551	488,436	9.83
2012	57,660	546,096	10.68

Source: Ministry of Social Development.

Chile Solidario sub-programmes as conceived at the origin were as follows:

(1) The Puente (Bridge) Programme, aimed at families in extreme poverty. It was run by municipalities and is administered and technically assisted by the Solidarity and Social Investment Fund (FOSIS).
(2) The Vinculos (Links) Programme, aimed at supporting adults and older adults living alone and vulnerable. It was a municipal programme and had the technical assistance of the National Service for the Elderly (SENAMA).
(3) The Calle (Street) Programme, aimed to work with adults who were homeless. It was a programme implemented by either municipalities, provincial governments and NGOs and management, and technical assistance came from the Ministry of Planning (MIDEPLAN).
(4) The Caminos (Roads) Programme, aimed at supporting children from families where situations of forced separation existed because of the enforcement order of any of its members. The programme was implemented by NGOs, and design and methodological support was provided by MIDEPLAN.

The cost of the programme over the time is also an important issue. In the following chart, the cost of sub-programme is detailed. In general, we can say that the general cost is low in relation to the purpose of alleviation of poverty in relation to the percentage of GDP that the government spends on social benefits.

Table 9.3 Expenditure of the Chilean Solidarity System (Millions of Pesos 2014)

	Bridge Programme	Links, Street and Roads Programmes	Bono Chile Solidario	Social benefit	Transfers to Other Programmes	Others	Total
2003	2,999	-	2,993	-	9,600	565	16,157
2004	6,256	-	6,739	-	36,397	927	50,319
2005	6,612	-	16,636	-	58,849	3,175	85,272
2006	6,726	1,263	16,969	-	61,457	3,296	89,711
2007	6,665	641	20,325	-	60,230	123	87,984
2008	6,127	2,169	17,450	-	57,937	4,827	88,509
2009	7,690	3,564	19,715	-	66,931	5,672	103,573
2010	7,696	4,720	20,888	-	64,663	561	98,528
2011	-	5,556	24,408	64,104	70,383	109	164,560
2012	7,677	6,489	24,362	81,019	61,214	3,813	184,575

Source: Ministry of social development.

However, even considering the programme as a success in the fight against poverty there is no significant evidence that Chile Solidario helped to increase average levels of employment and earnings of participants, although assessments have very restricted scope for data availability.[14] Thus, the programme helped the poor to survive but did not take the next step in terms of getting them out of poverty.

The origins of the Ministry of Planning can be found in the government of President Eduardo Frei Montalva (1964-1970), when the need for a technical organization dedicated to development planning at the national level arose. The Planning Office (ODEPLAN) was established and during the first two years, it worked without legal recognition and reported directly to the President of the Republic. In 1967, this new entity acquired decentralized public service status with its own assets. Regional Offices of Planning, which subsequently were renamed Regional Secretariats of Planning and Coordination (SERPLAC), and served as advisory bodies, the Technical Secretariat of the Regional Governor and the Regional Development Council were created.

In 1990 and by Decree Law No. 18,899 of 19 July, the National Planning Office was transformed into the Ministry of Planning and Cooperation, assigned with the mission to collaborate with the President of the Republic in the design and implementation policies, plans and programmes of national development, to propose public investment goals and evaluate investment projects financed by

---

14. Osvaldo Larrañaga, Dante Contreras & Cabezas Gustavo, *Políticas Contra la Pobreza: de Chile Solidario al Ingreso Ético Familiar*, Documento de Trabajo, Programa de las Naciones Unidas para el Desarrollo, 29 (Chile, Área de Reducción de la Pobreza y la Desigualdad, December 2014).

the State, and to coordinate the various public sector initiatives aimed at eradicating poverty. This included a national programme for overcoming poverty.

This effort to optimize public policies to benefit the neediest in the country motivated the creation, in 2002, of the Chile Solidario system, which provided comprehensive support to individuals and families living in extreme poverty. Three years later, the Secretary of State was responsible for developing, coordinating, disseminating and promoting nationwide the social protection system, which radically changed the focus of social policies, leaving behind a paternalistic view and replacing it with a rights approach.

In October 2011, Mideplan became the Ministry of Social Development, expanding its powers and positioning itself as the coordinating body of all Chilean social policies (social protection policies), coordinating intra-ministerial initiatives and overseeing its operation.

The creation of two new under-secretariats is one of the great innovations of this new portfolio.

The Under-secretariat of Social Services is responsible for coordinating the activities of all related services: the National Service for the Elderly (Senama), the National Corporation of Indigenous Development (Conadi), the Solidarity and Social Investment Fund (Fosis), the National Institute of Youth (Injuv) and the National Disability Service (Senadis). It also coordinates the whole system of social protection with other ministries.

The Under-secretariat of Social Evaluation, which enhances the impact of social policies, assessing and controlling existing social programmes, in order to oversee that public funds are spent properly and reach the intended beneficiaries, was also created.

Thus, the Ministry of Social Development embarked on a new journey, with a strong emphasis on fighting poverty and the needs of the most vulnerable and discriminated against in society.

The sub-system of Securities and Opportunities created in 2012 under Law No. 20.595, promotes the work developed by Chile Solidario in relation to the population in extreme poverty and the aforementioned vulnerable groups. In this context, the individuals and families belonging to the Chile Solidario programme at the end of 2012 will remain in the programme until the end of their participation. Currently, individuals and families can only enter the Securities and Opportunities programme, as the Chile Solidario programme is closing, leaving a group of 50,683 active beneficiary's families, and most of whom will finish in 2017.[15]

---

15. Ministry of Social Development, *Informe de Desarrollo Social 2014* (Santiago de Chile, 2014).

The total number of users on 31 December 2014 corresponded to 106,990 households, equivalent to 399,588 participants. Of this total, 55.7% were women and the remaining 44.3% were men.[16]

Since the reformulation of the programme, the sub-programmes have also been reformulated. The programmes run by the Ministry today are as follows:

(1) Chile Crece Contigo (Grows with You)
   In order to accompany, protect and support children from gestation and during their first years of life, Chile Grows with You was established in 2007. It is a comprehensive system for children with activities and services delivered by different government departments, coordinated by the Ministry of Social Development protection.
   It is part of the Intersectoral Social Protection System (Law 20,379) which brings together actions and social benefits for people living in situations of greater socioeconomic vulnerability.
   Children are first assisted through the Chile Grows with You programme as early as the first antenatal appointment in the public health system. They are then accompanied and supported during their development until they enter the school system. They also have guaranteed access to technical aids, nurseries and kindergartens
(2) Securities and Opportunities
   To address inequalities and open up more opportunities to women and men of different ages and conditions, the Ministry of Social Development has created programmes, actions and social benefits that make up the Social Protection System.[17]

Beneficiaries who participate in these programmes access in the first instance, psychosocial help, consisting of the permanent support of a professional who works with the family and/or person during the process. In addition, participants can access to employment assistance, also with the support of a professional, building capacity and improving work and employment opportunities.

Participants are guaranteed access to an economic contribution, through the delivery of a voucher and cash transfer to supplement income with which the person and/or family already receives. Access to social services and benefits are also guaranteed to support people according to their status and specific needs:

(1) Family Programme
   The Family Programme is aimed at individuals and families who are living in extreme poverty and are particularly vulnerable. It includes a

---

16. Ministry of Social Development, *Informe de Desarrollo Social 2015*, 112 (Santiago de Chile, 2015).
17. Social Protection System is a term used to refer to all the mechanisms and benefits of social protection provided by the State through the Ministry of Social Development.

set of actions, social services and benefits to improve the quality of life of individuals and families, contributing to the achievement of higher levels of welfare and social cohesion.

To meet this goal, the programme has employment and psychosocial support and management, social services and benefits, as well as bonds and money transfers.

The Solidarity and Social Investment (FOSIS), sees to the implementation at the local level by municipalities and governorates.

(2) Abriendo Caminos

The Abriendo Caminos programme aims to take preventive and remedial actions in the conditions of development of children and adolescent children of persons deprived of their freedom.

To this end, it promotes the development of skills and abilities that enable them to achieve better living conditions, through a strategy of comprehensive and personalized intervention. Thus, depending on the particularities, needs, resources and capabilities of each of the family members, the various actions and support are defined. The programme was introduced in 2008 and since 2012 has been run nationwide.

(3) Vinculos Programme (Links)

The Vinculos Programme provides comprehensive support to adults and adults over 65 years of age in conditions of vulnerability and social exclusion. It consists of a set of actions to meet directly the needs of people of one- or two-person households. Also, it creates the conditions for access to social protection community network, connecting the older population with public services and social networks in their community. The Links Programme provides its participants employment and psychosocial support.

9.1.3 The Mechanism for Measuring Poverty: A Determinant of Protection

One of the main relevant aspects of the Chilean mechanism is the way the targeting is done. This has been drastically modified with the reformulation of the programme.

In the first period of the Chile Solidario programme, the beneficiaries were selected by an individual mechanism through an individual survey of income called *Ficha de Proteccion Social* (FPS). However, this mechanism was found to be insufficient to meet the needs of selecting the poor, and the instrument was reformulated into a new one, keeping the individual approach, and renamed *Ficha Social* (FS).

This change is explained by a series of problems presented by the FPS, since for example, in the first government of Michelle Bachelet, many people gave false information in order to receive a benefit that under regular parameters would not be assigned to those applicants. A manifestation of this phenomenon could be seen in the different results presented by the FPS in relation to those collected in the CASEN survey; thus, the FPS recorded a greater number of disabled people present in households, fewer people by family and women's headship. These last two data were a manifestation of the omission of the husband as a member of the household, in order to be able to declare a lower income generation.[18]

Traditionally in Chile, poverty has been measured on the basis of household income. This form of income poverty measurement is an indirect measure of the well-being achieved by individuals and their households through the consumption of goods and services. This approach seeks to simplify the identification of those considered to be living under an acceptable standard of living, taking into account only one indicator. On the other hand, a multidimensional poverty measurement allows a direct measurement of the living conditions of the population, while measuring the situation of people and households in relation to different dimensions and indicators of well-being that are considered socially relevant. In this way, it makes it possible to identify deficiencies that affect people and their households in multiple dimensions, beyond their income, and to analyse the relative importance of such deficiencies in the living conditions of the population in poverty.[19] It is this redefinition that made Chile able to achieve greater certainty about who the poor are and thus to be able to better protect them.

The Social Registry of Homes (RSH) is the new system of support to the selection of users of social benefits, which replaced the FPS on 1 January 2016, and whose objective is to support the various user selection processes of benefits and social programmes, through the provision of a broad set of information, mainly from administrative records of the State, which includes the construction of a Socioeconomic Household Rating. (*Calificación Socioeconómica de los Hogares*).[20]

The database of the FP and the FPS is used in the new methodology to collate data on the range of households. This does not limit access to the household programme that would have filled only one survey. For the generation of payrolls corresponding to the year 2017, the Social Register of Households will be used, which contains a consolidated FPS and FS, plus all households that have registered with the registry since its establishment in January 2016.[21] As of

---

18. Osvaldo Larrañaga, Denise Falck, Rodrigo Herrera & Amanda Telias, *De la Ficha de Protección Social a la Reforma de la Focalización*. 10-11 (Santiago, Programa de las Naciones Unidas para el Desarrollo, 2014).
19. Ministry of Social Development, *Nueva Metodología de Medición de la Pobreza por Ingresos y Multidimensional*, Serie Documentos Metodológicos N° 28, 24 (Santiago de Chile, 2015).
20. Ministry of Social Development, *Informe de Desarrollo Social 2016*, 59 (Santiago de Chile, 2016).
21. Ministry of Social Development, *Informe de Desarrollo Social 2016*, 101 (Santiago de Chile, 2016).

July 2016, the RSH contains the entries of 12,530,003 people in 4,554,571 households, corresponding to 72.5% of the country's population.[22]

Thus, the Social Registry of Homes is the system of support for user selection of social benefits. It is a large database containing information on households, from administrative data held by the State and declared by them. The information held by the State comes from various institutions such as the National Civil Registry Service, the Internal Revenue Service, the Superintendent of Pensions, the Superintendent of Health, FONASA, the Chile School Register, among others. All households in the country may be a part on the register, regardless of their socio-economic status.

The number of people living in poverty by 2015 was estimated at 2,046,404 (equivalent to 11.7% of the population living in private households), while the number of people living in multidimensional poverty was estimated at 3,547,184 (20.9%). This last figure takes into account the measurement made with the extended methodology, that is, incorporating the indicators of environment and networks.[23]

It should be noted that although the methodology change in the selection of cohorts in 2015 and 2016 is an improvement in the identifying families in situations of extreme poverty, it is recognized that there is still room for improvement. The change made in it is indeed very significant and we are in a period of transition in which the figures that are shown are very relevant, and one must wait to see the effects of the multidimensional approach to be able to make a complete analysis.

9.2 ASSESSMENT OF CHILE SOLIDARIO ON THE BASIS OF THE PRINCIPLES

It is now necessary to carry out a review of the principles of ILO Recommendation No. 202 that is the object of this project in the light of the presentation and evolution of the mechanism of social protection of Chilean poverty.

As we have pointed out throughout this presentation, there has been an evolution in terms of legislation as well as public policy. On the one hand, Chile Solidario is a system of social protection that includes several programmes. On the other hand, it was transformed and renamed Seguridades y Oportunidades (Securities and Opportunities).

The evaluation of the principles will be made taking into account the evolution described and will take into account the revised version of the conditional money transfer programme for the poor and the extreme poor.

---

22. Ministry of Social Development, *Informe de Desarrollo Social 2016*, 70 (Santiago de Chile, 2016).
23. Ministry of Social Development, *Informe de Desarrollo Social 2016*, 15 (Santiago de Chile, 2016).

9.2.1 State Responsibility

According to R202, the State should be responsible for formulating, articulating and implementing, as well as supervising the programme. But in the Chilean case, it has also been responsible for the evaluation and reformulation of the same. All this in search of a better and greater coverage and specifying in an important way who are the vulnerable people and how to protect them. This State activity is carried out through the Ministry of Social Development.

It should be borne in mind that the level of benefits is guaranteed by the State budget and in the specific budget of the Ministry of Social Development.[24]

In its action, the ministry for the implementation of programmes and sub-programmes can act through private actors. In principle, this should be viewed positively considering the interaction in between different actors of the community and not only the State administration. However, it should be noted that these private activities are usually present in a commune or municipality so that differences can be created between services provided in the same region and all within the country. The benefits are the same for the whole country but not all the private actors are, so some regions might have a lower offer of protection if the public service cannot implement that specific programme.

The Ministry of Social Development plays an oversight role, guaranteeing the roll out of the programmes all over the country.

The principle is achieved by Chile; it has a structure, a ministry and a legal framework that can assure the implementation of a social protection floor. We must add that the Chile Solidario programme existed before R202, so actually all the recent improvement explained in the previous section shows that Chile has an advanced social protection floor.

9.2.2 Universality of Protection

Universality has been conceived by the doctrine of security in two ways. Universality, in a general way, is a principle that refers to total coverage. Full coverage must be understood in two senses: that the entire population is covered and on the other hand, that all social risks are covered. Thus, universality can be considered objectively, according to which all social contingencies are covered. But there is also a subjective conception of universality, according to which all inhabitants or residents must be protected.[25]

It should be kept in mind that through the conditional transfers of money such as Security and Opportunities, it seeks to protect people excluded from protection by the existing mechanisms of social security. Therefore, in itself the

---

24. The State has an annual budget law. It includes various funding lines for each ministry and then divides into each of the activities of each ministry.
25. Pablo Arellano Ortiz, *Lecciones de seguridad social*, 60 (Librotecnia, Santiago, 2015).

mechanism under study is not universal. The universality is obtained to the extent that the beneficiary is under the criterion of targeting.

Specific groups such as children as well as informal workers can participate in the programme as they meet the targeting criteria. It should be noted that in our view there may be incentives for certain groups, including informal workers, to remain in their State in order to benefit from State programmes.

If the person meets the targeting criteria, everyone has the right to be a part of the programmes and sub-programmes.

One of the most recent issues raised in Chile is the question of whether migrants are covered by social protection benefits. In this regard, the Chilean constitution as well as Chilean law does not make any reference to nationality or immigration status as a condition to be a beneficiary. This criterion has also been established by the Inter-American Court of Human Rights. Therefore, regular or regular immigrants benefit from the various social protection programmes in Chile.

The programmes are universal; all the people are included, as far as they meet the targeting criteria.

9.2.3 Entitlements Based on Law

In terms of the legal framework, since its inception, the transfer of benefits under Chilean Solidarity has been established by law. The reformulation of the programme in Securities and Opportunities is also contained in a law.

Table 9.4 Laws on Chile Solidario

Law No. 19.949	Establishes a System of Social Protection for Families in the Situation of Extreme Poverty Denominated 'Chile Solidario'. Official Journal, 5 June 2004.
Law No. 20.595	Create Family Ethical Income that Establishes Bonds and Conditional Transfers for Extreme Poverty Families and Creates Subsidy for Women's Employment. Official Journal 17 May 2012.

The rights in both cases, although they are contained in these laws, the actual effectiveness depends on the fulfilment by the beneficiaries of the criteria of targeting. That emphasizes the importance of a new mechanism that considers poverty from a multidimensional perspective and not only based on income.

The criteria of targeting as well as all the conditions in order to obtain the benefit are set by the law. At the same time, complaints and appeal procedures exist, as well as administrative controls in order to prevent any fraud from false beneficiaries. The controls of the conditions are strict, nevertheless, occasionally fraud is discovered.

In general, it can be said that the principle is fulfilled by Chile.

9.2.4 Adequacy and Predictability of Benefits

One criticism is that the amounts of benefits are very low considering the line of poverty. Within the reformulation, this has been taken into account. A more accurate evaluation of those who are poor and extremely poor is sought. It also redefines the criteria for estimating the poverty line.[26]

Another criticism is that there is no relevant reduction in the percentage of poverty and/or extreme poverty. There are even contradictory figures that reflect a slight increase in poverty in certain periods.

While the mechanism is a considerable aid to those in poverty, this is not enough to improve their situation. The main criticism does not point directly to the delivery of a conditional amount of money but to the absence of a link between the programme and the creation of employment. It is widely believed that this type of mechanism can be linked to the creation of jobs for the most vulnerable.

Possible beneficiaries must have to apply in order to obtain the benefits, either through Chile Solidario or Securities and Opportunities. The procedure is mainly completed at the community level by a social assistance officer at the Municipality. The programme is well known, and the procedure is clear for the future beneficiaries.

The amount of the benefits is very low, but so is the minimum wage. It is hard to say that the benefits provide a good standard of living. Actually, they facilitate survival, and if you are poor, you will remain in poverty. There is a need for a significant increase in the amounts.

9.2.5 Non-discrimination

The Chilean legal system does not establish differences of treatment between men and women. In this way, social security benefits must be governed by the constitutional norms in this matter.

---

26. The benefits are reviewed every year and indexed by the Consumer Price Index. The Consumer Price Index (CPI) is an aggregate indicator that estimates the monthly variation of the prices of goods and services consumed by households.

Table 9.5   Chilean Constitution

Chilean Constitution	
Article 1	People are born free and equal in dignity and rights.
Article 19, paragraph 2	Equality before the law. In Chile, there is no privileged person or group. In Chile, there are no slaves and the one who treads its territory is free. Men and women are equal by the law. Neither the law nor any authority can establish arbitrary differences.

Notwithstanding the above and reaffirming that there are no formal differences between men and women, Law No. 20.595 along with establishing the mechanism of Security and Opportunities have established a series of benefits aimed at working women. These are subsidies aiming to help women who work and working women with children.

One of the recent issues of debate in Chile is immigration. In relation to this issue, we must point out that social benefits are delivered regardless of the migrant's immigration status in Chile. However, it should be noted that there is an adequate number of bilateral social security agreements, relating to old age and health, which are not applicable to the benefits of this type of programmes because these agreements are mainly signed in relation to contributory benefits. Security and Opportunities is a non-contributory mechanism, so it is not included in such regulation.

Chile fulfils the principle and no beneficiary is discriminated by sex, age, nationality or any other condition. It is now difficult to find irregular migrant who has been granted with housing subsidies. This is a good example of how the benefits do not discriminate.

9.2.6   Financial Solidarity

The mechanism under study is State funding, so it is a non-contributory mechanism. The balance, responsibility and feasibility of the programme are borne by the State and its annual budget established by the annual budget law.

Not being a contributory mechanism, the contribution of the beneficiaries is zero, which has contributed to incentives not to participate in the labour market and potentially increase informality. As we have argued, in order to sustain the programme over time, it is necessary to be able to connect it with job creation policies.

The system will remain financially stable as it continues to be funded by taxes, as it is today.

9.2.7 Good Governance

Good governance is ensured by State responsibility. But it is not only that the State ensures that this principle is considered to be fulfilled. The evolution described above demonstrates that the system is constantly evaluated, and that adjustments have been made in order to provide better protection.

The evolution of the legislative framework has been in line with the follow-up carried out by the State. Despite this constant vigilance, a deficiency in the struggle regarding the social protection of informal workers can be noted, which has increased in recent years.

The mechanism of Securities and Opportunities fulfils the ideas of transparency, sustainability with good services and benefits. However, in relation to the coherence, the programme is lacking coordination with other public institutions in order to achieve a better protection of the unemployed, and to facilitate the return to work.

9.2.8 Coherence of Policies

In terms of coherence, the conditional transfer mechanism under analysis belongs to a set of public policies and social protection programmes. These social protection programmes fall within the remit of the Ministry of Social Development.

As to whether these policies are in line with the act of protection provided by other mechanisms, it must be indicated that the Ministry of Social Development coordinate with the Ministries of Labour and Health. As we have already noted, there is a deficiency in terms of linking the conditional transfer mechanism with job creation policies.

A manifestation of the coherence of public policies is precisely the change described, from Chile Solidario to Securities and Opportunities, since this change was motivated by a restructuring of the mechanism in order to improve the protection of the poor.

As it was mentioned above, the coherence of the mechanism lacks a better structure for the protection of the unemployed, particularly in order to help them to return to work. If this is not fulfilled the beneficiaries will remain in poverty, thus beginning a cycle of dependency on social benefits.

9.2.9 Social Participation and Freedom of Association

The State orders and directs the action of the mechanism without consultation with social actors.

In addition, it should be noted that in policies of social protection social partners are not included in their evaluation and formulation, nor in their implementation.

This is for several reasons. For example, since the benefits of the programme are non-contributory, it is very difficult to find them included in a collective agreement, and plus, in Chile there is a very low rate of union membership. Freedom of association is a very relevant problem for Chilean social law. It is possible to add on this point the recent labour reform of Law No. 20,940, which was published on 8 September 2016. This reform is a failed attempt to improve collective bargaining and to strengthen unions. The reform makes creating a union more difficult and also does not open the scope of negotiation enough, plus the negotiation is kept at the enterprise level, and negotiation by branch is desirable. We regrettably note that this law is a serious setback in terms of freedom of association.[27]

It is important to clarify that unions do not participate in the formulation and implementation of social protection policies. They are involved only in social policies that include formal dependent workers. However, it is possible to find the participation of civil society organizations in non-binding advisory roles in the formulation of policies.

The principle is met only partially. Civil society can participate but with a limited scope and participation. And, social partners, especially unions, have a very limited influence.

9.3 DISCUSSION OF LEGISLATIVE DEFICITS AND/OR IMPLEMENTATION FAILURES FLOWING FROM THE ASSESSMENT

The initial approach of the Chile Solidarity programme included a significant burden on the beneficiaries, particularly when basing the focus on only the perceived income. The reformulation of the programme as Securities and Opportunities views poverty from a more complete perspective: a multi-disciplinary approach.

This reformulation has involved a redirection of the focus with a new instrument, as already described. It has been found that during the implementation of Chile Solidario the participating families found it very difficult to get out of poverty, rather, they remained in that State. Following a new approach means giving families the tools to be more autonomous and thus to achieve better living conditions. This is the aim of the new approach, and an evaluation should be completed in a few years once the reformulation in fully in place. Within this, we note the need to articulate job creation policies with the security and opportunity programme.

---

27. An analysis of this reform can be obtained in: Pablo Arellano Ortiz, Severin Concha, Juan Pablo & Feres Nazarala María Ester (eds), *Reforma al Derecho Colectivo del Trabajo. Exámen crítico de la ley núm. 20.940* (Thomson Reuters 2016); Pablo Arellano Ortiz, Ricardo Liendo Roa, Francisco Y Walker Errazuriz, *Reforma Laboral Ley N°20.940, Moderniza las relaciones laborales* (Librotecnia, Santiago, 2016).

As for the principles of R202, it can be said that in general the reformulation of the Chilean programme into the Securities and Opportunities programme fulfil most of the principles. However, the coherence of the policies and the participation of the social actors are still lacking. In our opinion, this will not be introduced in the 1980s. If, for example, the collective bargaining regulation were reformulated, the participation of social partners would increase, but it could be a long time before this happens.

It is also worth considering the composition of the families that are part of the social protection programmes. A significant number are single-parent families, and in others it is the woman who is the breadwinner. Given that women earn less income in the same employment, and also in general only receive the minimum income, it is necessary to adopt more measures of positive discrimination in favour of women. Existing worker bonuses are not enough.

9.4 REFORMULATION OF THE PROGRAMME AND POLICY

As for the reformulation of this programme, the description shows that Chile Solidario's move to Security and Opportunity is undoubtedly an excellent example of how a government is aware of the need to reformulate public policies, generating in addition, the necessary legislative change for this. The current multi-disciplinary approach is no doubt consistent with the idea of better protecting vulnerable groups.

The different sub-programmes, in general, are in line to guarantee a minimum income and services to the most vulnerable in Chile. However, the level of the benefits is just over the poverty line. So, in order to make a change to this group the amount of the benefits needs to increase. Otherwise, they just will help the poor to stay poor, rather than helping them to escape the poverty trap.

As to whether or not this mechanism, in the Chilean version, complies with the requirements of Recommendation No. 202, is complex to evaluate. In terms of public policy and coverage delineation, the mechanism complies. However, in terms of the participation of trade union organizations and an effective improvement of the living conditions of the poor, there is still a long way to go.

BIBLIOGRAPHY

Arellano Ortiz, Pablo, Severin Concha, Juan Pablo & Feres Nazarala, María Ester (eds), *Reforma al Derecho Colectivo del Trabajo. Exámen crítico de la ley núm. 20.940* (Thomson Reuters 2016).

Arellano Ortiz, Pablo, Ricardo Liendo Roa, & Francisco Y Walker Errazuriz, *Reforma Laboral Ley N°20.940, Moderniza las relaciones laborales*, (Santiago, Librotecnia 2016).

Arellano Ortiz, Pablo, *Lecciones de seguridad social*, (Santiago, Librotecnia 2015).

Arellano Ortiz, Pablo, *Reto actual de las pensiones de vejez: 'Fin de las AFP?' Regreso a reparto?*, (Santiago, Librotecnia 2015).

Arellano Ortiz, Pablo, *Protection of Old Age in Chile*, 415-427 (Ulrich Becker, Frans Pennings and Tineke Dijkhoff eds, Kluwer 2013).

Arellano Ortiz, Pablo, *Universalism and Individualism in Chilean Pension Law: An Example of Extension of Coverage for Eastern Europe*, 219-231 (Roger Blanpain, William Bromwich, Olga Rymkevich & Iacopo Senatori eds, Kluwer 2012).

Arellano Ortiz, Pablo, *The Private Pension System. Critic Study Base on the Chilean Case* (Roger Blanpain & Michele Tiraboschi eds, Kluwer 2008).

CIEDESS, *Situación de la Informalidad en el Mercado Laboral Chileno, Boletín de Informalidad Laboral, Cifras a junio de 2016* (Santiago, Gerencia de Estudios November 2016).

CIEDESS, *Análisis y propuestas para incentivar la cotización de los trabajadores al sistema de pensiones chileno*, informe final (Santiago, 29 January 2015).

Cecchini, Simone & Aldo Madariaga, *Conditional Cash Transfer Programmes. The Recent Experiences in Latin America and the Caribbean*, Cuadernos de la CEPAL 95, Economic Commission for Latin America and the Caribbean (ECLAC) (Santiago, Chile United Nations, September 2011).

ECLAC, *Social Panorama of Latin America 2015* (Social Development Division and the Statistics Division of the Economic Commission for Latin America and the Caribbean 2016).

Fultz, Elaine & John Francis, *Cash Transfer Programmes, Poverty Reduction and Empowerment of Women: A Comparative Analysis Experiences from Brazil, Chile, India, Mexico and South Africa*, GED Working Paper 4/2013, Geneva Gender, Equality and Diversity Branch Conditions of Work and Equality Department, Social Protection Department (International Labour Office 2013).

Fundación Sol, *Los Verdaderos Sueldos de Chile*, Panorama Actual del Valor de la Fuerza de Trabajo Usando la NESI 2015, Documento de trabajo área Salarios y Desigualdad (Estudios de la Fundación SOL, Agosto 2016).

Larrañaga, Osvaldo, Dante Contreras & Gustavo Cabezas, *Políticas Contra la Pobreza: de Chile Solidario al Ingreso Ético Familiar*, Working paper Programmea de las Naciones Unidas para el Desarrollo-Chile, Área de Reducción de la Pobreza y la Desigualdad, Diciembre 2014.

Larrañaga, Osvaldo, Denise Falck, Rodrigo Herrera & Amanda Telias, *De la Ficha de Protección Social a la Reforma de la Focalización*. Working paper, Programmea de las Naciones Unidas para el Desarrollo-Chile, Área de Reducción de la Pobreza y la Desigualdad, Diciembre 2014.

ILO, *Social Protection Floor for a Fair and Inclusive Globalization. Report of the Social Protection Floor Advisory Group* (Geneva, International Labour Office 2011).

ILO, *Extending Social Security to All, A Guide Through Challenges and Options*, (International Labour Office, Social Security Department, 2010).

ILO, *El seguro social y la protección social*, Conferencia Internacional del Trabajo, 80a reunión, Memoria del Director General (Parte I), Ginebra, 1993.

Ministry of Social Development, *Informe de Desarrollo Social 2016* (Santiago de Chile 2016).

Ministry of Social Development, *Valor de la Canasta Básica de Alimentos y Líneas de Pobreza, Informe Mensual* (Santiago de Chile, November 2016).

Ministry of Social *Development, Informe de Desarrollo Social 2015* (Santiago de Chile 2015).

Ministry of Social Development, *Informe de Desarrollo Social 2014* (Santiago de Chile, 2014).

Ministry of Social Development, *Nueva Metodología de Medición de la Pobreza por Ingresos y Multidimensional*, Serie Documentos Metodológicos N°28 (Santiago de Chile 2015).

OECD, *Inequality Update 2016, Income Inequality Remains High in the Face of Weak Recovery* (Centre for Opportunity and Equality, 24 November 2016).

LEGISLATION

Law No. 19.949 Establece Un Sistema De Proteccion Social Para Familias En Situacion De Extrema Pobreza Denominado 'Chile Solidario' D.O. 5 June 2004.

Law No. 20.595 Crea El Ingreso Ético Familiar Que Establece Bonos Y Transferencias Condicionadas Para Las Familias De Pobreza Extrema Y Crea Subsidio Al Empleo De La Mujer D.O. 17 May 2012.

CHAPTER 10

Does Employment Guarantee Support a Social Protection Floor?: A Case Study of Mahatma Gandhi National Rural Employment Guarantee Scheme (MGNREGS) in India

Babu P. Remesh

10.1 INTRODUCTION

A central concern of ILO Recommendation No. 202 is the importance of providing 'income security' to people over the complete life cycle. Three out of the four basic social security guarantees highlighted in the Recommendation are related to 'income securities'. Referring to the desirability of providing 'income security' to the working poor and economically active population, the Recommendation states that member countries need to ensure 'basic income security, at least at a nationally defined minimum level, for persons in active age who are unable to earn sufficient income, in particular in cases of sickness, unemployment, maternity and disability'.

Against this backdrop, the following case study of Mahatma Gandhi National Rural Employment Guarantee Scheme (MGNREGS) in India helps us understand how a national level employment guarantee scheme can effectively support a social protection floor by ensuring a modicum level of income security for the whole rural population, on a self-selection basis.

MGNREGS is an innovative scheme that provides 100 days of guaranteed employment to all rural households in India and is now regarded as the world's largest employment guarantee programme. A major aspect that makes the scheme unique is its right-based approach, as it is backed by an Act (National

Rural Employment Guarantee Act (NREGA) 2005) passed by the Indian Parliament which, *inter alia*, makes the State legally bound to either provide the guaranteed employment to the rural population as and when demanded or to provide compensatory charges, as stipulated in the Act.

It is a fully State-funded scheme, open to all rural households in India, where access to the benefits of the scheme is purely demand-driven. The State is liable to provide employment to the needy, as and when demanded within a stipulated time period, and that, too, in a local place of work. Such a right-based approach makes MGNREGS a unique scheme, *vis-à-vis* the discretionary or conditional programmes for extending social protection (e.g., as in Latin American countries such as Mexico, Chile and Brazil). In an era when most of the low- and middle-income countries are shifting towards Conditional Cash Transfer (CCT) schemes, mainly to balance between the State's social protection commitments and fiscal constraints, this Indian scheme which assures a committed, continuing and ever expanding budget allocation for financing such a mammoth programme is considered as a bold step towards supporting a social protection floor in India.

Though India is not a signatory of ILO Convention No. 102 on Social Security (Minimum Standards), 1952, the Constitution of India and in its Directive Principles provide essential directions for various governments in the federal system to effectively address the matter of social protection. Accordingly, the country has many well-established social security schemes both at central and state levels covering a wide range of areas including basic education and health, employment creation and promotion, workers' social security, food and nutrition security, and social pensions. Some of these programmes are also legally supported[1] and thus follow a rights-based approach. Thus, notwithstanding India's non-signatory position *vis-a-vis* ILO Convention 102, there have been certain State initiatives that have truly reflected the spirit of the Convention.

It is important to note here that MGNREGS was initiated even before the advent of Recommendation No. 202 on Social Protection Floors and in fact, the details of the scheme were discussed in the preparatory reports submitted to ILO, prior to the adoption of Recommendation No. 202 and in the Third Inter-Ministerial Conference on Social Protection Policies held in Colombo in 2011, to which India was a signatory.

Thus, by dissecting the details of MGNREGS and examining the extent to which the spirit of NREG Act and MGNREGS reflect the principles of Recommendation No. 202, what we are attempting to do is to examine how the contents of a pre-existing scheme of employment guarantee in a low-income country go very closely with the ethos of an international guideline for creating a national floor for social protection.

A growing body of literature testifies that, since its inception, the MGNREGS has become a central pillar of India's national social protection floor, by

---

1. Ravi Srivastava, *A Social Protection Floor for India* (New Delhi: International Labour Organization 2013).

providing employment to more than 50 million rural households annually. It has also brought in revolutionary changes in the rural societies by assuring a certain level of income security, increasing rural wage rates, encouraging higher levels of work participation rates (especially for women and marginalized groups), creating durable assets for rural communities and so on.[2] Given this, it is worthwhile looking at how MGNREGS and its right-based entitlements worked in realizing social protection in practice for millions of rural poor in India.

10.2 MGNREGS: A PROFILE

India has a long history of welfare programmes for working poor and the unemployed. A frontrunner is the Rural Works Programmes initiated during early 1960s which already aimed at providing employment for 100 days. The other major interventions were the Rural Landless Employment Guarantee Programme initiated in 1980s, the Employment Assurance Scheme of 1990s and the *Sampoorna Gramin Rozgar Yojna* (Ehmke 2015[3]). Apart from these central programmes, there were also some State level schemes of a similar nature. For instance, in the late 1970s, the government of Maharashtra introduced a State level Act (Maharashtra Employment Guarantee Act 1977) providing some degree of employment guarantee for workers within the State of Maharashtra.

However, by early 2000s, there had been a growing apprehension about the inefficacy of most of these programmes, in the context of increasing reports of farmer suicides, distress migration and absolute poverty. Accordingly, country-wide campaigns for employment guarantee backed by grass-roots social organizations as well as national labour movements took place. Such movements also gelled with other campaigns such as the right to food campaign, the right to information campaign and so on. All these circumstances prompted the United Progressive Alliance (UPA) to include the employment guarantee as an agenda in their joint-election manifesto and subsequently in the Common Minimum Programme of the UPA government, when it came into power, in May 2004.

The passing of the National Rural Employment Guarantee Bill by the Indian Parliament in September 2005 is considered to be a landmark event in the recent history of social security interventions in India. Following this, the NREGA 2005 came into force. The Act essentially aims at addressing the problem of 'under employment' and the resultant economic deprivation of working poor in rural areas, by providing assured employment, albeit for some limited days in a year. By assuring a basic income security, the Act also effectively addressed the 'right

---

2. Ellen Ehmke, *National Experiences in Building Social Protection Floors: India's Mahatma Gandhi National Rural Employment Guarantee Scheme* (Geneva: International Labour Office 2015); Ashok Pankaj, *Right to Work and Rural India: Working of the Mahatma Gandhi National Employment Guarantee Scheme* (New Delhi: Sage Publishing 2012); Pramod Kumar and Dipanwita Chakraborty, *MGNREGA – Employment, Wages and Migration in Rural India* (Abington: Routledge 2016).
3. Ehmke, *supra* n. 2.

to food' concerns of rural poor, albeit in an indirect way. As per the provisions of this Act, the National Rural Employment Guarantee Scheme (NREGS) was launched in 2006. Subsequently, this scheme was renamed the Mahatma Gandhi National Rural Employment Guarantee Scheme (MGNREGS) in 2009.

As mentioned before, the MGNREGS stipulates that all rural households in India are legally entitled to demand 100 days of work per year, from the State. Only adult members of the rural households are eligible to apply for work under this scheme, and they should be willing to undertake certain unskilled manual work identified and arranged by the local government institutions (*Gram Sabhas and Gram Panchayats*). Once an applicant requests a job, the local government is liable to provide work to the job seeker, within fifteen days of application, and within a radius of 5 kilometres. If the authorities fail to provide the work within the prescribed time, the applicant must be compensated with an unemployment allowance. All the participating workers are paid a statutory minimum wage prescribed for the programme, without any discrimination across gender or social categories.

Essentially, MGNREGS is designed as a major social insurance scheme, where an 'employment guarantee' is effectively used as an active measure to help the rural poor.[4] As the scheme guarantees the 'right to work' for all rural households, it is hailed as one of the most effective interventions of the government of India to fight rural poverty.

The scheme is designed to alleviate poverty since poorest of the poor constitute its beneficiaries. Due to the 'unskilled and manual' nature of work offered under the scheme, only those who are in real need apply to the scheme. This brings in a 'self-targeting' or 'self-selection' feature to the scheme, as the non-poor and better off prefer not to take up work under this scheme. By design, the scheme envisages that if there are better opportunities, even those workers who are dependent on the scheme will readily move away from the NREGS. Thus, the work under the scheme is often a last resort employment option for its beneficiaries.

10.3 VIEWING MGNREGS THROUGH THE LENS OF NATIONAL SOCIAL PROTECTION FLOOR

MGNREGS is a scheme that came into existence a few years before the adoption of ILO Recommendation No. 202 on National Social Protection Floors. Nevertheless, even a cursory glance at the details of the scheme suggests that it truly reflects some of the basic principles enshrined in the Recommendation and thus qualifies to be considered as an ideal or desirable initiative to be showcased as reflecting the basic principles enshrined in Recommendation No. 202.

---

4. K.P. Kannan, *Social Security for the Working Poor in India: Two National Initiatives*, 53 (3) Development (2010).

The subsequent discussion on the efficacy of the MGNREGS with special reference to ILO Recommendation No. 202 relies mainly on available empirical evidence, research studies and reports on the performance of the scheme. Following the framework provided by Dijkhoff (2016), the analysis focuses on nine basic principles that underline ILO Recommendation 202. These are: (1) State responsibility; (2) universality of protection; (3) legal entitlements; (4) adequacy and predictability of benefits; (5) non-discrimination; (6) financial solidarity; (7) good governance; (8) coherence of policies; and (9) social participation.

10.3.1 State Responsibility

The central government of India at the time of passing of NREGA in 2005 played a crucial role in creating this national programme guaranteeing employment to the rural poor. But, unlike its earlier and crude version, the Maharashtra Employment Guarantee Act of 1977 (a State level Act guaranteeing employment for workers in Maharashtra), NREGA cannot be viewed as a fully State-initiated Act. Since late 1990s and in the early years of the twenty-first century, there was a massive campaign on the 'right to work' involving civil society organizations, social activists, rural workers and researchers. There was also an effective social campaign on the right to food, prompting the government to launch the National Food for Work Campaign (NFFWP) in 2001. All of these campaigns provided the backdrop required for demanding the enactment of a national law that provides a basic employment guarantee to the working poor. The political coalition in power at the time of the passing of NREGA was also supportive of such an intervention, as expanding social security measures for the labouring poor was one of the core concerns of the government's National Common Minimum Programme at the time. Accordingly, the government played a proactive role in launching and expanding NREGS with committed budget allocations. Given this backdrop, it is more appropriate to assert that the genesis of the programme owes itself to the particular historical context, when a long-drawn-out people's movement for realizing right-based employment guarantees was matched with a supportive stance from the ruling party/government at the centre.

Notwithstanding this overall supportive role of the State in creating this national programme, there had been strong resistance within bureaucracy and government, which necessitated the considerable dilution of certain provisions of the Act considerably *vis-à-vis* those listed in the 'citizen's draft' prepared by the advocacy groups.[5] The original provisions of the Act have been diluted primarily in three ways: (a) limiting the days of employment to 100 days; (b) limiting the benefits provided under the Act to households (not to individuals);

---

5. Ritika Khera and Nandini Nayak, *Women Workers and Perception of the National Rural Employment Guarantee Act*, 44 (43) Economic and Political Weekly (2009); Kannan, *supra* n. 4.

and (c) limiting the nature of work to 'manual work'. Even with all these dilutions, the introduction of NREGA is regarded as a landmark intervention, as it explicates the 'open-ended public commitment' of the Indian State to introduce a legally backed, national level social security programme.[6]

The functioning of MGNREGS is planned within the federal structure of Indian State, with specific functions attached to different levels of government (central government, state government and local government). As per section 3 of NREG Act, the States are responsible for providing work in accordance with the Scheme. Section 4 of the Act stipulates that every state government is required to introduce a scheme providing for not less than 100 days of guaranteed employment in a financial year, for those who demand work. The ultimate implementation of the scheme is vested with the local governments and *Gram Sabhas*, which are responsible for planning public works, as per needs of the job-seeking public and for implementing the execution of identified works.

The funding of the programme is largely met by the central government. About 90% of the total cost of the scheme is borne by the central government and remaining by the state governments. Statutorily, the central government is liable to provide 100% of wages for unskilled labour and 75% of the material costs (which include costs of employing skilled labour). The state governments are required to provide 25% of the material costs and 100% of the unemployment allowance. The cost of organizing the projects and workers are borne by the local governments (section 22 and sub-sections (1) & 2 of NREG Act 2005).

As per the Act, participatory planning at the village level is central to the implementation of MGNREGS, as the implementation of the scheme is vested with the elected local government *(Gram Panchayat)*, in close coordination with the *Gram Sabha*, a general body of all adults in the village (sections 16 & 17 of NREG Act 2005). Provisions for organizing 'monitoring and village committees', with the involvement of social activists, elected representatives of local bodies, grass-roots level organizations and participating workers of the programme, ensure a higher degree of transparency and social accountability in the implementation of the projects. The scheme also provides ample scope for public-private partnership, as it even allows the local governments to plan development work on private lands if such work improves overall livelihood options and employment prospects in a given locality.

10.3.2 Universality of Protection

MGNREGS is a scheme open to all adult members of rural households in India, who are willing to take up manual and unskilled employment. The beneficiaries are allowed to participate in the Scheme, as per their requirement on a

---

6. Kannan, *supra* n. 4; Puja Dutta et.al, *Does India's Employment Guarantee Scheme Guarantee Employment?*, 47 (16) Economic and Political Weekly (2012); Bhagirathi Panda, *National Rural Employment Guarantee Scheme: Development Practice at the Cross Roads*, 50 (23) Economic and Political Weekly (2015).

'self-selection basis'. The Scheme is operational across the entire country, except in those districts with a 100% urban population, and covers about two-thirds of the country's population.[7]

As per the estimates of recent a performance assessment report prepared by Ministry of Rural Development, the implementing Ministry of MGNREGS, on an average, around 50 million households work every year under MGNREGS.[8] In the first decade since its inception, 19,700 million days of employment were generated under the scheme. In 2014-2015, 40.8 million rural households accessed work under this scheme and the total number of days of employment generated was 1,600 million. All this suggests that the scheme has the potential to reach out to the vast majority of the population.

The Scheme being more pro-poor, it reaches the resource poor and vulnerable groups in society more efficiently. The employment guarantee of the scheme is much better than previous public work programmes.[9] The features of 'self-selection' and the delimiting of the work to manual operations ensure that only the needy are enrolled in the scheme. It has been found that the scheme shows higher participation rates among women, Scheduled Castes (SCs), Scheduled Tribes (STs) and Other Backward Castes (OBCs).

The programme is only available to adult members. This is a 'positive' delimitation or social protection gap, as it effectively checks the engagement of child labour. In MGNREGS, the children's welfare is ensured through the employment and income security provided to adults. Available empirical evidence also supports this argument by showing that the successful implementation of MGNREGS has led to nutritional improvement within households and has positively impacted on the schooling of the children of the beneficiaries.[10] All these highlight the potential of the scheme in improving the welfare of children through providing an employment guarantee to adult members of the family. Notwithstanding these positive results, there still exist some coverage gaps. Even a decade on from its inception, all registered workers under the scheme are not provided with 100 days of guaranteed employment. For instance, an in-depth study based on primary survey data from 16 major States in the country,[11] observe that MGNREGS has not been successful in providing 100 days of employment to all registered persons, thereby adversely affecting the scheme's potential to make a significant dent in rural poverty. Thus, in order to meet the objective of universality of social protection, it is desirable not only to

---

7. Pankaj, *supra* n. 2.
8. MoRD, *Mahatma Gandhi National Rural Employment Guarantee Act 2005: The Journey of a Decade* (New Delhi: Ministry of Rural Development, Government of India, 2016).
9. Srivastava, *supra* n. 1.
10. UNDP, *MGNREGA Sameeksha II: An Anthology of Research Studies (2012-2014)* (New Delhi: United Nations Development Programme 2015); Subha Mani, *Impact of the NREGS on Schooling and Intellectual Human Capital*, Proceedings of the International Conference on MGNREGA (IGIDR, Mumbai 2013).
11. Kumar and Chakraborty, *supra* n. 2.

increase the number of registered families under the scheme but also to ensure the provision of 100 days of employment to all registered households.

10.3.3 Legal Entitlements

The fact that MGNREGS is backed by a national law itself provides a right-based character to the Scheme. The targeted beneficiaries (i.e., adult members of the rural households in need of supplementary days of paid wage employment) enjoy several legal entitlements. As explained earlier, the three central entitlements as per the NREG Act are employment on demand, minimum wages and unemployment allowance.

As regards the employment guarantee, every rural household is legally entitled to seek employment for up to 100 days. The Act also stipulates a 'time-bound guarantee', i.e., once the employment is demanded, it must be provided within fifteen days of the request for work. The beneficiaries are also assured of employment within their locality i.e., within a radius of 5 kilometres from the applicant's residence, if possible, and in any case within the Revenue Block (consisting of a small number of closely located villages). If the work is provided further than 5 kilometres away, the workers are also entitled to a travel allowance, equal to 10% of the wages, in addition to the wages paid to them for their work.

The provision of a minimum wage on a par with the officially declared minimum wage for agricultural labourers in the given State is a crucial entitlement, which provides the scope for a national level floor of the minimum wage.[12] As per the Scheme, all workers with a job card are entitled to equal wages at the level of the minimum wage, leaving no scope for wage disparities between various groups of workers. This is a crucial feature which makes the Scheme unique and attractive, given the strikingly noticeable gender disparity in most of the other available work options in rural labour.

Another important entitlement is that unemployment allowance payable to a worker, who has sought work but who has not been provided with it by the local authorities. In this regard, the Act states that if a job seeker is not provided job within fifteen days, he/she should be compensated at the rate of one-quarter of the minimum wage for the initial thirty days, and one-half thereafter.

The Act stipulates that every workplace needs to provide drinking water, first aid facilities and shade. There are also entitlements which are female-friendly and/or aim at female empowerment. The Act stipulates that at least one-third of the beneficiaries should be women. The Act also provides for childcare facilities (e.g., crèches), when more than five children under 6 years of age are present in the workplace. The provision of such facilities enables women with small children to also participate in work.

---

12. Kamala Sankaran, *NREGA Wages: Ensuring Decent Work*, 46 (7) Economic and Political Weekly (2011).

In order to ensure transparency and accountability, the Act also stipulates for regular social audits and the proactive disclosure of information regarding these social audits. Provisions are there in the NREG Act 2005 for setting up appropriate mechanisms of redress for grievances (section 19 NREG). It is further clarified that grievance redressal is a specific function of the District Programme Officer (section 14 sub-section 3(g)).

All of the above facilitate greater transparency as well as a certain degree of beneficiary participation in the implementation of the employment guarantee scheme. Section 17 of the NREG Act 2005 insists on providing a social audit system, under which the *Gram Sabha* (the council of all adults in the village) is entrusted to carry out regular social audits of the work carried out by the *Gram Panchayats*. Further, the Operational Guidelines of MGNEGA 2013 clearly spell out the procedure to be followed for ensuring the proactive disclosure of information, which, *inter alia*, results in higher levels of transparency in implementation of the scheme. The number of complaints and appeals submitted under the Scheme is very low, till date, which may be due to multiple reasons, including: an absence of, or delay in, setting up mechanisms for redress of grievances; a lack of awareness on the part of beneficiaries about such arrangements; priorities attached by beneficiaries on accessing the employment under the Scheme (rather than going to the advanced level of complaining and correcting erroneous practices); and so on. Notwithstanding, it is reasonable to believe that the very existence of social auditing and the proactive disclosure of information act as prevention measures for corruption and malpractice.

10.3.4 Adequacy and Predictability of Benefits

As discussed elsewhere, by design, the scheme is intended to benefit those people who are the poorest of the poor due to the 'self-selection' feature and the delimitation of the scheme to unskilled manual work. Though the scheme is not strictly confined to households below the official poverty line, the self-selection feature of the scheme more or less makes it ideal and most suitable for those who belong to the Below Poverty Line (BPL) category. Still, there is empirical evidence suggesting that Scheme also reaches to those who are just above poverty line.[13]

The legal entitlement to employment or unemployment allowance stipulated in NREGA ensures a certain degree of predictability of benefits for the rural workers. Though the duration of employment guaranteed (maximum of 100 days) under the Scheme is inadequate considering the actual requirements of the unemployed in rural society, even this delimited guarantee of employment provides a modicum level of social security. The provision of unemployment allowance provides a minimum guarantee of a dole, if there is an unsatisfied job demand. Such an assurance is crucial for the labouring poor in a country with a

---

13. Kumar and Chakraborty, *supra* n. 2.

population of 1.2 billion, of which 377 million live in rural areas. During the first decade since its launch, the Scheme has proved to be an effective shock-absorbing mechanism in rural India, by helping millions of rural households to escape the trap of poverty. It is reported that in its first ten years of its existence, the scheme has reduced poverty by 32% for participant households, and has helped 14 million people to avoid falling into poverty.[14]

It has also been found that more than providing a modicum level of income/social security, the MGNREGS also enhances the dignity and social status of workers, as the functioning of the Scheme is deeply embedded within the local community, ensuring the active participation of beneficiaries at all levels, right from conceptualization to the implementation of development works. Essentially, this aspect brings a dimension of an 'empowerment guarantee', over and above the stated objective of 'employment guarantee'.[15]

Apart from inbuilt reviewing mechanisms such as social audits and mechanisms for redress, regular reviewing systems are also in place to examine the efficacy of MGNREGS. The nodal Ministry of the Scheme itself commissioned several research studies in the past, probing into the issues at the implementation levels and to highlight delivery gaps, leaks and malpractice, if any, in the implementation of the Scheme. The findings of these studies, summarized in two volumes (Sameeksha I & II), provide ample evidence of the scheme's credibility in terms of adequacy and predictability of benefits.[16]

Apart from the above positive aspects, the extant studies also point towards gaps in terms of coverage, full-provision of employment and (in) adequacy of benefits under the Scheme. A major issue that apropos the adequacy of benefits of MGNREGS is the difference between the wages paid under the Scheme and the minimum wages in various States or the actual wages paid for manual work in a particular State. Previously the MGNREGA wages were fixed on a par with the minimum wage of the State concerned. This system was abandoned in 2008 and since then the MGNREGA wages are fixed in relation to the consumer price index for agricultural labourers (CPIAL) in a particular State. Thus, the wage rates of the Scheme vary from State to State and often fall below the State minimum wage (or the actual wages prevailing), thereby making the Scheme unattractive to some of the beneficiaries, who could take up another employment option rather than joining NREGS. For instance, a recent PTI report titled *Revised MGNREGA wages put states in a quandary* (dated 3 April 2016) reports that the MGNREGA wages are below the State level wage in many of the States. The report adds that while giving its verdict on a dispute over a wage gap between NREGA and State level minimum wage, the Karnataka High Court, in July 2011,

---

14. Priyanka Kotamraju, *Keep Calm and Carry on MGNREGA*, BLink, The Hindu Business Line (28 Aug. 2015).
15. Reetika Khera, *Empowerment Guarantee Act*, 43 (35) Economic and Political Weekly, 2008.
16. MoRD, *MGNREGA Sameeksha: An Anthology of Research Studies of MGNREG Act, 2005, 2006-2012* (New Delhi: Orient Black Swan, 2012); UNDP, *supra* n. 10.

asked the Central Government to pay the rural job scheme workers the State minimum wage, including the arrears accumulated since 2008.

10.3.5 Non-discrimination

The Scheme is open to all rural households in the country without any discrimination, provided the member requesting the work is an adult with a MGNREGS job card issued by the local government. There is no restriction regarding the allocation of eligible work within a household. This provides a certain degree of flexibility for the households to suitably decide who needs to apply for employment under the Scheme, given the other options available to various members of the family at a particular point in time.

As MGNREGA provides for the payment of minimum wages and payment of equal wages for men and women, in effect, the Scheme's employment benefits are positively skewed towards female members of the family. Given the prevalence of the gender pay gap, in other employment options available in the rural economy, households often allocate more work to female members. Because of this, the participation rates of women in the programme are comparatively higher than men, and with respect to women's overall work participation rates.

The inclusive nature of the programme is also evident from the impressive rate of participation of workers belonging to scheduled castes and scheduled tribes. So far, it has been understood that the NREGS workplaces are free from the traditional patterns of social exclusion and discrimination in the labour market, as all the beneficiaries are treated equally, are assigned similar tasks (i.e., manual work for all) and are paid equally, irrespective of their caste, community and gender. Because of this, the Scheme truly reflects the underlying ethos of social inclusion as envisaged in the ILO Recommendation No. 202.

10.3.6 Financial Solidarity

The Scheme is fully financed by the government, and there are no charges levied on the beneficiaries. The central (union) government meets about 90% of the expenses and the remaining 10% is met by the respective state governments. There are also clear-cut directions apropos fund-sharing and the allocation of responsibility as per the nature of work and the type of payment to the beneficiaries. The central government is liable to meet 100% of the cost of wages for unskilled manual work, and 75% of the material cost of the schemes including payment of wages to skilled and semi-skilled workers. State governments are to meet 25% of material cost including the payment of wages to skilled and semi-skilled workers.

A total 100% of unemployment allowance is to be paid by the state government. This stipulation in fact acts as a penalty clause for those States which fail to provide employment as per demand and within the stipulated period.

Given the legal obligation on the respective governments to ensure the smooth functioning of the scheme, normally, some allocation for the Scheme is always planned in the annual budgets of the central and state governments. Subsequently, additional allocations are provided if the actual work-demands exceed the estimated work-demands.

The Scheme also provides ample scope for other governmental schemes and departments to pool their financial resources to supplement the resources for its running and for providing additional support to the participants of MGNREGS, thereby facilitating a greater degree of convergence of development/welfare schemes at the grass-roots level.

10.3.7 Good Governance

NREGA 2005 provides detailed guidelines for setting up a governance system for the implementation of the employment guarantee scheme set out in the Act. The Ministry of Rural Development is the nodal agency implementing MGNREGS. As per the guidelines set out in the Act, a Central Employment Guarantee Council is the apex advisory body, guiding the union government. At the State level, there are also similar Employment Guarantee Councils, providing all support for the scheme, including technical, financial and administrative support and guidance. At the district level, the *District Panchayats* (the body of elected representatives) are entrusted with the planning, implementation, monitoring and supervision of the Scheme. A specifically designated District Programme Coordinator leads the district level team to ensure smooth coordination and conduct of all activities under the scheme. Further down the system, a *Block Panchayat* (again a body of elected representatives) is responsible for the implementation and coordination of the system. A programme officer at this level coordinates with the *Gram Sabhas* and deals with major matters such as the selection of work, organization and the payment of wages. At the last and final level of governance, the elected local governments *(Gram Panchayats)* ensure the actual implementation of the scheme, in close coordination with *Gram Sabha*, a general body of all adults in the village. *Gram Sabhas* are the grass-roots level bodies responsible for the registration of beneficiaries and the identification/selection of work. The eligible beneficiaries are to register with the *Gram Panchayats*, which will have an array of development projects available to these job seekers. *Gram Panchayats* allocate 50% of these projects directly.

Thus, the implementation of the Scheme is essentially deeply embedded within the decentralized planning and governance system of India as per 73rd Amendment of the Constitution concerning the devolution of powers as per a three-tier Panchayati Raj system, in which the local governments are vested with special powers in designing and implementing welfare/development programmes at grass-roots level.

Apart from its underlying emphasis on 'beneficiary participation and decentralized planning', MGNREGS also attach considerable importance to ensure transparency in its governance and functioning. On the one hand, there are social audits and social accountability mechanisms to increase transparency and to enhance social participation (though these systems are yet to be utilized by the beneficiaries effectively). Regular assessment studies are conducted/commissioned by the nodal Ministry to uncover the gaps and to analyse the problems identified with the functioning of the programme. Transparency is also maintained by regularly sharing data, information and research findings with the general public through the Scheme's website.

There are also inbuilt mechanisms to check wage theft and to prevent the flow of income to non-participants. An e-financial management system (e-FMS) is already in place, covering about 94% of locations, at present. This system ensures that wages are credited directly into workers' accounts.

Notwithstanding all these good governance mechanisms, there have been reports of implementation issues, governance problems and leaks, and corrupt practices in the running of the scheme. However, given the fact that the scheme is legally backed and there are dedicated State resources available, and to be made available in the future, these issues can be effectively addressed in time to come.

10.3.8 Coherence of Policies

MGNREGS exhibits a lot of scope for convergence of social welfare measures and coherence of policies. The Scheme is often implemented in consonance with other pro-poor schemes, social protection measures and rural workfare programmes. These include public distribution systems, debt relief programmes, public housing schemes (e.g., *Indira Awas Yojana*), literacy and educational programmes (e.g., the rural literacy mission, *Sarva Shiksha Abhiyan*, and the Integrated Child Development Scheme). Such convergence of welfare measures, along with active the participation of *Panchayati Raj Institutions* (local governments) and *Gram Sabhas* provides MGNREGS with a stable and coherent platform, thereby enhancing its efficacy as a social shock absorbing mechanism.

The workers in MGNREGS are covered by the *Janashree Bima Yojana* (JBY) implemented by Ministry of Finance. This provides life coverage and disability benefits to the beneficiaries. The other benefit that is extended to the NREGS workers is the *Rashtriya Swasthya Bima Yojana* (RSBY), which is a national level health security programme that provides up to Indian Rupees (INR) 30,000 coverage for all registered families for meeting their inpatient medical charges.

In many States, NREGA activities are scheduled in view of the seasonality of agricultural and other rural work, to ensure that the employment provision in the scheme does not clash with peak periods of labour requirement in the rural economy. The soil and water conservation measures undertaken as part of MGNREGS are often found to result in the creation of productive assets for livelihood promotion, besides bringing about positive environmental outcomes.

There are also nutritive and educational benefits, for example, higher levels of food security, reduced school dropout rates, etc.[17] The active participation of people in *Gram Sabhas* is yet another by-product, which, *inter alia*, leads to enhanced participation of people in all development activities.[18] The other important benefits of the scheme include increased financial inclusion of the rural poor, enhanced work, increased participation of women, increased mobilization of rural labour and enhanced participation of the working poor in the overall political process.

10.3.9 Social Participation

MGNREGS also merits attention in terms of its role in enhancing social participation. As the organization and implementation is vested with the elected local governments in rural areas, in coordination with local communities (*Gram Sabhas*) and other development functionaries/agencies at the grass-roots level, by design itself, the Scheme ensures concerted participation of various social partners – ranging from bureaucrats to the actual beneficiaries of the scheme.

As discussed elsewhere, the passing of the NREGA 2005 itself needs to be seen as an outcome of a people's movement, whereby long and protracted public debates and campaigning led by civil society organizations, social activists, rural workers' organizations, researchers, intellectuals and political parties eventually prompted and pressurized the State to introduce this scheme of employment guarantee.

Effective functioning of the local governments (*Gram Sabhas*) is a prerequisite for the successful implementation of MGNREGS. The identification/selection of work and registering of eligible workers are fully entrusted to the local government and local community. The scheme also provides ample scope for participation of concerned individuals and social organizations, by actively involving them in monitoring and supervising its functioning, through the conducting of social audits. Thus, from the role of designers to that of watchdogs, the Scheme provides a myriad of opportunities for social participation for the effective and transparent implementation of the Scheme. Though the social participation rates are not very high to date, the Scheme, by design, has ample scope for promoting social participation and beneficiary involvement for its successful implementation.

---

17. Pankaj, *supra* n. 2; Sonalde Desai et al, *Mahatma Gandhi National Rural Employment Guarantee Act: A Catalyst for Rural Transformation* (New Delhi: National Council of Applied Economic Research, New Delhi, 2015); UNDP, *supra* n. 10.
18. Kumar and Chakrabory, *supra* n. 2.

10.4 PERFORMANCE ANALYSIS AND CONCLUSION

MGNREGS has been operational in India for more than a decade now, and there is a growing body of literature to support the argument that the Scheme has helped the rural poor in distress – through drought, crop failure and high unemployment. The element of the 'employment guarantee' of the Scheme has effectively acted as a social insurance to the poorest of the poor in the rural areas.

There are a number of empirical studies and reports that suggest that the Scheme has helped the working poor to enhance their income levels and to make them less poor or to cross the officially determined poverty line.[19] Further, it is also pointed out that the advent of this Scheme has brought with it various forms of empowerment among the rural workers.[20] First, as the Scheme provides employment as per the minimum wage rate set by the government, it has helped increase the overall wage rates in rural areas, for all casual and manual work, at least up to the level of NREGS wages. Thus, the availability of NREGS work (as a last resort) is found to add to the 'reservation wages' of the rural workers and has set a 'minimum floor of wages' thereby helping even those workers who are not directly participating in the Scheme.

Furthermore, the provision of equal wages to all participants without any discrimination under NREGS has reduced wage differentials between various groups of workers, especially between male and female workers. Yet another positive impact, pointed out by several studies, is the reduction in the 'distress out-migration' from rural to urban areas. As the Scheme provides a bare minimum level of employment in the native regions itself, with a stipulated minimum wage, it has acted as a deterrent for many rural workers contemplating migration to urban areas, in favour of taking up manual work. It is also widely acknowledged that given the right-based and legally assured nature of the Scheme and due to its stress on decentralized planning, 'bottom-up' and demand-driven approach, the NREGS has brought with it an overall sense of empowerment among the rural people (both participants and non-participants in the Scheme alike). The Scheme has also brought several spill-over gains to the economy, such as increasing numbers of women drawing cash incomes, more children going to school, an overall improvement in terms of the nutritive intake of rural families, more people opening bank accounts and so on.

The above list of the achievements of the Scheme is by no means meant to state that the NREGS is free from problems. There are several aspects where the Scheme needs to be further strengthened. The coverage of the programme is still not complete, given the fact that there exists a huge unmet demand (i.e., the gap between jobs demanded and provided). Many studies report that there exist huge gaps between jobs demanded and actually provided. There are also reports about the rationing of work as a common practice, which undermines other

---

19. UNDP, *supra* n. 10; Desai et al, *supra* n. 17; MoRD, *supra* n. 8.
20. Khera, *supra* n. 15; MoRD, *supra* n. 16; MoRD, *supra* n. 8; Dutta et.al, *supra* n. 6; Panda, *supra* n. 6; Kumar and Chakraborty, *supra* n. 2.

benefits such as employment gains and insurance benefits. The average number of days of employment provided per households is still below sixty.

There is also empirical evidence suggesting instances of corruption, leaks, entitlement gaps and malpractice. It is widely pointed out that, at present, the efficacy of the Scheme is being evaluated only in terms of its coverage, adequacy (in terms of geographical area/number of households covered, average days of employment provided per households) and timely provision of employment. So, the vigilance of the local communities and pressure groups is more or less at the level of first-generation issues (such as timely provision of employment, adequacy of employment days, adherence to the norm of minimum wage payments and so on). The other issues/aspects like the payment of unemployment allowance, the setting up of mechanisms for redress of grievances, the functioning of monitoring committees, etc., still remain unaddressed. For instance, the provisions such as maintaining crèches and ensuring basic facilities (water, shades etc.) in the workplace are not followed properly in many of the locations. Even then, neither the beneficiaries nor the concerned activists/pressure groups consider this as a major issue.

There also exist wide variations in the performance indices across States. Given this, it is important to hold more in-depth, State-specific enquiries to understand the coordinates that determine the success and failure in implementation. Such efforts will also help in identifying replicable methodologies from certain States and providing inputs for further strengthening the implementation strategies.

On the whole, it is evident from the foregoing analysis that MGNREGS truly qualifies as a good example of a national social protection floor, as envisaged in ILO Recommendation No. 202. It is a 'successful contemporary development practice'[21] with proven potential to change the rural social power structure and to empower the weaker groups in society.[22] Thus, it is extremely desirable to further strengthen this Scheme by addressing coverage gaps, leaks and practical issues at implementation level.

BIBLIOGRAPHY

Anand, Utkarsh, *Supreme Court Pulls up Centre over Delay in Wage Payments in NREGA* (The Indian Express, 14 May 2016).
Desai, Sonalde et.al, *Mahatma Gandhi National Rural Employment Guarantee Act: A Catalyst for Rural Transformation* (National Council of Applied Economic Research, New Delhi 2015).
Dijkhoff, Tineke, *Principles for a Social Protection Floor: Introductory Paper for the Case Studies*, Background Paper of the MPI/CICLASS Workshop on The

---

21. Panda, *supra* n. 6.
22. Mihir Sha, *Employment Guarantee, Civil Society and Indian Democracy*, Economic and Political Weekly, 42 (45-46), 2007; Khera, *supra* n. 15.

ILO Recommendation on Social Protection Floors: Basic Principles for Innovative Solutions to be held at Johannesburg, 12-13 September 2016 (2016).

Dutta, Puja et.al, *Does India's Employment Guarantee Scheme Guarantee Employment?* 47 (16) Economic and Political Weekly (21 April 2012).

Ehmke, Ellen, *National Experiences in Building Social Protection Floors: India's Mahatma Gandhi National Rural Employment Guarantee Scheme* Extension of Social Security Paper No. 49 (International Labour Office, Social Protection Department: Geneva 2015), http://www.social-protection.org/gimi/gess/ResourcePDF.action?ressource.ressourceId=53326 (Accessed on 15 February 2017).

Ghosh, Lopa, *Empowering Lives Through Mahatma Gandhi NREGA* (UNDP India, New Delhi 2011).

Kannan, K.P, *Social Security for the Working Poor in India: Two National Initiatives*, 53 (3) Development, 338-342 (2010).

Khera, Reetika, *Employment Guarantee and Migration* (The Hindu, 17 June 2006).

Khera, Reetika, *Empowerment Guarantee Act*, 43(35) Economic and Political Weekly (30 August 2008).

Khera, Reetika ed., *The Battle for Employment Guarantee* (Oxford University Press, New Delhi 2011).

Khera, Ritika & Nayak, Nandini *Women Workers and Perception of the National Rural Employment Guarantee Act*, 44 (43) Economic and Political Weekly (24 October 2009).

Kotamraju, Priyanka, *Keep Calm and Carry on MGNREGA* (BLink, The Hindu Business Line, 28 August, 2015).

Kumar, Pramod & Chakraborty, Dipanwita, *MGNREGA – Employment, Wages and Migration in Rural India* (Routlege, Abington 2016).

Mani, Subha, et al., *Impact of the NREGS on Schooling and Intellectual Human Capital*, Proceedings of the International Conference on MGNREGA (IGIDR, Mumbai 2013).

MoRD, *MGNREGA Sameeksha: An Anthology of Research Studies of MGNREG Act, 2005, 2006-2012* (Orient Black Swan, New Delhi 2012).

MoRD, *Mahatma Gandhi National Rural Employment Guarantee Act 2005: The Journey of a Decade* (Ministry of Rural Development, Government of India, New Delhi 2016).

Panda, Bhagirathi, *National Rural Employment Guarantee Scheme: Development Practice at the Cross Roads*, 50 (23) Economic and Political Weekly (2015).

Pankaj, Ashok, *Right to Work and Rural India: Working of the Mahatma Gandhi National Employment Guarantee Scheme* (Sage Publishing, New Delhi 2012).

Sankaran, Kamala *NREGA Wages: Ensuring Decent Work*, 46 (7) Economic and Political Weekly (12 February 2011).

Sha, Mihir *Employment Guarantee, Civil Society and Indian Democracy*, 42 (45-46) Economic and Political Weekly (2007).

Srivastava, Ravi *A Social Protection Floor for India* (International Labour Organization, New Delhi 2013).

UNDP, *MGNREGA Sameeksha II: An Anthology of Research Studies (2012-2014)* (United Nations Development Programme, New Delhi 2015).

CHAPTER 11
Namibia National Pension Scheme

Mathias Nyenti

11.1 INTRODUCTION

Namibia is classified as a medium human development and an upper middle-income country.[1] It has a population of 2.3 million, and this number is predicted to rise to 3 million by the year 2030.[2] About 40.1% of the population live in urban areas. The life expectancy at birth is currently 64.8 years and 17.3 years at the age of 60.[3] Despite the country's relatively high-income status, it is faced with unemployment, high informal sector employment, extreme poverty and inequalities in income distribution, general standard of living and quality of life.[4] The Namibia Labour Force Survey of 2014 estimates the unemployment rate at 28.1%.[5] A majority (60%) of employed persons are engaged in the informal sector, mainly in subsistence agriculture.[6] The poverty rate (proportion of the population living below the national poverty line) is 28.7%,[7] with 23.5% living on less than Namibian Dollars (NAD) 1.25 a day.[8] Up to 1.034 million (45.5% of

---

1. In 2014, Namibia was ranked at number 126 on the United Nations Development Programme Human development Index (*see*: United Nations Development Programme *Human Development Report 2015* (2015) 273).
2. United Nations Development Programme *Human Development Report 2015*, 236 (2015).
3. United Nations Development Programme *Human Development Report 2015*, 210 and 240 (2015).
4. *See*: National Planning Commission (Namibia) *Poverty and Deprivation in Namibia 2015*, 2.
5. Namibia Statistics Agency *Namibia Labour Force Survey 2014 Report*, 6 (2015).
6. National Planning Commission (Namibia) *Poverty and Deprivation in Namibia 2015*, 20.
7. National Planning Commission (Namibia) *Poverty and Deprivation in Namibia 2015*, 2; and National Planning Commission (Namibia) *Namibia Index of Multiple Deprivation*.
8. United Nations Development Programme *Human Development Report 2015*, 229 (2015).

the population) live in multidimensional poverty; 19.3% live near multidimensional poverty; and 13.4% live in severe multidimensional poverty.[9]

Namibia's Gross Domestic Product (GDP) is US Dollars (USD) 21.4 billion and GDP per capita of USD 9,276.[10] However, a Gini-coefficient of 61.3 indicates high-income inequalities with a high concentration of wealth.[11] There are geographic or spatial differences in the incidence of poverty, with higher levels in rural areas. The rural northern regions of Kavango, Ohangwena, and Oshikoto make up half of the national population living in poverty (they account for 21%, 15% and 14% of the national population in poverty, respectively, with more than half of the population in Kavango classified as poor).[12] The high incidence of poverty in these regions is also due to the prevalence of subsistence farming in the areas, employing 58.3% of the population in Kavango, 53.3% in Ohangwena, and 44.3% in Oshikoto.[13]

Namibia has various social protection measures in place, including social assistance, social insurance, and occupational and private pension provision. Social assistance consists of cash transfer schemes, housing and living expense allowances for vulnerable groups, food-for work programmes, and free access to primary health care and basic education.[14] Social insurance schemes are the Maternity, Sick Leave and Death Benefit Fund, and the Employees Compensation Fund, under the Social Security Commission; and the Motor Vehicle Accident Fund.

Social assistance cash transfer schemes include the National Pension Scheme (which provides a basic social grant/old-age pension, disability grant and funeral benefit for recipients of the old-age pension and disability grant), grants for orphaned and vulnerable children (place of safety allowance, special maintenance allowance, maintenance grant, and foster parent allowance), and a war veterans' grant. Namibia's cash transfer schemes were implemented before the development of the Social Protection Floor Initiative and the adoption of the ILO Recommendation No. 202 on National Social Protection Floors (hereinafter 'Recommendation 202').[15] However, they seek to realize the objectives of the

---

9. United Nations Development Programme *Human Development Report 2015*, 229 (2015). Multidimensional poverty is made up of several factors that constitute poor people's experience of deprivation (e.g., poor health, lack of education, inadequate living standard, lack of income etc.).
10. United Nations Development Programme *Human Development Report 2015*, 248 (2015).
11. United Nations Development Programme *Human Development Report 2015*, 218 (2015).
12. National Planning Commission (Namibia) *Poverty and Deprivation in Namibia 2015*, 2.
13. National Planning Commission (Namibia) *Poverty and Deprivation in Namibia 2015*, 4.
14. *See*: B.M. Chiripanhura and M. Nino-Zarazua, *Social Safety Nets in Namibia: Structure, Effectiveness and the Possibility for a Universal Cash Transfer Scheme* (2013) accessed at https://www.bon.com.na/CMSTemplates/Bon/Files/bon.com.na/88/8836bf27-7f47-4b0c-9744-f124611e6abb.pdf (5 Aug. 2016).
15. The old-age pension was introduced in 1949 but was reserved for whites only. It was extended to black Namibians in 1973. *See*: S. Devereux, *Social Pensions in Namibia and South Africa* IDS Discussion Paper 379 (February 2001) for more on the history of the old-age pension.

Initiative/Recommendation.[16] In addition, Namibia is a member of the ILO and aims to establish a comprehensive national social protection floor. This is evidenced by the Namibia Social Protection Floor Assessment Report published in 2014 with the technical assistance of the ILO.[17]

The basic social grant/old-age pension as a cash transfer scheme for the elderly serves the requirement of Recommendation 202 for Namibia to establish and maintain a social protection floor comprising basic income security, at least at a nationally defined minimum level for older persons in accordance with its national circumstances.

The old-age pension has a marked effect on poverty for beneficiaries. The most recent Namibia Household Income and Expenditure Survey indicates that pensions are the main source of income for 11.1% of households. There is a large difference between urban and rural households, as the pension is the main source of income for 4.5% of urban households and 16.1% of rural households.[18]

---

16. The objective of the Social Protection Floors Recommendation (No. 202), 2012 is to provide guidance to Members to: (a) establish and maintain, as applicable, social protection floors as a fundamental element of their national social security systems; and (b) implement social protection floors within strategies for the extension of social security that progressively ensure higher levels of social security to as many people as possible, guided by ILO social security standards (Art. 1.1 of Recommendation 202). The Recommendation defines social protection floors as nationally defined sets of basic social security guarantees which secure protection aimed at preventing or alleviating poverty, vulnerability and social exclusion (Art. 1.2 of Recommendation 202). The Recommendation requires Members, in accordance with national circumstances, to establish as quickly as possible and maintain their social protection floors comprising basic social security guarantees. The guarantees should ensure at a minimum that, over the life cycle, all in need have access to essential health care and to basic income security which together secure effective access to goods and services defined as necessary at the national level (Art. 4 of Recommendation 202). The social protection floors should comprise at least the following basic social security guarantees: (a) access to a nationally defined set of goods and services, constituting essential health care, including maternity care, that meets the criteria of availability, accessibility, acceptability, and quality; (b) basic income security for children, at least at a nationally defined minimum level, providing access to nutrition, education, care and any other necessary goods and services; (c) basic income security, at least at a nationally defined minimum level, for persons in active age who are unable to earn sufficient income, in particular in cases of sickness, unemployment, maternity, and disability; and (d) basic income security, at least at a nationally defined minimum level, for older persons.
17. International Labour Office and Oxford Policy Management, *Namibia Social Protection Floor Assessment Report* (2014). The Assessment Report was in implementation of Priority 2b, Outcome 6 of the Decent Work Country Programme of Namibia (2010-2014) which required the government, in collaboration with workers and employers, to 'improve the knowledge and information base on the coverage and performance of their social security system'. The report was also due to the request by the Parliament of Namibia for a comprehensive review of social protection programmes.
18. Namibia Statistics Agency *Namibia Household Income and Expenditure Survey 2009/2010*, 8.

Namibia currently has a low old-age dependency ratio of 8.8 per 100, according to the 2011 Census; and 5.9 per 100, according to the 2015 Human Development Report.[19] This implies that there will not be any fiscal pressures on the State due to the old-age pension in the short term. However, the old age dependency ratio is projected to increase to 7.6 per 100 in 2025, and to 24.5 per 100 by 2050.[20] The expected increase in the old age population and higher dependency ratio has led to renewed calls for the introduction of narrower targeting of the old-age (and disability) pension so as to improve financial sustainability.[21] Additional challenges to the effectiveness of the old-age pension include Namibia's low population density, which makes the equitable and cost-effective delivery of benefits and services problematic; as well as administrative barriers that restrict access.[22]

11.2 ASSESSMENT OF THE OLD-AGE PENSION ON THE BASIS OF THE PRINCIPLES

Although it was introduced before the adoption of ILO Recommendation 202, many of the principles listed in the Recommendation have been applied in the establishment and implementation of the old-age pension.

11.2.1 State Responsibility

The Recommendation 202 allocates the overall and primary responsibility of giving effect to it to Member States.[23] One specific responsibility on Member States is the establishment and maintenance of national social protection floors.[24] Member States are also required to establish the basic social security guarantees by law,[25] and to formulate and implement social protection floor strategies.[26] Member States are further responsible for monitoring the developments of the social protection floor and for defining proper monitoring mechanisms.[27]

---

19. See: International Labour Office and Oxford Policy Management, *Namibia Social Protection Floor Assessment Report* (2014) 14; and United Nations Development Programme, *Human Development Report 2015*, 236 (2015).
20. See: International Labour Office and Oxford Policy Management, *Namibia Social Protection Floor Assessment Report*, 14 (2014).
21. International Labour Office and Oxford Policy Management, *Namibia Social Protection Floor Assessment Report*, 50 (2014).
22. International Labour Office and Oxford Policy Management, *Namibia Social Protection Floor Assessment Report*, 167 (2014).
23. Article 3 of Recommendation 202.
24. Article 4 of Recommendation 202.
25. Article 7 of Recommendation 202.
26. Article 13 of Recommendation 202.
27. Article 19 of Recommendation 202.

In relation to the old-age pension, Namibia satisfies its overall and primary responsibility of establishing and maintaining a social protection floor comprising basic income security – at least at a nationally defined minimum level – for older persons. The old-age pension scheme in Namibia began in 1949 when eligibility for South African non-contributory State pensions was extended to white Namibians.[28] The pension was continued under the national pension scheme when it was established by the National Pensions Act in 1992. Payment of the pension is guaranteed by the State since it is funded by the government through national budgetary allocations.[29] The Office of the Prime Minister and the Ministry of Poverty Eradication and Social Welfare undertake general supervision of the national pension scheme.[30] The Directorate of Social Welfare in the Ministry administers the Scheme.[31] The Minister appoints District Pension Officers in each of the designated pension regions/districts. Pension Officers have the responsibility for receiving, registering, investigating, and submitting applications for national pensions to the Permanent Secretary of the Ministry.[32]

However, the government has privatized the administration and distribution of the old-age grant. Since 2011, this has been undertaken by Epupa Investment Technology, a private company (before 2011, it was carried out by another private company, United Africa Group).[33] A contract between Epupa Investment Technology and the government provides guidelines for the administration of the grant. It has been held that the privatization of the administration and distribution of the old-age grant brought about efficiency gains since biometric identification of recipients was introduced, which reduced wastefulness as only beneficiaries or their procurators received the pension.[34] Transaction costs are also relatively low, as government pays NAD 16.25 per transaction to Epupa, which is 2.7% of the value of a basic pension.[35]

---

28. S. Devereux, *Social Pensions in Namibia and South Africa* IDS Discussion Paper 379, 1 (February 2001).
29. *See*: Budget Statement Presented by Calle Schlettwein, MP, Minister of Finance, 26 (25 Feb. 2016).
30. *See* s. 5 of the National Pensions Act; U. Dempers, *Social Protection in Namibia – Civil Society Perspective!* presentation at the SASPEN/PSP/FES Social Protection Colloquium (Lusaka, Zambia, 12 May 2016) accessed at http://www.saspen.org/home/wp-content/uploads/2016/04/Uhuru-Dempers_PRESENTATION_Lusaka-Socialprotect ion-Colloqu ium_SASPEN-PSP-FES_24022016.pdf (11 Aug. 2016); Social Security Administration/ International Social Security Association, *Social Security Programs Throughout the World: Africa 2015*, 159; and E. Schleberger, *Namibia's Universal Pension Scheme: Trends and Challenges*, 11 (International Labour Office ESS Paper No. 6, 2002).
31. Social Security Administration/International Social Security Association, *Social Security Programs Throughout the World: Africa 2015*, 159.
32. Section 11 of the National Pensions Act.
33. International Labour Office and Oxford Policy Management, *Namibia Social Protection Floor Assessment Report*, 164 (2014).
34. When the administration of the grant was privatized, the United Africa Group introduced biometric identification of recipients to prevent fraud (*see*: B.M. Chiripanhura and M. Nino-Zarazua, *Social Safety Nets in Namibia: Structure, Effectiveness and the Possibility for*

On the other hand, privatization led to a reduction in the number of access points (pay points), especially in rural areas, which made it difficult – if not impossible – for some elderly people to access their pensions. Privatization has also led to 'significant transaction costs to the recipients, resulting in reduced access and possibly coverage'.[36]

11.2.2 Universality of Protection

The old-age pension is a universal cash transfer of NAD 1,100 (about USD 82) per month paid to persons who are 60 years of age and older. In addition to the age requirement, a person will be eligible for the pension if he/she is a citizen or permanent resident non-citizen of Namibia (i.e., an immigrant) and lives in the country.[37] This means that temporary residents, such as migrant workers, are excluded.

With the exception of Employees Compensation Fund, self-employed workers have access to social insurance schemes on a voluntary basis.[38] This means informal sector workers are able to contribute towards retirement insurance. However, the high levels of unemployment and employment in subsistence farming implies that a large number of persons do not have access to social insurance benefits and rely on the old age pension when they reach the age of 60 years. Since the old-age pension is a universal scheme, it is accessible by every citizen or non-citizen with permanent residence status who meets the age requirement. The pension is received by 98.4% of older persons, meaning that almost every older person has access to the pension.[39] Some of the reasons advanced for the lack of 100% coverage include the long distances across the country that pension administrators have to travel, the isolation of some communities, and the illiteracy of qualifying persons.[40]

---

a *Universal Cash Transfer Scheme*, 4, accessed at https://www.bon.com.na/CMSTemplates/Bon/Files/bon.com.na/88/8836bf27-7f47-4b0c-9744-f124611e6abb.pdf (5 Aug. 2016).

35. International Labour Office and Oxford Policy Management, *Namibia Social Protection Floor Assessment Report*, 174 (2014).
36. B.M. Chiripanhura and M. Nino-Zarazua, *Social Safety Nets in Namibia: Structure, Effectiveness and the Possibility for a Universal Cash Transfer Scheme*, 4, accessed at https://www.bon.com.na/CMSTemplates/Bon/Files/bon.com.na/88/8836bf27-7f47-4b0c-9744-f124611e6abb.pdf (5 Aug. 2016).
37. Section 3 of the National Pensions Act 10 of 1992.
38. *See* the Social Security Act 34 of 1994.
39. *See*: United Nations Development Programme, *Human Development Report 2015*, 49 (2015).
40. *See*: B.M. Chiripanhura and M. Nino-Zarazua, *Social Safety Nets in Namibia: Structure, Effectiveness and the Possibility for a Universal Cash Transfer Scheme*, accessed at https://www.bon.com.na/CMSTemplates/Bon/Files/bon.com.na/88/8836bf27-7f47-4b0c-9744-f124611e6abb.pdf (5 Aug. 2016).

11.2.3 Entitlements Based on Law (Incl. Inspection, Enforcement, Effective and Accessible Complaint, and Appeal Procedures)

Article 7 of Recommendation 202 states that basic social security guarantees should be established by law. National laws and regulations should specify the range, qualifying conditions and levels of the benefits giving effect to these guarantees. Impartial, transparent, effective, simple, rapid, accessible and inexpensive complaint and appeal procedures should also be specified. Access to complaint and appeal procedures should be free of charge to the applicant. Systems should be in place that enhance compliance with national legal frameworks.

The old-age pension is regulated by legislation, the National Pensions Act of 1992. The Act outlines the following:

- Categories of benefits paid: the Act provides for the payment of basic State pensions, pensions for the blind, disability pensions, as well as additional and supplementary allowances (including carer's allowance).[41]
- Persons entitled to national pensions: in terms of Article 3(1), a person is entitled to the national pension if he or she satisfies the Permanent Secretary that he or she is an aged, blind or disabled person; that at the time of his or her application for a national pension, he or she is ordinarily resident in Namibia; and that he or she is a Namibian citizen; or has been lawfully admitted to Namibia for permanent residence and had been so resident in Namibia for a continuous period immediately preceding the date of his or her application for a national pension.
- Procedures for application for a national pension: a person who is eligible for a national pension is required to apply in the form determined by the Permanent Secretary to the district pension officer of the district or area where he or she is ordinarily resident. He/she must furnish such particulars as may be prescribed or as such a district pension officer may require.[42]
- Modalities for the suspension, cancellation and administration of national pensions: the Permanent Secretary is empowered to cancel the payment of any national pension if a pensioner, for any reason, ceases to be a Namibian citizen; or is a permanent resident who has ceased to be ordinarily resident in Namibia; or fails to furnish the Permanent Secretary with proof of his or her Namibian citizenship when required to do so; or has failed to collect his or her national pension for a continuous period exceeding six months.[43]

---

41. *See* s. 2(1) of the National Pensions Act.
42. Section 4(1) of the National Pensions Act.
43. Section 2(1) of the National Pensions Act.

However, one area where the requirement that national laws and regulations should specify levels of the benefits is not applied is the failure to gazette decisions on national pension increases as provided in terms of the relevant legislation.[44] This is regarded as providing a basis for uncertainty, also about the pension increase implementation date.[45]

The Act also outlines complaint and appeal procedures. According to section 7, any decision made, or action taken, by the Permanent Secretary in the administration of the Act is subject to appeal to the Minister. In giving effect to this provision, the service delivery charter of the Directorate of Social Services states that a person who is unhappy with decisions or responses from pension administrative offices should contact the Complaints Coordinator in the Office of the Permanent Secretary in the Ministry, for forwarding on the complaint to the Director of Social Welfare. Where they are not satisfied with the response from the Director, a person can 'consult' the Permanent Secretary in the Ministry. In the final instance, if they are still dissatisfied with the response of the Permanent Secretary, they can lodge a complaint with the Ombudsman.[46]

There are few complaints to the Ombudsman relating to the administration of the old-age pension. Although the Ombudsman received 2,438 complaints in 2014 (3,961 in 2015), complaints about pensions made up 3% of complaints to the Ombudsman (about seventy-three).[47] This was down from 5% in 2009 and 4% in 2010.[48] Complaints about the administration of pensions are free of charge. In addition, a State-funded legal aid scheme under the Ministry of Justice offers legal assistance and representation to indigent persons who wish to seek redress before the Ombudsman for human rights violations.[49]

However, concerns have been raised about the double internal 'review' process (Complaints Coordinator to Director of Social Welfare to Permanent Secretary), the technical capacity of the Ombudsman to handle social assistance cases, and whether effective access to a fair appeals process is possible in view of the size of the country.[50] The Ombudsman has confirmed that its complaints

---

44. *See*, for example, the announcement of the NAD 100 increase in the old-age pension for 2016 in the Budget Statement Presented by Calle Schlettwein, MP, Minister of Finance, 26 (25 Feb. 2016).
45. International Labour Office and Oxford Policy Management, *Namibia Social Protection Floor Assessment Report*, 157 (2014).
46. International Labour Office and Oxford Policy Management, *Namibia Social Protection Floor Assessment Report*, 158 (2014).
47. Ombudsman Namibia, *Annual Report 2015*, 24 and 62.
48. International Labour Office and Oxford Policy Management, *Namibia Social Protection Floor Assessment Report*, 161 and 182 (2014).
49. *See*: Committee on Economic, Social and Cultural Rights, *Consideration of Reports Submitted by States Parties under Articles 16 and 17 of the International Covenant on Economic, Social and Cultural Rights: Initial Reports of States Parties Due in 1997 – Namibia*, 13 (13 Feb. 2015).
50. International Labour Office and Oxford Policy Management, *Namibia Social Protection Floor Assessment Report*, 158 (2014).

procedures are not yet accessible to all citizens, especially in rural areas.[51] The Ombudsman was able to resolve 68% of complaints in 2014 and 73% of complaints in 2015.[52] This implies that although complaints and appeals procedures are set out in the National Pensions Act, their efficiency and accessibility are not guaranteed, since they are not impartial, transparent, effective, simple, swift, and accessible.

International standards on efficient and accessible complaints and appeals procedures point to the need for (*inter alia*) the establishment of independent and impartial courts or tribunals,[53] sequential and complementary reviews and appeals procedures,[54] the provision of reasonable time limits for reviews (complaints) and appeals,[55] the need for expeditious and simple proceedings,[56] the

---

51. Ombudsman Namibia, *Annual Report 2015*, 3.
52. Ombudsman Namibia, *Annual Report 2015*, 25.
53. The ILO has held that in accordance with Convention No. 102, the right of appeal should be guaranteed against decisions of a social security administration either to a court of a general jurisdiction or to a special tribunal. It is of the opinion that this fundamental right is intended to guarantee that courts and judges are impartial and have judicial independence to decide disputes according to the facts and the law, including freedom from improper internal and external influence (ILO, *Social security and the rule of law*, General Survey concerning social security instruments in light of the 2008 Declaration on Social Justice for a Fair Globalization, Report of the Committee of Experts on the Application of Conventions and Recommendations (Arts 19, 22 and 35 of the Constitution) Report III (Part 1B), International Labour Conference, 100th Session, 2011, paras 406 and 433 (2011)).
54. Efficient and accessible complaints and appeals procedures require an institutional separation between administrative accountability, review and revision, on the one hand; and a wholly independent, substantive system of appeals, on the other. According to the ILO: '... social security disputes are settled in two stages: a first complaint phase, generally before the higher level administrative body within the social security institutions, and a second stage of appeal against the decision of the administrative body, generally before an administrative, judicial, labour or social security court or tribunal.' It further held that '... the concept of appeal further implies the settlement of the dispute by an authority that is independent of the administration that reviewed the initial complaint. Merely guaranteeing the right to seek review of the decision by the same administrative authority *would not therefore be sufficient to constitute an appeal procedure* under Convention No. 102. In addition, in the absence of special appeal procedures against the decisions of an administrative authority responsible to the government which rules in the first and last resort, the Committee has previously observed that the safeguards provided for in the Convention could nonetheless be ensured by the application of the general rules governing the right of appeal to the ordinary courts insofar as these rules permit the review or annulment of any administrative ruling in the cases covered by Article 70' (ILO, *Social security and the rule of law*, paras 406 and 434).
55. The ILO suggests that although its standards do not prescribe the length of the period that should be available to the claimant to lodge a complaint, the Committee of Experts considers that such period should be of a reasonable duration (ILO, *Social Security and the Rule of Law*, para. 418).
56. According to the ILO, the general principles set out in international social security instruments, which call for recourse procedures to be rapid, militate in favour of the harmonization of the applicable procedural law throughout dispute settlement procedures in social security matters. It adds that in certain cases, due to the, at times, inadequate

guarantee of representation and legal assistance,[57] and the provision of effective (enforceable) remedies.[58]

To meet the requirements of Recommendation 202, the internal complaints procedures must be shortened to a one-step process either by the Director of Social Welfare or by the Permanent Secretary. As the Ombudsman has remarked:

> it is therefore imperative that ministries, offices etc. should introduce internal complaint procedures to resolve these issues which citizens may have against them, where they started. Some of these issues are simple enquiries ... which can be resolved internally, speedily and at no cost.[59]

The Ombudsman also needs to extend the reach of its services, especially in rural areas, in order to improve accessibility. It plans to establish regional and satellite offices in some under-served areas.[60]

11.2.4 Adequacy and Predictability of Benefits (Accessibility, Sufficiency, and Responsiveness to Specific Needs)

Namibia defines poverty as the percentage of people in a specific area whose annual equivalent consumption per adult is below the poverty line. In 2010, the poverty line was NAD 3,330.48 (about USD 456) per annum for the lower threshold and NAD 4,535.52 (about USD 621) for the upper threshold. An adult is considered to be living in poverty when his/her annual equivalent consumption is below the upper boundary of the poverty line. A person is considered to be living in extreme poverty when the annual equivalent consumption is below the lower threshold of the poverty line. The incidence of poverty is the proportion of the population whose consumption is below the poverty line.[61]

---

guarantees relating to the impartiality and independence of the administrative bodies that examine complaints in the first resort, emphasis should be placed on observance during the complaint procedures of certain fundamental principles, which should therefore be reinforced, such as the right to obtain a rapid and reasoned decision. This is because one of the most important principles of regular proceedings, namely the prompt rendition of justice, is also crucial in social security matters, since claimants often have to rely on benefits to survive. This underscores the need to establish a procedure for the rapid solution of cases where the urgency is manifest (ILO, *Social Security and the Rule of Law*, para. 436).

57. The ILO has proposed that during the resolution of a dispute, both parties should be guaranteed the right to engage a lawyer or other qualified representative of their choice. The ILO also advocates for the provision of free legal aid and legal assistance in social security disputes (ILO, *Social Security and the Rule of Law*, para. 436).
58. In terms of ILO standards, the right to a fair trial further guarantees that any decision has to be legally enforceable (ILO *Social Security and the Rule of Law* para. 433).
59. Ombudsman Namibia, *Annual Report 2014*, 4.
60. Ombudsman Namibia, *Annual Report 2015*, 24.
61. *See*: National Planning Commission (Namibia), *Namibia Index of Multiple Deprivation*.

The old-age pension is paid to prevent poverty among the elderly.[62] Therefore, the level of the benefit is pegged at a point where the poverty of beneficiaries is reduced. The value of the old-age pension is NAD 1,100 (about USD 73) per month in 2016. As Namibia's Minister of Finance has stated:

> At this level of grants, our senior citizens are placed above the national poverty line, making the grants an effective and credible shield against poverty and vulnerability.[63]

In addition to reducing poverty amongst beneficiaries, the old-age pension also promotes the dignity of elderly persons. The debates in the National Assembly on the adoption of the National Pensions Act reveal that the objective of the pension is to enable beneficiaries '... to clothe themselves and to feed themselves'.[64] This is in line with Article 4 of Recommendation 202, which states that the various benefits should together secure, over the life cycle, effective access to goods and services defined as necessary at the national level.

The debates also stated that the pension is to be administered by the elderly themselves and spent at their own discretion. They should have the freedom to administer their pensions themselves and arrange their priorities as they see fit.[65] The pension also enhances the social and economic standing of pensioners in their households,[66] thereby further promoting their dignity. This satisfies Article 8, which requires that benefits to facilitate a life lived with dignity. The Article provides that the minimum income level to facilitate a life lived with dignity may be defined as a set of necessary goods and services, or as a national poverty line, or income threshold for social assistance, or in any other way, and may take into account regional differences. Since the old-age pension level is above the poverty line, it provides recipients with the opportunity to live a life of dignity.

The level of the old-age pension is regularly reviewed to maintain the real value of the benefit. When Namibia was declared independent in 1990, there were different old-age pension amounts for the various races. There was thus a need to equalize the pension amounts in accordance with the equality and freedom from discrimination clauses of the Constitution.[67] The standard pension

---

62. *See*: B.M. Chiripanhura and M. Nino-Zarazua, *Social Safety Nets in Namibia: Structure, Effectiveness and the Possibility for a Universal Cash Transfer*, 3, accessed at https://www.bon.com.na/CMSTemplates/Bon/Files/bon.com.na/88/8836bf27-7f47-4b0c-9744-f124611e6abb.pdf (5 Aug. 2016).
63. *See*: Budget Statement Presented by Calle Schlettwein, MP, Minister of Finance, 26 (25 Feb. 2016).
64. Republic of Namibia, *Debates of the National Assembly* (vol. 20) 1992, 75.
65. Republic of Namibia, *Debates of the National Assembly* (vol. 20) 1992, 70.
66. *See*: B.M. Chiripanhura and M. Nino-Zarazua, *Social Safety Nets in Namibia: Structure, Effectiveness and the Possibility for a Universal Cash Transfer Scheme*, 5, accessed at https://www.bon.com.na/CMSTemplates/Bon/Files/bon.com.na/88/8836bf27-7f47-4b0c-9744-f124611e6abb.pdf (5 Aug. 2016).
67. Article 10 of the Constitution of Namibia guarantees equality and freedom from discrimination as fundamental rights.

amount was set at NAD 92 per month in October 1990 and was increased to NAD 120 in 1992 (the top rate was NAD 382). However, in 1994, the amount of the old-age pension was equalized at NAD 120 for everyone, which was increased to NAD 135 in May 1994 and to NAD 160 in 1996. In 2008 and 2009, it stood at NAD 450 and was increased to NAD 500 in 2010. From April 2013, the old-age pension amounted to NAD 600, and was increased to NAD 1,000 in 2015. It now stands at NAD 1,100 per month in 2016, with provision made for an additional NAD 100 per month (to NAD 1,200) in the next budget.[68]

Almost every person aged 60 years and above in Namibia receives the old-age pension (98.4%).[69] Challenges to the effectiveness of the old-age pension scheme include Namibia's low population density of 2.6 persons per square kilometre which makes the equitable and cost-effective delivery of benefits and services problematic. The 2009/10 Namibia Household Income and Expenditure Survey revealed that 33% of households live within 1 kilometre from the nearest pension pay point, 43% live between 2 and 5 kilometres from it, and 9% live more than 20 kilometres away from the pension pay point.[70] The situation is worst in the Karas, Otjozondjupa, and Kunene regions, with 39%, 33%, and 23% of households respectively travelling more than 20 kilometres to the nearest pension pay point. Access to the old-age pension is further limited by administrative barriers. Some commentators have stated that:

> The costs to clients of complying with requirements and receiving benefits, including monetary and time costs, can be significant. In principle, long travel distances to administrative offices and delivery points, complex requirements (for example, the extensive documentation from various sources that is required), and under-capacitated and untrained bureaucracies (resulting in long waiting times and failure to pay benefits) could impose substantial costs on clients, and could be an obstacle to accessing benefits and at other times significantly reduce the real value of the benefits.[71]

The costs to clients of complying with requirements and receiving benefits reduce the amount of benefits that beneficiaries take home since such costs are set against the pension. Therefore, these costs negatively affect the value of their benefits thereby reducing the pension.

---

68. *See*: S. Devereux, *Social Pensions in Namibia and South Africa*, IDS Discussion Paper 379, 10-11 (February 2001); B.M. Chiripanhura and M. Nino-Zarazua, *Social Safety Nets in Namibia: Structure, Effectiveness and the Possibility for a Universal Cash Transfer Scheme*, 4, accessed at https://www.bon.com.na/CMSTemplates/Bon/Files/bon.com.na/88/8836bf27-7f47-4b0c-9744-f124611e6abb.pdf (5 Aug. 2016).; and Budget Statement Presented by Calle Schlettwein, MP, Minister of Finance, 26. (25 Feb. 2016).
69. *See*: United Nations Development Programme, *Human Development Report 2015*, 49 (2015).
70. Namibia Statistics Agency, *Namibia Household Income and Expenditure Survey 2009/2010*, 96.
71. International Labour Office and Oxford Policy Management, *Namibia Social Protection Floor Assessment Report* 167 (2014).

Although it is deemed to be otherwise effective, there are also a few issues with the old-age pension disbursement process. The main issue relates to the fingerprints of recipients who receive benefits at cash pay points becoming unreadable for biometric identification on the payment system of the delivery institution (Epupa Investment Technology). This can lead to delays in the payment of the pension or the need for procurators to be appointed to receive the pension on behalf of the beneficiary.[72]

As discussed above, the regulation of the old-age pension in legislation makes it predictable. The only part of the benefit that is not predictable is the regular increases that are not gazetted as required by legislation.

11.2.5 Non-discrimination (Including Gender, Nationality, and Status of Employment)

The old-age pension is a universal and unconditional benefit of NAD 1,100 per month paid to every Namibian citizen or permanent resident, irrespective of (prior) employment status. This implies that there is no discrimination between males and females, between citizens and permanent resident non-citizens, or between (former) workers and the unemployed. However, temporary and irregular non-citizens are excluded. The age of eligibility for the pension was equalized at independence in 1990 due to constitutional requirements. Before then, females became eligible at the age of 60 years, while males could only qualify at the age of 65 years.[73] Section 10 of Namibia's Constitution states that all persons shall be equal before the law, and that no persons may be discriminated against on the grounds of sex, race, colour, ethnic origin, religion, creed, or social or economic status. Section 5 further states that fundamental rights and freedoms enshrined in the Constitution must be respected and upheld by the Executive, Legislature, and Judiciary; all organs of the government and its agencies; and, where applicable to them, by all natural and legal persons in Namibia; and shall be enforceable by the Courts in the prescribed manner. As a result of the above, the old-age pension is equally accessible to males and females as well as citizens and permanent residents. However, the reduction in the number of access points – especially in rural areas – that has made it difficult for some elderly people to access their pensions, means beneficiaries in the affected areas are discriminated against in terms of equal access to the pension.

---

72. International Labour Office and Oxford Policy Management, *Namibia Social Protection Floor Assessment Report* 165 (2014).
73. S. Devereux, *Social Pensions in Namibia and South Africa*, IDS Discussion Paper 379, 9 (February 2001).

11.2.6 Financial Solidarity

As a universal, unconditional, and non-contributory cash transfer scheme, the old-age pension is wholly financed through general taxes in terms of budgetary allocations to the Ministry of Poverty Eradication, and Social Welfare.[74] Beneficiaries are not required to have been previously employed or to have made any contributions to the scheme. The solidarity of the Namibian people with recipients of the old-age pension (and other social assistance schemes) is evident in the 2016 budget and the Medium-term Expenditure Framework (April 2015-March 2018) having as one of their objectives the improvement of the welfare of Namibians in an inclusive and sustainable manner.[75] In addition, poverty eradication and the improvement of social welfare (which include the old-age pension) has been listed as one of the priority areas of national development.[76] Some of the issues currently undertaken include the definition Ministry of Poverty Eradication and Social Welfare of an integrated package of cross-cutting instruments for driving back the frontiers of poverty and vulnerability, and the improvement of the quality and coverage of social safety nets (including the increase in the old-age pension in 2016).[77]

The prioritization of the old-age pension and other social assistance schemes in the Medium-term Expenditure Framework, despite doubts about the long-term sustainability of the schemes (also due to their increase in real terms),[78] and the maintenance of its universal and unconditional nature, further point to financial solidarity with the beneficiaries of these schemes.

11.2.7 Good Governance

Efforts have been made to respect the rights and dignity of pensioners. The Directorate of Social Welfare in the Ministry of Poverty Eradication and Social Welfare has a service charter setting out methods of telephonic, written, and personal contact with officials, and key values of the Directorate (customer

---

74. See, for example, Budget Statement Presented by Calle Schlettwein, MP, Minister of Finance (25 Feb. 2016); and Republic of Namibia, *Estimates of Revenue, Income and Expenditure 01 April 2015 to 31 March 2018*.
75. Budget Statement presented by Calle Schlettwein, MP, Minister of Finance, 11 (25 Feb. 2016).
76. Budget Statement presented by Calle Schlettwein, MP, Minister of Finance, 6 (25 Feb. 2016).
77. Budget Statement presented by Calle Schlettwein, MP, Minister of Finance, 7-8 (25 Feb. 2016).
78. B.M. Chiripanhura and M. Nino-Zarazua, *Social Safety Nets in Namibia: Structure, Effectiveness and the Possibility for a Universal Cash Transfer Scheme*, 6, accessed at https://www.bon.com.na/CMSTemplates/Bon/Files/bon.com.na/88/8836bf27-7f47-4b0c-9744-f124611e6abb.pdf (5 Aug. 2016).

Chapter 11: Namibia National Pension Scheme

service orientation, sensitivity, recognition, transparency, integrity, and accountability).[79] The contract between Epupa Investment Technology and the government also contains provisions promoting the rights and dignity of pensioners. It states that Epupa must: 'provide and maintain in good working order, suitable, payment-and-computer equipment and equip pay out units with ATM type instrument fitted with dispensers. The contractor shall also disseminate information concerning the pay days, pay times and pay-points for the districts'. It is also the responsibility of Epupa to ensure that 'pay-points and service points are accessible to old and disabled persons and personnel are available to assist where required'.[80]

The good governance requirements on Epupa are deemed to be implemented in practice as there are limited complaints about the timeliness of paymasters and the length of queues, with the general impression of the payment process being that it is quite effective (there are indications that paymasters are generally on time and that the time taken to complete the process and the length of queues are acceptable).[81]

However, as discussed earlier, the number of pay points was reduced with the privatization of the delivery of pensions, resulting in some pensioners walking long distances to pay points. However, the pension payment process is considered to be effective. Pension pay points at offices of the Ministry of Poverty Alleviation and Social Welfare are generally good, with seated waiting areas and ablution facilities. The only concerns are the absence of ablution facilities in some Namibia Post Office (NamPost) pay points and the lack of buildings (and therefore ablution facilities) in rural pay points.[82]

Since the pension scheme is wholly financed by the State, diversity of methods and approaches is mostly in terms of payment modalities. The administration and distribution of the old-age pension has been privatized and is undertaken by a private company, Epupa Investment Technology. As a result, the company undertakes the payment of most pensions with others paid through banks and NamPost.[83]

Transparent, accountable, and sound financial management and administration of the old-age pension scheme, and financial, fiscal, and economic sustainability with due regard to social justice and equity are ensured as the

---

79. International Labour Office and Oxford Policy Management, *Namibia Social Protection Floor Assessment Report*, 159 (2014).
80. Excerpt from the contract between the Government of Namibia and Epupa Investment Technology as quoted in International Labour Office and Oxford Policy Management, *Namibia Social Protection Floor Assessment Report*, 160 (2014).
81. International Labour Office and Oxford Policy Management, *Namibia Social Protection Floor Assessment Report*, 165 (2014).
82. International Labour Office and Oxford Policy Management, *Namibia Social Protection Floor Assessment Report*, 165 (2014).
83. International Labour Office and Oxford Policy Management, *Namibia Social Protection Floor Assessment Report*, 178-179 (2014).

scheme is wholly financed by the State through the Ministry of Poverty Eradication and Social Welfare. There have been recent calls for the introduction of narrower targeting of the old-age (and disability) pension so as to improve financial sustainability.[84] However, the old-age pension and other social assistance schemes have been prioritized in the Medium-term Expenditure Framework.[85] The old-age pension is also transparent since it is wholly financed through general taxes in terms of budgetary allocations to the Ministry of Poverty Eradication and Social Welfare. Allocations to the scheme are outlined in the annual Budget Statements and the Estimates of Revenue, Income and Expenditure.[86]

There is coherence between the old-age pension delivery institutions. The Office of the Prime Minister manages the social grant database. The Ministry of Poverty Eradication and Social Welfare collates information on pension recipients and forwards it to regions and districts every month. Regional and district offices of the Ministry and Epupa Investment Technology then effect payment of the pensions. In addition, the Ministry of Home Affairs and Immigration is involved in the provision of identity documents and birth certificates necessary for application for pensions. However, the capacity of the Ministry of Home Affairs and Immigration is not the same all over the country, and it provides little assistance to grant recipients.[87] The multiplicity of responsible ministries in the pension application process that are not located in a single place limits coherence across institutions dealing with the pension.

The Ministry of Poverty Eradication and Social Welfare is mandated to undertake regular monitoring of the implementation of the old-age pension scheme. Section 12(1) of the National Pensions Act states that the Permanent Secretary or the district pension officer may conduct an inquiry into any matter relating to a national pension. At present, Epupa Investment Technology collects pay point information and submits this to the Ministry. In addition, the Ministry's regional and local offices submit monthly activity reports. Although these are considered to be important for planning and identifying problems in the system, there is little indication that these are captured and analysed to assess service delivery and to improve planning.[88]

There is limited evidence of fraud, which is also due to the introduction of biometric identification of recipients by United Africa Group when it took over

---

84. International Labour Office and Oxford Policy Management, *Namibia Social Protection Floor Assessment Report*, 50 (2014).
85. *See*: Budget Statement presented by Calle Schlettwein, MP, Minister of Finance (25 Feb. 2016).
86. *See*, for example, Budget Statement presented by Calle Schlettwein, MP, Minister of Finance (25 Feb. 2016); and Republic of Namibia, *Estimates of Revenue, Income and Expenditure 01 April 2015 to 31 March 2018*.
87. International Labour Office and Oxford Policy Management, *Namibia Social Protection Floor Assessment Report*, 167 (2014).
88. International Labour Office and Oxford Policy Management, *Namibia Social Protection Floor Assessment Report*, 181 and 183 (2014).

Chapter 11: Namibia National Pension Scheme

the administration of the grant. However, the absence of electronic data capturing in the Social Assistance System by the relevant ministries makes the system susceptible to fraud.[89]

11.2.8 Coherence of Policies

Recommendation 202 states that social protection floors should comprise at least the following basic social security guarantees: (a) access to a nationally defined set of goods and services, constituting essential health care, including maternity care, that meets the criteria of availability, accessibility, acceptability, and quality; (b) basic income security for children, at least at a nationally defined minimum level, providing access to nutrition, education, care, and any other necessary goods and services; (c) basic income security, at least at a nationally defined minimum level, for persons in active age who are unable to earn sufficient income, in particular in cases of sickness, unemployment, maternity, and disability; and (d) basic income security, at least at a nationally defined minimum level, for older persons. Together with the old-age pension, there are various social protection measures adopted by Namibia that are aimed at creating a social protection floor. These include social grants for children, a disability grant, a war veterans' grant, labour market-linked transfers, and social insurance schemes.

Grants and allowances aimed at protecting orphaned and vulnerable children are the Child Maintenance Grant, the Foster Parent Grant, the Places of Safety Allowance, and the Special Maintenance Grant. The Child Maintenance Grant is paid to a Namibian citizen or permanent resident who is the biological parent of a child younger than 18 years of age, is a spouse receiving the disability or old-age grant, is deceased, or is serving a jail term of not less than six months. Children older than 7 years of age must attend school.[90] The amount of the grant was NAD 250 per month in 2015. The Foster Parent Grant is paid to a citizen or permanent resident who cares for a child who is placed in their custody. The Foster Parent Grant was also NAD 250 per month in 2015. The Places of Safety Allowance of NAD 10 per day is given to a person or family who care for a child under the age of 21 who was placed by the Commissioner of Child Welfare, or was placed in the place of safety under the terms of the Children's Act or the Criminal Procedure Act of 1977. The Special Maintenance Grant of NAD 250 per month is paid to the caregiver of a child under 16 years of age who has a disability.

Children's grants have low coverage rates, with only about 146,249 children out of a total child population of 958,716 (15% of children) receiving a

---

89. International Labour Office and Oxford Policy Management, *Namibia Social Protection Floor Assessment Report*, 171-172 and 182 (2014).
90. Social Security Administration/International Social Security Association, *Social Security Programs Throughout the World: Africa 2015*, 161.

grant in 2013.[91] The high rate of poverty means that a large proportion of poor children have no access to the child grants and allowances. Some of the barriers to accessing the grants include the transport costs associated with the grant application process; a lack of awareness and the incorrect application of eligibility criteria; bureaucratic challenges such as misplaced files, the perceived inefficiency of officials, and the need for repeat visits; and problems with essential documentation, especially birth and death certificates.[92]

Measures for persons of active age who are unable to earn sufficient income include the disability pension, labour market-linked transfers, and social insurance schemes. The disability pension is paid to every citizen or permanent resident who has a disability.[93] The amount of the disability pension is NAD 1,100 in 2016 and is paid to any person aged 16 years or older who has a disability (temporary or permanent) or has been diagnosed with AIDS by a doctor in the public health care system.[94] Coverage of the disability pension is estimated to be 95%.[95] The funeral grant is paid to all recipients of the old-age and disability pensions. The cost of a funeral up to NAD 3,000 is paid directly to the undertaker to ensure a dignified burial of pensioners and disabled people, which contributes to income security for older persons.[96]

Labour market-linked transfers are food-for-work/cash-for-food programmes, public works programmes, and informal sector and micro-enterprise support. Food-for-work programmes are mostly implemented during droughts or floods. The programmes require participants to take part in an economic or development activity to receive food. Participants also gain experience that improves their future labour market engagement.[97] Support is provided by the government for the creation of employment in the informal sector.[98] Some of this includes the provision of credit and business training to small enterprises by the Namibia Development Corporation. Non-governmental organizations also assist rural households with small loans to those who want to start small businesses. The Ministry of Gender Equality and Child Welfare also operates an initiative to

---

91. *See*: International Labour Office and Oxford Policy Management, *Namibia Social Protection Floor Assessment Report* 65.
92. Ministry of Gender Equality and Child Welfare (Namibia) The Effectiveness of Child Welfare Grants in Namibia Study Findings and Technical Notes, X (2010).
93. *See* ss 2 and 3 of the National Pensions Act.
94. Social Security Administration/International Social Security Association, *Social Security Programs Throughout the World: Africa 2015*, 158.
95. *See*: International Labour Office and Oxford Policy Management, *Namibia Social Protection Floor Assessment Report* 60.
96. Social Security Administration/International Social Security Association, *Social Security Programs Throughout the World: Africa 2015*, 158; and B.M. Chiripanhura and M. Nino-Zarazua, *Social Safety Nets in Namibia: Structure, Effectiveness and the Possibility for a Universal Cash Transfer Scheme*, 7, accessed at https://www.bon.com.na/CMSTemplates/Bon/Files/bon.com.na/88/8836bf27-7f47-4b0c-9744-f124611e6abb.pdf (5 Aug. 2016).
97. *Ibid*, 17.
98. *Ibid*, 18.

promote entrepreneurship and employment creation by offering an income generating activity grant to deserving individuals.

Social insurance schemes are the Maternity, Sick Leave and Death Benefit (MSD) Fund and the Employees Compensation Fund under the Social Security Commission; and the Motor Vehicle Accident Fund. The schemes administered by the Social Security Commission are accessible to both employees and the self-employed. The MSD Fund provides retirement, disability, survivors', sickness, and maternity benefits. The Employees Compensation Fund provides benefits to employees (including apprentices) whose earnings are up to a prescribed limit. The Fund pays out disability benefits (temporary and permanent), medical, and survivors' benefits to employees who are injured or contract a disease at work.

The war veterans' pension is an additional measure guaranteeing basic income security for some for older persons. A beneficiary must be a Namibian citizen who was involved in the armed struggle for independence and is resident in Namibia.[99] The amount of the pension was NAD 2,200 in 2015.[100]

11.2.9 Social Participation (Both in the Design and Administration of a Scheme) and Freedom of Association

Namibia's Constitution guarantees freedom of association, including freedom to form and join trade unions.[101] In realizing this right, trade unions operate freely in the country and they are involved in current discussions aimed at developing a social protection floor in Namibia. An example is the inclusion of the Namibian Employers Federation, the Trade Union Congress of Namibia, and the National Union of Namibian Workers in the National Consultative Working Group that was undertaking the Namibia Social Protection Floor Assessment in 2013 and 2014.[102] The social partners are thus instrumental in the development of Namibia's social protection floor as the National Consultative Working Group is said to have 'offered a platform and an opportunity for Namibian institutions and actors to learn from each other, and helped build consensus on key aspects of Namibia's social protection system'.[103]

Despite their current inclusion in the development of the social protection floor, there is no indication of the involvement of social partners in the extension of the old-age pension to Namibia in the 1940s. In addition, as a non-contributory scheme funded entirely by the government through the national

---

99. *Ibid*, 11.
100. Social Security Administration/International Social Security Association, *Social Security Programs Throughout the World: Africa 2015*, 158.
101. Article 21 of the Namibian Constitution.
102. *See*: International Labour Office and Oxford Policy Management, *Namibia Social Protection Floor Assessment Report* iv.
103. *See*: International Labour Office and Oxford Policy Management, *Namibia Social Protection Floor Assessment Report* iv.

budget, social partners are not involved in the determination of the level of the pension or increases. This is done by the Ministry of Finance and adopted by the National Assembly.[104] The administration of the pension is undertaken by the Ministry of Poverty Alleviation and Social Welfare, Epupa Investment Technology and Namibia Post. However, there is some involvement of social partners (i.e., representatives of old persons) in the administration of the pension. Research indicates that in some regions, pay point committees led by local elders have been established. An example is where the Kunene South Welfare Organization set up sub-committees at the Fransfontein, Anker, and Khorixas pay points to improve payment facilities and amenities.[105] The Organization receives donations from local government and other organizations to improve pay point facilities. The Organization also funds an NAD 500 food parcel as an additional death benefit and a food parcel in December through contributions from pensioners.[106]

11.3 LEGISLATIVE DEFICITS AND/OR IMPLEMENTATION FAILURES OF THE OLD-AGE PENSION

The National Pensions Act of 1992 established the old-age pension. It also regulates the categories of benefits paid, the persons entitled to national pensions, the procedures for the application for a national pension, and modalities for the suspension, cancellation, and administration of national pensions. However, decisions on national pension increases are not provided in terms of any law, leading to uncertainty, also about the pension increase implementation date.

The old-age pension is a universal pension for citizens and permanent residents aged 60 years and older. This means that every older person in Namibia is entitled to the pension. The pension is received by 98.4% of old persons. It thus satisfies the requirements of universality of protection and of accessibility. Some of the reasons advanced for the failures in universality of protection and accessibility include the large distances across the country that pension administrators have to travel, isolation of some communities, illiteracy among some qualifying persons, and administrative barriers (including costs to clients of complying with requirements and receiving benefits, long travel distances to administrative offices and delivery points, and complex application requirements). It may also be due to self-targeting, with eligible but well-off persons not applying for the grant.

---

104. *See*, for example, the Budget Statement Presented by Calle Schlettwein, MP, Minister of Finance (25 Feb. 2016).
105. International Labour Office and Oxford Policy Management, *Namibia Social Protection Floor Assessment Report*, 165 (2014).
106. International Labour Office and Oxford Policy Management, *Namibia Social Protection Floor Assessment Report*, 166 (2014).

In addition, although the National Pensions Act outlines complaint and appeal procedures, their efficiency and accessibility are not guaranteed since they are not impartial, transparent, effective, simple, rapid, accessible, and inexpensive. This is because they fail to meet the requirements of Recommendation 202 and other international instruments on efficient and accessible complaints and appeals procedures which point to the need for (*inter alia*) the establishment of independent and impartial courts or tribunals, sequential, and complementary reviews and appeals procedures, the provision of reasonable time limits for reviews (complaints) and appeals, the need for expeditious and simple proceedings, the guarantee of representation and legal assistance, and the provision of effective (enforceable) remedies.

Proper governance of the pension scheme is facilitated through (amongst others) coherence between the old-age pension delivery institutions. However, the capacity of the Ministry of Home Affairs and Immigration, which provides identity documents and birth certificates necessary for application for the pension, is uneven and it affords little assistance to grant recipients. The coherence of delivery institutions is further limited by the fact that the multitude of responsible ministries in the pension application process are not located in a single place. Good governance is also adversely affected by the lack of regular monitoring of the implementation of the old-age pension scheme. Although Epupa Investment Technology collects pay point information and submits this to the Ministry of Poverty Eradication and Social Welfare and the Ministry's regional and local offices submit monthly activity reports, these are not captured and analysed to assess service delivery and to improve planning.

Trade unions operate freely in Namibia in line with the Constitution's guarantee of freedom of association, including freedom to form and join trade unions. The social partners are involved in current discussions aimed at developing a social protection floor in Namibia. However, they were not involved in the extension of the old-age pension to Namibia in the 1940s. They are also not involved in the determination of the level of the pension or increases, as this is done by the government through the National Assembly. On the other hand, community-based organizations (such as the Kunene South Welfare Organization) play a role in the administration of the pension.

11.4 CONCLUSIONS

As a universal scheme, the old-age pension largely complies with Namibia's obligations in terms of Recommendation 202 to establish and maintain a social protection floor comprising basic income security, at least at a nationally defined minimum level for older persons in accordance with its national circumstances. The establishment and implementation of the pension fully conforms to many of the principles listed in the Recommendation: State responsibility; adequacy and predictability of benefits (accessibility, sufficiency, and responsiveness to the specific needs); non-discrimination (including gender, nationality, status of employment); financial solidarity; and coherence of policies.

However, some of the listed principles have not been fully applied. These relate to universality of protection; entitlements based on law (including inspection, enforcement, effective and accessible complaint and appeal procedures); good governance; and social participation (both in the design and administration of a scheme) and freedom of association. The lack of full application of the principles entails that not all old people who are in need of the old-age pension are able to receive it. This is contrary to the prescripts of Recommendation 202, which states that Members should, in accordance with national circumstances, establish as quickly as possible and maintain their social protection floors comprising basic social security guarantees. The guarantees should ensure at a minimum that, over the life cycle, all in need have access to essential health care and to basic income security which together secure effective access to goods and services defined as necessary at the national level. There is thus a need for Namibia to adequately apply the principles that are not currently fully applied to enable every older person in Namibia who is in need of the old-age pension to have access to it in practice.

Possible interventions include increasing the number of pay points (especially in isolated rural areas), undertaking education campaigns to inform eligible persons about the pension, reducing the costs to applicants of complying with requirements, and receiving benefits. The current complaint and appeal procedures should also be reformed to ensure that they are impartial, transparent, effective, simple, rapid, accessible, and inexpensive. Improved coordination between the various institutions involved in pension administration and delivery should be promoted. This should include the improved capacity of the Ministry of Home Affairs and Immigration in the provision of identity documents and birth certificates. This could be facilitated by locating all the institutions in a single place. Good governance can be achieved through the regular monitoring of the implementation of the pension scheme. Pay point information by Epupa Investment Technology and monthly activity reports by regional and local offices of the Ministry of Poverty Eradication and Social Welfare should be captured and analysed to assess service delivery and to improve planning of the scheme. Representatives of older persons should be involved in the planning and implementation of the scheme, as they have been instrumental in improving payment facilities and amenities at pay points.

BIBLIOGRAPHY

Publications

Budget Statement presented by Calle Schlettwein, MP, Minister of Finance (25 February 2016).

Chiripanhura, B.M. and M. Nino-Zarazua, *Social Safety Nets in Namibia: Structure, Effectiveness and the Possibility for a Universal Cash Transfer Scheme*, (2013) accessed at https://www.,bon.com.na/CMSTemplates/Bon/Files/bon.com.na/88/8836bf27-7f47-4b0c-9744-f124611e6abb.pdf (5 August 2016).

Committee on Economic, Social and Cultural Rights, *Consideration of Reports Submitted by States Parties under Articles 16 and 17 of the International Covenant on Economic, Social and Cultural Rights: Initial Reports of States Parties Due in 1997 – Namibia* (13 February 2015).

Dempers, U., *Social Protection in Namibia – Civil Society Perspective!*, presentation at the SASPEN/PSP/FES Social Protection Colloquium (Lusaka, Zambia, 12 May 2016) accessed at http://www.saspen.org/home/wp-content/uploads/2016/04/Uhuru-Dempers_ PRESENTATION_Lusaka-Socialprotection-Colloquium_SASPEN-PSP-FES_24022016.pdf (11 August 2016).

Devereux, S., *Social Pensions in Namibia and South Africa*, IDS Discussion Paper 379 (February 2001) for more on the history of the old age pension.

ILO, *Social Security and the Rule of Law* (General Survey concerning social security instruments in light of the 2008 Declaration on Social Justice for a Fair Globalization) (Report of the Committee of Experts on the Application of Conventions and Recommendations (Articles 19, 22 and 35 of the Constitution) Report III (Part 1B)) International Labour Conference, 100th Session, 2011 (2011).

International Labour Office and Oxford Policy Management, *Namibia Social Protection Floor Assessment Report* (2014).

Ministry of Gender Equality and Child Welfare (Namibia), *The Effectiveness of Child Welfare Grants in Namibia Study: Findings and Technical Notes* (2010).

Namibia Statistics Agency, *Namibia Household Income and Expenditure Survey 2009/2010*, 8.

Namibia Statistics Agency, *Namibia Labour Force Survey 2014 Report* (2015).

National Planning Commission (Namibia), *Namibia Index of Multiple Deprivation*.

National Planning Commission (Namibia), *Poverty and Deprivation in Namibia 2015*.

Ombudsman Namibia, *Annual Report 2015*, 24 and 62.

Republic of Namibia, *Debates of the National Assembly* (vol. 20) 1992.

Republic of Namibia, *Estimates of Revenue, Income and Expenditure 01 April 2015 to 31 March 2018*.

Schleberger, E., *Namibia's Universal Pension Scheme: Trends and Challenges* (International Labour Office ESS Paper No. 6 (2002).

Social Security Administration/International Social Security Association, *Social Security Programs Throughout the World: Africa 2015*.

United Nations Development Programme, *Human Development Report 2015* (2015).

CHAPTER 12

Old-Age Allowance Scheme in Thailand

Worawet Suwanrada

12.1 INTRODUCTION

Thai society has faced demographic change in last four decades. Thai women have fewer children on average than women in other countries. At the same time, Thai people live longer. Since the introduction of voluntary family planning-based population policy in the late 1970s, the fertility level has decreased. According to the Survey of Population Change conducted by Thailand's National Statistical Office,[1] the total fertility rate (TFR) decreased from 4.9 in 1974-1976 to 2.7 in 1985-1986, and from 2.0 in 1995-1996 to 1.7 in 2005-2006. The office of the National Economic and Social Development Board (NESDB) has estimated that TFR will fall to 1.5 by 2021.

Simultaneously, life expectancy of both Thai males and females has been on the increase. Male life expectancy at birth has increased from approximately 63.8 in 1974-1976 to 68.9 in 1985-1986, and 77.6 in 2005-2006. On the other hand, female life expectancy at birth has also increased from 58.0 in 1974-1976 to 63.8 in 1985-1986, and 69.9 in 2005-2006. The NESDB has estimated that female life expectancy at birth will increase to 77.7 and 79.4 by 2011 and 2021 respectively, and that of males will increase to 70.6 and 72.8 by the same dates.

As a result of a decline in fertility rates and an increase in life expectancy, Thai society is now an aging society. The number and proportion of older population (generally defined as the population aged 60 and over in Thailand) has continued to rise since 1980. According to the National Population and Housing Census conducted by the National Statistical Office, from 1970, the proportion of the older population increased from 4.9% in 1970 to 5.5% in 1980,

---

1. The 2005-2006 Survey of Population Changes, National Statistical Office of Thailand.

7.4% in 1990, 9.5% in 2000, and 13.2% in 2010. From the NESDB population projection, the proportion of the older population will continue to rise to 18.4% in 2020, 25.9% in 2030, and 32.1% in 2040.

Together with the increase in the proportion of older people, the number and the proportion of both the working-age population (aged 15-59 years) and children are decreasing. Consequently, there is an age-structure imbalance between older persons and those of working age. This implies that the Thai labour market will be enormously affected by population ageing and the decline in fertility rates. In particular, the continuous decrease in the working population results directly in the shrinking of labour supply and leads ultimately to labour shortage. The apparent increase in foreign workers, especially from neighbouring countries in some industrial sectors such as fisheries, construction, agriculture and services sectors, reflects more or less the currently dwindling manpower in Thailand.

During last two decades, in order to maintain older persons' economic security, the Thai government has focused particularly on the old-age allowance system, such that, since its establishment in 1993, it has been revised several times by various cabinets. Indeed, before April 2009, the old-age allowance system consisted initially of means-tested system among various social assistance schemes for specific vulnerable groups of the population. Only the underprivileged elderly were eligible to receive the allowance.

Later, the philosophy behind allowance allocation shifted in favour of a more universal scheme. Save some specific groups who are enjoying officially equivalent public benefits from the government, all older Thai people are entitled to receive the old-age allowance. The informal working population (i.e., informal workers, housewives) in particular is expected to benefit from this scheme.

Thus, this system can be regarded as an important element of a national social protection floor, which aims to guarantee a universal minimum level of old-age economic security for older people in Thailand. Every eligible older person is able to register to receive this benefit at their local authority office. In addition, the level of old-age allowance has been changed from a flat rate to multiple rates according to the age of the beneficiaries. Nevertheless, the old-age allowance system coexists with the other non-contributory and contributory public pension schemes.

Thailand has already ratified the social security (minimum standard) convention (No. 102), but the government has not yet explicitly used the ILO Recommendation on Social Protection Floors (Recommendation No. 202) as a source of inspiration for reforming old-age allowance. The question can be raised as to what the future holds for the old-age allowance. However, at the end of 2015, the Council of the Ministers officially approved the proposal of Ministry of Finance to set up the National Pension Committee whose function is to overview all pension schemes in Thailand. Currently, the bill is under the scrutiny of the Office of the Council of the State. The position of the Thai government regarding Recommendation No. 202 and the old-age allowance as

Chapter 12: Old-Age Allowance Scheme in Thailand

an element of the social protection floor shall be clearer after this legislative process.

This chapter consists of five sections. First is the introduction. The second section is about the historical background and development of old-age allowance scheme in Thailand. Some remarks on the scheme's impact on older persons shall be described in the third section. The fourth section included in it contributes to the assessment of the old-age allowance scheme on the basis of nine principles as explained in Chapter 2: State responsibility, universality of protection, entitlement based on law, adequacy and predictability of benefits, non-discrimination, financial solidarity, good governance, coherence of policies, and social participation. The last section is about existing problems and issues of this scheme.

12.2 HISTORICAL BACKGROUND, DEVELOPMENT AND CONTEXT OF THE OLD-AGE ALLOWANCE SCHEME[2]

12.2.1 Historical Background and Development of the Scheme

The old-age allowance system was launched in 1993 under the Department of Public Assistance (DPA hereafter) in the Ministry of the Interior. The objective of the scheme was to provide financial assistance to the unprivileged elderly, defined as those of at least 60 years of age without enough income to meet necessary expenses, unable to work, abandoned, or with no caregivers. In the beginning, as the representative of DPA, the villages' public welfare assistance committee had the role in identifying the eligible elderly. At the outset, the level of allowance was only THB 200 per head per month. The committee allocated the allowance to the eligible elderly directly. Suwanrada[3] mentioned that the number of recipients was initially only 20,000.

As illustrated in Table 12.1, from 1993 to 2004, the system underwent some minor changes regarding eligibility, amount of allowance, responsibility for the system, the targeting process, and administration. In 2000, the amount of pension was raised to THB 300 per head per month. The local administrative organizations started to play an important role in the targeting process, and the methods of payment of the pension have since diversified (i.e., through an authorized person, postal cheque, and bank account transfer). In 2002, in the reorganization of government ministries, the DPA became part of the Ministry of Social Development and Human Security. Nevertheless, two changes relating the eligibility and targeting process should be noted. First, the priority was given

---

2. This part has been drawn from W. Suwanrada, *The Old-Age Allowance System in Thailand, Recent Developments in the Role and Design of Social Protection Programmes: A Policy Dialogue, Expert Workshop and South-South Learning Event*, Poverty in Focus Number 25, Poverty Practice (Bureau for Development Policy, UNDP 2013).
3. W. Suwanrada, *Poverty and Financial Security of the Elderly in Thailand*, 33. No. 1-4 Ageing International, 50-61 (2009).

to the underprivileged elderly and who could not readily access public services. Second, the members of the community could join the targeting committee. During this period, the number of recipients increased to 110,850 in 1995, and to 318,000 in 2000. From 1999 to 2004, the number remained quite stable at approximately 400,000 recipients.

In 2005, the allowance underwent a big change due to the wave of decentralization. The old-age allowance programme was transferred to the Department of Local Administration (DOLA) in the Ministry of the Interior, which takes care of budget provision to local authorities. The authority of targeting was decentralized to the local authorities. In addition, the participation of the community in the targeting process in the form of community councils or community meetings was legally accepted. Moreover, local authorities could top up the amount of the allowance, if it could exhibit financial competency. Unfortunately, in practice, the top-up facility was not being used by any local authority. In 2006, the amount of allowance was raised to THB 500 per month per head. After the decentralization of the targeting process, the number of recipients increased dramatically to 527,083 in 2005, and almost doubled to 1,073,190 in 2006. The number rose to 1,755,178 in 2007 and 2008.

Although the local governments and communities have played an important role in the targeting system as shown in Figure 12.1, it seems that the targeting inefficiency problem is, to a certain extent, serious. Prachuabmoh et al. found that more than 50% of underprivileged elderly living below the poverty line and without support from their families did not receive the allowance.[4] As the national government had not invested in building the institutional capacity of the targeting system and there were no national guidelines, the approach of the local authorities with regard to targeting was very diverse: some undertook strict targeting but some allocated the allowance to all the elderly. Further, local authorities treated the meaning of 'community meeting' differently. Local authorities faced difficulties in selecting beneficiaries, but could not clearly explain why one older person had been selected but not another. Favouritism by local officials was often appealed.[5]

---

4. V. Prachuabmoh et al. *Research Report on Monitoring and Evaluation of the Second Elderly National Plan 2002-2022* (Bangkok: College of Population Studies, Chulalongkorn University, 2009).
5. Quated by W. Suwanrada and W. Dharmapriya. Development of the Old-Age Allowance System in Thailand: Challenges and Policy Implications, in *Social Protection for Older Persons: Social Pensions in Asia* 153-167 (S.W. Handayani and B. Babajanian eds., Philippines, Asian Development Bank, 2012).

Chapter 12: Old-Age Allowance Scheme in Thailand

Table 12.1   Changes to Old-Age Allowance After its Establishment and Before 2009

Year	Eligibility of Beneficiaries Thai Nationality, 60 Years Old +	Targeting Mechanism	Pension Amount
1993	A. Living in the village, where the Village Social Assistance Centre was located B. (i) abandoned (ii) without caregivers, (iii) poor or (iv) cannot work	Village Social Assistance Committee (VSAC) nominates the name of beneficiaries according to assigned quota.	THB 200
2000	B.	VSAC and/or Local Authorities selected beneficiaries and made an ordered list.	THB 300
2002	B. C. Elderly with the characteristics above and cannot access public services, or lives in a remote area – prioritized.	Local Committee: Members are more diverse. Regional and local officials, civil society, elderly, etc.	THB 300
2005	B. C.	Community Council or	THB 300
2006		Community Meeting (*Prachakom*)	THB 500

Source: Suwanrada 2012.[6]

---

6. W. Suwanrada, *Old-Age Allowance System in Thailand, Recent Developments in the Role and Design of Social Protection Programmes: A Policy Dialogue*, Expert Workshop and South-South Learning Event 3-5 December 2012 (Brasilia, Brazil, 2012).

Figure 12.1 Targeting Process of the Old-Age Allowance System Before 2009

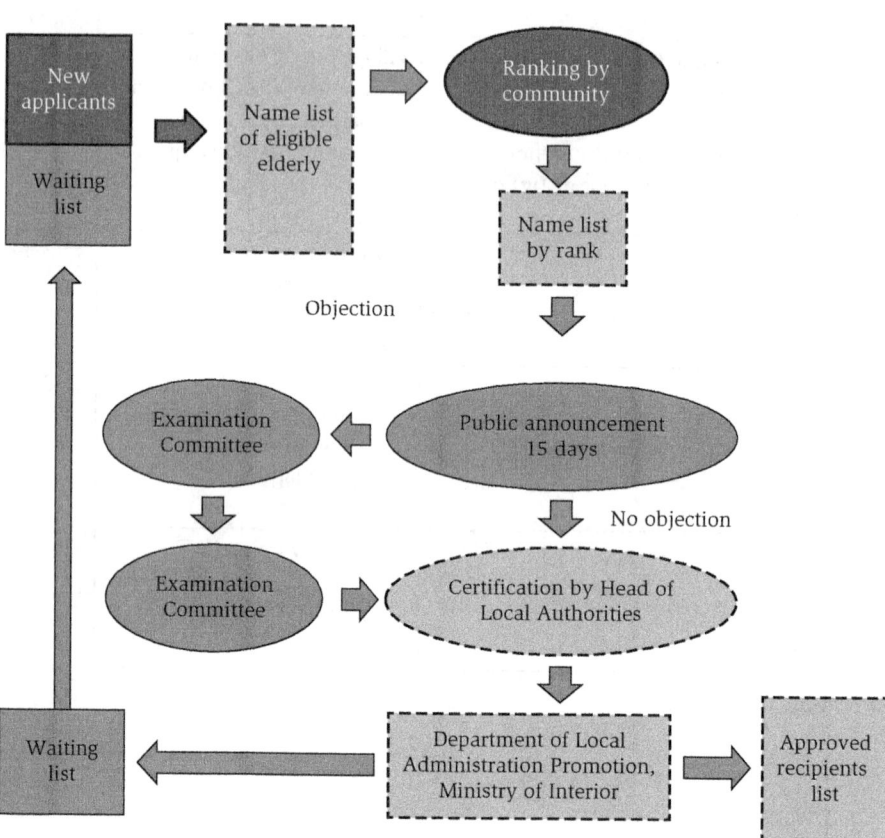

Source: W. Suwanrada, *Economic Situation of the Elderly in Thailand* in *The Synthesis of Body of Knowledge on Thai Elderly from 2003-2007* (C. Wichawut, et al. Foundation of Thai Gerontology Research and Development and Health Systems Research Institute, Bangkok: TQP Printing House 2009); T. Sakunphanit and W. Suwanrada *500 Baht Universal Pension Scheme*, in *Sharing Innovative Experiences: Successful Social Protection Floor Experiences* 401-415 (United Nations Development Programme eds., New York, Special Unit for South-South Cooperation, 2011).

The biggest change was made in 2009, when the old-age allowance was expanded to all elderly Thai people, aged 60 or older, who are not living in public homes for the elderly or do not receive permanent income through a salary or pension (i.e., excluding central, local or public enterprise pension recipients, social security fund old-age benefit recipients, and government employed persons) are included in the system. The number of recipients in this universalization of old-age allowance reached 5,652,863 recipients in 2010, 6,784,734 recipients in 2012, and increased to 7,996,332 recipients in 2016.[7] Not only has the number of recipients increased, but also the government budget for the old-age allowance. According to Table 12.2, the proportion of the total older population who are also beneficiaries during last eight years is approximately 82.6%. The government budget for the scheme has increased from THB 21,963 million in 2009 to THB 63,098 million in 2016, which accounts for 2.32% of the national government annual budget.

Table 12.2   Coverage of Old-Age Allowance Scheme After 2009

Fiscal Year	No. of Recipients	Budget (THB)	No. of Older Population	Coverage (%)
2009	5,448,443	21,963,075,000	7,176,819	76.1
2010	5,652,893	32,779,232,400	7,493,227	78.1
2011	6,521,749	37,893,398,000	7,811,450	83.4
2012	6,784,734	52,535,425,200	8,170,909	84.0
2013	7,308,315	58,347,043,200	8,734,101	89.4
2014	7,664,599	60,999,878,400	9,110,754	85.4
2015	7,749,138	61,879,284,200	9,455,777	85.1
2016	7,996,332	63,098,546,400	10,014,699	79.8

Source: Department of Older Persons, Ministry of Social Development and Human Security and Official Statistics Registration Systems, Ministry of Interior, 2017.

In principle, the elderly or the authorized representative must register with the local authorities, where he or she is registered as residing. The registration procedure will be annually, in November. In practice, some local authorities provide mobile units to facilitate the registration of the elderly. The documents required for registration are an identification card, residence registration book, bank account (if applicable), and proxy form (if applicable). Upon completing the approval process, the qualified older person will start to receive pension from October of the next year. The method of payment can be chosen from the following. First, the cash can be received directly from the local authority office; second, an authorized representative can receive the cash directly from the local authority office; third, the pension can be transferred into the elderly person's bank account; and fourth, the pension can be transferred to the bank account of an authorized representative.

In 2012, the Yinluck Shinawatra Cabinet approved a change in the pension rate to the multiple rate system. Formally, it was a single rate of THB 500 per head per month. Currently, the monthly pension amount varies by age of recipient, namely, THB 600 (USD 16.99) per month for those aged 60-69, THB 700 (USD 19.83) per month for those aged 70-79, THB 800 (USD 22.66) per

---

7. Department of Older Persons, Ministry of Social Development and Human Security (2017).

month for those aged 80-89, and THB 1,000 (USD 28.33) per month for those aged 90 and older.[8]

12.2.2 Context of Old-Age Allowance Scheme in the Public Pension Systems

Figure 12.2 illustrates the entirety of public pension systems in Thailand. The Old-Age Allowance Scheme is a part of the Thai public pension systems. There are four major characteristics of current public pension schemes in Thailand. First, the whole pension system consists of an occupational (or labour status)-based pension system (for formal sector's working population, see employees) and an old-age allowance system. Second, universal coverage is covered by Old-Age Allowance System for the elderly who are not a part of the occupational-based pension system. Third, Thai public pension schemes have both non-contributory and contributory schemes, which comprise both a defined benefits system and a defined contribution system. Fourth, there is no single pension authority to regulate and monitor all subsystems at present. Details on some of the sub-systems are included in Table 12.3.

Figure 12.2 Entire Picture of Public Pension Schemes in Thailand: At Present

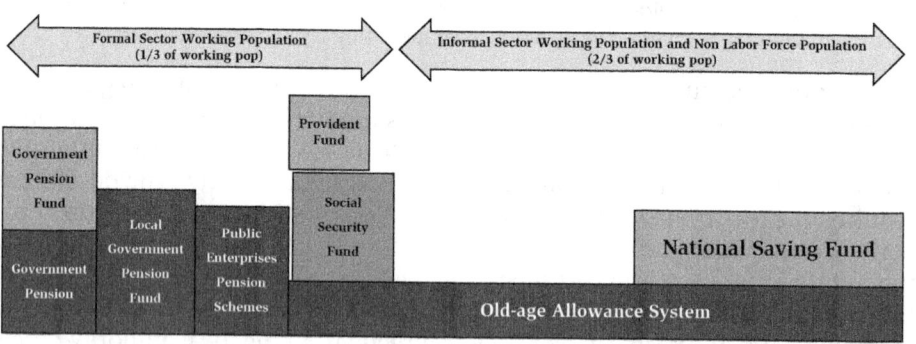

Source: Compiled by the author.

---

8. USD 1 = THB 35.2980 (annual reference rate of Commercial Banks in Bangkok Metropolis in 2016, Bank of Thailand).

Table 12.3 Main Public Pension Systems in Thailand

System	Target Group	Sub System (and/or Relevant Legal Basis)	Financing Method	Benefits
Social Security Fund	**Private Employees** (This compulsory scheme includes not only old-age benefits for private employees but also other benefits for other events, i.e., illness, childbirth, disability, old age, assistance for the family, death and unemployment)	-	- Contributory system - Defined Benefits - Insured Employees: 5% - Employer: 5% - Government: 2.75% of his/her monthly wages (be limited to THB 15,000 /month)	Old-age benefits = 20% of average monthly income of last 60 months before retirement (Conditions: must be 55 years old and have paid contributions for 180 months). In case of contribution of more than 180 months, 1% will be added to every 12 months of contributions. If contribution periods are shorter than 180 months, he/she will receive lump sum payment for retirement (gratuity).

System	Target Group	Sub System (and/or Relevant Legal Basis)	Financing Method	Benefits
Civil Service Pension System	Central and regional government officials	**Traditional Pension from National Budget** (Government Pension Act)	-Non-contributory -Tax Financing	Amount of pension per month (depends mainly on level of wages before retirement and working periods; eligible for pensions if working periods are over 25 years)
		Government Pension Fund (Government Pension Fund Act)	- Contributory System -Defined Contribution -Individual: 3% -Government: 3% of his/her monthly wages	Lump sum payment (depends on individual and government contributions and their financial benefits)
	Local Government Officials	(Local Government Officials Pension Act)	-Non-contributory -Tax Financing	Amount of pension per month (depends mainly on level of wages before retirement and working periods; eligible for pensions if working periods are over 25 years)

System	Target Group	Sub System (and/or Relevant Legal Basis)	Financing Method	Benefits
National Saving Fund Scheme	Any of the working population, aged 20-59 who does not yet have old-age security under any scheme, such as government official pensions, government pension fund, or a social security fund.	-	-Voluntary -Contributory, -With co-contribution by the government	Contribution: monthly, namely THB 50 or THB 100. Co-contribution: under 30 years of age, 50%; if 30-50 years of age, 80%; and 50-59, 100% of the member's contribution. Benefits: money received at 60 in individual account shall be annuitized. Additional Saving: up to THB 1,000 accepted but this saving shall not be co-contributed by the government

Source: Table 7.3 in W. Suwanrada, in *Global Aging Issues and Policies: Understanding the Importance of Comprehending and Studying the Aging Process* (Boni Li et al., Charles C. Thomas Publisher, USA, 2013). The author added more details on the National Saving Fund Scheme.

12.3 ECONOMIC AND SOCIAL IMPACT OF OLD-AGE ALLOWANCE

Although the old-age allowance system has been implemented for a long time in Thailand, studies on the impact of the allowance are still limited.

Using the National Statistical Office's National Survey on Older Persons over a number of years, Knodel, Prachuabmoh and Chayovan and Knodel, Teerawichitchainan, Prachuabmoh, and Pothisiri have confirmed the percentage of persons aged 60 and older who received any income regardless of the amount during the previous twelve months from a variety of potential sources during 1994-2014, as shown in Table 12.4.[9] Work is one of a number of possible

---

9. J. Knodel, B. Teerawichitchainan, V. Prachuabmoh and W. Pothisiri, *The Situation of Thailand's Older Population: An Update based on the 2014 Survey of Older Persons in Thailand* (Help Age International, 2015); J. Knodel, V. Prachuabmoh and N. Chayovan, *The*

sources of income for older Thai people. The researchers also mentioned that, prior to the 2009 expansion of the Old-Age Allowance scheme, the most common source of income for older persons was their children. However, after 2009, the percentage that reportedly received some from children was still high but was slightly less than the percentage reporting that they received an old-age allowance from the government. It is quite apparent that the proportion of beneficiaries of the old-age allowance scheme has increased over the last two decades. The proportion was only 0.5% in 1994 but has increased to 84.9%, according to the latest survey.

Table 12.4 Sources and Main Source of Income of Older Population in Thailand (%)

Income Source	Percent Receiving Any Income from the Following Source					Main Source of Current Income			
	1994	2002	2007	2011	2014	1944	2007	2011	2014
Work	38.0	37.7	37.8	42.7	38.8	31.5	28.9	35.1	33.8
Pension	4.1	4.3	5.4	7.5	6.3	4.0	4.4	6.0	4.8
Old-age allowance	0.5	3.0	24.4	81.4	84.9	0.0	2.8	11.4	14.9
Interest, saving, rent	17.1	18.0	31.7	35.7	n.a.	1.7	2.9	2.6	3.8
Spouse	21.4	17.4	23.3	21.4	25.2	4.6	6.1	3.1	4.3
Children	84.5	77.2	82.7	78.5	78.9	54.1	52.3	40.1	36.8
Relatives	11.4	6.9	11.0	8.9	10.0	2.4	2.3	1.5	1.4
Other	8.8	2.6	1.5	2.5	1.6	1.7	0.5	0.2	0.2
Total	-	-	-	-	-	100.0	100.0	100.0	100.00

Source: For 1994, 2002, 2007 and 2011 from Table 4.2 in J. Knodel, V. Prachuabmoh and N. Chayovan, *The Changing Well-being of Thai Elderly: An update from the 2011 Survey of Older Persons in Thailand* (College of Population Studies, Chulalongkorn University and Help Age International 2013). For 2014 from J. Knodel, Teerawichitchainan, Prachuabmoh and Pothisiri, *The Situation of Thailand's Older Population: An Update based on the 2014 Survey of Older Persons in Thailand* (Help Age International 2015).

On the other hand, Knodel, Teerawichitchainan, Prachuabmoh, and Pothisiri also emphasized that although almost all elderly people have more than one source of income, in most cases these sources differ considerably in their

---

Changing Well-being of Thai Elderly: An Update from the 2011 Survey of Older Persons in Thailand (College of Population Studies, Chulalongkorn University and Help Age International 2013).

importance.[10] For all surveys, the elderly still report that children are the most important source of income. However, there exists a relatively small minority reporting old-age allowance as their main source of income. The proportion of older persons who have claimed that old-age allowance has become their main source of income has increased over the last two decades as well. The proportion was extremely low in 1994 but has increased to 14.9%, according to the results of the latest survey. This reflects the fact that, although the amount of the benefit is not so high (i.e., THB 500 or THB 600-THB 1,000 per head per month), it is quite substantial for people who are extremely poor.

Suwanrada and Dharmapriya used micro data from the Socio-economic Survey in 2009 to consider the income poverty reduction effect of the old-age allowance by hypothetically excluding the old-age allowance (and disability assistance from the government) from household income and calculating the change in numbers of households living below the poverty line (THB 1,586 2009), as shown in Table 12.5.[11] The old-age allowance programme seems to reduce the numbers of poor households by about 1.3% of the total number of households. In addition, it also reduces the number of older persons living alone below the poverty line by about 3.3%, and the number of two-person elderly households by about 6%. The results confirm that the old-age allowance programme effects a reduction in income poverty, especially among underprivileged older persons.

Table 12.5 Income Poverty Reduction of Old Age Allowance (in 2009)

Type of Household	Number of Households Whose Average Household Income per Head Was Below Poverty Line (THB 1,586)	
	Current Situation (as in Survey)	Hypothetical Calculation After Excluding Old-Age Allowance from Household Income
All households	1,621,536	1,877,013
	8.28%	9.6%
One elderly living alone	20,112	47,029
	2.48%	5.8%

---

10. *Ibid.*
11. W. Suwanrada and W. Dharmapriya Development of the Old-Age Allowance System in Thailand: Challenges and Policy Implications, in *Social Protection for Older Persons: Social Pensions in Asia* 153-167 (S.W. Handayani and B. Babajanian eds., Philippines, Asian Development Bank, 2012).

Type of Household	Number of Households Whose Average Household Income per Head Was Below Poverty Line (THB 1,586)	
	Current Situation (as in Survey)	Hypothetical Calculation After Excluding Old-Age Allowance from Household Income
Two-elderly households	73,717	117,427
	10.19%	16.2%

Source: Adapted by the author using Table 6.6 in W. Suwanrada and W. Dharmapriya *Development of the Old-Age Allowance System in Thailand: Challenges and Policy Implications* in Social Protection for Older Persons: Social Pensions in Asia 153-167 (S.W. Handayani and B. Babajanian eds., Philippines, Asian Development Bank, 2012).

Notes: % shows above means the proportion of households whose average household income per head was below the poverty line in comparison with equivalent households in total.

Suwanrada and Dharmapriya also emphasize the social impact and institutional impact of the old-age allowance.[12] Although the amount of the pension is not high as such, older persons use it to meet their basic needs, especially basic expenditures such as food, clothing, and medicine. It also financially helps older persons who have been left behind by family members who have migrated to the city in search of better economic opportunities. In some cases, the pension is used for their grandchildren who have been left behind. In addition, although health coverage for older persons shall be guaranteed by the Universal Coverage Scheme, the allowance relieves some of the burden of the cost of accessing health facilities because of the limitations of public transport system, especially in sub-rural and rural areas. Moreover, the pension enabled older persons to participate in social events with dignity as they can spend the money on donations (mostly to Buddhist temples), or can make social contributions on important occasions, including religious festivals, marriage, funerals, etc. For institutional impacts, Suwanrada and Dharmapriya have insisted that the change to universal coverage of old-age allowance limits social cost incurred from conflicts within community, corruption and possible favouritism under the means-tested system.[13]

Using a questionnaire put to 2,256 elderly persons from an original survey taken in thirty communities or villages in four sub-districts within three Northern provinces, Chiangmai, Lampoon and Maehongson, Suwanrada W. and P. Leetrakul explored the impact of the old-age allowance at the individual and household levels, and its impact on the community economy.[14] Taking old-age allowance as one source of income, they confirmed that old-age allowance is the

---

12. Ibid.
13. Ibid.
14. W. Suwanrada and P. Leetrakul (2014).

main source of income of 43.80% of all older persons in four sub-districts. In addition, the allowance makes an impact at the both individual (the elderly themselves) and household levels as follows. The old-age allowance can reduce the poverty rate among the older persons by approximately 13.20%. Essentially, the old-age allowance enables older persons receiving it to attain a higher income that takes them above the poverty line. In addition, the allowance has facilitated a more effective income distribution among older persons. Moreover, the benefits of old-age allowance have been transmitted to the family of the elderly as well. The old-age allowance can reduce the household's poverty rate by approximately 17.07%. Those households enjoy a higher average household income above the poverty line when the older person, as one of the household's number, receives the old-age allowance. In the same manner, the allowance has facilitated better income distribution among households as well.

In terms of expenditure, Suwanrada W. and P. Leetrakul confirmed that in the sub-districts when the older persons have received the allowances, they tend to spend money on the following items:[15]

(1) food;
(2) donations – which in most cases is for merit-making;
(3) public utilities, rent, and house maintenance;
(4) medical expenses; and
(5) contributions for cremation expenses.

For some specific households, similar to all cases, they tend to spend money first on food and donations. However, the next priority of each group is somewhat different, for example, the elderly living with only their spouse tend to spend the money on social relations, whereas the elderly living with their grandchildren tend to spend the money on looking after their grandchildren.

In addition, the impact of the old-age allowance on community economy has been estimated from older persons' spending behaviour.[16] According to their research, there is both spending which will contribute to community economy and spending that flows out of the community. The study found that when the elderly spend their old-age allowance, 53.27% of spending shall at least circulate once within the community, while 16.73% will flow out of the community. The ambiguous part is approximately 27.91% because this part is income transfer to others in various forms, for example, donations, social expenses, and family support. Its impact on the community economy depends on the behaviour of the transferee's consumption behaviour as well. Finally, 2.08% will be used for savings and insurance, which will not contribute to the community economy in the short term.

---

15. *Ibid.*
16. *Ibid.*

12.4 ASSESSMENT OF THE OLD-AGE ALLOWANCE SCHEME ON THE BASIS OF NINE PRINCIPLES

12.4.1 State Responsibility

12.4.1.1 Establishment and Maintenance

In the Constitution of the Kingdom of Thailand B.E. 2550 (2007), the State responsibility for the establishment and maintenance of the old-age allowance scheme under section 53 of Part 9 Rights to Pubic Health Services and Welfare from the State and Directive Principles of Fundamental State Policies reads as follows:

> Section 53. A Person who is over sixty years of age and has insufficient income on which to live shall have the right to receive such welfare and public facilities as suitable for his or her dignity as well as appropriate aids to be provided by the State.

In addition, the responsibility of the State for the design of the future public pension system is clearly stated in section 84(4) as well:

> Section 84(4). The State shall pursue directive principles of State policies in relation to the economy to provide savings for the people and State officials living in old age.

Moreover, the role of the government in providing the old-age allowance to older persons is mentioned explicitly in section 11 of the Act on the Elderly B.E. 2546 (2003). It states that the government must guarantee the right of older persons to access the following protection, promotion, and support:

(1) medical and public health services for the elderly which take account of convenience and rapid access;
(2) education, religion, and useful information and news relevant to them;
(3) suitable jobs or occupational training;
(4) self-development and participation in social activities, facilitating a togetherness as a network or community;
(5) facilities and security measures especially for the elderly in buildings, public places, vehicles, and other public services;
(6) appropriate support for the payment transport fares;
(7) exemption from entry fees to government buildings;
(8) assistance for any elderly person at risk torture, unlawful exploitation or abandonment;
(9) the provision of advice and consultation on other proceeding in connection with a case or the resolution of family problems;
(10) extensive provision of housing, food, and clothing where necessary;
(11) extensive and fair provision of monthly old-age allowance;
(12) assistance in holding traditional funerals; and

(13) other matters.

Thus, we can confirm the fact that section 11(11) of the Act on the Elderly B.E. 2546 secures basic income security in old-age as suggested in the ILO Recommendation on Social Protection Floors. However, some issues around implementation, financing, and delivery system of old-age allowance are not mentioned in the Act on the Elderly.

Besides the guarantee of the government on providing monthly old-age allowance to older persons, under the Act on the Elderly, the so-called National Committee on the Elderly (hereafter, NCE) has been established. The authority and responsibility of the NCE relating to old-age allowance are mainly:

(1) to set up policies and principal plans on protection, promotion, and support of status, roles, and activities of the elderly under the Cabinet's approval;
(2) to set up a framework for implementing the policies and principal plans subject to (1), including coordinating, monitoring, and evaluating the results of such policies and principal plans; and
(3) to propose to the Cabinet the recommendations and observations on promulgation or revision of legislation on protection, promotion and support of status, role and activities of the elderly.

The NCE consists of:

(1) the Prime Minister as Chairman;
(2) the Minister of Social Development and Human Security as First Deputy Chairman;
(3) the President of the Senior Citizens Council of Thailand under the Royal Patronage of Her Royal Highness the Princess Mother as Second Deputy Chairman;
(4) the Permanent Secretary for Finance, the Permanent Secretary for Foreign Affairs, the Permanent Secretary for Social Development and Human Security, the Permanent Secretary for the Interior, the Permanent Secretary for Labour, the Permanent Secretary for Education, the Permanent Secretary for Public Health, the Deputy Provincial Governor of Bangkok Metropolitan, the Director of the Bureau of the Budget, the Secretary General of the Nation Economic and Social Development Board, the President of the National Council on Social Welfare of Thailand under His Majesty's Royal Patronage, and the Secretary General of the Thai Red Cross Society, as ex officio member;
(5) not more than five qualified members appointed by the Cabinet from representatives of private entities involved in the work of protection, promotion and support of status, roles and activities of the elderly;
(6) not more than five qualified members appointed by the Cabinet. The Director General of the Department of Older Persons in the Ministry of

Social Development and Human Security acts as a Member-cum-Secretary. The Director of the Bureau of Empowerment of Vulnerable Groups in the Ministry of Social Development and Human Security and the Director of the Institute of Geriatric Medicine, the Department of Medical Services in the Ministry of Public Health, act as Assistant Secretaries.

The NCE had a role in providing guidelines and rules for implementing and maintaining the old-age allowance system. In order to proceed with its implementation, the Committee enacted the Order of the NCE on Old-Age Allowance Payment Criteria in 2009, clarifying the whole process of the old-age allowance system, including the eligibility of recipients, the application process, the procedure for the consideration of applicants' eligibility, payment methods, the termination of payment, and the delegation of authority on the old-age allowance payment to local authorities.

12.4.1.2 Implementation

In practice, the central government has delegated the authority on the payment of the old-age allowance to local authorities. Thus, the local authorities including municipalities, sub-district administrative organizations, Bangkok Metropolitan, and Pataya City are the providers of the old-age allowance. Based on the Order of the NCE on Old-age allowance Payment Criteria in 2009, the legal framework for implementing the provision of the old-age allowance was set up in the form of the Order of Ministry of the Interior on the Payment of Old-Age Allowance by Local Authorities B.E. 2552 (2009) by the Ministry of the Interior, who has direct responsibility for the supervision of local authorities. The contents of this Order consist of beneficiary eligibility, application processes, payment methods, the termination of pension payment, monitoring and recording, and budgeting. Annually, local authorities are able to propose the budget for eligible applicants to the DOLA in the Ministry of the Interior. The annual budget shall be allocated to local authorities based on the number of eligible applicants in the form of specific grants for old-age allowance.

12.4.1.3 Monitoring Mechanisms

There are two channels through which the central government – in this case the NCE – can monitor the old-age allowance scheme. First, the Director General of the Department of Older Persons in the Ministry of Social Development and Human Security, who acts as a Member-cum-Secretary, has an obligation to report the current situation (e.g., the number of recipients, budget, etc.), issues, problems and proposals, collated from all local authorities by the DOLA in the Ministry of the Interior, to the NCE's regular meeting. The Prime Minister and the other members of NCE can monitor the implementation of old-age allowance policy through this kind of national committee system.

Second, the NCE can monitor the old-age allowance scheme in term of coverage through the process of the National Plan on the Elderly's monitoring and evaluation. Currently, the Thai government is using the 2nd National Plan on the Elderly (2002-2021). The long-term plan is evaluated once every five years. This current plan has already been evaluated twice – in 2007 and 2012. The National Plan on the Elderly is a roadmap for all focal points on elderly issues. It provides a platform for integration and coordination among Ministries and related organizations. This long-term plan is also an important mechanism for monitoring and evaluating the progression of policy responses on elderly issues.

In the 2nd plan, there are five strategies in total, as shown in Table 12.6: the strategy on readiness preparation of the people for quality ageing; the strategy on the promotion and development of the elderly; the strategy on social safeguards for the elderly; the strategy on the management of the development of the national comprehensive system for undertakings and developing the personnel for the elderly involving missions; and the strategy on processing, upgrading, and disseminating knowledge to the elderly and the national monitoring of implementation of NPE. Under each strategy, there are measures to be implemented by related government organizations. According to the latest evaluation in 2012, only 51% of key performance indicators that had been set out in the 2nd plan has been met. The progression on the preparedness for quality ageing and social protection for the elderly seems to be very slow.

The measure relating to the old-age allowance is that on income security under the third strategy 'on the social safeguards for the elderly'. Under this measure, a key performance indicator, namely 'the proportion of older persons receiving government pension or old-age allowance monthly', shall be monitored once in every five years by the NCE.

Table 12.6 Entire Picture of National Plan on the Elderly

Strategy	Measures
Strategy on readiness preparation of the people for their quality ageing	1. Measures on income security for old age. 2. Measures on education and lifelong learning. 3. Measures on raising social conscience on the respect for, and recognition of, valuable contribution and dignity of the elderly.
Strategy on the elderly promotion and development	1. Measures on health promotion, prevention against disease, and primary self-care. 2. Measures on encouraging the joining of groups and strengthening the elderly representative organizations. 3. Measures on the promotion of employment and income of the elderly.

Strategy	Measures
	4. Measures on the promotion of the skilled elderly. 5. Measures on the promotion and support of all classes of the mass media to include the elderly involving programmes and support for the elderly to facilitate access to knowledge and data, information and news. 6. Measures on the promotion and provision of enabling and friendly housing and environment.
Strategy on the social safeguards for the elderly	1. Measures on income security. 2. Measures on health security. 3. Measures on their families, caregivers, and protection. 4. Measures on the service system and supportive networks.
Strategy on management of developing the national comprehensive system for undertakings and developing the personnel for the elderly involving missions	1. Measures on management of developing the national. comprehensive system for the elderly involving undertakings. 2. Measures on promoting and supporting personnel for the elderly.
Strategy on processing, upgrading and disseminating knowledge on the elderly and the national monitoring of implementation of NPE	1. Measures on encouraging and supporting gerontology researches for the purpose of formulating policies and developing services and undertakings useful to the elderly. 2. Measures on the consecutive and effective monitoring of NPE. 3. Measures on upgrading and updating the database on the elderly, whereby the significant database shall be accessible and easy to search.

Source: V. Prachuabmoh et al. *Research Report on Monitoring and Evaluation of the Second Elderly National Plan 2002-2022* (Bangkok: College of Population Studies, Chulalongkorn University 2009).

12.4.2 Universality of Protection

The personal scope of the old-age allowance scheme is quite broad. According to the Order of Ministry of the Interior on the Payment of Old-Age Allowance by Local Authorities B.E. 2552 (2009), the requirements of beneficiaries are as follows:

(1) Thai nationality;
(2) registering residency with the relevant local authority;
(3) being aged 60 years or older and registering and applying for old-age allowance to the local authority; and

(4) must not be receiving a pension or equivalent benefits from national governmental organizations, public enterprises, or local authorities.

This scheme excludes mainly only government sector pensioners and older persons being cared in public residential homes. These groups of older persons' income security (government officials' pension scheme) and livelihood are already respectively secured by the government. However, the current old-age allowance scheme's coverage has been expanded to include as many Thai older people as possible as recommended by the ILO Recommendation on social protection floors. Even the working population in the informal sector or housewives can enjoy the benefits of this scheme.

However, we must note that this old-age allowance scheme itself is still not universal in terms of provision to all older persons. However, it successfully ensures all Thai older persons are financially secure in old age. This old-age allowance does not show universality in terms of pension but it achieves universality of protection. Nevertheless, this system still excludes both legal and illegal immigrants. The argument for expanding its coverage to immigrants still falls on deaf ears.

12.4.3 Entitlement Based on Law

The entitlement to old-age allowance benefits is clearly prescribed by the Order of the NCE on Old-age allowance Payment Criteria 2009 and the Order of Ministry of the Interior on the Payment of Old-Age Allowance by Local Authorities 2009. The Order of the NCE on Old-age allowance Payment Criteria is not the law adopted by Parliament. It can be changed any time by the Chairman of the Committee, namely the Prime Minister. Of course, the Order of Ministry of the Interior on the Payment of Old-Age Allowance by Local Authorities 2009 can be changed as well by the Minister of the Interior, but it must not violate the Order of NCE.

The Order sets out clearly the system including the range and qualifying conditions. It must be noted that, regarding the level of the old-age allowance, the amount can be changed by the approval of the Cabinet. In addition, the level of old-age allowance has not been yet defined by the nationally defined minimum level of money such as the monetary value of a set of necessary goods and services, national poverty lines or income threshold for social assistance, or any other comparable thresholds established by national law.

It is still far from the Recommendation's expectation. The details of the legal framework are described in Table 12.7. In addition, the routine calendar for the implementation process of Old-Age Allowance Payment under the Order of Ministry of the Interior on the Payment of Old-Age Allowance by Local Authorities B.E. 2552 (2009) is visualized in Table 12.8.

12.4.4 Complaint and Appeal Procedures

Basically, the old-age allowance system was changed from a targeting system to a universal system in 2009, thus there were no longer complaints about targeting inefficiency or inclusion and exclusion errors. However, in the Order of Ministry of the Interior on the Payment of Old-Age Allowance by Local Authorities B.E. 2552 (2009), the local authorities must announce publicly the list of the qualified persons based on the aforementioned eligibility criteria in not less than fifteen days since their application for the allowance. If there is no objection to the list of the qualified recipients, the local authorities shall submit the list to the DOLA in the Ministry of the Interior for budgeting. If there are any objections, local authorities must re-examine the qualifications of the applicants, against whom objections have been raised.

Table 12.7 *Main Features of the Order of Ministry of the Interior on the Payment of Old-Age Allowance by Local Authorities B.E. 2552 (2009)*

Features	Details
Qualifications of eligible beneficiaries	1. Thai nationality. 2. Registering residency with relevant local authority. 3. Being aged 60 years or older and registering and applying for old-age allowance to the local authority. 4. Must not be receiving a pension or equivalent benefits from national governmental organizations, public enterprises or local authorities, i.e., pensioner or beneficiaries of equivalent welfare, the elderly in public or local public assistance facilities, income or compensation earners, except disability or HIV/Aids patients who are receiving an allowance according to the Order of Ministry of the Interior on the Payment of Allowance by Local Authorities B.E. 2548.
Application processes	**When and where** – In November (the second month of the fiscal year), the persons who will turn 60 years old in the next fiscal year must apply to the local authority's office on the basis of registered residency.

Chapter 12: Old-Age Allowance Scheme in Thailand

Features	Details
Application processes	Note that, 1. The elderly cannot process the registration by themselves; they can delegate the application to others by letter of attorney. 2. In case the beneficiary moves into and newly registers residency in another local authority, he or she shall receive the allowance from the former local authority until the end of fiscal year. Simultaneously, before the end of fiscal year, he or she must apply for the allowance to the local authority in the area to which he or she has moved.
	Required Documents 1. ID card or any other identification card issued by governmental organizations and a photocopy of same. 2. Residence Registration Book. 3. Bank passbook (in cases where the elderly person requests a money transfer).
Amount of Pension	THB 500 per month or any other amount approved by the Cabinet.
Payment Method	The beneficiaries shall receive a monthly allowance (before the 10th of each month) by cash or money transfer to a bank account. The authorized person shall receive it in the same manner.
Termination of Payment	The payment shall be terminated when: 1 the beneficiaries pass away; 2 the beneficiaries receive a pension or equivalent benefits from national governmental organizations, public enterprises or local authorities; or 3 the beneficiaries waive the claim to the allowance.

Source: The Order of Ministry of Interior on the Payment of Old-Age Allowance by Local Authorities B.E. 2552 (2009), compiled by the author.

Table 12.8 *Calendar for the Process of Old-Age Allowance Payment under the Order of Ministry of the Interior on the Payment of Old-Age Allowance by Local Authorities B.E. 2552 (2009)*

Start of Fiscal Year 't + 1'	Year 't', October	Local authorities examine the current (living) status of the beneficiaries by self-report, certification or registration database search.
	Year 't', November	New applicants apply for the allowance at local authorities' offices.

	Year 't + 1', February	Local authorities send the lists of eligible beneficiaries to the DOLA, Ministry of the Interior for the fiscal year 't + 2' budget proposal.
		Budgeting process and budget approval.
Start of Fiscal Year 't + 2'	Year 't + 1', October	New applicants, who applied in previous fiscal year, start to receive old-age allowance.

Source: The Order of Ministry of Interior on the Payment of Old-Age Allowance by Local Authorities B.E. 2552 (2009), compiled by the author.

12.4.5 Adequacy and Predictability of Benefits

In the Order of Ministry of the Interior on the Payment of Old-Age Allowance by Local Authorities B.E. 2552 (2009), the amount of benefits is prescribed as follows: THB 500 per month or any other amount approved by the Cabinet. The order provides a room for amendment of benefits in the future. After the change from the targeting system to the universal system in 2009, the amount of benefits was THB 500 per head per month. In 2012, the Yinluck Shinawatra Cabinet has approved the change of pension rate to the multiple rate system. Formally, it was unified rate, namely THB 500 per head per month. Currently, the monthly pension amount varies by age of recipient, namely, THB 600 per month for those aged 60-69, THB 700 per month for those aged 70-79, THB 800 per month for those aged 80-89, and THB 1,000 per month for those aged 90 years and older.

As shown in Table 12.9, the amount of old-age benefits is quite far from a nationally defined minimum level such as the official poverty line. Comparing with poverty line (THB 2,647) in 2014, the minimum (THB 600 or USD 16.99) and maximum (THB 1,000 or USD 28.33) level of old-age benefits account only for 22.6% and 37.77% of the poverty line respectively. However, we must note at least two issues when we discuss adequacy based on the poverty line.

The first issue is the existence of a universal health security scheme. Besides retired government officials, nearly all older Thai people enjoy free medical services from this scheme. The government allocates a fixed amount of the per capita budget annually for this scheme, i.e., in the fiscal year 2016, it was THB 3,028.94 per head. This implies that, excluding medical expenses from the definition of a nationally defined minimum level, the aforementioned proportion shall be hypothetically higher.

The second issue is about the scope of the poverty line. The poverty line consists two parts; minimum expenditure for food and non-food. If we consider minimum expenditure for food as a nationally defined minimum level, the old-age allowance shall cover more than 50% of it. However, the current level of old-age allowance may secure a minimum standard of living, but it does not facilitate life in dignity. Moreover, at present, there is absolutely no automatic adjustment with the change in the cost of living. In addition, any change in its level is left to arbitrary approval of Cabinet. It cannot be predicted.

Table 12.9   Official Poverty Line of Thailand After 2004

Year	2004	2006	2007	2008	2009	2010	2011	2012	2013	2014
Poverty Line (THB)	1,719	1,934	2,006	2,172	2,174	2,285	2,415	2,492	2,572	2,647

Source: Data of The Household Socio-Economic Survey, National Statistical Office, Processing by the Development Indicators database and social NESDB, Office of The NESDB.

12.4.6   Non-discrimination

Based on principle (d) 'non-discrimination, gender equality and responsiveness to special needs', the Order of Ministry of the Interior on the Payment of Old-Age Allowance by Local Authorities B.E. 2552 (2009) provides for equality of treatment between women and men, on the level of income, economic activities, disadvantaged, and non-disadvantaged groups.

However, this legislative framework excludes those older persons receiving a pension or equivalent benefit from national governmental organizations, public enterprises, or local authorities, i.e., pensioners or beneficiaries of equivalent welfare, the elderly in public or local public assistance facilities, income or compensation earners. Retired government officials shall receive a monthly old-age allowance from another scheme. In other words, among the non-retired older population of government officials, all older persons are treated equally in principle. People engaged in informal economic activities are included in the scheme at the same time as retired private sector employees. We must note that, nevertheless, this order is still not applicable to foreign individuals and only partially to older Thai people without official identification cards or documents.

Moreover, the disability or HIV/Aids patients who are receiving an allowance according to the Order of Ministry of the Interior on the Payment of Allowance by Local Authorities B.E. 2548 are also included in this scheme. They can claim old-age allowance as an older person and enjoy specific benefits according to their additional qualifications.

12.4.7 Financial Solidarity

The Old-Age Allowance scheme is non-contributory. Its source of funding is the national budget, mostly taxation. In order to implement this scheme, local authorities, including municipalities and sub-district administrative organizations, receive a budget from central government through the DOLA in the Ministry of the Interior, in the form of 'specific grants' based on the number of qualified older persons proposed by each individual local authority. There are two debates surrounding the financial solidarity of the old-age allowance.

First, as a result of rapid demographic change in Thailand, the potential support ratio is decreasing continuously, namely from approximately 4 currently to 2 in the near future. The financial burden borne by future generations will be higher. Second, there is a financial conflict between central government and local authorities because of specific grant allocations for the old-age allowance, even though local authorities allocating the old-age allowance to older persons on behalf of central government is one of the local authorities' objectives. The central government (specifically speaking the NCE) has initiated the old-age allowance's universalization scheme and delegates its implementation to local authorities. The central government takes it for granted and decreases the general subsidy to local authorities. Therefore, the allocation of the 'old-age allowance' more or less supersedes other objectives of local authorities.

Figure 12.3 Continuous Decrease in Potential Support Ratio

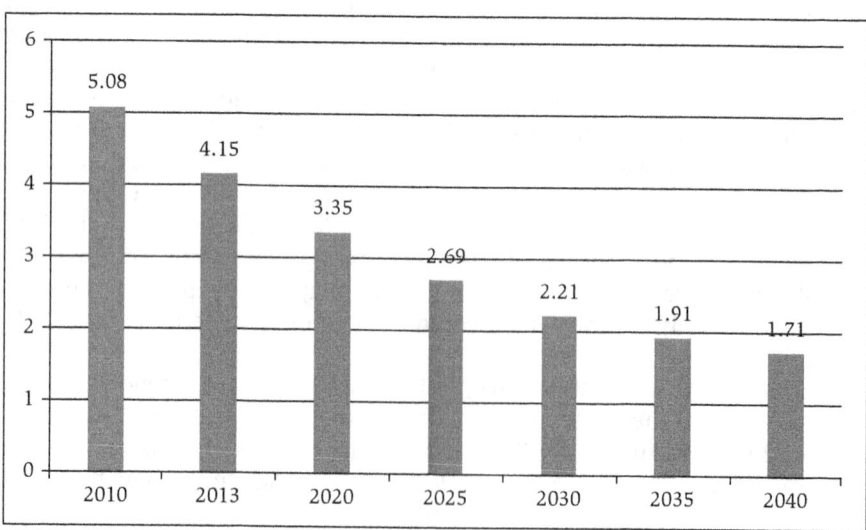

Source: National Economic and Social Development Board, Population Projection in Thailand: 2010-2040, calculated by the author.

12.4.8 Coherence of Policies

The old-age allowance scheme is related to other policies directly and indirectly. First, the beneficiaries of this scheme are entitled to be eligible for the other social assistance schemes, namely the disability allowance and HIV/Aids patients' allowance under the Order of Ministry of the Interior on the Payment of Allowance by Local Authorities B.E. 2548.

Second, the beneficiaries of other contributory public pension schemes, namely the Social Security Fund scheme (which mainly focuses on employees in the private sector), the National Saving Fund (which focuses on the unemployed population), are eligible to receive the old-age allowance. In other words, an older person can receive old-age allowance as a basic right and additionally enjoy pension benefits from his/her affiliated contributory pension system. Therefore, these rules truly reflect the existence of the old-age allowance as social protection floor among various old-age benefits.

Third, the beneficiaries of old-age allowance scheme are not excluded from enjoying financial access to the Elderly Fund to attain some money for occupational purposes. Under the Act on the Elderly B.E. 2546, the so-called Elderly Fund was established to promote older people's work and the social activities of senior citizens' clubs. It provides financial loans to older persons who are running small business and allocates budgets on a project-by-project basis to support the social activities of senior citizens. The beneficiaries of the old-age allowance scheme are still eligible for this government scheme.

12.4.9 Social Participation

Social participation and involvement have taken place both on a legal basis and voluntarily in some processes of the old-age allowance scheme. Some examples of social participation are as follows. At the policy formulation stage, as a Member of the NCE by law, non-politicians and non-government official Members have the chance to participate in policy formulation and routine decision-making processes and to impart some wisdom on scheme improvement, including the level of benefits issue. Such Members are the President of the Senior Citizens Council of Thailand under the Royal Patronage of Her Royal Highness the Princess Mother as Second Deputy Chairman; some qualified Members appointed by the Cabinet from representatives of private entities or non-profit organizations involved in the work of protection, promotion and support of status, roles and activities of the elderly; and some qualified Members appointed by the Cabinet, who are mostly academics.

In addition, there exists another channel, namely the National Older Persons Assembly, which allows older persons from different walks of life to participate and voice their opinions on specific issues of the elderly. The Department of Older Persons in the Ministry of Social Development and Human Security acts as a Member-cum-Secretary of the NCE is the facilitator of this event. Although this event is not mandatory by law, the resolutions of the Assembly are proposed on the agenda for consideration in the NCE.

12.4.10 Good Governance

After reviewing the aforementioned principles, we can confirm that there exist some elements reflecting good governance in the current old-age allowance system. For instance, the scheme forces local authorities to pay more attention and give more importance to older persons. The scheme provides many methods of delivery to take account of the diversification of older persons' characteristics. Moreover, the current system ensures regular monitoring of the system through the process of regular reporting, i.e., on the number of recipients, budget utilization, etc., to the National Committee of the Elderly.

Once in every five years, the system is evaluated by the National Plan for Elderly's monitoring and evaluation system. In addition, there exists coherence in the current system with other social protection schemes, such as the social security scheme, the Elderly Fund, the disability allowance, and the HIV/Aids patients' allowance, etc. However, there are still some elements of the system which do not reflect good governance. For example, there still remains a lack of respect for the dignity of older persons covered in the scheme in terms of level of benefits.

The current level of old-age allowance does not ensure a nationally defined minimum level. There are no regular actuarial studies performed in view of the sustainability of the scheme. The old-age allowance's specific grant crowds out subsidy from the national government to local authorities. It causes more or less fiscal negative externalities to other outlays of local authorities' government spending.

12.5 CHALLENGES OF OLD-AGE ALLOWANCE IN THE FUTURE

In the period of military government after the coup in May 2014, the National Reform Assembly (NRA) has played an important role in indicating future direction and driving some important emergent policies to be legalized and/or implemented to cope with population ageing. NRA has proposed four important aspects and specific issues for emergent reform. They are: the economic aspect (pension reform and economic reform for vitality); the health aspect (promoting the strengthening of the community-based long-term care system, including in urban areas); the environment aspect (achieving a safe living environment at home and constructing age-friendly communities, promoting social housing, and enabling ageing business and industries); and the social aspect (promoting the preparedness of, and empowering, individuals, families, communities, public and private sectors; increasing the value of older persons).

Among these proposals, the direction on old-age allowance reform has been mentioned as well. The agenda raised in the NRA proposal are as follows.

First, the position of old-age allowance should be officially changed to a 'basic pension' (of course, as a national social protection floor). Second, in order to guarantee the basic pension's status and to avoid from arbitrary political change, the legal status should be upgraded from the order of Ministry to the Basic Pension Act, which shall bring the old-age allowance scheme's legal status in line with the Recommendations for Social Protection Floors. Third, a single pension authority should be established. Nevertheless, the fiscal sustainability issue has been raised as a future concern in the proposals of NRA. However, the level of benefits debate is still pending.

Currently, in the fiscal year 2016, public expenditure for old-age allowance accounts for THB 63,098 million, which is 2.32% of national government annual budget. While the older population is increasing and the working population is decreasing, the fiscal burden on future generations from old-age allowance has been highlighted as another concern. Another concern relates to the position of old-age allowance as a basic pension. As mentioned in the previous section, Thailand has fragmented pension systems for sub-groups of population. Unfortunately, there is no pension authority to overview all systems simultaneously and to draw an entire picture of pension system. The lack of such a pension authority may be an obstacle to promoting the old-age allowance scheme and to transforming it into a sustainable basic pension that is a social protection floor of all other pension schemes.

BIBLIOGRAPHY

Knodel, J. and N. Chayovan. (2008). *Population Ageing and the Well-Being of Older Persons in Thailand: Past Trends, Current Situation and Future Challenges*. Bangkok: UNFPA Thailand and Asia and the Pacific Regional Office.

Knodel, J., V. Prachuabmoh and N. Chayovan. (2013). *The Changing Well-Being of Thai Elderly: An Update from the 2011 Survey of Older Persons in Thailand* (College of Population Studies, Chulalongkorn University and Help Age International).

Knodel, J., B. Teerawichitchainan, V. Prachuabmoh and W. Pothisiri. (2015). *The Situation of Thailand's Older Population: An Update Based on the 2014 Survey of Older Persons in Thailand*, Help Age International.

National Economic and Social Development Board. (2007). *Population Projections for Thailand 2000-2030*. Bangkok: Office of the National Economic and Social Development Board.

National Statistical Office. (2007). *Report on the 2007 Survey of the Older Persons in Thailand*. Bangkok: Thana Press.

Prachuabmoh. V. et al. (2009). *Research Report on Monitoring and Evaluation of the Second Elderly National Plan 2002-2022*. Bangkok: College of Population Studies. Chulalongkorn University.

National Statistical Office. (2007, 2011). *Report on Public Opinions on Knowledge and Attitudes Towards the Elderly*. Bangkok: Ministry of Social Development and Human Security, College of Population Studies Chulalongkorn University and National Statistical Office.

Sakunphanit T. and W. Suwanrada. (2011). '500 Baht Universal Pension Scheme', in United Nations Development Programme (eds), *Sharing Innovative Experiences: Successful Social Protection Floor Experiences*. New York, Special Unit for South-South Cooperation, 401-415.

Suwanrada, W. (2007). *National Pension System*. Bangkok: Chulalongkorn University Printing House.

Suwanrada W. and A. Kamwachirapitak. (2007). *Current Situation Analysis of the Old-Age Allowances System in Thailand*, Research Report submitted to Thailand Research Fund (Project Number: PDG5030208), August 2007.

Suwanrada W. (2008). *National Pension System, Research Book No. 8, Textbook Development Project*, Document Services Center, Faculty of Economics, Chulalongkorn University, March 2008.

Suwanrada, W. and A. Kamwachirapitak. (2008). *Problems of Old Age Allowance System in Thailand*. Bangkok: Chulalongkorn University Press.

Suwanrada, W. (2009). *'Poverty and Financial Security of the Elderly in Thailand'*, Ageing International, Volume 33. No. 1-4, 50-61.

Suwanrada,W. (2009). Economic Situation of the Elderly in Thailand. In Chuenta Wichawut, et al. *The Synthesis of Body of Knowledge on Thai Elderly from 2003-2007*. Foundation of Thai Gerontology Research and Development and Health Systems Research Institute. Bangkok: TQP Printing House.

Suwanrada, W. and W. Chadoevit. (2009). *National Pension: Old Age Welfare. Foundation of Thai Genrontology Research and Development*. Bangkok: TQP Printing House.

Suwanrada W. and W. Dharmapriya. (2012). 'Development of the Old-Age Allowance System in Thailand: Challenges and Policy Implications' in Sri Wening Handayani and Babken Babajanian (eds). *Social Protection for Older Persons: Social Pensions in Asia*. Philippines, Asian Development Bank, 153-167.

Suwanrada W. (2013). in Boni Li et al., *Global Aging Issues and Policies: Understanding the Importance of Comprehending and Studying the Aging Process*, Charles C. Thomas Publisher, USA.

Suwanrada W. (2013). 'Old Age Allowance System in Thailand', in Fabio V.S., Radhika L. and H. Ryan et al., *Recent Developments in the Role and Design of Social Protection Programmes: A Policy Dialogue*, Expert Workshop and South-South Learning Event, Poverty in Focus, No. 25, IPC-IG, UNDP.

PART III Conclusions

CHAPTER 13
A Framework of Principles as a Policy and Assessment Tool: Conclusions

Tineke Dijkhoff & Letlhokwa George Mpedi

13.1 INTRODUCTION

The relevance and importance of the International Labour Organization (hereinafter 'the ILO') Social Protection Floors Recommendation 2001 of 2012 (hereinafter 'the Recommendation') in the ongoing national and global endeavours to ensure social protection for all members of society cannot be emphasized enough. As apparent from the Recommendation and the discussions contained in the preceding chapters, social protection is a human right and not a privilege that should be enjoyed by every living human being. It provides a plan through which countries of the world can design and/or redesign their social protection systems for the benefit of those individuals who live within their respective jurisdictions. As apparent from the discussions in the various case studies contained in the book, there are countries that already have schemes germane to what the Recommendation seeks to achieve. These schemes, which generally predate the Recommendation, are key to the realization of what is required of their respective countries to progressively extend the reach of social protection to those persons who are excluded and marginalized by the current system.

This chapter filters and critically discusses the pitfalls and challenges facing countries and their respective schemes used as case studies. It highlights the lessons (to be) learnt from the selected case studies. In addition, the chapter pronounces on the compliance of the various schemes with the identified principles contained in the Recommendation. This is followed by some concluding observations on the legislative deficits and implementation failures as well as challenges experienced and faced by the schemes considered in the case studies.

13.2 PRINCIPLES

13.2.1 State Responsibility

As shown in the book, the State has a fundamental role to play in the social protection provisioning endeavours. This role, as elaborated in the case studies on Mexico,[1] South Africa,[2] and Thailand,[3] is multifaceted in the sense that the State can serve as a regulator, administrator and provider or supplier. The lesson to be learnt is that, each and every State has a duty to ensure that the social protection floors are set and, this is the case, irrespective of its financial might. The principle of progressive realization of social protection accommodates any and every State. It is not a ground that States can use to shirk their social protection responsibilities. However, as apparent from the case studies, private actors are often involved in the social protection provisioning endeavours. This has positive and negative results. As shown in the case of Namibia,[4] the privatization of the administration of the State old-age pension has made the scheme efficient and reduced wastefulness. On the other hand, this has increased the transaction costs to the pension recipient.[5] This is undesirable seeing that the majority of the old-age allowance recipients are indigent.

An example of the privatization of some of the aspects of the social assistance scheme, which were initially handled by the State, can be found in South Africa, where the disbursement of the social grants is handled by private actors.[6] This has, similarly to the case of Namibia,[7] yielded positive and negative results. The privatized payment of social grants, soon to be insourced, granted many social grants recipients with an opportunity to receive their grants through its well-developed banking system.[8] In the processes, this resulted in problems such as illicit deductions from the banking accounts of the social grant recipients.[9] Based on these experiences, it is crucial that States endeavour to avoid the slavish privatization of social protection schemes. Most importantly, privatization should benefit and not impose undue hardship on the social protection beneficiaries. In addition, any challenges identified, stemming from the privatized system, must be addressed swiftly. To identify challenges in the administration of social protections schemes, the States need to have effective monitoring and evaluation programmes and processes in place. As implied in the case study on Thailand,[10] to be operative, the monitoring and evaluation of schemes

---

1. Chapter 6 (Mexico).
2. Chapter 5 (South Africa).
3. Chapter 12 (Thailand).
4. Chapter 11 (Namibia).
5. Ibid.
6. See Chapter 5 (South Africa).
7. See Chapter 11 (Namibia).
8. Chapter 5 (South Africa).
9. Ibid.
10. Chapter 12 (Thailand).

Chapter 13: A Framework of Principles as a Policy and Assessment Tool

need to be carried out on a regular basis. This is not always the case in some jurisdictions. As shown in the case study on Tunisia, the regular monitoring of the National Programme for Assistance to Families in Need has been neglected by the State.[11]

A careful review of the case studies on the various roles played by the State leads one to the conclusion that the different schemes discussed in the book do conform to the State responsibility principle. Having said that, there is scope for improvement, particularly in countries where private actors are engaged in the social provisioning endeavours. Furthermore, in some cases, the monitoring and evaluation of the schemes require urgent attention.

13.2.2 Universality of Protection

What does universal protection entail and how can it be achieved? According to Behrendt et al., in Chapter 3, '[t]o achieve universal protection, Member States should provide, at least, the basic social security guarantees to at least all residents and all children, subject to country's existing international obligations.' The foregoing insights offered by Behrendt et al., it is opined, answer the above-mentioned question. In addition, they are expedient for assessing whether a social protection scheme complies with the universality of protection principle. Based on these observations, it would appear that none of the case studies discussed in this book fit in with the universality of protection principle. This view stems largely from the fact that none of the schemes discussed cover all residents. For instance, while it is true that the Namibian old-age pension is conceived and operated as a universal cash transfer scheme, the truth of the matter is that, as argued by the relevant case study, it is provided only to eligible citizens and permanent residents of the country.[12]

The Thai old-age allowance can be singled out, alongside the Namibian experience, to illustrate the point made earlier. While it is admirable that the aforementioned allowance can, as pointed out in the relevant case study, be accessed by informal sector workers and housewives, it is, at the same time, not available to documented migrants. Those schemes, which have been designed and introduced for the benefit of children, do not cover all children. The South African and the Argentinian case studies highlight this point succinctly.[13] Another example of the schemes covered in this volume, which fail to meet the universality of protection principle, is the Indian Mahatma Gandhi National Rural Employment Scheme.[14] This scheme guarantees 100 days of employment. However, in reality it stands accused of not having been true to its promise. According to the relevant case study, not all registered persons are successful in

---

11. Chapter 8 (Tunisia).
12. Chapter 11 (Namibia).
13. Chapter 5 (South Africa) and Chapter 7 (Argentina).
14. Chapter 10 (India).

securing the 100 days of employment.[15] Furthermore, the number of families registered in terms of the scheme needs to be increased. In other words, the scope of coverage needs to be broadened to cover more needy rural families.[16]

Countries covered in this book need to work towards complying with the universality principle. This will entail ensuring that their respective social protection schemes, especially those geared at forming the social protection floors, provides the basic guarantees to all residents and children as desired in the Recommendation. This, in the spirit of the principle of progressive realization, need not be achieved overnight. In any event, many developing countries cannot afford to that.

13.2.3 Entitlement Based on Law

The various schemes discussed in the case studies are unashamedly founded in law. Most importantly, the legislative framework of all the schemes covered predates the Recommendation. In some case studies, legal entitlement can be traced to the Constitution. The South African Constitution, which recognizes social protection as a fundamental right, is a case in point. The legal entitlement to benefits, as illustrated in, for example, the case studies on the Old-Age Allowance Scheme in Thailand and Namibian National Pension Scheme, is important in the sense that the applicable laws generally outline the available benefits; personal and, in some instances, territorial scope of coverage; applicable procedures and instances that would lead to the suspension of benefits; and complaints and appeal procedures. Another point to be noted is that the right to social protection, as illustrated in some of the case studies, is interlinked with certain rights such as the right to dignity, right to health, right to housing, right to education, and right to food.[17]

The schemes considered in the book do, in the main, meet this principle. However, it should be cautioned that in a majority of instances, particularly in developing countries, the mere fact that entitlement is outlined in the statute books does not automatically mean that that is the case in practice. Often, beneficiaries (prospective and current) fail to enforce their legal entitlements due to inaccessible social protection dispute resolution mechanisms. This could be due to the lack of free social protection dispute resolution mechanisms. In addition, some of the social protection laws are often not published in all the languages used in the country and understood by the indigent members of the society – especially the minorities.

---

15. *Ibid.*
16. *Ibid.*
17. *See*, for example, Chapter 3 and Chapter 4.

13.2.4 Adequacy and Predictability of Benefits

The adequacy and predictability of benefits need to be kept in check if benefits are to provide meaningful social protection. Schemes covered in this book strive to extend social protection by, *inter alia*, enabling the recipients to live a life of dignity.[18] They also endeavour to empower social protection beneficiaries to access other rights such as the right to food,[19] the right to health, and the right to education.[20] However, a common challenge that emerges from the case studies is that the value of the benefits offered is generally low. This undermines the potential of the schemes to provide the beneficiaries with an adequate standard of living.[21]

It should be acknowledged that some of the schemes discussed in this book do, based on an objective and transparent process, review and adjust the value of the benefits they provide on a regular basis to ensure that they maintain their real value.[22] This is not, generally speaking, the case with the other schemes. For instance, the allocation of the cash benefit in the case of the Tunisian Cash Transfer Programme is dependent on a subjective assessment,[23] and the level of the benefit in Thai 500 Bath Pension Scheme is subject to the arbitrary approval of the Cabinet.[24]

In order to render the benefits provided to be predictable, the legislative framework of countries such as South Africa and Namibia require that the level of benefits be specified and published in a Government Gazette.[25] Regrettably, Namibia fails to gazette the pronouncements on the national pension increment.[26] Another point worth noting, which is of relevance, is that the South African Child Support Grant is disbursed as a matter of right and not a privilege. It follows a rights-based approach to social protection provisioning. The South African method ensures that social benefits are distributed as an entitlement that is not dependent on the colours of the ruling party of the day. The State has to ensure that the benefit is adequately budgeted for.

13.2.5 Non-discrimination

The principle of non-discrimination can be discerned from the various schemes discussed in the case studies. The pertinent legislative framework of some of the schemes proscribes unfair discrimination on the basis of, *inter alia*, gender, sex,

---

18. *See* Chapter 11 (Namibia).
19. *See* Chapter 4.
20. *See* Chapter 3 (Implementation of Social Protection Floors).
21. *See*, for example, Chapter 5 (South Africa), Chapter 7 (Argentina) and Chapter 9 (Chile).
22. *See* Chapter 5 (South Africa) and Chapter 11 (Namibia).
23. Chapter 8 (Tunisia).
24. Chapter 12 (Thailand).
25. Chapter 5 (South Africa) and Chapter 11 (Namibia).
26. Chapter 11 (Namibia).

and race. Schemes such as the Indian Mahatma Gandhi National Rural Employment Scheme and the Tunisian National Programme for Assistance to Families have built in some affirmative action's measures in favour of women. This is significant – particularly when one considers the fact that women are often among the vulnerable members of the society.

What is of notable concern is that many schemes exclude and marginalize non-citizens from their scope of coverage. The Namibian National Pension Scheme and Thai Old-Age Allowance Scheme are notable examples. In addition, the rural poor are invariably deprived of the same service as the one available to their urban counterparts. The point is that the relevant schemes are frequently based in urban areas much to the neglect of the rural far-flung locations.[27]

13.2.6 Financial Solidarity

The benefits disbursed by the various schemes discussed in the book are non-contributory. They are funded by means of general taxes which are collected by the State. This ensures financial solidarity – particularly between the rich and poor.[28]

13.2.7 Good Governance

The principle of good governance, as illustrated in the book, requires that the schemes be administered in an accountable and transparent manner.[29] Second, there is a connection between good governance and monitoring, adjudication, and enforcement mechanisms.[30] This is crucial to, among others, keep the bureaucratic powers in control. To do that effectively, the rights such as those concerning access to information and just administrative action are of utmost importance.[31] In addition, it is crucial that the information collected concerning the (prospective) beneficiaries is protected.[32] This entails the protection of the current and future beneficiaries' personal details. This is even more pressing when States strive for the greater use of technology in their quest for efficiency and in instances where the administration and disbursement of the schemes is outsourced. Thus, the right to privacy should be guaranteed and protected.

Another point to be noted, which is linked to good governance, is financial sustainability.[33] This requires, *inter alia*, regular audits and actuarial reviews.[34]

---

27. *See*, for example, Chapter 5 (South Africa).
28. *See*, for example, Chapter 5 (South Africa).
29. *See*, for example, Chapter 3 (Implementation of Social Protection Floors), Chapter 5 (South Africa) and Chapter 10 (India).
30. Chapter 3 (Implementation of Social Protection Floors).
31. *See*, for example, Chapter 5 (South Africa).
32. Chapter 3 (Implementation of Social Protection Floors).
33. *Ibid.*
34. *See*, for example, Chapter 5 (South Africa) and Chapter 6 (Mexico).

Chapter 13: A Framework of Principles as a Policy and Assessment Tool

It is regrettable there are programmes that are not subjected to regular actuarial evaluations. Such an omission places the financial sustainability of the schemes in jeopardy. The Thai Old-Age Allowance Scheme and Mexican Conditional Cash Transfers for Families and Children are examples of such schemes.[35] Furthermore, schemes such as the Mexican Conditional Cash Transfers for Families and Children and Tunisian National Programme for Assistance to Families in Need are reportedly undermined by poor management, lack of transparency, and corruption.[36]

13.2.8 Coherence of Policies

As apparent from the case studies, the schemes considered display cracks in terms of policy coherence and coordination. These gaps include poor collaboration between government departments involved in social protection matters,[37] lack of measures aimed at the prevention of destitution,[38] and (re)integration into the society (e.g., freeing the beneficiaries from the clutches of poverty).[39] A further point to be noted, which can be distilled from the discussion on social protection floors and the right to food,[40] is that policy makers in their quest to craft coherent policies need to ensure that social policies embrace matters connected to social protection in the broader sense, such as food security, as initially envisaged in the social protection floors initiative papers.

13.2.9 Social Participation

Social participation, in most of the schemes covered in this book, takes different forms, and these include planning community development and citizen opinion (Mexico);[41] grass-roots level participation (India);[42] Senior Citizens Council and National Older Persons Assembly;[43] and legally sanctioned public participation.[44] Parties involved include the general public, beneficiaries, private institutions, academics, employers, workers (including informal sector workers represented by trade unions), and government and non-governmental organizations.[45] It should be mentioned that not all schemes discussed in the

---

35. Chapter 6 (Mexico) and Chapter 12 (Thailand).
36. Chapter 6 (Mexico) and Chapter 8 (Tunisia).
37. Chapter 5 (South Africa).
38. *Ibid.*
39. Chapter 5 (South Africa) and Chapter 6 (Mexico).
40. Chapter 4 (Social Protection Floors and the Right to Food).
41. Chapter 6 (Mexico).
42. Chapter 10 (India).
43. Chapter 12 (Thailand).
44. Chapter 5 (South Africa).
45. *See*, for example, Chapter 5 (South Africa), Chapter 6 (Mexico) and Chapter 10 (India).

book are fully compliant with the social participation principle. For instance, the scope of civil society participation is reported to be limited in Chile.[46]

13.3 LEGISLATIVE DEFICITS AND IMPLEMENTATION FAILURES

A number of key legislative deficits and implementation failures have been identified and require urgent attention. These include the following: a dearth of a comprehensive and coherent legislative framework; weak monitoring, enforcement, and adjudication mechanisms; a lack of requisite documentation to unlock access to benefits; poor social policy coherence and involvement of social actors; the absence of services in rural areas; corruption, fraud, and poor levels of service; a lack of transparency; and deficient information sharing services.

13.4 CONCLUSION

The conclusion to be drawn from the preceding discussion is that the set of principles drawn from the Recommendation and elaborated in Chapter 2 and Chapter 3, is a useful tool through which social protection schemes, particularly those that are already in existence, can be evaluated and their effectiveness measured. This framework consisting of nine principles comprises all fundamental rules a social protection floor should comply with to be in accordance with the human rights to social protection. The framework of principles reflects the notion of social justice and the call of the Declaration of Human rights for adequate life standards.

The framework could also be used in identifying gaps in the relevant social protection schemes and crafting solutions towards addressing such deficiencies. In addition, the Recommendation is a welcomed instrument for informing the policy-making process aiming at the development of a sustainable and adequate national social protection floor as a basis for higher levels of protection.

---

46. Chapter 9 (Chile).

Appendix: R202 – Social Protection Floors Recommendation, 2012 (No. 202)

Recommendation concerning National Floors of Social ProtectionAdoption: Geneva, 101st ILC session (14 Jun 2012) - Status: Up-to-date instrument.

Preamble

The General Conference of the International Labour Organization,
Having been convened at Geneva by the Governing Body of the International Labour Office, and having met in its 101st Session on 30 May 2012, and
Reaffirming that the right to social security is a human right, and
Acknowledging that the right to social security is, along with promoting employment, an economic and social necessity for development and progress, and
Recognizing that social security is an important tool to prevent and reduce poverty, inequality, social exclusion and social insecurity, to promote equal opportunity and gender and racial equality, and to support the transition from informal to formal employment, and
Considering that social security is an investment in people that empowers them to adjust to changes in the economy and in the labour market, and that social security systems act as automatic social and economic stabilizers, help stimulate aggregate demand in times of crisis and beyond, and help support a transition to a more sustainable economy, and
Considering that the prioritization of policies aimed at sustainable long-term growth associated with social inclusion helps overcome extreme poverty and reduces social inequalities and differences within and among regions, and
Recognizing that the transition to formal employment and the establishment of sustainable social security systems are mutually supportive, and
Recalling that the Declaration of Philadelphia recognizes the solemn obligation of the International Labour Organization to contribute to "achiev[ing] ... the

Appendix

extension of social security measures to provide a basic income to all in need of such protection and comprehensive medical care", and

Considering the Universal Declaration of Human Rights, in particular Articles 22 and 25, and the International Covenant on Economic, Social and Cultural Rights, in particular Articles 9, 11 and 12, and

Considering also ILO social security standards, in particular the Social Security (Minimum Standards) Convention, 1952 (No. 102), the Income Security Recommendation, 1944 (No. 67), and the Medical Care Recommendation, 1944 (No. 69), and noting that these standards are of continuing relevance and continue to be important references for social security systems, and

Recalling that the ILO Declaration on Social Justice for a Fair Globalization recognizes that "the commitments and efforts of Members and the Organization to implement the ILO's constitutional mandate, including through international labour standards, and to place full and productive employment and decent work at the centre of economic and social policies, should be based on ... (ii) developing and enhancing measures of social protection ... which are sustainable and adapted to national circumstances, including ... the extension of social security to all", and

Considering the resolution and Conclusions concerning the recurrent discussion on social protection (social security) adopted by the International Labour Conference at its 100th Session (2011), which recognize the need for a Recommendation complementing existing ILO social security standards and providing guidance to Members in building social protection floors tailored to national circumstances and levels of development, as part of comprehensive social security systems, and

Having decided upon the adoption of certain proposals with regard to social protection floors, which are the subject of the fourth item on the agenda of the session, and

Having determined that these proposals shall take the form of a Recommendation;

adopts this fourteenth day of June of the year two thousand and twelve the following Recommendation, which may be cited as the Social Protection Floors Recommendation, 2012.

I. OBJECTIVES, SCOPE AND PRINCIPLES

1. This Recommendation provides guidance to Members to:
    (a) establish and maintain, as applicable, social protection floors as a fundamental element of their national social security systems; and
    (b) implement social protection floors within strategies for the extension of social security that progressively ensure higher levels of social security to as many people as possible, guided by ILO social security standards.

Appendix

2. For the purpose of this Recommendation, social protection floors are nationally defined sets of basic social security guarantees which secure protection aimed at preventing or alleviating poverty, vulnerability and social exclusion.
3. Recognizing the overall and primary responsibility of the State in giving effect to this Recommendation, Members should apply the following principles:
   (a) universality of protection, based on social solidarity;
   (b) entitlement to benefits prescribed by national law;
   (c) adequacy and predictability of benefits;
   (d) non-discrimination, gender equality and responsiveness to special needs;
   (e) social inclusion, including of persons in the informal economy;
   (f) respect for the rights and dignity of people covered by the social security guarantees;
   (g) progressive realization, including by setting targets and time frames;
   (h) solidarity in financing while seeking to achieve an optimal balance between the responsibilities and interests among those who finance and benefit from social security schemes;
   (i) consideration of diversity of methods and approaches, including of financing mechanisms and delivery systems;
   (j) transparent, accountable and sound financial management and administration;
   (k) financial, fiscal and economic sustainability with due regard to social justice and equity;
   (l) coherence with social, economic and employment policies;
   (m) coherence across institutions responsible for delivery of social protection;
   (n) high-quality public services that enhance the delivery of social security systems;
   (o) efficiency and accessibility of complaint and appeal procedures;
   (p) regular monitoring of implementation, and periodic evaluation;
   (q) full respect for collective bargaining and freedom of association for all workers; and
   (r) tripartite participation with representative organizations of employers and workers, as well as consultation with other relevant and representative organizations of persons concerned.

Appendix

II. NATIONAL SOCIAL PROTECTION FLOORS

4. Members should, in accordance with national circumstances, establish as quickly as possible and maintain their social protection floors comprising basic social security guarantees. The guarantees should ensure at a minimum that, over the life cycle, all in need have access to essential health care and to basic income security which together secure effective access to goods and services defined as necessary at the national level.
5. The social protection floors referred to in Paragraph 4 should comprise at least the following basic social security guarantees:
   (a) access to a nationally defined set of goods and services, constituting essential health care, including maternity care, that meets the criteria of availability, accessibility, acceptability and quality;
   (b) basic income security for children, at least at a nationally defined minimum level, providing access to nutrition, education, care and any other necessary goods and services;
   (c) basic income security, at least at a nationally defined minimum level, for persons in active age who are unable to earn sufficient income, in particular in cases of sickness, unemployment, maternity and disability; and
   (d) basic income security, at least at a nationally defined minimum level, for older persons.
6. Subject to their existing international obligations, Members should provide the basic social security guarantees referred to in this Recommendation to at least all residents and children, as defined in national laws and regulations.
7. Basic social security guarantees should be established by law. National laws and regulations should specify the range, qualifying conditions and levels of the benefits giving effect to these guarantees. Impartial, transparent, effective, simple, rapid, accessible and inexpensive complaint and appeal procedures should also be specified. Access to complaint and appeal procedures should be free of charge to the applicant. Systems should be in place that enhance compliance with national legal frameworks.
8. When defining the basic social security guarantees, Members should give due consideration to the following:
   (a) persons in need of health care should not face hardship and an increased risk of poverty due to the financial consequences of accessing essential health care. Free prenatal and postnatal medical care for the most vulnerable should also be considered;
   (b) basic income security should allow life in dignity. Nationally defined minimum levels of income may correspond to the monetary value of a set of necessary goods and services, national poverty lines, income thresholds for social assistance or other comparable

Appendix

thresholds established by national law or practice, and may take into account regional differences;

(c) the levels of basic social security guarantees should be regularly reviewed through a transparent procedure that is established by national laws, regulations or practice, as appropriate; and

(d) in regard to the establishment and review of the levels of these guarantees, tripartite participation with representative organizations of employers and workers, as well as consultation with other relevant and representative organizations of persons concerned, should be ensured.

9.

(1) In providing the basic social security guarantees, Members should consider different approaches with a view to implementing the most effective and efficient combination of benefits and schemes in the national context.

(2) Benefits may include child and family benefits, sickness and healthcare benefits, maternity benefits, disability benefits, old-age benefits, survivors' benefits, unemployment benefits and employment guarantees, and employment injury benefits as well as any other social benefits in cash or in kind.

(3) Schemes providing such benefits may include universal benefit schemes, social insurance schemes, social assistance schemes, negative income tax schemes, public employment schemes and employment support schemes.

10. In designing and implementing national social protection floors, Members should:

(a) combine preventive, promotional and active measures, benefits and social services;

(b) promote productive economic activity and formal employment through considering policies that include public procurement, government credit provisions, labour inspection, labour market policies and tax incentives, and that promote education, vocational training, productive skills and employability; and

(c) ensure coordination with other policies that enhance formal employment, income generation, education, literacy, vocational training, skills and employability, that reduce precariousness, and that promote secure work, entrepreneurship and sustainable enterprises within a decent work framework.

11.

(1) Members should consider using a variety of different methods to mobilize the necessary resources to ensure financial, fiscal and economic sustainability of national social protection floors, taking into account the contributory capacities of different population groups. Such methods may include, individually or in combination, effective

enforcement of tax and contribution obligations, reprioritizing expenditure, or a broader and sufficiently progressive revenue base.
(2) In applying such methods, Members should consider the need to implement measures to prevent fraud, tax evasion and non-payment of contributions.
12. National social protection floors should be financed by national resources. Members whose economic and fiscal capacities are insufficient to implement the guarantees may seek international cooperation and support that complement their own efforts.

III. NATIONAL STRATEGIES FOR THE EXTENSION OF SOCIAL SECURITY

13.
(1) Members should formulate and implement national social security extension strategies, based on national consultations through effective social dialogue and social participation. National strategies should:
   (a) prioritize the implementation of social protection floors as a starting point for countries that do not have a minimum level of social security guarantees, and as a fundamental element of their national social security systems; and
   (b) seek to provide higher levels of protection to as many people as possible, reflecting economic and fiscal capacities of Members, and as soon as possible.
(2) For this purpose, Members should progressively build and maintain comprehensive and adequate social security systems coherent with national policy objectives and seek to coordinate social security policies with other public policies.
14. When formulating and implementing national social security extension strategies, Members should:
   (a) set objectives reflecting national priorities;
   (b) identify gaps in, and barriers to, protection;
   (c) seek to close gaps in protection through appropriate and effectively coordinated schemes, whether contributory or non-contributory, or both, including through the extension of existing contributory schemes to all concerned persons with contributory capacity;
   (d) complement social security with active labour market policies, including vocational training or other measures, as appropriate;
   (e) specify financial requirements and resources as well as the time frame and sequencing for the progressive achievement of the objectives; and

(f) raise awareness about their social protection floors and their extension strategies, and undertake information programmes, including through social dialogue.
15. Social security extension strategies should apply to persons both in the formal and informal economy and support the growth of formal employment and the reduction of informality, and should be consistent with, and conducive to, the implementation of the social, economic and environmental development plans of Members.
16. Social security extension strategies should ensure support for disadvantaged groups and people with special needs.
17. When building comprehensive social security systems reflecting national objectives, priorities and economic and fiscal capacities, Members should aim to achieve the range and levels of benefits set out in the Social Security (Minimum Standards) Convention, 1952 (No. 102), or in other ILO social security Conventions and Recommendations setting out more advanced standards.
18. Members should consider ratifying, as early as national circumstances allow, the Social Security (Minimum Standards) Convention, 1952 (No. 102). Furthermore, Members should consider ratifying, or giving effect to, as applicable, other ILO social security Conventions and Recommendations setting out more advanced standards.

IV. MONITORING

19. Members should monitor progress in implementing social protection floors and achieving other objectives of national social security extension strategies through appropriate nationally defined mechanisms, including tripartite participation with representative organizations of employers and workers, as well as consultation with other relevant and representative organizations of persons concerned.
20. Members should regularly convene national consultations to assess progress and discuss policies for the further horizontal and vertical extension of social security.
21. For the purpose of Paragraph 19, Members should regularly collect, compile, analyse and publish an appropriate range of social security data, statistics and indicators, disaggregated, in particular, by gender.
22. In developing or revising the concepts, definitions and methodology used in the production of social security data, statistics and indicators, Members should take into consideration relevant guidance provided by the International Labour Organization, in particular, as appropriate, the resolution concerning the development of social security statistics adopted by the Ninth International Conference of Labour Statisticians.

Appendix

23. Members should establish a legal framework to secure and protect private individual information contained in their social security data systems.
24.
(1) Members are encouraged to exchange information, experiences and expertise on social security strategies, policies and practices among themselves and with the International Labour Office.
(2) In implementing this Recommendation, Members may seek technical assistance from the International Labour Organization and other relevant international organizations in accordance with their respective mandates.

STUDIES IN EMPLOYMENT AND SOCIAL POLICY

1. W. Beck, L. van der Maesen & A. Walker (eds), *The Social Quality of Europe*, 1997 (ISBN 90-411-0456-9).
2. R. Blanpain, M. Colucci, C. Engels, F. Hendrickx, L. Salas & E. De Smyter, *Institutional Changes and European Social Policies after the Treaty of Amsterdam*, 1998 (ISBN 90-411-1018-6).
3. V. Lo: *Law and Industrial Relations: China and Japan after World War II*, 1998 (ISBN 90-411-1075-5).
4. A. Den Exter & H. Hermans (eds), *The Right to Health Care in Several European Countries*, 1998 (ISBN 90-411-1087-9).
5. M. Biagi (ed.), *Job Creation and Labour Law from Protection towards Pro-Action*, 2000 (ISBN 90-411-1432-7).
6. W. Beck, L. van der Maesen, F. Thomése & A. Walker (eds), *Social Quality: A Vision for Europe*, 2000 (ISBN 90-411-1523-4).
7. F. Pennings, *Introduction to European Social Law*, 3rd ed., 2001 (ISBN 90-411-1628-1).
8. J. Murray, *Transnational Labour Regulation: The ILO and EC Compared*, 2001 (ISBN 90-411-1583-8).
9. R. Blanpain & C. Engels (eds), *The ILO and Social Challenges of the 21st Century*, 2001 (ISBN 90-411-1572-2).
10. M. Biagi (ed.), *Towards a European Model of Industrial Relations? Building on the First Report of the European Commission*, 2001 (ISBN 90-411-1653-2).
11. J. Clasen (ed.), *What Future for Social Security? Debates and Reforms in National and Cross-National Perspective*, 2001 (ISBN 90-411-1671-0).
12. A. Numhauser-Henning (ed.), *Legal Perspectives on Equal Treatment and Non-Discrimination*, 2001 (ISBN 90-411-1665-6).
13. R. Blanpain (ed.), *Labour Law, Human Rights and Social Justice* 2001 (ISBN 90-411-1697-4).
14. M.-C. Kuo, H.F. Zacher & H.-S. Chan (eds), *Reform and Perspectives on Social Insurance: Lessons from the East and West*, 2002 (ISBN 90-411-1819-5).
15. P. Foubert, *The Legal Protection of the Pregnant Worker in the European Community*, 2002 (ISBN 90-411-1842-X).
16. M. Biagi (ed.), *Quality of Work and Employee Involvement in Europe*, 2002 (ISBN 90-411-1885-3).
17. F. Pennings, *Dutch Social Security Law in an International Context*, 2002 (ISBN 90-411-1887-X).

18. T. Carney & G. Ramia, *From Rights to Management: Contract, New Public Management and Employment Services*, 2002 (ISBN 90-411-1889-6).
19. R. Blanpain & M. Colucci, *European Labour and Social Security Law, Glossary*, 2002 (ISBN 90-411-1905-1).
20. I.U. Zeytinoglu (ed.), *Flexible Work Arrangements: Conceptualizations and International Experiences*, 2002 (ISBN 90-411-1947-7).
21. J. Berghman, A. Nagelkerke, M. Boos, R. Doeschot & G. Vonk (eds), *Social Security in Transition*, 2002 (ISBN 90-411-1969-8).
22. R. Blanpain, *The Legal Status of Sportsmen and Sportswomen under International, European and Belgian National and Regional Law*, 2003 (ISBN 90-411-1980-9).
23. R. Blanpain & M. Weiss (eds), *Changing Industrial Relations & Modernisation of Labour Law, Liber Amicorum in Honour of Professor Marco Biagi*, 2003 (ISBN 90-411-2008-4).
24. J. Malmberg (ed.), *Effective Enforcement of EC Labour Law*, 2003 (ISBN 90-411-2160-9).
25. M. De Vos (ed.), *A Decade Beyond Maastricht: The European Social Dialogue Revisited*, 2003 (ISBN 90-411-2163-3).
26. M. Sewerynski (ed.), *Collective Agreements and Individual Contracts of Employment*, 2003 (ISBN 90-411-2190-0).
27. R. Blanpain & M. Van Gestel, *Use and Monitoring of E-Mail, Intranet and Internet Facilities at Work: Law and Practice*, 2004 (ISBN 90-411-22-66-4).
28. A. C. Neal (ed.), *The Changing Face of European Labour Law and Social Policy*, 2004 (ISBN 90-411-2312-1).
29. E. Sol & M. Westerveld (eds), *Contractualism in Employment Services: A New Form of Welfare State Governance*, 2005 (ISBN 90-411-2405-5).
30. F. Pennings (ed.), *Between Soft and Hard Law – The Impact of International Social Security Standards on National Social Security Law*, 2006 (ISBN 978-90-411-2491-3).
31. L. Dickens & A. C. Neal (eds), *The Changing Institutional Face of British Employment Relations*, 2006 (ISBN 978-90-411-2541-5).
32. G. Sebardt, *Redundancy and the Swedish Model in an International Context*, 2006 (ISBN 978-90-411-2503-3).
33. A.M. witkowski, *Charter of Social Rights of the Council of Europe*, 2007 (ISBN 978-90-411-2608-5).
34. M. Sargeant (ed.), *The Law on Age Discrimination in the EU*, 2008 (ISBN 978-90-411-2522-4).
35. G. Di Domenico & S. Spattini (eds), *New European Approaches to Long-Term Unemployment: What Role for Public Employment Services and What Market for Private Stakeholders?*, 2008 (ISBN 978-90-411-2614-6.)
36. C. Welz, *The European Social Dialogue under Articles 138 and 139 of the EC Treaty: Actors, Processes, Outcomes*, 2008 (ISBN 978-90-411-2744-0).
37. M. Rönnmar (ed.), *EU Industrial Relations v. National Industrial Relations: Comparative and Interdisciplinary Perspectives*, 2008 (ISBN 978-90-411-2770-9).

38. F. Pennings, Y. Konijn & A. Veldman (eds), *Social Responsibility in Labour Relations: European and Comparative Perspectives*, 2008 (ISBN 978-90-411-2783-9).
39. F. Pennings & C. Bosse (eds), *The Protection of Working Relationships: A Comparative Study*, 2011 (ISBN 978-90-411-3289-5).
40. S. Devetzi & S. Stendahl (eds), *Too Sick to Work?: Social Security Reference in Europe for Persons with Reduced Earnings Capacity*, 2011 (ISBN 978-90-411-3426-4).
41. U. Becker, F. Pennings & T. Dijkhoff (eds), *International Standard-Setting and Innovations in Social Security*, 2013 (ISBN 978-90-411-3233-8).
42. E. Ales (ed.), *Health and Safety at Work: European and Comparative Perspective*, 2013 (ISBN 978-90-411-4661-8).
43. F. Pennings, T. Erhag & S. Stendahl (eds), *Non-public Actors in Social Security Administration: A Comparative Study*, 2013 (ISBN 978-90-411-4917-6).
44. A. Neal (ed.), *Cross-Currents in Modern Chinese Labour Law*, 2014 (ISBN 978-90-411-4763-9).
45. B. Waas (ed.), *The Right to Strike: A Comparative View*, 2014 (ISBN 978-90-411-5007-3).
46. A. Ojeda-Avilés, *Transnational Labour Law*, 2015 (ISBN 978-90-411-5858-1).
47. A. Numhauser-Henning & M. Rönnmar, *Age Discrimination and Labour-Law: Comparative and Conceptual Perspectives in the EU and Beyond*, 2015 (ISBN 978-90-411-4979-4).
48. A. Perulli & T. Treu (eds), *Enterprise and Social Rights*, 2017 (ISBN 978-90-411-8234-0).
49. Dr F.C.A. van Haasteren, *Decent Flexibility: The Impact of ILO Convention 181 and the Regulation on Temporary Agency Work*, 2017 (ISBN 978-90-411-9236-3).
50. T. Dijkhoff & L.G. Mpedi (eds), *Recommendation on Social Protection Floors: Basic Principles for Innovative Solutions*, 2018 (ISBN 978-90-411-8623-2).